moments of seeing

Reflections from an Ordinary Life

also by Katrina Kenison

Mitten Strings for God:
Reflections for Mothers
in a Hurry

Meditations from the Mat:
Daily Reflections on the Path of Yoga
(with Rolf Gates)

The Gift of an Ordinary Day:
A Mother's Memoir

Magical Journey:
An Apprenticeship in Contentment

moments of seeing

Reflections from an Ordinary Life

KATRINA KENISON

EARTH SKY + WATER, LLC
PUBLISHING

Grateful acknowledgment is made to the following to reprint the material specified below:

"The Peace of Wild Things" from *The Selected Poems of Wendell Berry* by Wendell Berry. Copyright © 1999 by Wendell Berry. Reprinted by permission of Counterpoint Press, Berkeley, CA.

"I Want to Say Something So Simply" from *Evidence: Poems* by Mary Oliver, published by Beacon Press, Boston. Copyright © 2009 by Mary Oliver, used herewith by permission of the Charlotte Sheedy Literary Agency.

"Like Snow" from *New and Collected Poems* by Wendell Berry. Copyright c 2012 by Wendell Berry. Reprinted by permission of Counterpoint Press, Berkeley, CA.

Lines from "A Blessing for One Who Is Exhausted" and from "A Blessing for the Senses" from *To Bless the Space Between Us* by John O'Donohue. Copyright © 2008 by John O'Donohue. Reprinted by permission of The Doubleday Broadway Publishing Group, New York, NY.

"Irreverent Baking" by Maya Stein. Copyright © 2011 Maya Stein. Used by permission of Maya Stein. www.mayastein.com.

"Otherwise" from *Otherwise: New and Selected Poems* by Jane Kenyon Copyright © 1996 by The Estate of Jane Kenyon. Reprinted by permission of Graywolf Press, St. Paul, MN.

Excerpt from "Circle of the One" by John Squadra. From *This Ecstasy*. Copyright © 2004 by John Squadra. Heron Dance Press, North Ferrisburgh, VT.

Published in the United States by Earth Sky + Water, LLC.

Earth Sky + Water, LLC
PO Box 60
Wilton, NH 03086
www.earthskywater.net

ISBN-13: 9781621262169

For more information visit www.katrinakenison.com

Printed in the United States of America

First edition: October 2016

Book design by Ellen Klempner-Béguin
Cover painting by Sue Callihan, www.suecallihan.com

For my readers, who have walked this path with me

What is the meaning of life? That was all—a simple question; one that tended to close in on one with years, the great revelation had never come. The great revelation perhaps never did come. Instead, there were little daily miracles, illuminations, matches struck unexpectedly in the dark; here was one.
—Virginia Woolf, *To the Lighthouse*

I keep writing about the ordinary because for me it's the home of the extraordinary, the only home.
—Phillip Levine

contents

2011

*We write to taste life twice, in the moment
and in retrospect.*
— *Anais Nin*

—·— introduction —·—

Early in the summer of 2009, my publisher gave me a
to-do list. It had been almost ten years since my first book,
Mitten Strings for God, had been published. And in that
decade, thanks to the Internet and the arrival of social
media, the entire landscape of publishing had changed. To
connect with readers in this new world, my young publicist
patiently explained, I would need a platform.

I had spent much of the previous year holed up in
my house writing a memoir I wasn't sure anyone would
actually want to read. *The Gift of an Ordinary Day* was
my attempt to capture some of the last moments of our
family's life as it had always been: two parents and two
kids all living together under one roof. Suddenly, as my
older son was finishing high school and my younger one
confronted the challenges of his freshman year, I found

myself profoundly aware of life's fleetingness. I knew my task as a parent was to let go. At the same time, my heart was urging me to hold on, tight, to each precious moment. Writing that book had been a private, consuming way to do both at once.

But now the time had come to send this quiet little memoir out into the world. "Get yourself a website," the publicist instructed. "Start a blog." It's hard to fathom now, but in techno-time, 2009 was an eon ago. I didn't even have a Facebook account, and only a vague idea of what a blog was. I had never actually seen one.

A few weeks before my son Henry headed back to college, he designed a simple website for me and showed me how to create a post. I dutifully wrote a few paragraphs about how it felt to have a book published. With Henry looking over my shoulder, I cut and pasted it into my new dashboard and hit "publish." And I wondered how long I would be expected to keep this thing going.

Much as I might wish to set a timer, type away for twenty or thirty minutes, and have something ready to tweak and post, that's just not me. I've always been a slow writer. I still am. I can easily spend a day pondering and writing and revising a blog post. And as time passed and my book came out and the world moved on, there was no real way to justify the many hours I continued to spend perched on a kitchen stool writing essays that might be read by a small handful of people who happened to Google my name and land on my website.

And yet it wasn't long before I realized I'd come to

love taking time out of the busyness of life to sit quietly and reflect on the meaning of life. There was something deeply satisfying about simply writing in the moment and of the moment, without any great plan or plot or deadline. I could experiment, or I could pour my thoughts out onto the page, or I could just sit and wait patiently for words to come, gathering up my feelings and trying to make some sense of them.

So, I continued. I wrote of my ordinary days, searching for the story beneath the story in a way I hoped might bring depth and meaning to the experiences of others as well. And in the process, something wonderful happened. What began as an assignment was transformed into a conversation—with myself, yes, but even more importantly, with *you,* a compassionate, generous community of readers and fellow travelers on this twisting path through life. With each passing week, the circle expanded. Pretty soon, you were writing back, offering glimpses of your own lives and passions and predicaments. Reading your thoughtful comments, I was pretty sure I wasn't the only one feeling grateful for the space we shared and for this deepening sense of connection with kindred spirits.

Now, seven years later, with your encouragement, I've gathered many of these pieces together into this book. I'm a little shocked at how long it is. And, in fact, I left a lot of stuff out. The book reviews, the exchange of letters with my friend and writing colleague Margaret Roach, the essays about food — you can find them online, but they didn't seem to fit here. (I did, however, include all the recipes in an appendix at the end.)

What's left is a patchwork record of a particular time—moments of seeing. I don't write about one thing, but rather about anything: snatches of life as it's being lived, thoughts as they come, fleeting ruminations, family moments, inner struggles, small revelations. Ordinariness. The Chinese have a notion that a good life is one in which not much happens. A person who has survived illness or disaster or who's suffered a great loss understands the truth of these words immediately. But so does any mother who's raised children to adulthood. We know, in the very depths of our being, that a quiet day is a good day. Drama has its place, of course, and our children's victories supply brief thrills. But the highs are fleeting, and we hope the lows won't last. By contrast, a dinner table on a weeknight, with every seat filled, can feel like the most beautiful place on earth. To really value life is to know: the best moments are often the ones we might miss altogether if we weren't paying attention. Writing is a way of fully inhabiting those moments and, too, of making sure they don't disappear. A photograph captures an image and records a memory, but only words can evoke the ephemeral contents of a heart. Only words can begin with the everyday and move us toward the infinite.

I've spent the last two months reading through and editing every piece I've written over the last seven years. I wanted to make sure, first, that they would hold up well enough to warrant a collection. But I was also curious to see just what the whole lot of them, read chronologically, might reveal. What I found is a string of days, a random collection of memories that surely would have vanished if not for the hours I spent on that kitchen stool, searching for words with which to hold them.

But I also see the arc of a life in transition. From one day to the next, change can seem incremental. Take a step back, though, and what comes into focus are lives transformed by time. In 2009, with one son in college and the other in boarding school, much of my life still revolved around the comings and goings of my children. Every visit home was cause for celebration, every parting poignant. Not yet accustomed to the newly emptied nest, I took refuge in the page, wrestling with my feelings of loss, searching for some new sense of direction, and, too, trying to make peace with the fact that some things that mattered very much to me hadn't gone as planned.

Our younger son had struggled in high school, had benefited enormously from nine weeks in a wilderness therapy program, had eagerly embraced a fresh start in a new school, and yet was still making some impulsive choices. There were many times when I was full of hope for his future. And there were others when I would find myself awake at 3 am, staring at the ceiling, wondering if he was simply getting better at masking his feelings.

At the time, his story was not mine to tell. He was a teenager who needed me to respect his privacy. What I *could* write about, however, was my own painful understanding that the only real work I could do was on myself. I couldn't control my son or fix his life or choose his destiny. But I could make sure I held up my own end of our relationship. I could honor his efforts and seek help for myself when I needed it. I could surrender to uncertainty. I could learn to work more gracefully with all the things I couldn't change. And I could share these efforts, in the belief that every one of us is engaged in some kind of similar enterprise, learning to trust life's current to carry us rather than trying to swim upstream.

In the years since I began writing these pieces, I've accompanied two close friends through their final days and grieved their deaths. I fulfilled a long-held dream and became a yoga teacher, and then I stopped teaching yoga as arthritis made even simple poses inaccessible to me. I wrote and published a second book, which had its beginnings in these pieces. I gave up running, and I got two new hips, which I hope will one day carry me back up mountains and into forward lunges. Our family mourned the loss of one dog and adopted another. One son graduated from college and embarked on a career as a musician. The other followed a rockier path into adulthood and has arrived in his twenties with a remarkably clear sense of who he is: sober, grateful, and happily employed at the same wilderness-therapy program that afforded him that much-needed "time out" at age sixteen.

Meanwhile, my husband and I have grown older. The empty nest has become a cozy, familiar place. Our family, scattered geographically, is in some ways closer than ever, the angst of adolescence a memory now, receding. I talk to both my sons nearly every day, grateful for these new, refreshingly open adult relationships that bring joy to us all.

"Everything vanishes," says James Salter, "except that which is written down." I believe this to be so. These pieces bear it out. Because I write about people close to me, there is much I cannot say, boundaries I honor with care. But it turns out there is still, always, an intimate, worthwhile story to tell. A story about the grace of a certain kind of surrender and about the courage of forgiveness. Of finding beauty in life as it is, even when it's not exactly what we'd choose. A story of learning to see blessings hiding in plain sight and learning to absorb losses with more resilience and deeper faith. A story of moments to be endured and moments I'd give anything to live again. I can write about all of this. And I do. The work on the page and the work on the self, it turns out, is one in the same, never really finished. Until, of course, it is. But I see this now: the themes all along, in the soul and in the writing, have remained the same. Acceptance, gratitude, love.

My heartfelt thanks to all of you who have joined me on this path—some of you since the very beginning— to read and write and share this magical journey that is everyday life. May we continue to travel well together, to support one another along the way, and to celebrate the gift of all our ordinary days.

Everything that is not written down disappears except for certain imperishable moments, people and scenes.
— *James Salter*

—·— book happiness —·—

A few days ago, a writer friend sent me a lovely e-mail, acknowledging my upcoming publication date and wishing me much "book-related happiness."

She caught me by surprise, for we've been so taken up this week with the stuff of life that no one has been thinking much about my book. I've received one finished copy of *The Gift of an Ordinary Day* from the publisher, so I know it finally exists. I'm nervous and excited to send this book into the world at last.

But we also have lots else going on: welcoming Henry home for a few days between the end of his summer job in Maine and his return to college next week, and getting Jack ready to head back to school as well.

We're trying to squeeze in a few last swims, a dinner with our old neighbors, an overnight stay at a friend's

Vermont cabin. Tonight, though, the four of us are just sitting around in the kitchen, watching the U.S. Tennis Open on TV and chatting.

Jack's been playing tennis almost every day this summer and is an enthusiastic student of the game. He's multitasking, watching Andy Roddick's match while also making neat stacks of note cards and envelopes. (Jack's been working for Steve's company this summer, too, packing cards and rolling posters.) Henry's trying to load new software onto his laptop. Steve's narrating the tennis match and serving up coffee ice cream. I'm typing, pausing when the guys whoop to watch replays of the important points.

And what I realize, sitting here with my family a few days before my memoir is officially published, is that my happiness in this moment is not book related, but life related. Nearly grown children safe at home and within arm's reach. A tangle of leggy black-eyed Susans in a vase on the table. Our dog, Gracie, content and underfoot. My cheerful, wisecracking husband trying to make the kids laugh.

A book's publication is a major life event to be sure, but the "gift" I've spent the last two years writing about is really just exactly this and nothing more: a fleeting moment hallowed by attention.

Another friend, whose gentle, loving husband died of a stroke a couple of months ago, wrote me this morning that today would have been his birthday. Years ago, we celebrated his fiftieth on an island in Maine, with lobster on the beach, champagne at sunset, a bonfire, toddlers running barefoot through the sand—one of those perfect, golden occasions that you think your life will be full of, if you do things right.

And then years go by, and suddenly you see that the occasions are different, and people are missing, and you feel older and sadder and wiser. And yet, despite the tally of losses—a list that grows only longer with the passing of time—you still find ways to be grateful and joyful. Our whole family is at home tonight, a rarity now. The moon is nearly full in a clear early September sky. We will have four more days and nights together, every bed full and lots of dishes to do. It's not much, and yet it's everything. It's life as it is. And it does make me happy.

September 2009

———·—— a book is born ——·———

Publication date for *The Gift of an Ordinary Day* came and went, my new book's arrival in stores eclipsed in our house by the fact that Henry was heading back to college, and summer really was coming to an end. I said good-bye to him at 5:30 this morning, as he and his dad were leaving for the airport and as I was leaving myself, to drive to Boston for a TV interview on a national news channel.

It was dark when we all left the house. I drove south in silence, on empty highways, watching the sky grow light. This was Labor Day, and it seemed the whole world was sleeping in. The sun rose, and I calmed the butterflies in my stomach by telling myself that no one was even awake at this hour, let alone watching the news on TV.

A few hours later I was back in New Hampshire, standing across from the general store in Francestown in the midst of a holiday crowd as we awaited the beginning of the annual Labor Day Parade. It was a glorious late summer day, and in this part of the world anyway, Francestown was the place to be. There were artisans selling crafts, an ice cream social in full swing inside the church, sheep to visit and felted slippers to buy, used-book tables to browse, and a flea market full of unexpected treasures. Jack arrived with some friends. I ran into my brother and his wife and their small children, neighbors, all sorts of familiar faces.

The theme of this year's parade was "The Games People Play," and folks had created floats paying homage to everything from Scrabble to dominoes, tug-of-war redneck-style (lots of mud involved) to hangman—with a real gallows and noose. In a nod to twentieth-century reality, one float featured a ratty old sofa occupied by a bunch of teenaged boys playing video games.

Every vintage fire truck within thirty miles had been spruced up and brought over, along with a few antique cars, showy horses, and marching bands. There was even an 1860 horse-drawn hearse on display, complete with a tiny coffin riding in the back. The Temple Cloggers danced by, followed by a team of quick-stepping toe tappers of every age and body type.

Jack had said he didn't care much about watching this hokey old small-town parade; we've come every year for the last five, ever since we moved to New Hampshire, and the novelty has worn thin for him.

But in the end, he couldn't resist the pleasure of seeing it all through his two-year-old cousin's eyes. Gabriel waved and clapped for every man, woman and child, every animal and vintage car and siren-blower. And I realized that I was having as much fun watching sixteen-year-old Jack watch two-year-old Gabe watch his first parade as I was having watching the parade itself. Which is why hokey small-town parades live on, I guess, and why they are so special.

Part of a parade's appeal is about dusting off some cherished relics from the past and bringing them back out into the light of day. There's a particular satisfaction to be found in coming together and making things, and in sharing some town-wide spectacle and pomp and noise. But a parade is also about bringing along the next generation, instilling in them a sense of what really matters in life: tradition, community, an appreciation for the places in which we live, our shared history, and the people who are our neighbors.

Later, back at home, I rummaged around in the freezer for something I could make for dinner. Steve and Jack and I had planned to go to a nice restaurant to celebrate my book's publication date, but in the end no one was really in the mood. Henry was gone, and we sort of missed him already. Jack was heading back to school in the morning. It was getting late and we were all tired. I didn't really need dinner out at the end of this long, full day. We'd had

a parade, after all, and that turned out to be enough.
September 2009

——•—— bookstores and hydrangeas ——•——

It seemed fitting that my first reading for *The Gift of an Ordinary Day* take place in our old hometown of Winchester, Massachusetts. My husband, Steve, and I first met Judy Manzo the week she bought Book Ends Bookstore, nearly seventeen years ago. She didn't know anything about selling books, she confessed to us, but she did know a lot of people in town. She figured she'd do fine if she just ordered five copies of any book a customer requested. It was a start. Judy was a quick learner, and it wasn't long before she had turned this sleepy suburban bookstore into a lively cultural center and the go-to place in town for gifts, cards, books, and news of local authors and book groups.

I did my first author event ever, for *Mitten Strings for God,* there ten years ago, nervous and shaky and not at all sure I had anything to say that others might want to hear. It was only a tiny bit easier this time. (Maybe opening night jitters never go away?)

Judy had been selling my book for a week, sending e-mails, advertising, keeping the stack high on the front table. Old friends appeared, as did strangers who had already bought books and arrived eager to talk. After my reading, three friends took me out for Chinese food, and then I spent the night at the home of a former neighbor, sitting up late, drinking tea and catching up on all the news in town.

We've been gone from Winchester for five years now, and yet in most of the ways that really count, the town still feels as much like home as ever. Our friendships endure. And it feels wonderful, always, to be welcomed back so warmly. As Jack and I have come at last to agree, moving just made our world bigger—we didn't give up one life in favor of another one so much as expand and stretch our lives so that they include more: more friends, more people, more places to care about, a broader definition of the "good life."

Our old house is empty for now. The new owners are spending this year overseas. It's strange to see it there, dark and hollow and unlived in. The gardens are overgrown, the grass a little long, the dark green paint starting to peel. But the hydrangeas that Steve and the boys and I planted as frail saplings on several successive Mother's Days many years ago are full-size trees now, in extravagant bloom and bent nearly to the ground beneath their weighty burdens of blossoms.

"You might as well cut some," my old next-door neighbor said in the morning. "No one is going to mind." And so it was that I stood in the yard that we left five years ago, scissors in hand, cutting flowers from trees I planted that no longer belong to me. How strange it felt, to be there again, doing what I used to do. I clipped a huge armful, and then my two friends and I headed up the hill to pick raspberries, just as we always used to do in early September.

Two hours later, driving back to New Hampshire with a trunk full of hydrangeas and hands stained with berry juice, I thought about how grateful I am for life as it is right now, a life that allows me to embrace two places, not one; that is enriched by friends and loved ones in two towns; and that has taught me so much about change and resilience and holding on and letting go.

Back at home in our "new" house, I filled vases with hydrangeas cut at the "old" house, watered the garden, put away groceries, reclaimed my space. And the next day, on the spur of the moment, I pulled over at a roadside nursery and bought a wispy hydrangea sapling to plant here, just outside the screened porch.

The weekend has been busy—three more book signings in two days—but there was still time for a walk this afternoon when I got home from the last bookstore. Steve and I grabbed a trash bag, whistled for Gracie, and headed out to hike our forty-five-minute loop through the woods and up the road to our house. We picked up beer bottles along the way, empty cigarette packs, crushed soda cans. By the time we got back to the house, our bag was full and the roadside looked beautiful again. Home, after all, isn't just the house. It's the town itself, the road where we live, the trail through the woods that we walk nearly every day. Taking care of this place, even if it's just to pick up litter, feels like a good way to express our appreciation for all we've found here.

And then Steve dug a hole, our neighbor Debbie came down to lend a hand, and we got our new little tree into the ground, well watered and staked. It looks just right there. Next year when it's time to cut hydrangeas, I won't have to look farther than our own front yard.

September 2009

———•—— a widening circle ——•———

It's been a month since *The Gift of an Ordinary Day* was published. No bestseller lists, no rave reviews in the *New York Times,* no calls from Oprah. There are still lots of unsold books piled on bookstore tables across the land. And yet, to my mind anyway, the book already feels like a success, thanks to all the readers who have discovered it, read it, and taken the time to write to me and say something like, "I'm glad you wrote this book and I'm glad I found it."

Sitting on the couch in my kitchen all those months ago, typing away, it was easy to pretend no one would ever actually read what I was writing. With that mindset, I could confess my doubts and fears about growing older, admit that I once hid my seventh grader's clothes, wrestle with my emotions as the day approached for my older son to leave home, make lists of the mundane things I'm grateful for. Often, at the end of the day, I would wonder if I was just wasting my time, trying to put words to all these private thoughts and feelings. When the book finally came out and I headed off to visit bookstores and do interviews, I sort of felt as if I were running around in my pajamas—not totally naked, but oddly exposed and vulnerable.

Then the first letter arrived in my inbox, from a woman in California, just my age. "You and I are kindred spirits and I am sure we would be fast friends if we were to meet," she wrote. "After spending an emotional afternoon yesterday finalizing the college list with my senior son and husband, who is quite opinionated about what he is willing to pay for, I had the good fortune to spend a half an hour wandering around a bookstore. Finding *The Gift of an Ordinary Day* was like stumbling upon a vintage Valentino gown in a thrift shop. I couldn't wait to get home and read the chapter on 'Applying.'"

Tracy went on to tell me a bit about her family and how my words had seemed to validate some of the things she already felt to be true. That relationships matter, for example. That it's ok to be quiet and still. That sometimes just taking a long deep breath is more important than accomplishing something on a list. At the end of her long e-mail, Tracy wrote, "I think we feel the same way about life." I had to agree.

Last night, my new friend who I've never met held a gathering for a group of women at her house outside of Los Angeles. They were meeting to discuss *The Gift of an Ordinary Day* with one another and to put together care packages for their kids in college. Since Tracy's daughter is in Cairo for the semester (and, as she learned the hard way, shipping anything to Cairo costs a fortune), she had offered to put together a package for my son Henry, who's in school in Minnesota. "Hope he will like a bunch of kooky stuff from California," she wrote the other day.

Meanwhile, Tracy is sending copies of my book to her friends from all over. And the conversation among a group of women scattered across the country is expanding by the day. Yesterday, I opened my e-mail to find a note from yet another kindred spirit. The words touched my heart: "While reading your book, so many of my thoughts and realizations found not only companionship but validation and hope. Thank you for becoming my 'partner' with your book, comforting me with your words and easing my way to surrender. I know that this process won't be easy or quick, but I'm on my way."

Today, I'm sitting on the couch in my kitchen, computer balanced on my knees, looking out at the same mountains that inspired me and my husband to put down roots in this small New England town five years ago. But all of a sudden, I feel a part of a larger community, too, a widening circle of new friends with stories to share and words of support and encouragement to exchange. Someday we may all meet in person somewhere, to walk on a beach, cook dinner, and compare notes face to face. Who knows? But until then, I'm grateful to know we're already connected—through written words, through shared sensibilities, through our common hopes and dreams for ourselves and for our children.

May the conversation continue. I am so glad to know you!

October 2009

——·—— writing class ——·——

Sixteen autumns ago, when my younger son, Jack, was a baby, I took a writing class in Harvard Square. Wednesday morning was the high point of my week. I would riffle through my closet, trying to pull together an outfit that wasn't stained with spit-up and that didn't shout out "suburban housewife," the babysitter would arrive, and I would jump into my car and head down Mass Ave., thrilled to have an excuse to buy a new notebook and a nice pen, to be out and about without an infant in a stroller or strapped on my back, happy instead to be part of the hustle and bustle of undergraduates and academics in the Square.

I made a point of getting into town early on those fall mornings, so I could linger over a pot of strong mint tea at Algiers and put the finishing touches on my piece for the week. Sometimes, I wrote the whole thing right there in the hour before class, notebook balanced on a teeny, tippy table in the window, scribbling down the events of the hours I had just lived through—waking up before dawn with a toddler in our bed, changing the baby, finding a private moment with my husband, greeting the day.

Our class, held in a dusty first-floor classroom at the Cambridge Center for Adult Education, was led by a woman with a weirdly wonderful name. Mopsy Strange Kennedy was something of an ageless, enigmatic, beloved Cambridge institution. With her head of wild, dyed-red hair, heavily lined eyes, snug boucle sweaters and miniskirts, she was scattered and zany and kind—an unlikely but unfailingly generous cheerleader for a bunch of aspiring writers. And she managed to set a tone each week that was some kind of magical amalgam of therapy session, cocktail party, and staged reading. She gave us provocative assignments ("Write the biography of your hair"), which we were free to do or not, and loads of encouragement. She found something to like in every piece and, buoyed aloft by her enthusiasm, even the shyest among us found the courage to read our work aloud.

We were a varied lot: jovial retirees filling time, serious students dedicated to their craft, unemployed twenty-somethings in search of themselves, zesty post-menopausal women eager to write new life chapters, and me, a former New York literary editor morphed into an exhausted young suburban mom. My entire publishing career had been built on the belief that I was better at ushering the work of "real" writers into the world than trying to say something of my own. Writing still seemed a bit presumptuous of me, as if I was trying to show off or get away with something. And yet, sitting around the table in that warm, safe room, I realized I had nothing to prove or to fear. It was possible to write for the joy of it. And it was just as possible, and just as satisfying, to be an open-hearted listener to my classmates' humble efforts. We were all in it together, trusting one another with our stories.

Week after week, for want of a more compelling subject, I found myself writing about the life I was living in that moment—my first attempt to make jam, the last of the tomatoes in the garden and my bouquet of nasturtiums on the windowsill, my young sons, myself.

"You have a perfect life," a classmate said to me once over coffee after class. Her remark surprised me. *Perfect* it most definitely was not. And yet, by teaching myself to pay attention to the way things actually were, by caring enough about the textures and mundane details of my days to write about them, I was beginning to find a voice. I was also discovering in my own ordinary life a kind of grace, or sanctity, that I had never quite noticed or appreciated before. To me, the most compelling and challenging subject of all, it seemed, was the present moment. Could I ever live it fully? Could I capture it, perhaps even hold onto it, by finding words to describe it?

Yesterday, my mom and I paid a visit to Mopsy's class. My mother had found her own writing voice in that room a few years after I left the class, and she'd made lasting friendships there at a time of transitions and losses in her life. "Go take Mopsy's workshop," I'd advised her, and so she did. And she began to write about her complicated marriage, her sadness, her hopes for the future. It was quite a treat, all these years later, to return as alumnae visitors. One of my mother's classmates (still a loyal attendee after thirteen years) had invited both of us to come together, and the timing was perfect. My mom has an essay she wrote in this month's edition of *The Sun* magazine. I had my new book to bring along. We could return as two published writers.

This time, I left home at 7 am and drove to Harvard Square from New Hampshire. And all the way down the highway, I thought about how important that long-ago class had been to me at a time when I wondered if I had anything at all to say. What I'd come to realize, sitting alone with my notebook in Algiers, or reading aloud to a group of kind-hearted souls, is that as long as we write what we love, it is worth doing, if only to honor that which is beautiful and precious and fleeting in our lives. The file folder in my desk drawer from that autumn sixteen years ago holds a stack of fading pages, brief word pictures of my life as it was then, a life that seems so distant in time that I can reach out and touch it only by reading those words. How grateful I am now that I paused then, in the midst of a great deal of exhaustion and exhilaration and tedium, and wrote some things down.

October 2009

——·—— Halloween shopping ——·——

Every year since my younger son, Jack, was three or so, we have tried on Halloween masks together. It was always Jack's holiday, the plans for some elaborate costume taking shape weeks in advance, the scarier the better.

When he was really young, he was happy to go trick-or-treating in whatever sweet little outfit I dreamed up for him—a tiny vampire, a tiger, a pumpkin. But the age of innocence didn't last long. He wanted to be terrifying.

Whereas Henry was content to paw through a bag of castoff clothes or to grab an old dress out of my closet and stick a witch hat on his head at the last minute, Jack wanted a full-bore, frontal-assault sort of costume, the kind that could not possibly be homemade, that absolutely had to be store-bought, preferably dripping fake blood. He wanted a knife or a spear or a hatchet to carry and would not be caught dead putting a jacket on over his black flowing garments, no matter how chilly Halloween night turned out to be. The costume ruled.

Yesterday morning, before Jack and I drove back to his high school in Massachusetts, we set out early with a shopping list he'd made the night before—all the things he's discovered he can't live without these days. Tea bags, boxes of cereal, Clearasil, a hot-water heater. We were efficiently checking things off the list—until we found ourselves alone in the Halloween section of Wal-Mart. It was hard to resist pausing to critique this year's batch of outrageous masks. Jack pulled a clown mask over his head, and I slipped on a piece of zombie headgear, complete with creepy little arms dangling from the sides. Pretty soon, we had tried on every mask on the shelf and contemplated a few mullet wigs as well.

Last year at this time, Jack and I were pretty much at a stand-off. His sixteenth year hasn't been easy for any of us, a time of growth and transformation, but of challenge and worry, as well, in equal measure. We've fought about everything. We've steered clear of each other some days; on others we found ourselves engaged in long, intense heart-to-heart talks. And we've also worked hard over the last few months, each in our own ways, to find new, healthier ways to communicate. Slowly, we're reestablishing trust, agreeing on new boundaries, grateful for each new piece of common ground. In a few weeks, he'll turn seventeen. He's happy, doing well in school, nearly grown up. It is easy, for the moment anyway, for us to actually enjoy each other's company.

Jack didn't buy a mask for Halloween. But our detour down the costume aisle brought back good memories for us both. I realize that what I remember most clearly now is not all the actual costumes of his childhood, but rather our annual trips together in search of the perfect mask. And how, year after year, I—a fully-grown woman—willingly tried on one ghoul and ghost face after another for my son.

How much fun we had together, when I wasn't in a rush to get the job done or to get somewhere else, but slowed down to his pace instead, and took the time to play and ponder along with him. That's what we did yesterday. It felt, for a few minutes, as if he were just a little kid again.

"We've always done this," he said, as we left the Halloween aisle and headed off in search of batteries and earbuds. "Wouldn't miss it," I answered.

October 2009

—·— still learning —·—

Five years ago today, my husband and I signed the papers on the property we now call home. I remember that day well, how nervous I was, already second-guessing myself and fearful we were doing the wrong thing. It was a gorgeous October day, cloudless and crisp, just a few leaves left on the trees.

We finished the closing and drove up from town to our new land and our dilapidated little cottage. Sitting outside that autumn morning next to my reluctant partner in this questionable real-estate venture, sipping a weak takeout coffee, I tried hard to make the moment special. We had just bought ourselves a house, after all, and ten acres of rocky fields, and a lovely view of Pack Monadnock. But neither of us was feeling very excited. There was, obviously, no turning back. But we weren't quite sure how to go forward.

Would we actually live here, in the old mouse-ridden, bat-infested cottage? It seemed so isolated and remote that morning, so meager and rundown compared to the solid suburban home we'd left behind. Everything sagged – our spirits, the scaly old roof, the rickety left-behind chairs we'd just lugged out of the house and set down in the grass, which needed mowing. I wondered if we would actually be happy here, whether we would be able to fix up the house, let alone our battered psyches, tested by several years of indecision, a job loss (his), restlessness (mine), and midlife questions (ours). Would we ever feel "at home" again anywhere? Was there any way to know for sure that this quiet New Hampshire hilltop was where we were really meant to be?

Yesterday, Steve and I raked leaves. The view across the mountains is completely familiar now and yet always surprising. Washed with color on a perfect fall afternoon, the spectacle of dappled mountain against blue sky still holds me in thrall. Henry, home from college for fall break, was reading in the hammock, idly tossing a tennis ball for Gracie. Day by day, I've been cutting back the garden, pulling out the annuals, cleaning up the beds. But the chrysanthemums are still blooming and the kitchen herbs continue to thrive. The place looks pretty good. Everywhere I turn, I see something that we have planted, built, or tended—and also something that still needs to be done.

As we hauled a huge tarp load of leaves down through the field to our growing burn pile, I asked my husband, "If you had the chance to do it all over again, knowing what you know now, would you have stayed put, or are you glad that we moved and ended up here?"

"Moving made me less afraid of the unknown," he said. "And a lot more open to change. But even apart from that, I can finally say I'm glad we did it. Life here is better than I expected. And even if we'd never moved at all, our lives would have changed anyway."

Hypothetical questions are silly. But I knew our house "anniversary" was coming up today, and I couldn't resist asking. I feel lucky to be here, too, and grateful for the lessons we've learned along the way. Leaving one home and making another one was a way to stretch ourselves, to sift through a lot of our assumptions about what it means to live well, to figure out what's important and hold on to that, while letting go of a lot that we'd always thought we needed.

The thing is, even now, after giving up one way of life in one place for another life elsewhere; after tearing down a house and building a new house from scratch and moving in; after sending one son off to college and getting the other midway through high school; after writing a book about all that and sharing our struggles, I *still* feel as if I'm sorting all this stuff out.

I still have to figure out what really matters, every single day. Change is still scary to me, even though we've lived through plenty of it. And yet, my life is also filled with joy and countless things to be grateful for. Mornings, I get up eager to see what the day will bring. At night I step outside, look up at the stars, and feel glad to be where I am.

This week, I've been surprised that the leaves have already fallen here, that frost came so early, that I still miss Henry so much when he's not around, that Jack is so tall and so funny and still, at times, so unreadable. Tonight, I was even surprised that the simple dinner I'd planned took me so long to prepare. (You'd think I'd know by now that it's impossible for me to make dinner in twenty minutes, no matter what the recipe gives for a prep time.)

And then, sitting around the table—our last night together before Henry goes back to school—I was surprised that everything seemed at once so wonderful and so painfully bittersweet. Sometimes I wonder: will all of this, any of it, ever start to feel like old hat? Or will I always be an amateur, continually taken by surprise by the twists and turns of my own life?

Maybe no one's a pro. I do take some comfort in that thought, the possibility that really we're all just feeling our way here, trying our best to be decent parents, partners, friends, daughters, and sons.

Long experience of living on the planet doesn't necessarily make anyone great at being a human being, but our devotion to the work can take us far. Good intentions count. Small steps in the right direction lead to more right steps. Kindness is always a good choice, no matter what else is going on. Five years after making the leap, I'm glad we landed here. And I'm also well aware that the challenge of crafting a good life doesn't end with a house being built, or a son growing up, or a book being completed. It's ongoing, for as long as we are willing and able to grow and to learn and to change. And being a passionate amateur is perfectly ok.

October 2009

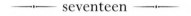 seventeen

My baby turned seventeen yesterday. Of course, he hasn't been a baby for a very long time and yet because he is my youngest, I can't help but think of him that way. Even now. Even though he is six feet tall, doing math that's beyond my comprehension, and creating a life in which he is increasingly, and (mostly) appropriately, independent. Sometimes it's hard for me to know exactly where my sphere of influence ends these days, when to speak up, when to hold my tongue and remember it's time for him to be making his own choices.

Yesterday morning, Jack drove his dad and me to our favorite breakfast spot. The sun poured in, onto our favorite table. We ordered coffees all around (he's drinking coffee; I'm saying nothing), and our talk turned to nationalism and liberalism and conservatism, monarchies and democracies (he's taking European history). His grasp of these concepts was reasonably solid and he was eager to share his new knowledge of how the past has come to inform our present (he's got some pretty well-informed opinions). I found myself listening carefully, learning things I hadn't known. Over pancakes and omelets, we asked questions (but not too many), had some laughs, got a pretty good glimpse of what's going on in our younger son's mind these days.

I'd written him a long birthday letter, for which I'd been mercilessly teased (I'm accused of going on and on in these annual missives), and so I'd already expressed how proud I am to be his mom, how glad I am that he's happy, thriving, working hard in school. So we didn't talk about any of that at breakfast or make much of the fact that his sixteenth year has been a rather wild ride.

A year ago, his dad and I were really worried about him, and he was really mad at us. He spent his sixteenth birthday at a friend's house. That weekend, I was half relieved to get a break from the fighting and half heartbroken that, for the first time ever, we weren't together on his birthday, blowing out candles and offering him our wishes for the year to come. Lying in bed that night, wide awake and sad, I did make a wish of my own, though.

In the afternoon yesterday, Steve and Jack hit some tennis balls. It was an unseasonable 70 degrees outside, tee-shirt weather, and I was happy to sit on the grass by the courts and read a book. The two of them are well matched, but this game wasn't about who could beat whom. It was just two guys who love to play and who enjoy each other's company. I got to watch, and to listen as they complimented each other's best shots. The sun shone. My husband and my son played with the grace and good humor you'd expect from two good friends, but not necessarily from a teenaged boy and his father. They whacked the ball hard, returned it again and again, reveled in their dance. I lay my book down, kicked back, and closed my eyes, listening to the sound of the ball, the easy laughter. Sometimes, wishes come true.

November 2009

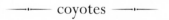

If you live in the country, you know the sound: the high, frantic yipping and yowling of coyotes working themselves into a frenzy around a kill. Last night, the yelps jolted me out of a sound sleep, heart pounding. Gracie already had her nose to the open bedroom window, on high alert. Steve, wide awake too, took my hand, and we listened in tense silence as the wild dogs went at it, the unearthly, piercing calls rising and falling and rising again in the field just below our house. Later, after the racket had stopped, I lay awake for a long time, shaken by this stark reminder that the world is multi-layered, more complicated and perilous than I like to admit to myself by light of day.

The flags are flying at half-mast here in our small town, though we are hundreds of miles from the military base at Fort Hood, where thirteen innocent people were shot this week and many others injured in a mass shooting. Driving up to Agway to buy a bag of birdseed, I look at that lowered flag and it hits me again: life is fragile; it turns on a dime. For any of us, at any time, tragedy may be no more than a heartbeat away. There's no way to know, nothing to be done either, other than be grateful for every good moment we're blessed to have, even as we carry those who suffer in our hearts. This week, it seems to me that death is just a little more present than usual.

A mile from our house, on a road I travel every day, a car crossed the center line in broad daylight, hit a pickup truck head-on, and killed the driver instantly. This morning, Steve called from the office with news that one of his best friends has died suddenly, unexpectedly, alone in a hotel room. I turn on the computer and see a headline first: "Swine flu has killed 540 children." And I pause to allow the statistic to assume meaning, knowing that behind the number are parents, siblings, friends, whose lives are irreparably changed. Meanwhile, my mother sits with her dying sister in Florida, trying to figure out how, after seventy-four years, you say good-bye to someone who arrived on the planet before you did and has always been right there, across the hall or at the end of a phone line, since the day you were born.

The coyotes' eerie yelps have echoed in my mind as I've gone about my business today, pondering death and carrying on with life, as people always do. Watering the houseplants, answering e-mails, changing the sheets on the bed, I am also aware, almost painfully so, of the fleetingness of things. What if a meaningful life is simply one in which the person doing the living is really paying attention?

I'm not quite sure how to respond to the painful truth of tragedies that aren't mine, exactly, but that are part of my world nonetheless. It does feel important to pay attention, if only to pause in my own daily doings to honor the suffering of all those whose lives have been taken or irreparably damaged. Empathy is what makes us human.

And so, not quite knowing what else to do, I stop in the parking lot at Agway, before the lowered flag, and say a prayer for the Fort Hood families. It's a small, private gesture, insignificant, I know. And yet it feels necessary, too.

I rebuckle my seat belt, drive the two miles into town, and then slow the car as I pass the spot where a stranger died a few days ago, just because he glanced down for a second, or answered his cell phone, or turned his gaze away from the road to watch a flock of geese heading south.

I stand at the kitchen sink, and I remember my husband's friend dancing at our wedding twenty-one years ago after making a silly, affectionate toast. I talk to my mom on the phone and then think back to an autumn picnic just two Octobers ago, when my mother and I, and my cousin and my aunt, all sat together on the banks of Norway Pond sharing sandwiches from the Hancock store. We knew even then that the cancer wasn't going to go away, that sometime in the future we would look back and savor the memory of that mild, golden day.

Somehow, we have to live knowing we will die. And so we count on the little things—which really aren't so little—to hold us in place and to give us some perspective: love, memory, hope, and faith. We reach out to embrace the present moment, imperfect as it is. "I have a bit of a girl-friend these days," one son confided today, surprising me.

"I think I did pretty well on my big test," the other reports over the phone.

My husband comes home, we feed the dog, pour a glass of wine, light a fire. I bring dinner to the table and we start talking things over. Life feels fragile and sacred and good. It is all of that, and more.

November 2009

—·—— dinner out ——·—

The year my mom turned sixty, my dad had the bright idea to whisk her off to a dental conference to celebrate. My mother, who never asks for much of anything, was, to put it mildly, underwhelmed. She'd thought he was planning a romantic getaway for the big 6-0. A night in a chain hotel in Baltimore wasn't what she had in mind. So my brother and I leapt in at the eleventh hour and took her out for a leisurely dinner at a very nice restaurant, just the three of us. My dad got the point pretty fast. To this day I think he still feels a little sheepish about how badly he blew it, but a tradition was born that night. My brother, John, and I had staked our claim.

Last night, we took my mom out for her thirteenth birthday dinner. I think we're so protective of this annual ritual because it's the only time that we ever find ourselves in this particular configuration—my mother and her two grown children. The three of us look forward to this night together; in truth, we enjoy it even more than we can admit to our respective spouses, who for this one occasion, are not invited. We love having one another all to ourselves, the chance to chat off-the-record about goings on in the family, the freedom to order whatever we want, including three separate desserts. We always have champagne.

As we lifted our glasses last night to my mom's seventy-third birthday, the three of us agreed that on her seventy-fifth, we will take our celebration to a charming inn somewhere and stay over night. Why not? None of us is getting any younger, and with every passing year the times that we do have to spend together seem even more special. My mom made us promise that when she's "dead and gone," as she bluntly put it, the two of us will still get together every year on her birthday, have a good meal, and carry on in her memory. We laughed and promised we would, and said we hoped there'd be many more years before anyone is ordering a drink to place in front of an empty chair.

The other morning a friend came by for tea, and we were talking about how hard it is, at times, to be at peace with the fact that our kids' childhoods really are over. There's no rolling back the clock to recapture even a moment of the past. All we can do is pay attention to the present, try not to repeat our old mistakes, love well *now*, even if we didn't always do such a great job *then*.

Sometimes, I miss my sons as the little boys they once were so much that it hurts. For years, we were so close, so tangled up with each other, that everything I thought or did in the course of a day was, in one way or another, all about them. But Jack turned seventeen a couple of weeks ago. Next month, Henry will be twenty. They are almost men, busy and preoccupied with their lives. My job now isn't to shape my days around theirs but to create a new rhythm for myself, to find a new sense of purpose altogether. I'm working on that. Life is busy and interesting and challenging in new ways. I'm getting better all the time at letting go.

But sitting with my brother and my mom last night, I allowed myself to imagine a future in which my own two fully-grown sons might insist on having me all to themselves for an evening. I could see myself climbing into one of their cars, being driven to a restaurant of their choosing, where the three of us would linger over decaf and dessert. We would talk about their spouses, the grandchildren, and how things are going for them at work and at home. I have no idea how to make that dream a reality, other than to do what my own mother has done all these years for me and my brother: Listen well. Love unconditionally. Laugh a lot. Believe in us.

November 2009

—·— thankful —·—

"Thanksgiving is really over," my friend Patti wrote yesterday. "All that's left are yams." I know what she means. In our house, it's a Tupperware container a third full of brothless turkey soup that no one looks forward to facing again.

When I was growing up, my parents put on Thanksgiving dinner for the whole extended family. My mother would pull out her spiral-bound Thanksgiving notebook days in advance and begin making lists and trying to pin down numbers. Thanksgiving for thirty was a weeklong enterprise that involved moving the furniture around, sliding leaves into tables, ironing tablecloths, grocery shopping with two carts, staying up late the night before, peeling potatoes and butternut squash. By ten in the morning the relatives would begin to arrive, bearing home-baked pies and braided loaves and tins of homemade fudge.

My Grammie Kenison always brought apple pie and a loaf of her airy white bread, perfect for sandwiches the next day. If the forecast promised clear skies, her brother, Great-Uncle Woodrow, would come, too. Woodrow could be counted on for his famous raspberry pie, made with berries he'd picked in July and frozen heaped into a pie plate for this very occasion. My dad churned two kinds of ice cream in the garage and roasted a huge turkey on the Weber, while my mom tended a second bird in the oven. It was my job to wash the grapes, make the clam dip, stuff celery, arrange olives and sweet gherkin pickles on the lazy Susan. The aunts and grandmothers chatted in the kitchen. The men would retreat, beers in hand, to the den and football on the TV. Eventually my brother and I would be shooed outside with all the cousins for "fresh air before dinner."

The meal I remember from my childhood was on the table, without fail, between one and two in the afternoon. Heads would bow while a grandparent said the grace, remembering those who had died, giving thanks for the health of those gathered round, blessing the food, the family, the day. The menu never varied: turkey and stuffing, mashed potatoes and baked sweet potatoes, gravy and cranberry sauce, creamed onions and boiled peas, squash, sliced bread, marshmallow salad. Four kinds of pie.

Every year was the best year ever, every dish the best it

had ever been—even the year a wild windstorm blew the power out and my parents managed to cook the entire meal in the fireplace and on the grill. Always, someone would say that we'd eaten too fast, given how much time and work had gone into all the preparation. Always, someone who claimed to be too full to swallow one more bite would agree to seconds anyway, just to make it last.

And then, just as the rest of us were slowing down, loosening belts or unbuttoning pants, Uncles Roger and Chet, who saw each other but once a year, for the Thanksgiving feast, would, by some unspoken signal, face off. The bowls of mashed potatoes and stuffing would be passed down the table, the plates filled again, and the two of them would set to work, this annual competition for the greatest stomach capacity as much a ritual part of our day back then as the Macy's parade or the fruitcake that no one ever ate but that everyone insisted my mom had to make anyway, so it would be there for breakfast the morning after.

Somehow, by the time the last car pulled out of the driveway and disappeared into the night, the kitchen would be restored to order, the dishes done, the turkey carcass encased in foil and tucked into the fridge surrounded by precarious stacks of leftovers. My parents made the whole thing look easy. And as a result, although I am now a middle-aged mother of two nearly grown children and fancy myself a good cook, I have never cooked a turkey in my life.

Last week, my mom and dad produced their forty-eighth Thanksgiving dinner. It's been a long time since we hosted the whole clan. Death and circumstance and the passage of time have separated us. And this year, with Henry in Minnesota and my brother at his wife's family's house, there were just five of us at the table, as small a Thanksgiving as any of us has ever had. We edited a little: no fruitcake, no creamed onions or clam dip or homemade ice cream. But otherwise, the meal was the one I've eaten all my life. Jack and Steve and I held hands with my mom and dad, said grace together, and then we each spoke in turn about what we're grateful for. My dad had tears in his eyes as he said, "I'm just glad that we can still do this."

Earlier in the day, I'd taken a walk and passed a house where a dozen or more family members were engaged in a ragtag football game out on the lawn. For an instant then, I found myself feeling sad, yearning for the good old days, the gaggle of aunts and uncles and cousins, the holiday as major production. But it really was just for an instant. We've had that, I reminded myself. We've lived it, loved it, and come now to a different part of life's journey. And back at the house, at that very moment, my parents were putting the finishing touches on Thanksgiving dinner, as they have for as long as I've been on the planet.

The five of us lingered at the table for a long time, enjoying one another's company as well as the meal. We raised a glass to the missing ones and the departed ones and we savored what was ours to savor in the moment. And then, in no time at all, Steve and Jack and I had the dishes done. We whiled away the afternoon, talked to the relatives on the phone, played Scrabble and Bananagrams, nicked away at the pie.

In the morning, my mom and I divvied up the remains of the bird. By evening, we three were home again, stock simmering on our own stove, Thanksgiving abundance carrying us right through the weekend. Today Jack went back to school, Steve took one last biscuit and the final bit of soup to work for his lunch, and another Thanksgiving holiday came to an end. Someday, I know, I'll be the one following my mom's old recipes and Steve will be trying to recreate my dad's special nest of charcoal on the grill. But right now, I'm grateful, above all, for this: the fact that I'm still somebody's daughter.

November 2009

———·—— scatter the darkness ——·——

If you're lucky, life affords you a few moments when you feel as if you are where you are meant to be, doing exactly what you are meant to do. Once in a while such a moment coincides with one of your children having that very same experience at the very same time. So it was yesterday afternoon as the lights dimmed for the final St. Olaf Christmas Festival concert of this year.

My husband and I had flown from New Hampshire to Minnesota for this Sunday afternoon performance. As the lights dimmed, the audience hushed, and the orchestra musicians finished tuning. The cavernous gymnasium grew silent, reverent. Five choirs filed in and took their places. I didn't expect to cry and yet when the violin section's first notes rang out, sudden tears rolled down my cheeks. The expectant silence gave way to ascendant harmonies; it was as if the air itself vibrated with sound. There is something about seeing and hearing over six hundred student musicians all joined together in a hymn of praise that can prompt a mother's already-full heart to, well, overflow.

A couple of hours earlier we'd talked with Henry over lunch about whether he was still thinking of studying music abroad for a semester next year. "Not in the fall," he'd said definitively. "There's no way I'd miss Christmas Fest."

Peering through the dimmed auditorium to pick him out in the crowd just before the stage lights came back up—second row from the back on the long risers, dressed in a scarlet robe, eyes trained on the conductor—I understood. Playing piano for a musical, performing in a jazz ensemble, rehearsing with singers, jamming with friends—these are all things my son loves to do. But one discovery he's made since he left home, went off to college, auditioned for a choir, and began to take voice lessons is that nothing makes him feel more alive than to join his own singing voice with others'.

Judging from the level of commitment and the talents of the St. Olaf choirs, he is not alone in that. For two breathtaking hours those of us in the audience were swept along on a spiritual journey in song. Most of us had traveled some distance to be there; now, thanks to these gifted young musicians, we were truly transported. In a world that too often seems bleak and overburdened, here was redemption, hope, and light.

"Scatter the darkness," a banner above the performers proclaimed. Tiny white bulbs outlined the Christmas trees on each side of the stage and shone like stars above. Voices soared. Slowly, sumptuously, the hymns and carols gathered in strength and power, weaving shimmering tapestries of sound. My son sang. We were there to hear every note. How glad I was in that moment—for him, for us, and most of all, for new passions discovered, claimed, and realized.

December 2009

 snow day

First snow. And Gracie and I are the first ones in the woods this afternoon, breaking the trail. I am sweating in my jacket in no time, heart pounding as I trudge up the path. It feels good to have my snowshoes on again, and it's also sobering to realize how out of shape I am. I stand in my tracks for a moment, catch my breath, listen to the silence, quiet the thoughts racing through my head. *Just be here,* I remind myself.

When we woke to the sound of snowplows this morning, I was excited and then a little sad. There's nothing better on a dark December morning than being the messenger to sleeping teenagers, getting to whisper those magical words, "No school today." I missed my boys this morning, missed having them lounging around in sweats and tee shirts while the snow fell outside, missed the leisurely breakfast, the afternoon shoveling, the coziness of being snowed in with the kids. Jack called when he finished classes, and then Henry called, and that helped a bit. But snow days are not what they used to be.

Out in the woods, the snow is already deep, still falling soundlessly, relentlessly, transforming the world. I stick out my tongue, catch a few feathery flakes, and feel the brief sting of melt, the flutter of snow dampening my eyelashes, my cheeks. A reminder that no matter how old I am or how much my life changes, things can still feel new and fresh. Wonder doesn't expire. And by the time I get home, I feel better—rejuvenated, ready for a cup of tea, able to face the empty house, the quiet, the stillness of a December dusk.

December 2009

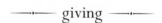

—·— giving —·—

Every month, my neighbor Debbie brings me her copy of *Yoga Journal* after she's read it. This small gesture is one of so many kindnesses Debbie extends to me that, I'm embarrassed to admit, sometimes I don't even remember to say thank you.

Among other things, Debbie entertains our dog Gracie for a few hours a day, fills our bird feeder when it's empty, waters my houseplants when I go away, sweeps our garage, brings me inspiring quotes to read and a still-warm croissant from the bakery, just because.

Sometimes I also forget that Debbie lives with chronic pain, the debilitating aftereffects of her near-fatal bout with E. coli nearly ten years ago. My friend doesn't talk much about her health. She's an expert at deflecting that mundane question, "How are you?" Only when I notice that she's walking more slowly than usual or bending down on one knee to rest does it occur to me—she's not mentioning it, but physically she feels lousy.

I don't think I'm totally oblivious. It's more that Debbie is so focused out, and she does such a good job of taking care of the people and animals in her life, that I don't always notice what else is going on—namely, that she's hurting. One thing I've begun to see, however, is that giving to others is Debbie's way of taking her mind off her own discomfort.

A couple of weeks ago, while paging through the most recent issue of *Yoga Journal* one night, I came across a review of a book called *29 Gifts*. Author Cami Walker had spiraled into a depression after she was diagnosed with multiple sclerosis. Two years later—angry, alone, and addicted to painkillers—she was advised by a South African healer to give something away every day for twenty-nine days. The gifts didn't have to be large, or even material, he explained, but they did need to be offered with love and with consciousness. For Walker, this simple practice was transformational, the first steps on her own healing journey.

The idea of giving a small unexpected gift each day

during the month of December was so appealing that I decided to give it a try. The next day, December 1, I bought a couple of chocolate Santas, just so I wouldn't go into the exercise empty-handed. And then, without much more thought than that, I began. The gifts I've given over the last few weeks are nothing special really—a box of treats mailed to a son at school, a vintage copy of "Heidi" sent to a friend's nine-year-old daughter, homemade granola to our neighbors, candy to a niece and nephew, a letter written to someone feeling low, a pint of Ben & Jerry's Strawberry Cheesecake ice cream to Debbie.

But being on the lookout for gift-giving opportunities has subtly changed the way I move through my days. Giving, not surprisingly, creates a sense of abundance. It's fun. And it's also sort of magical. Taking an extra moment to make eye contact and say something kind to a shopkeeper or a waiter, I get the gift of their response in return. Calling an old friend to say hello, I get the gift of her surprise and pleasure on the other end of the line. Offering dinner to friends, I receive the gift of their appreciation. Meanwhile, I notice a fresh current of energy in my life. A few days ago, an odd, long-out-of-print book arrived in the mail, specially ordered for me by a friend in Minnesota because he knew it would make me laugh. Gifts are flowing both ways.

During this Christmas season, as we choose presents for our loved ones, we're reminded that it's not really the gift itself but the act of giving that makes the world a brighter place. Giving to others, we can't help but be more aware of the blessings in our own lives. Gratitude bubbles up. So does joy. Pretty soon we realize we don't need a holiday to inspire generosity. We can give just for the pleasure of bringing a smile to someone's face or a little more love into the world.

Eighteen days into my month of giving, I think I'm coming to understand Debbie a bit better. Giving and doing for others is her spiritual practice. It is a decision she makes, day by day and moment by moment, to choose gratitude over self-pity, generosity over pain, light over darkness. She's an inspiring teacher. And I'm lucky to be her student as well as her neighbor and her friend.

December 2009

*This is the first, the wildest and the wisest thing
I know: that the soul exists and is built entirely
out of attentiveness.*
— Mary Oliver

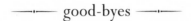 good-byes

The house is so quiet. I had planned to spend the afternoon putting Christmas decorations away, vacuuming the dog hair and grit from the floor, stripping sheets off the kids' beds, the guest-room bed, the pullout couch. (We had a full house here last night.) But I know that when I get up from my spot at the kitchen table and begin those tasks, it will mean the holiday we've had together really is over.

When I went to bed last night around 11:30, Henry and a couple of his former high-school classmates were sprawled on the couch with afghans, watching old episodes of *The West Wing*. Jack was upstairs chatting on the phone with a friend. My eighteen-year-old niece, Caitlin, who's been staying with us for a week, was putting the finishing touches on her college applications. The fire we'd nursed all afternoon was burning to embers in the fireplace, the dishwasher was running its second load, a pile of sodden boots sat in a widening puddle by the back door, an unfinished game of Bananagrams lay abandoned on the table, laptops and iPods were scattered about the kitchen. The place looked lived in, definitely.

Early this morning we said good-bye to Henry's best friend, I took Henry and Caitlin to the airport, and Jack left as well, to drive back to school with his dad. I am behind on everything, with two weeks' worth of un-answered e-mails on my computer, a deadline to meet, an empty refrigerator. It's been days since I exercised or picked up a book or wrote so much as a word. There's plenty to do. And yet, alone for the first time in weeks, I'm a bit unsettled by the silence, almost bereft, already missing everybody.

One thing I've found this year is that the partings don't get much easier, no matter how many times my sons come home and go away again. But I've also learned how important it is to appreciate all the moments of their being here, even when those moments are not exactly the bliss-ful "family time" I always envision. The house gets messy, best-laid plans go awry, the days fly by too fast, and suddenly it's time to haul out the suitcases again, grab the last load from the dryer, say good-bye.

I guess there's never going to be quite enough time, no matter how long their visits last—not enough time to do all the things I look forward to doing or to launch all the conversations I hope to have or even to relax into our old, comfortable routines. Certainly most of the things Jack and I used to fight about and wrangle over seem silly now, a waste of precious opportunity. And if Henry never does stand up straight or chew with his mouth closed, so be it. Instead of being bothered by things that used to drive me crazy, I'm aware that our time together is short, my sons' imminent departures always right around the corner. And so I remind myself to see what's good and to appreciate what is. At seventeen and twenty, my children have their own ideas about what they want to do and when and how. I'm learning to accept that, too. To simply say "I love you," rather than, "Why don't you. . ."

We didn't read Truman Capote's *A Christmas Memory* this year, or sing carols, or walk the New Year's labyrinth at Town Hall. We never made it to the movies nor did we even manage to shoot a family photo before everyone scattered out the door—all things that were on my holiday agenda. But we did light candles last night and hold hands for one grace around the dinner table. We rang in 2010 together, had lots of laughs and wonderful visits with family and friends, and bestowed sweet hugs and kisses all around this morning as we went our separate ways.

Upstairs, the scent of Old Spice still lingers. Snow is falling. The empty house settles into late afternoon shadow. And I allow myself this thought: the time we did have, though not as I'd imagined it would be, was perfect as it was. And the quiet now—it is perfect, too.

January 2010

———·—— loss and love ——·———

One after the other, my aunt's husband of fifty-nine years and her three grown children spoke about what they remembered and what they would miss. It was bitterly cold in Florida on Saturday, all rain and bluster. My dad had gone over to my aunt and uncle's house early, to staple plastic sheeting around the screened lanai and install a rented space heater to keep the guests warm.

"I want music," my aunt had told my mother some months ago, and so my mom hired a singer and we had "Amazing Grace." Also at my aunt's request, the portrait she had painted of her beloved dog hung in a place of honor on the kitchen wall. There was a reading from the Bible, the 23rd psalm; she had wanted that, too.

Otherwise, for the first time in their lives, her family was on its own. Together, without the guiding hand of the one who really ought to have been there calling the shots, my mom and my uncle and cousins created a memorial service that felt fitting and true.

This is what we do when our loved ones die. We attend to details, send cards and flowers, change plans, book plane tickets. We cook and rent chairs and search for old photos and call the caterer. We get busy, and then we gather ourselves together and try to make some sense of it all. My mother had baked a cheesecake, found a poem, arranged for a meal, asked my son Henry to compile two CDs' worth of music. And when it was her turn to speak, she stood up in the living room and tried to put into words how it felt to lose the last person on earth whom she'd known her entire life, her big sister.

My uncle wrote a eulogy and somehow found the strength to deliver it. He recalled the day he saw my aunt for the first time, in the lunch line at the University of New Hampshire in the fall of 1948. She was blonde, movie-star beautiful, had been voted Kampus Kitten that freshman year. "I'm going to marry that girl," my uncle told his buddy. He did, and until the day she died, he marveled at the way her smile still lit up the room.

"She was the nicest person I ever knew," he said at the end, his eyes full of tears, and then he said it again, to make sure we all knew how important her kindness was to him.

"My mom was always there, every time I woke up after one of my surgeries," recalled my cousin Carol, who lost a leg to cancer at age eleven and has endured many more surgeries in the forty-plus years since. "Sitting by my bed, just waiting with me."

My cousin Sue described a hot summer day, a ride on the swan boats in the Public Garden in Boston with her two young sons and her mom. Nothing special really, except that those boys are grown now and launched on lives of their own. But years ago they experienced a special moment together, and they have all cherished the memory ever since.

Behind Sue, on the bookshelf, stood a blurry photograph—two sweaty little boys on a boat, a weary young mother, a grandmother whose face was alight with joy. "Every spring, when the swan boats return," Sue promised us and herself, "I'm going to make sure to go again, and to remember the happiness of that day."

"We had an ongoing, private conversation," my cousin Don revealed when it was his turn. "My mom and I could talk about anything, but we shared a curiosity about spiritual things, mysteries, the afterlife . . . We always wondered about what would come next. I guess my mom knows the answer now."

My aunt was an artist, and her watercolors fill the walls of her modest home. Months ago, she affixed small stickers to the frames, ensuring that each child and grandchild would receive his or her rightful inheritances. But I have been thinking these last two days of my aunt's real legacy. Of what it is that any of us leave behind when we go. The "stuff" doesn't really mean much. Most of us yearn for less of it in our homes, in our lives. What counts in the end is love.

My uncle's romanticized recollections to the contrary, my aunt was not a perfect wife and mother. Their family life wasn't perfect either. Whose is? Yet I found deep consolation in the course of that cold, rainy hour, as my aunt's husband and children offered their memories. What had endured for them, what they shared with the rest of us, was the knowledge that they had been loved—loved unconditionally and completely—for who they are.

I have been worried about a son this week. Giving in to my own fear, I wrote him an e-mail I regretted as soon as I sent it. I spun hurt and anger when I should have been restitching the frayed seam of our love. We are working now to set things right, my son and I, to repair what has been torn between us. I feel some urgency about this. And I will do my best to write and speak with more care in the future.

Death is, among other things, a stark reminder of what really matters in the long run. It's not the book written, the picture painted, the money earned, saved, or spent. It's certainly not being right, or convincing another to see your point of view. And so, I realized this morning that I owed Jack an apology.

"I'm sorry, I love you, please forgive me." These words don't fix a problem but they do bring love back into the heart and center of a relationship. And isn't this really the only legacy worth leaving? The knowledge that no matter how many other things we've done or not done along the way, we have loved with all our hearts, as best we can, from one moment to the next.

January 2010

——•—— asking for help ——•——

Yesterday afternoon I got a call from a mother in distress. The woman was a stranger to me, a single mom struggling through tough times with a troubled teenaged son. My younger son went through his own tough time at age sixteen. So I knew right away how things were for her—the helplessness, the worry, the anger, the isolation, the sleepless nights. Of course, it always helps to talk with a person who's already lived through the terrifying thing you're enduring in the moment. I was glad someone had given her my number and that she'd found the courage to call. I listened as best I could while driving down the highway, and then I offered her the only advice I felt qualified to give: get help.

It seems like such a simple thing, asking for help. And yet it can be so hard. Hard to admit, "What I'm doing isn't working." Or, "I have a problem that's bigger than I am." Or, "I have no idea what to do next."

Revealing the cracks—in our family life, in a relationship, in our own carefully crafted personas—means showing just how vulnerable we really are. Most of us have a lot invested in putting a good face on things, a message our children internalize early and master by adolescence. They get pretty good at acting as if they don't care, even when things are falling apart around them. Even when, inside, they are as lost and scared as we are.

I've learned a few life lessons from both of my teen-aged sons and most of them can be boiled down to the first lines of the Serenity Prayer, adopted years ago by twelve-step programs. If you are sharing your house with someone between the ages of fourteen and eighteen or so, you might think about taping these words up on your bathroom mirror, too:

God grant me the serenity to accept the things I cannot change; courage to change the things I can; and wisdom to know the difference.

In one way or another motherhood seems to demand

that we live these words every single day. For much of last year, the operative word for me was "courage." "Courage to change the things I can" means courage to admit that things aren't working, and that we have a responsibility to our children and to ourselves to find a better way. Sometimes, the first step on that path is the willingness to say, "We need a hand here." And then we are called to summon in ourselves yet another dose of courage. The courage to follow through, and to make hard choices and sometimes painful changes. The courage to be the best parents we can be, moment to moment, even when that means letting go of a vision of the way things "ought" to be.

Asking for help ourselves, we lead the way for our children. We affirm our own faith in the world, and we strengthen theirs a little, too, by acknowledging, "We can't do this alone." And then by saying, "The help we need is here."

"I have to go now," I finally said to my caller, promising that we would speak again. I was meeting my son to watch him play squash, a sport he discovered this winter and has taken up with a passion. I'd never even seen a squash match till a few weeks ago, when I Googled one on YouTube, so I'd know just what it was that Jack was so excited about. Yesterday we sat together and watched the varsity team, as he explained squash strategy and how to score. By the time he entered the court to play, I had my bearings. I sat with his best friend, who cheered him on in true best-friend spirit and who kindly gave me a bit of play-by-play as the match progressed.

Afterward, over dinner, we talked about how much has happened in a year, how much better things are now, how excited Jack feels as he looks into the future, wondering where he'll go to college, what he'll end up doing with his life, what might be just around the corner.

These days, I'm working with the "wisdom" part of that prayer. My sons are both so close to being grown up. And being their parent now means remembering that how they each "turn out" isn't up to me or my husband. It's up to them.

Wisdom is about knowing what I still need to keep hold of—our family values, basic agreements for living together in the house when the kids are at home, and confidence in their good judgment when they're not. It still means consequences that are directly related to poor decisions. And it means knowing what I must let go of: the idea that it's my job to make the world right for my children. It's up to each of them now to find their way in the world as it is.

I also have to trust that my sons have learned the most important lessons I had to teach them. Including the one that can save us all: "Ask for help."

February 2010

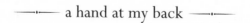 a hand at my back

I walked in off the street to a yoga class billed as "Sweet

Vinyassa." It's been a week of new places and new faces, from the moment I arrived last Wednesday night on the doorstep of a friend I'd never met in La Canada, California, to this morning, when I found myself asked to bend over backward and let go.

A week after my book *The Gift of an Ordinary Day* came out, an e-mail appeared in my in-box: "You and I are kindred spirits," it read, "and we would be fast friends if we were to meet." Fast forward six months—and my husband and I were unpacking our bags in Tracy's guest bedroom.

Tracy and I continued to write back and forth after that first letter, and from the very beginning something clicked. We became friends even without meeting. And so when she invited me to come to California, to stay at her house and speak to a large parent education group in her town, a voice inside me whispered, "Just say yes."

I haven't been to California for twenty years. The thought of speaking in front of strangers makes my palms sweat. Leaving my home is always hard for me. I've never stayed over night with someone I didn't already know. And yet . . .

I turned fifty-one last fall and something inside me shifted. After years of putting off travel, adventure, experiences that might take me out of my comfort zone, I finally began to ask myself: If not now, when? Facing up to the hard, cold fact of over half a century on the planet, I also had to confront the truth that anything I put off now might not ever happen at all. So I made a vow to myself on my birthday last year to accept the adventures that are offered to me, even if they do make my palms sweat.

And so, last Monday I bought myself a gray silk suit on sale for half price (the most beautiful, grown-up thing I've ever owned), and on Wednesday morning my husband, Steve, and I got up early, shoveled ten inches of fresh snow away from the garage door, and headed for the airport. In the last few days, thanks to Tracy's vision, hard work, and hospitality, I have given a talk to two hundred smart, incredibly welcoming women. I've spoken at a bookstore, signed well over a hundred copies of my book, and been the guest of honor at the loveliest ladies' tea party imaginable. I took a hike into the Southern California mountains with a group of women who felt like old friends before we'd panted our way up the first hill. And I had the joy of sitting down at the end of a long day, kicking off my shoes and getting to know my e-mail pen pal really well, face-to-face at last.

After photos and hugs and good-byes in La Canada on Saturday morning, it was on to Los Angeles, to meet another e-mail friend, writer and Zen teacher Karen Maezen Miller, whose book *Hand Wash Cold* will come out this spring. After two months of e-mails back and forth, and books exchanged and read avidly, Maezen and I took all of about thirty seconds to feel at ease with each other in person. We walked through her one-hundred-year-old Japanese garden, ate orange muffins, jumped into her nifty electric car, and made our way into the city for a dharma talk at the Zen center that is her spiritual home.

"This is really my life?" I thought, as Steve and I took

our places, sitting cross-legged on plump round pillows at the Hazy Moon Zen Center in Los Angeles, the only "civilians" amid a room full of Buddhist monks with shaved heads and long black robes. And yet, after three days of nonstop talking and smiling, it was a relief to be silent, to bow and to sit and to listen. To be reminded that the only moment is the present moment, the beautiful gift of right here and right now. Sun poured through the windows. Silence ripened. My mind, nothing but busy for weeks and weeks, grew quiet at last.

Now, with the "work" part of this trip behind me, I'm on holiday in the tiny town of Ojai, California, enjoying a bit of vacation with Steve at a homey bed and breakfast. It feels good to relax and exhale, to be the anonymous, invisible *me* rather than the author of a book, to take long walks, read a novel on the porch, wander through the farmer's market. And yet, even here, the opportunity to stretch presents itself.

"Just bend your knees and allow yourself to let go," the yoga teacher suggested to me this morning. She'd picked me, the stranger who'd just happened to show up in class, to demonstrate a backbend. No, I'd never done one before. But after a week of letting go and having faith that wherever I was, was exactly where I was meant to be, bending over backward didn't seem all that scary.

Two pairs of strong hands supported my back as I reached my arms up over my head and started to go over. And moments later I was in a place I'd never been before, palms on the floor, heart lifted, feet planted, backbending.

Tonight, as I sit in front of a cozy fire in our Ojai B&B, far from home, typing these words, I feel a little bit like I did this morning when I bent over backward. Which is to say, I'm reminded that life is one big invitation to say "yes" and then let go.

What I loved most about this week was not the book sales and accolades from readers (nice as they were!), but rather that sense of support, right there for me whenever I needed it most. There was a moment as I stood in front of the crowd giving my talk, when my legs stopped shaking and I began to sense instead the warm, supportive energy in the room. I realized it then and was made aware of it again this morning in a yoga class where I knew not a soul: let go, and you'll be caught. Let go, and then feel the relief of knowing there will a hand at your back if you need it, ready to hold you, to guide you, to make sure you don't fall over, or fall apart, or fall through the cracks.

Speaking to a room full of women was sort of like bending over backward. In each case, I met myself in a new place, thanks to some help from strangers who were just friends I hadn't met yet.

February 2010

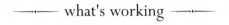

—·— what's working —·—

It started as I was stepping out of the bathtub the other morning. I slipped, one leg in, the other out, into a sort of bare-butt split that landed me down hard on the tile floor. The only real injury I sustained was a badly stubbed middle toe. But within two hours, the bruise was a brilliant black and purple and it hurt to walk. I couldn't put on a shoe. My toe swelled and pulsed, as if my heart were beating inside it.

Wincing, I made it to my book group that evening and to a meeting the next morning. But by then a few other things were going wrong. Jack had called, in some trouble at school. A wild storm of gusty wind and heavy snow had knocked out the power not only at our house, but at three hundred thousand other rural New England homes. I drove around for a while on slippery roads, buying coffees I didn't really want, in search of Internet access at cafes with Wi-Fi so I could get some work done. No luck.

That night, as it became clear that power wouldn't be restored any time soon, Steve and I returned to our cold, dark house, fumbled around for a flashlight, and gathered up a few things. The house plants were dry as bone. A week's worth of dirty laundry was piled in the bedroom – the contents of our California suitcases. I thought of the bags of summer raspberries and blueberries thawing in the freezer and wondered why we hadn't bought a generator after last year's ice storm. (But aren't generators a bit like umbrellas? Who buys one when it's not raining?) Camped out at a friend's house, I discovered that the "contact" part of my website hadn't been functioning for a while, and that all e-mails addressed to me were apparently disappearing into some vast spam file in the sky.

By the end of yesterday, crews had removed the fallen

trees from our road, and the electricity was back, though it turned out that our heating system had failed. Wearing long underwear, a hat, and my down parka, I fired up the gas stove, flushed the toilets, watered the poor plants, and began to unpack and set the house to rights. My neighbor Debbie stopped by to fill her water jugs from our tap and see how we were making out.

"So many things aren't working!" I complained, feeling exhausted and annoyed and sorry for myself.

"Yes," she answered cheerfully. "But think how many things ARE working!"

Of course, she had me. Beyond the window, huge snow-flakes were drifting slowly down, softening the hard edges of the world. Inside, the water was running again, and a flick of the switch brought light. All over town, people were still waiting for power, and ours was restored. My toe had just about shrunk back to normal size. Most of the food in the freezer was still frozen. And after a few phone calls and a $200 emergency visit from the heating contractor, I knew we would soon be warm again, too.

I scooped up the pile of laundry from the floor—bright summer shorts and tee shirts, so out of place here, in the middle of a snowstorm. And then I had to smile. Suddenly, instead of seeing a pile of dirty clothes, I saw a reminder of our week's worth of west-coast adventures and good times with friends old and new. I looked around at our house, cold still, but just fine, full of books and paintings and blankets and tables and chairs. . .the stuff of home. I could rummage around in the refrigerator and find enough food for dinner. The e-mails would wait.

Yeah, a few things in my life aren't working. But I don't have to look far to see plenty that are. Today, the house is warm. My son Henry somehow fixed my website from afar and even managed to retrieve the missing e-mails. My toe has healed enough for me to put on sneakers. After a good night's sleep in my own bed, I'm feeling decidedly more cheerful.

Debbie, an E. coli survivor who understands more about living with discomfort than anyone I know, just completed twelve weeks of IV iron treatments and still spends quite a few hours a week curled up with a heating pad, breathing through the recurring pain in her intestines. She makes a daily practice of ignoring what's not working and focusing instead on what is. As always, I learn from her example. Someday, maybe, I'll get it.

March 2010

———·——— dining alone ———·———

I am in New York City for two nights, serving as a judge on a literary panel. Today has been a long day, nine hours in a hotel conference room. By the time our group is released from duty just before 6, I'm ready to get outside and seize the last minutes of sunlight on the first day of the year that truly feels like spring.

I walk twenty blocks or so with my coat flapping open, cell phone pressed to my ear, checking in with every family member. Then I slip my phone into my pocket and watch Times Square grow even brighter as night falls, a vast neon panorama of news and temptation and blandishment. For a while it's fun just to be swept along by the tide of humanity, gazing into shop windows and considering my options.

Not knowing how long my meeting would run or how tired I'd feel after trying to be articulate all day, I haven't made a plan for the evening. But now, watching the world go by—families, couples, groups of friends—I feel a little unmoored, wishing for company. I think about going to a show, scoring a last-minute ticket at the half-price booth, but I've been sitting for hours. Actually, dinner and bed sound even more appealing. There was a time when I would have given anything to even have such a choice. Now I wonder if I'm settling for too little, behaving like a boring, middle-aged mother cut adrift, when I should be savoring my freedom by taking advantage of some big-city experience.

Twenty-five years ago, I was an editor in New York, young and ambitious and poor, putting a life together on a salary of $11,500 a year. One day during my first few months in the city, my boss paused at my desk around lunch time and asked what I was doing. "Reading a manuscript," I said, through a mouthful of tuna-fish sandwich.

"I don't want to see you here, eating in the office," he admonished, surprising me. "Your job is to get out there, meet people, and hustle. The best stuff always happens at lunch." In those days, even junior editors had expense accounts, but until Cork Smith gave me a little kick in the butt and told me to pick up the phone and start using mine, I wasn't quite sure what to do with it.

As it turned out, my publishing lunches kept me from starving. Knowing I would get a decent meal at noon, which would cost the equivalent of my own food budget for an entire week, I could subsist on a grapefruit and English muffin for breakfast, and a small salad from the Korean grocer on the corner for dinner. Once a day, I stuffed myself. If I was careful, I could just manage to pay my bills.

"You certainly eat a lot, for such a small person," I recall one elderly literary agent observing. No doubt I nodded, demure, not telling her that my next proper meal was twenty-four hours away.

I think of those days now, as I sit down to a solitary Saturday night dinner in a French bistro in midtown Manhattan. It's a first for me: a restaurant meal without the easy company of a spouse or child or friend along to split an entree, make conversation, share the moment, pay the tip. I have a magazine in my purse, but it's too dim in the restaurant for reading—no chance of hiding out after all. The waiter whisks away the other place setting at the table, hands me a menu, and I'm on my own. I take a quick survey, relieved to spot a middle-aged man nursing a glass of red wine, a single woman at a banquette against the wall, my compatriots in solitude.

The memories of my long-ago weekends in New York are still fresh. I'd put my sneakers on and walk the city for hours, soaking it in—smells, sounds, images, and glimpses of how other people lived. The bustling restaurants and alluring boutiques were way off limits—the Sunday *New York Times* was my one big indulgence. I often wondered back then what being truly "grown up" would feel like, whether I would ever be one of those casual, perfectly turned out women with the right sunglasses, jacket, and shoes. Whether I would ever wander into a sidewalk cafe for Sunday brunch without a thought for how deeply those scrambled eggs would dent my paycheck. At twenty-five, I was working hard to fake it till I made it, a small-town girl with a passion for books, a mostly empty Rolodex, and a minuscule alcove of an apartment on West 83rd—an address that surprised and thrilled me every time I wrote it out.

Now, twenty-six years later, I confront the truth: I will never have the right shoes. And most fashionable sunglasses look ridiculous on me. But I also realize that it doesn't matter much anymore. One good thing about turning fifty is the realization that we don't have to impress anybody. No one notices or cares what kind of shoes I wear.

Still, a part of me feels a little exposed and uncomfortable here, claiming a valuable piece of New York real estate—a restaurant table—all to myself. I order a glass of white wine and look around. Turns out that the other two previously solitary diners aren't alone after all—a delicately beautiful red-haired woman has joined the man, full of apology for her tardiness, and the lone woman's husband has returned from the restroom. I am the only unaccompanied person in the room.

"We can smile, breathe, walk, and eat our meals in a way that allows us to be in touch with the abundance of happiness that is available," writes Buddhist philosopher Thich Nhat Han. "We are very good at preparing to live, but not very good at living. We know how to sacrifice ten years for a diploma and we are willing to work very hard to get a job, a car, a house, and so on. But we have difficulty remembering that we are alive in the present moment, the only moment there is for us to be alive."

All of a sudden, it occurs to me that at twenty-five, much as I would have liked a date, I also would have been quite excited to eat a restaurant meal alone. How grateful I would have been back then to be able to just enjoy my food, without having to act like I knew what I was talking about or feigning interest in someone's mediocre first novel.

And so, in an instant, I make a decision: I will eat this particular meal in a way that allows me to be in touch with the abundance of happiness that is available. I'm here, I'm alone, and I am going to fully experience the experience. My salad arrives, and I savor every bite of lettuce and warm goat cheese. I smile at the waiter, observe my fellow diners, take in the convivial atmosphere, the clatter of silverware, the low din of voices, the exuberance of the two artfully dressed young French women seated next to me, tucking into their steak frites. I linger over a dish of mussels, with undistracted appreciation.

Happiness, it turns out, is available after all. By the time dessert arrives (I never order dessert!), I no longer feel unmoored, but intimately, joyfully connected. Alive in the moment, grateful for what is, full and content and ready for the long walk back to my hotel. Tomorrow at this time, I will be back at home in my own kitchen, making a meal and setting the table for two. Tonight, though, I am dining alone.

March 2010

————— spring break —————

Every year since our sons were very young, our family has come to Florida for a week of visits with the grandparents and a welcome respite from the back side of winter.

Yesterday morning, we stepped out our back door at 4:30 am into a torrent of freezing rain, gusting wind, and slush. In darkness, eyes still sleep-sandy, we made our way along the empty, icy roads to the airport—bright lights, security lines, hot Starbucks coffee.

As always, the contrasts of the day astonished me. It is surreal to wake up in one familiar place and go to sleep hours later in another. My parents' airy, modern home on a densely populated saltwater canal couldn't be more different from our own snug wooden house in New Hampshire. In the course of one day we exchange dirty snow and still-bare trees for lush green lawn, bougainvillea, and rustling palms; fleeces and boots and gloves for shorts and tee shirts and bare feet. Drum fish commence their percussive mating call in the water beyond the open bedroom windows, the temperature is a mild 68 degrees, the kitchen fruit bowl overflows with strawberries, avocados, cantaloupe.

There isn't much to do here—no beach nearby, no cool sights to see or touristy events to attend. When the boys were little we would treat them to a Little Rascals video, go out for a pancake breakfast, set up coloring books outdoors, play games of Clue. A trip to the Dairy Queen or a round of miniature golf might be the focus of the day. Yet year after year we'd return, content to do pretty much the same things we did the year before—spending a few days with Steve's parents three hours north of my folks, visiting my aunt and uncle, relaxing with my mom. Meanwhile, our sons grew up. Over time, Netflix movies replaced the Little Rascals, video games edged out board games, laptops took the place of coloring books and crayons. Pancakes and Dairy Queen are still part of the agenda, though they don't elicit the excitement they once did.

Waking up this morning on the foldout couch in the den, to the smell of fresh coffee and the low coo of mourning doves, I was overcome with a sense of the long, slow passage of time. How much has changed in our lives, even as this one annual ritual has held. The privilege of being both mother and daughter in this house will come to an end, I know. The day will soon arrive when our boys will no longer choose a visit to grandma as a spring-break destination. My parents, now in their seventies, cannot be our hosts forever. There are plenty more changes in store.

And so I'm grateful for every morning we find ourselves here in any family combination, waking to birdsong and the sounds of my mom making coffee in the kitchen. In recent years, Steve's father has passed away and his mother has declined into the advanced stages of Alzheimer's. My aunt, sick for several years, passed in December. Our sons, at different schools, have different vacation schedules now, without a single day of overlap. The family vacation of old has been transformed this year into a new, staggered arrangement of comings and goings. Everyone will get here eventually, but not at the same time. This week, Jack is with us. Henry will arrive for his own spring break soon after his dad and brother head back north. For a few days in between boys' visits, my mom and I will be alone together—rarely possible when both boys were still at home, but a special perk of this new life chapter.

Slowly, I'm learning to accept—no, to *appreciate*—the possibilities of our new reality. Needed less by my own children these days, I'm free to create new, closer relationships with my parents. At seventeen, the age Jack is now, I considered an evening spent home alone with my mom and dad as some kind of social failure on my part. Now, at fifty-one, it's a rare treat.

Last summer, my feelings were often bruised by the sight of my son, pacing back and forth in the driveway, cell phone pressed to his ear, trying to make a plan, any plan, that would get him out of the house for the night. What I should have remembered is that life is transformation. The present moment is always in the process of becoming something else, just as our children are always growing and changing, becoming fuller expressions of themselves. They flee our presence as if preprogrammed to do so. And then, if we keep the door open, they return, in time, by their own volition. Tonight, the old cribbage board has been taken out of the closet. As I sit here typing, Jack and Steve are side by side on the couch, shuffling cards, laughing, talking in their own peculiar shorthand. We are three generations here under one roof, not quite a complete family, but content with one another's company. Sort of like old times, but different.

March 2010

———— *Mad Men* ————

I remember shaking a bit as I told the librarian that she could call my mother. Twelve years old, I had just made the bold move of rejecting my old stomping ground, the Children's Room, and venturing instead into the adult stacks. After an hour spent browsing shelves of murder mysteries and thrillers, I'd settled on John le Carré's *The Spy Who Came in From the Cold*. Its black cover with bold white type struck me as quite sophisticated; the jacket references to British double agents, murder, and the Cold War held promise of a world I was eager to enter and comprehend.

But now I'd encountered trouble at the checkout desk. The elderly librarian shook her head in disapproval, looked down at me, and pronounced the book "unsuitable for children." Taken aback—and then even more determined to walk out of there with that novel under my arm—I blurted out the first thing that came into my head: "I'm sure my mother would say it's fine." And then I held my breath as the librarian, calling my bluff, dialed the number. Truth was, I had no idea how my mother would handle this stern gatekeeper's attempt to guard my innocence.

A moment later, I was signing my name on a small tan card. My mom, as it turned out, would let me read anything.

Le Carré's intrigue was pretty much lost on me; I don't think I even finished the book. But I never forgot that moment in the library, when I realized for the first time that my mother believed I could decide for myself what was appropriate and what wasn't.

We talked about that the other night, when my son Jack said he'd like to watch *Mad Men* with us. My mom and I got hooked on this series, about an advertising agency in the early 1960s, the last time we were together; this week, she'd ordered season two for us to watch. But I wasn't quite comfortable with the idea of exposing my son to, well, all that callous licentiousness—the drinking; the urgent, casual sex; the smoking; the cynicism; the disdainful treatment of women.

At seventeen, he is definitely not sheltered and hardly innocent. He's gotten into his share of adolescent trouble and hit a few guardrails, literally and figuratively. I know a lot about his life, but I'm not naive enough to think for a minute that I know everything. Along the way, he's watched movies, plenty of them, that would make me blanch. I've read books he's recommended to me, and then, coming across passages that make me blush, I've struggled to make peace with the fact that he was there before me, reading the same page. Sex, murder, drugs, depravity—they are part of the typical American's entertainment diet, and my kids are no exception.

Sometimes, it's hard to believe we are the same family that managed to keep our television unplugged and shut away in a cupboard for years on end. One neighborhood boy, shocked to learn there was no TV to watch at our house, once said to my son Henry, "No TV? What do you DO over here?" Having never known anything else, my son simply said, "We just live." And so we did, for quite a long time.

But of course the media crept in as the kids grew up. And my desire to protect my children from the shadow side of our human existence evolved, over time, into something more pragmatic: the realization that, rather than avoid the darkness, they must each be equipped to meet it. We develop the tools and inner resources we need to understand life by experiencing it head on, both the beautiful and the ugly, the dark and the light, the good and the evil. Growing up means figuring out who we are in relation to everything else, and the "everything else" in our culture includes some pretty nasty stuff.

I remember sitting at a publishing dinner years ago next to the writer Robert Stone. Having just finished reading and being disturbed by his bleak, hard-edged novel *Children of Light,* I asked him about his vividly explicit sex scenes, often fueled by drugs and alcohol. Did he write all that from personal experience? I wondered. Stone paused, took a sip of his drink, and than answered dryly, "I write all that stuff so that I don't have to do it."

Perhaps it is the same, to some extent, for all of us—we watch the movies we watch, read the books we read, so that we can explore the vast reaches and outer limits of the human condition without actually having to go there ourselves. Experiences without consequences.

My mom laughed when I admitted that the idea of my nearly grown son watching *Mad Men* made me a little queasy. It's been almost forty years, after all, since she herself made peace with the fact that a child's innocence, precious as it may be, is inevitably transformed by curiosity. We humans hunger to know the dark side. And then, knowing, we are called upon to make our own choices about who to be, how to live, what's right and wrong.

And so it was that the three of us power-watched *Mad Men,* season two, together. Jack and I piled into my mom's king-sized bed for three nights in a row, propped up on the pillows, ice cream at hand, and were captivated by a lot of really bad behavior, compellingly dramatized. And I realized, of course, what my own mom already knew: he could handle it. So could I.

March 2010

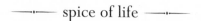 spice of life ——·——

They have a few things in common, my two sons. There

were a couple of long-ago, fondly remembered years when backyard baseball, MLB Showdown, and Magic cards were mutually beloved pastimes. They both recall the same antipathy toward a certain elementary school language teacher. They share a passion for music, and sometimes, after dinner, Jack will tune up his guitar, and they will play jazz together. They are big on Jon Stewart (the two of them will sit at breakfast, a laptop open between them, watching last night's *Daily Show* as they eat their cereal). They love *House;* the Beatles; our dog, Gracie; pancakes; the Peanut Buster Parfait at Dairy Queen; the state of Maine. They hold a reverence for tradition, adore their little cousins, and look forward to big family dinners. At this moment, I'm pretty sure that Jason Mraz's "I'm Yours" can be found on both of their iPods.

But the thing that most amazes me about the two human beings I gave birth to twenty and seventeen years ago is how different they are. It's as if the God of Parenthood set out to see how wildly diverse he could be within one gene pool—and then succeeded to create two opposite-ends-of-the-spectrum guys. As one of their early babysitters, a sweet young Hungarian girl, once said after a long night of trying to accommodate two utterly opposing agendas and temperaments, "Take these two little boys, put them in a pot, stir them both together, then you have a reasonable child."

And yet, for years our family life was all about trying to make things work for both of them. We shared a house, a life, a schedule, and somehow we needed to get to the baseball games and the piano recitals, come up with one homemade Halloween costume and buy one gross-out scary mask, kiss one boy good night before he conked out in his bed and produce a multi-chapter good-night saga for the other, give up on the idea of hand-me-down clothes in order to allow each to pursue his own particular style. (You can't require the boy who wants to wear bright orange to dress in his older brother's sage green castoffs.)

It's easier now. They've grown up, gotten drivers' licenses, attend different schools in different states, and increasingly live their own lives. But I do kind of miss the old negotiations and the juggling, not to mention the variety of our days. Henry and Jack, together, were a spicy mix. Raising them, living with them, wasn't always easy but it was always interesting. Being their parents stretched us in ways I'm not sure I fully appreciated in the moment, when I was being asked to test out yet another original board game created by Jack or to attend one more puppet show produced by Henry in the bedroom. But now, looking back, I realize that the activities they poured their hearts into when they were very young were the precursors of their passions today.

Jack would spend hours painstakingly making masks, inventing playing cards, drawing whacky animated figures on tiny pieces of paper to make a flip book. A few weeks ago, he e-mailed me his first animation project.

Henry conducted symphonies behind closed doors, a

chopstick in his hand, his tape player turned as loud as it would go. He would corral the neighborhood kids to perform in his musical productions, assemble notebooks of his favorite show tunes, envision musical revues. The other night he carried his laptop into my bedroom to play me a recording of a song he performed last month at a school concert, the only jazz number in an evening of classical music.

I was talking on the phone yesterday with my friend Carole. Our children grew up together. I remember her Alex at ten, masterminding the construction of a K'NEX ball machine in our playroom. Today he's a computer science major at Princeton. "Isn't it amazing," I said, "that our kids are so capable? That they have totally surpassed us in so many ways, doing exactly the things that, given who they are, we would have expected them to do?"

Carole admitted that, when it comes to math, Alex has been out of her league since he was in eighth grade. But she knew what I meant. Our grown children are just coming into themselves, finally beginning to realize those ambitions that first took shape years ago in the long, dream-filled hours of childhood.

Being a witness to this process of claiming and becoming is turning out to be one of the high points of parenting young adults. If your children are still small, pay attention to the messes they're making. Notice how they spend their time when there's nothing much to do. You may be catching glimpses of their futures.

March 2010

——·—— being there ——·——

I had coffee with an old friend on Saturday, a friend I feared might have vanished for good. Tragedy rearranges a life, irrevocably and often in unforeseeable ways. Eight years ago my dear friend Lisa's oldest son, Morgan, was killed while trying to stop a fight near his college campus. He was twenty-one years old, captain of the Bates lacrosse team, three months shy of graduating with honors, engaged to the girl of his dreams.

I first met Lisa when we brought our son Henry to her kindergarten classroom and tentatively showed her a thick file of test results confirming physical and cognitive delays that the doctors said could keep him from ever succeeding in a "normal" class. It was she who, upon meeting Henry, set the file aside, looked into the soul of our sweet, painfully shy, small-for-his-age five-year-old, and saw what was already perfect. Instead of comparing him to his more rugged peers, she met him exactly where he was.

"I think he will be fine," she said to us. And then she began to help us see all the ways he truly was. When Jack came along three years later, too rambunctious to sit quietly in circle time, she simply moved her class outdoors and began to reenvision kindergarten mornings as adventures for the body and the heart as well as an education for the mind.

By then, she and I were already friends. But it was even more than that; we were *every-day friends,* the way two little kids are best pals, completely current with each other's ups and downs and always eagerly planning our next playdate, be it a long run on the bike path after school or skinny-dipping on an overnight canoe trip to a deserted island.

Our friendship expanded early on to include my husband, Steve, and her longtime partner and soon-to-be husband, Kerby. There were couples' weekends away on the coast of Maine, birthday dinners and New Year's Eve celebrations, movies and books shared, and family campouts at the lake with our boys.

Two years after Lisa moved to New Hampshire to live with Kerby, and soon after Morgan's death, we pulled up roots and built a house in the same small town, certain our friendship would continue here, both in shared grief and also in healing, with a long, slow accumulation of good times and cherished memories. Ours was a conversation that, once started, felt as if it would go on forever. There was so much to talk about —love, loss, children, marriage, Mary Oliver's poetry, reincarnation, the meaning of life...

The death of a child is also the death of a small civilization. The intact family shatters, its old solid form vanished forever. And the ripples spread out from there. Friends and loved ones may gather round, willing to share the journey or to bear part of the load. But grief etches its own bleak road map. Sometimes the path leads away from love and connection into lonely uncharted territory. As poet Wendell Berry has written, "I don't believe that grief passes away. It has its time and place forever. More time is added to it; it becomes a story within a story. But grief and griever alike endure."

Endure, yes. But things are never what they once were. And in the years since her son's death, Lisa and I have grown apart. For me that's been another loss. Every once in a while, we run into each other at the gym. Occasionally, Steve and I have dinner with her and her husband. And yet, the bond of our old friendship, once so intimate and strong, has been thinned and stretched over time by sadness and by attempts to ward off that sadness. I have mourned the loss of Lisa's son and also the loss of my own beloved friend, as she turned away and disappeared from my life almost completely over these last difficult years.

I've felt the helplessness of knowing that nothing I could do or say would change things or make them better. Grief is grief. There is no right way to be sad. But there is a right way to love: without judgment, without expectation, but by simply making an ongoing effort to put ourselves in the shoes of another, to feel and witness for ourselves their suffering.

And somewhere along the way, as my attempts to get together with my friend failed and as the phone calls got fewer and farther between, I started to realize that sometimes even a well-intentioned attempt at comfort doesn't bring much comfort at all. My task wasn't to convince her to come take a walk with me, but to imaginatively, compassionately, quietly strive to bridge the gap between two realities: between someone who has endured great loss and someone who has not.

Hard as it was to accept my friend's silence, and hurt as my own feelings were at times, I kept reminding myself: I cannot know what it feels like to be her. I have not lost a child, have not had to bear that pain and then learn how to keep on living. My hope for myself was that I could somehow figure out how to be a true friend to Lisa anyway, even from a distance. That I could somehow continue to love her and to be present for her—if not face-to-face, then at least in spirit.

Over coffee the other day, Lisa told me that there came a day last summer when she finally just stopped in her tracks and asked God where he was. The answer was not too long in coming, a new spiritual path literally opening at her feet. Eight months later, she is intent on crafting a different life, one in which grief and connection coexist. It's a work in process, this hard work of prayer and practice and rebuilding from the ground floor up.

And so it was that we two met at last and began the joyful, tearful task of reunion. We ordered lattes, and then there was so much to say all at once that we forgot to drink them. Once we both got started crying, we couldn't stop—till we started laughing at ourselves through the tears. And in that moment it hit me hard—how much I've missed her and how deeply, profoundly grateful I am to have her back.

It felt amazing, after all this time, to finally get to say everything we each had been waiting for such a long time to say. She wanted to apologize. I wanted her to know she didn't need to. For the truth is, my friend has taught me how to hold a place for someone in my heart, even when that person's own heart is otherwise engaged. So often this is our real challenge: to grow in compassion, to keep on loving, to somehow be there for another, even from a distance, a distance that may feel at times like a very long arm's length away.

The next day, Lisa was going to attend Morgan's fiancée's baby shower. Her late son's beautiful girlfriend got married last summer. She is expecting a boy. She wants Lisa to be part of his life. And so, just like old times, the two of us finished our cold coffee and went shopping. Together, we picked out a music box for the unborn child who will not be Lisa's grandson, but who will arrive with her blessing and be the recipient of all the love she has to offer him. She knows, for sure, that's what Morgan would have wanted.

As we stood there at the counter, watching the store owner wrap this special gift for a special baby, we could only marvel at life, all these unexpected twists and turns. The inevitability of both death and birth, and the hard, transformative lessons to be learned from a loved one's suffering. No doubt I will need to be reminded again and again, but today I can say this with conviction: being present to another's pain and sadness, in whatever way we can, teaches us the true meaning of patience, compassion, and faith. Grief and griever alike endure. And so does love.

April 2010

—·— second journey —·—

*The call to a second journey usually commences when unexpected
change is thrust upon you, causing a crisis of feelings so great
that you are stopped in your tracks.*
—Joan Anderson, *The Second Journey*

I first read those words about nine months ago, sitting alone
in an empty kitchen and having wondered for weeks just
what I was meant to do next, now that the house was built,
the long-awaited book finally written and published, the
children nearly grown.

This weekend I went to meet the woman who wrote
them, the woman who once ran away from home to spend
a year in a cottage by the sea in order to find her way back
to her own true self, a self long since lost to the demands
of marriage, motherhood, career, and the needs of others.

Packing the car on Friday afternoon, I still wasn't quite
sure what I was looking for on my own "Second Journey"
retreat or why I was going off to spend a weekend with a
group of strangers on Cape Cod. I had more than enough
to do right at home—weeds to pull and herbs to plant, a
manuscript to read for a friend, a husband who preferred
to have me around, a to-do list filling the whole right
page of my calendar.

And yet. The ache I've felt deep in my breast this year
has not been assuaged by any of the small, worthy tasks
that fill my days. I do all I can in all directions and then
I lie awake at night worrying about things beyond my

control. I meditate in the morning, practice living in the moment, and yet find myself fighting against a deep sadness for moments already gone. I love the people in my life and yet feel bruised again and again by unsettling, difficult conversations. I reach out to my teenaged son and feel not connection but more distance, our relationship raw and tender to the touch. I answer my e-mails, read a little, write a little, spend time with my family, take lunch to a friend. The days are busy and full and good. Still, the question nibbles at my edges: *What now?*

Saturday afternoon, standing barefoot on the beach, I glimpsed the beginnings of an answer. Part of the ache, I know, comes from my own sense of still not being quite up to the job of being me. Not a good enough mother, wife, or friend, no matter how much I care or what I do. Not a good enough writer, or yoga student, or meditator, no matter how hard I try. Not a good enough public speaker, or checkbook balancer, or wage earner, no matter how much effort I put in.

I know that where I see lack and failure, others may see competence. But I compile my own secret list of insecurities and shortcomings, certain that what seems to come so easily and naturally to others must be harder for me. I want to be better at living my life than I am these days. To feel sufficient, more certain of what I'm meant to do now and how I'm meant to be.

We had arrived on the Outer Banks by boat, rolling our pant legs up high, holding our shoes in our hands, and hopping into the clear, icy water one by one to wade ashore. With a knowing twinkle in her eye, Joan had given us each our marching orders back at the dock, along with our bag lunches. "Don't talk," she said. We were to go in search of solitude and silence.

Out here, both were easy to find. A few steps along the beach and I was already alone, heading out toward the breaks, the surf, the wide open stretches of dune and shore grass and wild water. The sun was warm, the wind so fierce it whipped stinging needles of sand onto every little bit of exposed flesh. My face burned. My eyes watered. But what is a pilgrimage without a little pain?

For four hours or so I wandered the lip of the beach in silence, shedding layers of extra clothing along with layers of identity, feeling, thoughts, and inner chatter. There was nothing to do but walk and look and wonder, nowhere to go except where my feet carried me. No sooner had I taken a step than the next wave rolled in, erasing my footprints from the sand. The scouring, relentless wind washed my mind empty of thought and judgment and doubt. Step-by-step, moment-by-moment, I relaxed. First into a kind of inner stillness. Then, into peace. And from there, it was not much of a leap to contentment.

How satisfying it is to disappear and then to be found by the world. How exhilarating to be relieved of all expectation and commitment, and then to rediscover your own bare-naked self. What a relief to lighten my psychic load, to let go of all the worries and judgments and doubts I lug around with me day after day. What a blessing to see what it is that remains after everything heavy and useless and outgrown has been dropped and left along the way. What a gift to be slowly but surely filled right up to the brim again with love—love for my life as it is, for myself as I am, for the world as it is.

I adore Joan Anderson's books of self-discovery and renewal. I love her willingness to laugh at herself even through tears of confusion and despair, her generosity of spirit, her eagerness to share what she's learned with the rest of us restless, middle-aged seekers. And I am so grateful now that when I first wrote to her, months ago, she answered my letter. "Come to the beach," she wrote back.

I said I would. There is not a woman among us who couldn't use a weekend away, a walk on the shore, a good night's sleep alone in a bed far from home. I feel lucky to have had all those things this weekend, along with the most precious gift of all—time to just be, without one bit of pressure to do.

In the end, I did find what I was looking for out there on the Outer Banks: a bit of hope. Hope that things will work out for the best. Hope that when the going gets rough, as it always does, I will remember who I am, that I'll be gentler with myself, that I'll draw strength from the truth I already know: love is what enlarges and sustains us. Love saves us from ourselves. Love is pure, positive energy. Love really is all we need.

Joan gave us much this weekend, from a candle-lit lobster dinner in her home to wine and wisdom, belly laughs, and yoga on the beach. But I think the words I treasure most now that I'm home again were not hers, but ones

she shared by Robert Frost. Asked near the end of his long life if he had hope for the future, Frost replied: "Yes. And even for the past, that it will turn out to have been all right for what it was. Something that I can accept—mistakes made by the self I had to be, or was not able to be."
May 2010

———·——— present moment ———·———

They are home at last, both sons. And I'm perched here at the kitchen table for about two brief minutes before the potatoes boil. (Three men in the house means the menu is pretty much a given: grilled steaks and mashed potatoes for dinner.) All afternoon, I thought there would be an hour or so to sit down and write, but I'd forgotten how quickly a day flies by when the house is full. There is no time to gaze out the window, daydreaming sentences.

I can tell already that the rhythms are going to be different around here this summer. It may take me a while to adjust. My yoga mat sits untouched on the floor between the living room and the kitchen. I haven't answered a single e-mail or meditated or gotten back to the guy who wants to schedule a reading. The *New York Times* has not been touched by me, but sits on the coffee table in a mangled jumble of poor newspaper-folding technique. Boys.

I've made several rounds of breakfast, taken a run with Henry, done a huge load of grocery shopping, washed lots of sheets and soggy towels, heard detailed synopses of the latest episodes of *The Office,* bought two quarts of freshly picked strawberries at the farmers' market, cut peonies and irises from the garden, set the porch table, cooked a welcome-home feast for Jack. I can't quite believe it's dinner time again already, that I feel this tired, and that I never got any "real" work done today, let alone a downward dog or a long deep breath.

And I feel renewed admiration for every woman who manages a busy household, spends time with her family, and still finds time to write and read and think. I am in something close to awe of every woman who works outside the home and who manages to take care of the people in the home as well. I bow to all the women who juggle way more than I do—raising children and earning a living and tending to those in need—and who, nevertheless, also honor their commitments to themselves and their inner lives.

The soul work we do is so subtle, so easily postponed to another day, so low, sometimes, on the list of priorities. There is always so much that *must* be done that we tend to let go of those things that feel like self-indulgent extras. It seems impossible, at times, to find room in our busy, demanding lives to allow for stillness and time alone and regeneration. Reflection has become a luxury. Today, there's been more hustle and bustle and conversation going on in my own house than we've seen here in months. There are piles everywhere. Plans being made, tennis rackets and shoes proliferating, dirty glasses filling the sink. I'm still amazed at how much sheer space they take up, these grown kids of mine.

And yet, I have to say: tonight feels like a party. My three favorite people in the world are right here, my husband and our two sons. At least I have the presence of mind to pay attention, to be grateful, to remember that this really is IT—the life I have, the best life there is, the present moment.

June 2010

—·— homecomings —·—

It's been six years since we moved away from the neighborhood where Henry and Jack grew up. And although we've returned for many visits with friends and former neighbors, our roots are elsewhere now. Our boys, eleven and fourteen when they last spent a night in our old house, are young men of seventeen and twenty. And our current life in New Hampshire (one son halfway through college, the other finishing high school) bears no resemblance to the one we left behind (two little boys in the backyard playing catch until dark).

Year by year, as our family has shaped new rituals and memories in a new place, I've struggled to make my peace with Thomas Wolfe's famous pronouncement, "You can't go home again." (Well, you can't, not in any literal sense. The day you sign those closing papers and hand over all the keys, what was once yours no longer is.)

And yet, lately I've experienced one homecoming after another, homecomings at once unexpected, wonderful, and profound. In fact, I'm typing these words while sitting on the porch of our former next-door neighbor's house, gazing across the driveway at our own old green house, solid and quiet and still on this hot summer afternoon.

A few months ago Jack was invited to participate in a four-days-a-week training program in Boston this summer—long hours, hard work, lots to learn. "If you really want to do this," I told him at the time, "we can figure out a way to make it work."

He gave it some thought and said yes. And I started pondering the logistics. I looked into summer sublets on Craigslist and put out feelers to every friend within fifteen miles of the city. A few promising leads fizzled. And then our former next-door neighbors and best friends from across the driveway offered us their house. They would be in South Africa and could use a house sitter. We were welcome to move in, water the plants, and take care of the cat for the month they would be gone.

Last Sunday night, Jack and I let ourselves into the house where he had spent some of the happiest hours of his childhood playing with his two best buddies, Nick and Will.

"This feels pretty weird," we said in unison, as we flicked on lights and called out to Millie, whom we met as a kitten on the day she came home from the shelter years ago. Our friends were halfway across the world by the time we showed up, and neither of us quite knew what to do in their house without them in it. I put some food in the fridge, opened the windows, unpacked my bag, and then tossed and turned all night, feeling like a trespasser in my best friend's bedroom.

Jack, veteran of countless sleepovers here and epic games of hide-and-seek, knows every nook and cranny of this house. But in the morning he told me he'd had trouble settling down himself. He was at a bit of a loss, missing his friend and not quite comfortable sprawled out in Nick's bed instead of in a sleeping bag on the floor, his usual childhood spot.

As it turns out, our old house is empty this summer as well. The owners are abroad for a year; the house, silent and still. And so it's been all too easy to imagine that, any minute now, we'll just saunter across the driveway and be at "home" again. From the outside, everything looks as it did when we lived there. Which means I can fool myself into thinking that, inside, my dishes are stacked in the cupboards as always, our family photos are still on the walls, Steve is working away in his upstairs office, Henry's picking out tunes on the piano in the living room.

All during our first day here, I had to remind myself: those weeds in the garden over there are not mine to pull, the blueberries ripening by the garage, not ours to pick, even if no one else is around to harvest them. Jack has felt the tug in a different way. The other night, looking over at our old house as dusk fell, he mused, "If I ever get rich enough to build my own house, I think I'll make it exactly like this one. And then it would always feel like I was back home again."

Meanwhile, we are making ourselves at home again next door. After a few days in Carol's kitchen, I know where the pot holders are and how to use her coffee maker. The *New York Times* is on the front lawn by the time I take Jack to his train at seven. I've gone back to my old yoga studio for class each morning, taken long walks with old friends, visited the local farmers' markets (better than ever), and bought Jack a pizza at Joe's (exactly the same).

It's amazing how comfortable we've come to feel, how at home we are here in our old world, even after all this time away. It seemed perfectly natural for Jack's pal Will, who grew up in the house behind ours, to saunter through the front door last night and say "hi." Within five minutes those two six-foot-tall guys were down on the floor, practicing a wrestling hold, sweaty and laughing as if they were ten and eleven again.

Two days ago, I took a stroll through our old backyard and recalled the planting of every bush and perennial and tree. Remembering all the hours of hard work Steve and I put in over the course of our thirteen years here, trying to create our own version of paradise, I allowed myself a weepy moment at the sight of the weed-choked gardens and untended beds, as overgrown and rampant with vines as Sleeping Beauty's entangled castle. But then, all of a sudden, something in me lightened, and I think I let that particular sadness go for good.

It occurred to me that this old, odd house that was our home for so long—built as a barn in 1850, gutted and turned into a house for humans in 1923—has withstood both love and neglect, family life and family deaths, homecomings and goings for over a century and a half.

A hundred years from now, it will stand there still, holding its own silent counsel. Like all those who came before us and all those who will come after, we were just a few mortals passing through. No big deal in the grand scheme of things.

And yet, the seeds we sowed during our own brief time here were not just for the vegetables and flowers that brought us so much passing pleasure, but also seeds of love and friendship that continue to bear fruit in our lives today, despite the passage of time and the challenges of distance. The day we moved away six years ago—a day that I saw at the time as a wrenching finale to our sons' childhoods and the life we'd known—was in fact no such thing. It was just a day. Life transforming itself the way it does: this happens, and then that happens. In Buddhism it is said that all causes and conditions are related, that the world exists in a state of interdependence. Because one thing arises, another arises; because of this, that.

And so it occurs to me now that I was mistaken to ever think of life as a simple series of endings and beginnings. How self-defeating, to try so hard to grab hold of those things I wanted to keep intact, with the idea that permanence just might be possible.

Sitting here by myself, looking across the driveway at the empty shell of a house that was once stuffed full of us—but that is now the center of another family's universe—I think I finally get it: home really is the place where I am right now, if I choose to make it so. And if I'm awake and open, and loving what is, then I am always at home, no matter what roof is above my head or what

return address I write in the upper corner of an envelope.
June 2010

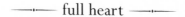 full heart

There were lots of ribbons and bows. But it wasn't about the gifts. It was about the pure, untrammeled beauty of a little girl celebrating her first birthday and just waking up to the pleasures of pink party hats, presents to open, a spoonful of ice cream, a bite of cake. We gathered in the living room, cousins and aunts and uncles and grandparents, neighbors and friends, snapping photos and marveling.

Just a year ago, Angelique arrived in our midst. Today she is an essential member of the family, this powerful pint-sized personality exquisitely packaged and growing up before our eyes. On the verge of walking, tossing her new red ball, laughing at her three-year-old brother, Gabriel, reveling in her moment. Brief as my tiny niece's time on earth has been, it's hard to remember what the world was like before she was in it.

Then: my husband's buzzing cell phone, a relentless caller, Steve finally giving in, disappearing down the hall, returning with news to whisper in my ear. A car crash, an eighteen-year-old girl dead.

Two weeks ago, Steve gave the graduation speech at High Mowing, Henry's alma mater. Huddled under umbrellas, our family watched as she and all the other soaked, exuberant high-school seniors tossed their caps into the air, whooped, and hugged before turning to receive congratulations from the crowd.

How quickly a moment turns upon itself, from joy to grief, from light to dark, from life to death. How to hold, on the bright summer afternoon of a child's first birthday, the sudden, senseless death of another child, one just coming into her young adulthood?

You put an arm around your own seventeen-year-old son, pull him close, and give silent thanks for his life. You say a private, wordless prayer for a family devastated by loss. You see in your mind's eye a photograph of a lovely girl with long brown hair, laughing as she danced with her classmates around the May Pole. You try to understand how it is that such a girl, with all her life to live before her, could so suddenly be gone. You carry forks and plates out to the porch, hug your dad, and watch your kid brother, now a father of two, cook the burgers on the grill. You smile when your sister-in-law sweeps her beautiful children into her arms and kisses their round, fat cheeks, and you choose to spare her the day's dose of grief.

All week, I've been wondering: how are we meant to do this? How can we learn to carry both the preciousness of life and the inevitability of death in our hearts at the same time?

At the end of Thornton Wilder's play *Our Town,* Emily, who has died in childbirth, is given the opportunity to return to earth and live one day of her life over again. She deliberately chooses an ordinary day, her twelfth birthday—a day of eggs and bacon cooking, sunflowers in the garden, a postcard album from the boy next door, something on the table wrapped in yellow paper that once belonged to her grandmother. To Emily, now an outsider looking in at the life she once took for granted, every minute detail of this long-forgotten day is cause for both delight and heartbreak.

So clearly does she see the fleeting, ineffable beauty of what is. So urgent is her wish for connection, meaning, recognition. But her distracted mother—rushing around to get breakfast on the table and her children hustled off to school— is oblivious. Gently, appealing to her mother to wake up and really see her, Emily implores, "Just for a moment now we're all together—Mama, just for a moment, let's be happy. Let's look at one another."

I have read this soliloquy so many times over the years— never without tears in my eyes—that I pretty much know it by heart. And yet, again and again, I have to remind myself: Just for a moment now, we're all here. Just for a moment, let's be happy. Let's look at each other.

And so on Sunday afternoon, with a heart full of sadness and confusion and gratitude all mixed up together, I did the best I could. I looked at our big extended family— my brother and sister-in-law and all her folks; my petite, feisty niece and my earnest, easygoing nephew; my own dear parents; my husband of twenty-two years, our six-foot-tall son. When Henry called in from his summer job in Maine, we passed the phone around. Three-year-old Gabriel ate the first hamburger of his life. Angelique tolerated her party hat. Plates were filled, food eaten, pink frosted cupcakes handed out to all takers.

"Oh earth," Emily cries when she can bear the poignancy of her visit no longer, "you're too wonderful for anyone to realize you!"

Turning to the wise, omniscient Stage Manager, she asks, "Do any human beings ever realize life while they live it—every, every minute?"

"No," he says quietly. And then, "Saints and poets maybe—they do some."

How I aspire to be one of those poets. To allow myself to know the ache of sadness, but to remember as well that life offers us good reason in each and every day to be love-struck. To learn to see by learning to write. To "realize life," as Emily would say, by truly inhabiting every moment that's granted me, without ever holding on too tight to what's already passing, changing, turning into some new, endlessly surprising present.

July 2010

——·—— fireworks ——·——

I dug the fire pit out in our yard five years ago, the week we moved into the old red cottage on our New Hampshire hilltop. It was sweltering hot, and no one was happy. The tiny, uninsulated upstairs bedrooms were unbearable. We plugged fans into every available 1923 wall outlet, then crossed our fingers and prayed we wouldn't blow out the ancient wiring. But it didn't help. The effect was more convection oven than cross breeze.

Desperation inspired us to have our first party in our new house. We needed something to distract us from the mold, the carpenter ants, the bats, the heat, the sleepless nights, and our overwhelming sense of buyer's remorse. It didn't make much sense to sit around in the small airless house; the view across the field to the mountains was the real draw anyway. And so I picked a spot out there, dug a little clearing and rimmed it with rocks, and stacked a few logs in the center.

That night there were just a handful of us—Steve and the boys and me, three of our friends—sitting by the fire, watching the sparks spiral up into the darkness as fireflies danced through the tall grass beyond. It was nothing short of magical, a peaceful moment of deliverance after a long, sweaty, terrible week, when every member of my family wished nothing more than to roll back the clock, do it all over again, and stay put—in our old suburban life in our familiar, comfortable, well-ventilated house.

What I remember most clearly about sitting by the fire that early summer night was the feeling—well, perhaps it was really just more of a hope—that at long last we were taking the first step into what we would come to love in our new life. Surely, I believed then, we would have many more such evenings—bonfires on the hilltop; easy, impromptu parties; countless reasons to gather our friends together to share food and laughter and to celebrate life's simple pleasures. In short order that summer, we pulled together a solstice party, a Father's Day brunch, a birthday, a cookout on the Fourth of July, a few pre-theater suppers in honor of our new proximity to the summer-stock playhouse a mile up the road, various other spontaneous get-togethers.

And then, reality set in. Summer came to an end, cold weather arrived, and we began the long, exhausting, and expensive project of moving out of the cottage, tearing it down, designing a new house, getting it built, choosing paint and fixtures, moving again, unpacking, settling in.

It all took so much longer than we ever imagined it would. Meanwhile, the kids grew up. Life got even more complicated. The party we meant to have when the house was finally finished, months later than anticipated, never happened. We were too wiped out to think about one more project.

Five years passed before we had another real party on this hilltop, Steve's sixtieth birthday last June. I was so out of practice that I planned and obsessed for weeks, wondering where people would sit, how many bottles of wine to buy and how many chairs to borrow, whether we should rearrange all the furniture, rent a table, get a new grill. It rained for days before, it rained on the day of, and it rained for a week after. That night, people stood up to eat. We squeezed into the kitchen, clustered in the living room, managed to have a fine time despite the weather. But it took a year before I could face the idea of putting myself through all that angst again.

This year, the Fourth of July fireworks were scheduled for Monday night at the high school just down the hill and across the valley from us—which means that the best view in town is from our back yard. It's been months since we've had more than four people at our dinner table. The fire pit that I was certain would be the center of countless memorable gatherings hasn't been used, not even once, since our very first summer here, when it seemed—for a few weeks anyway—to be at the very center of our life.

Clearly, it was time. So last week I sent off a few e-mails and made a few calls: Come over for a potluck dinner and fireworks. It used to be that such an invitation would always include the line "Bring the kids." These days, of course, the kids drive themselves, and whether they'll actually show up is by no means a given.

But the word went out. I wrote a to-do list, went food shopping, and hoped for a crowd. Jack and a friend spent a sweaty couple of hours digging out the old, overgrown fire pit, making it bigger and better than before. They laid an ambitious fire, stacked enough wood for a long night of revelry, and arranged all the benches and chairs we have into a semicircle. They set up the badminton net, at my insistence. Just in case.

And as it happened, we lucked out. Teenagers, parents, old friends and new ones—they all came. Coolers were carried into the kitchen and unloaded. The table filled with food—salads and watermelon and pasta. Steaks and chicken and hamburgers and hot dogs arrived for the grill. "Thank you," Jack said to me in passing, "for having some normal food here." (He meant the Coke and ginger ale and corn chips and bottled salsa that I rarely buy. But at a certain point, well, what you really want is for everyone present to feel happy and well fed.)

There was a moment, a kind of Mrs. Dalloway moment, when I just stopped, stood stock-still, and looked around at the loveliness of the scene. The men were in the kitchen, drinking beer. The women were outside, chatting. The boys were juggling—a skill they all learned together in sixth and seventh grade and suddenly, spontaneously, decided to revive at ages seventeen and eighteen. Clubs flew through the air. A fiercely competitive badminton game was in progress. A group of girls sat at the picnic table, deep in conversation.

Just a few minutes later, of course, this evanescent bubble would pop and vanish forever. Steve would carry the first platters in from the grill, the teenagers would troop in to fill their plates, and one tableau would transform itself into another, and another after that. Dinner served and eaten, talk and laughter carried through the air, dishes loaded into the dishwasher, lemon cake sliced onto paper plates, darkness falling.

Jack touched a match to the fire. The fireworks lit up the sky. We passed the bug spray around and sprawled out on blankets spread across the grass. Marshmallows were set aflame, s'mores made and devoured. The last time we did this, my children were still children. I don't know why we waited so long to find our way back here, to this ritual we created, loved, and yet abandoned all too easily—for what? Lack of time? Lack of energy? Lack of belief in the enduring magic of a campfire and friends with whom to share it?

Today, I promise myself this: More time for fun. More

spur of the moment parties, before it's too late and the younger generation is up and out and gone for good. More fires outside, more s'mores, more reasons to celebrate the joy of being alive, of raising children to young adulthood, of spending time with those young adults—who, after all, are still learning from us, each and every day, what it means to live a good life.

July 2010

——·—— the peace of wild things ——·——

We bike seven and a half miles up the road from our house, past hay fields and horses and silent, collapsing barns. It is my favorite route from home, a long, lovely panorama of wild gardens, moss-covered stone walls, old country houses set low to the ground, rolling pastures, and sun-dappled woods. The morning air is patchy, stunningly hot in the clear stretches, deliciously cool in the greenish darkness of shade, the trees arching over the road like a canopy as we sail along beneath, single file, each keeping our own counsel.

At the end of the road and at the top of the steepest hill: breakfast. Blueberry pancakes with maple syrup and wonderful coffee. Summer food, served outdoors. The picnic table with its broad green umbrella; the *New York Times,* sticky with syrup; old friends sitting across from us, telling the stories that always make us laugh. The voluptuous apricot day lilies with their pale yellow throats and lobed anthers, each ruffled bloom as sensual as a centerfold.

Sated, we ride through town to the pond, park the bikes, peel off our shorts and sweaty tee shirts, swim out. Dark deep water, the silvered reflection of clouds on the still surface, the rim of trees along the far shore. Floating on my back, suspended in stillness with my face turned to the sun, I'm glad to be where I am: awake to this one lovely moment in a lovely summer day.

Later, by the white light of the computer, I read a friend's e-mail. This time, her chemo isn't working.

All night I lie awake in bed, staring at a shadow on the ceiling and thinking about miracles. Who gets one? I wonder. And how do we carry on with grace when the miracles we hope for fail to materialize? In the morning, heavy-hearted, I slip out of bed and step into the garden, barefoot, to watch the sun come up, to hear the birds' chatter. And then, back inside, I take one book from the shelf and turn to a poem that gives words both to loss and to solace.

The Peace of Wild Things
When despair grows in me
and I wake in the night at the least sound
in fear of what my life and my children's lives may be,
I go and lie down where the wood drake
rests in his beauty on the water, and the great heron feeds.
I come into the peace of wild things
who do not tax their lives with forethought
of grief. I come into the presence of still water.

And I feel above me the day-blind stars
waiting for their light. For a time
I rest in the grace of the world, and am free.
—Wendell Berry
July 2010

—·— logistics —·—

I promised Henry that if he took a job working as a counselor and pianist at a remote music camp this summer, we'd figure out some way to get him to the orthodontist every month. This despite the fact that he has one day off a week, the day off happens to be Sunday, and we live three and a half hours away from Sweden, Maine, where he is senior counselor to a cabin full of fourteen-year-old aspiring musicians.

And the fact is, it did take me a full sixteen hours to drive to Maine last week, pick up Henry, drive him to a dock on the shores of Lake Winnipesaukee, meet the kindly vacationing orthodontist who was willing to see my son on the deck of his boat, drive back to Maine, drop Henry off in the woods, turn around, and drive home.

I assured Jack that if he wanted to accept an internship with a physical trainer this summer, we'd figure out a way to make it work. This despite the fact that his program runs from 7:30 am to 4:30 pm, Monday through Thursday, and we live two hours away from the studio in downtown Boston where Jack is getting an intense, hands-on course in anatomy, bodywork, Chinese meridians, flexibility, and resistance stretching.

And yes, making it work has meant house-sitting for three weeks in our old neighborhood and then scrambling among our friends to find unused beds and spare keys, parking permits, and welcome mats.

But the thing I realized this morning, as I awoke on a swaybacked pullout couch in a friend's borrowed Harvard Square apartment, is that I will never again be called upon to perform the jobs I'm doing these days—acting as chauffeur and roommate to my two sons. The braces will come off at last. We will break down and get another car. Apartments will be sublet for summer jobs. The kids will be older. They will find their own way.

Really, both of them are doing that already. All I'm providing here is a helping hand, easing the logistics in enterprises that are very much their own doing. I guess that's why, despite a few inconveniences, I feel grateful to be needed and why I am treasuring every moment of this unusually rootless summer. A lobster roll on the dock and a few hours with Henry in the car was reward enough for the long drive to Maine and back. Every game of Bananagrams or early morning conversation or stroll through Harvard Square with Jack feels special. I don't mind at all the fact that I'm living out of an L. L. Bean bag in Cambridge this week instead of waking up in my own bed.

Soon enough, this summer will end. The only thing I know for sure about next summer is that it will be different. And so I say yes to long drives, to a bag of clothes in the back of the car, and to doing whatever it takes to make things work for right now.

July 2010

—·—— Parents' Day ——·—

You'd think I would be used to it by now, the fact that my children have grown up.

Yet time after time the bittersweet truth hits me again in some new and unexpected way. A memory surfaces, vivid and fresh as this morning's sunrise—Henry at twelve, wearing a too-big Hawaiian shirt and a pair of dark sunglasses, playing Steely Dan's "Time Out of Mind" on the piano; or Jack, fourteen and all intensity and focus, as he reaches down to turn up his amp for a guitar solo on "Autumn Leaves."

And in a flash my eyes fill with tears and my heart swells up, as I realize how far we've already traveled from those moments. Life rushes forward. Except for those rare and precious circumstances when it affords us, instead, a poignant opportunity to circle back—back to a place we've been before, a place that's stayed the same even while we ourselves have changed and grown and moved on.

Nine years ago Saturday, Steve and Jack and I drove into the woods of western Maine for our first Parents' Day at Camp Encore/Coda. We took our seats in the dimness of an old post-and-beam barn on the shores of a quiet pond, and we watched Henry, age eleven, play jazz keyboards for the first time in his life. The song was Herbie Hancock's "Watermelon Man." He took a little solo, glanced out to where we sat in the audience, and flashed us a grin.

Music camp had been my idea, not his. Three weeks earlier, we'd delivered our shy little boy into the hands of a couple of friendly college students who promised him a fine time in Starfish cabin. And then we hugged him good-bye and left him there, eager and frightened, with a nervous stomachache and a black trunk full of carefully labeled shorts and tee shirts, pre-addressed and stamped envelopes for letters home, bug spray and sweatshirts and music books.

As we pulled out onto the dirt road that day and headed home, I realized that my own stomach felt kind of queasy. And I wondered if, in my desire to expand our son's world and build his confidence, I'd perhaps pushed a little too hard and a little too soon. It wasn't until we returned a few weeks later and saw him standing on the corner of the Old Music Hall stage, holding his own in a jazz band comprised of a bunch of other eleven-year-old kids, a look of pure joy on his face, that I knew for sure: painful as it had been to insist that our boy leave home for the first time in his life, the journey now belonged to him.

Jump forward nine years. It is Saturday, and I am in the audience at Parents' Day again. My son is a senior counselor, with piano students of his own to teach, a jazz workshop to lead, concerts to perform, and camp musicals to play. The memories come rushing back as I sit in the old barn—all the years we have returned to this camp that both our sons came, in their own turn, to love.

All the times we've gone through the very same ritual, arriving at the gate early on a midsummer morning, parking the car in a freshly mown field, following the signs into camp, eyes peeled for one of our boys.

How strange and wonderful it always was, to sit in a shed in the deep woods of Maine, listening to children and teenagers and adults all making music together. A handful of young string musicians performing the Brandenburg concertos with exquisite nuance. A group of kids in shorts and tee shirts, intently focused on their conductor as they sing Joni Mitchell's "Woodstock" in six-part harmony. A big band comprised of musicians whose average age is fourteen, swinging through intricate jazz arrangements with the panache and creativity of pros.

It's been four years since Henry's last summer here, when he spent seven weeks working his tail off as a CIT. Three years since Jack played lead guitar in the Zappa Rock Band. Camp vanished all too quickly in life's rear-view mirror, another part of childhood that had been lived and loved and left behind. And so, part of what gives rise to so much emotion on this particular morning is my own sharp awareness of time passing. It is not ex-actly jealousy I feel as I watch a new generation of parents greeting their children, exclaiming over summer tans, growth spurts, and shaggy hair. I had my turn. And yet I'm overcome, as I walk up the familiar path and hear the sound of a solitary violin being tuned in a practice cab-in, both with gratitude for this unexpected homecoming and, at the same time, with a profound, heartbreaking sense of how much is already over.

My challenge now—as it seems to be every day this summer—is to release my hold on what was, so that I can be grateful and at peace with what is. How well I remember the acute, visceral joy of these camp reunions. But there is a different joy awaiting me here now, if I can allow myself to feel it. Not the joy of bringing a much-missed child home at the end of the weekend, but rather the joy of being a mother who has done her job, and who is now being offered a glimpse of her grown-up son doing his.

July 2010

———·——— disconnecting ———·———

It is August and the goldenrod is in bloom alongside the road. Last night I lay in bed, windows opened wide, and listened to the thrum of crickets, a symphonic prelude to summer's end. I think back to all the things I was so sure I'd do this summer, to the private to-do list I wrote for myself the first week of June, and realize I've made little progress on any of those projects. What have I been doing all this time?

The fact that I've managed to write a few essays, answer most of my e-mail, read and sometimes comment on the blogs of a few friends and fellow writers, and stay current with my pals on Facebook doesn't exactly fill me with a sense of accomplishment. And yet, I tell myself, I've been busy—many days, really, *really* busy—just trying to keep up with the flow of news and information and communication that shows up on my computer screen each morning.

Over the weekend, Jack and Steve and I visited my parents in Maine. Cell phone reception is spotty and there is no Internet out on the spit of land where their house nestles on a ledge, surrounded by water on three sides. We didn't do very much—the guys played tennis on a neighbor's court, we went to the farmers' market and to the pancake breakfast at the library, took walks, read books, cooked and ate and cleaned up. The three days we spent hanging around the house seemed long and leisurely, in the best way.

It occurred to me that, for the first time all summer, it really and truly actually *felt* like summer. And then I realized why: my computer was sitting untouched in a straw bag in the bedroom. Freed from its siren call, unable to click, tweet, type, or browse, I was forced to give my complete, undistracted attention to the physical world before my eyes and at my fingertips.

Sky. Water. Flowers. Family. Books. A pad of paper and a pen. It felt strange and sort of wonderful to curl up on the couch and write by hand, in different colors of ink, on big sheets of blank paper. I doodled, sketched, and created a brand-new, A to Z, pie-in-the-sky to-do list—in color. Instead of making me anxious, the process was strangely calming, as if in committing all these random thoughts and ideas to paper I was already moving a step closer toward realizing some of them.

What happened to us this weekend in Maine seemed almost like an awakening. Time expanded. Each moment felt fat and full and rich. Meanwhile, something inside me relaxed and let go. The really surprising thing is that, without the ability to so much as check my e-mail, the vague anxiety I've had for weeks about not ever being caught up or on top of things disappeared altogether.

I read a bound galley I should have read weeks ago and wrote a quote for it (better late than never). I came up with an idea for a new writing project—another task that has had me stumped all summer. It wasn't so much that I was actually getting anything "done," but rather that I could feel myself coming back in touch at last with that small, capricious part of me that observes and imagines and creates from the inside out.

Driving home on Sunday afternoon, we were quiet in the car. Jack stretched out in the back seat, reading *Slaughterhouse Five* without his earbuds in. A rarity. Steve drove, without the radio on. I sat beside him, absorbed in thought. It felt as if our days of disconnection had, in fact, reconnected us. And so I had to wonder: How have the ingrained habits of my wired life imperceptibly altered my relationship with my innermost self and with the people I love? As we grow ever more accustomed to and dependent on our technology, what do we trade away in return for speed and ease, distraction and efficiency? What have we already lost?

Week after next, Henry will be done with his summer job, Jack will come home from Boston, and the four of us will spend a week together, as we always do in August, on a lake in Maine. A couple of years ago, bowing to pressure from the guests, the owner of the rustic old camp we return to year after year installed Wi-Fi in the main lodge. The change was subtle at first. Fewer people played Scrabble after dinner. The teenagers seemed to lose interest in flirting and chatting with one another over the perennially unfinished jigsaw puzzles and began texting with friends back home instead. There was room at the game tables. The place grew quieter. The books on the shelves were largely untouched. The guy who was always looking for a game of bridge didn't bother to get out his deck of cards. Last year, we looked around one night and laughed: the couches were full of people, and all of them were gazing at their laptops.

This year, I've decided that my vacation will be a vacation from my computer as well. Although we're long past the stage where we can make such a call for our kids, I'm hoping they'll consider taking a break from Facebook and YouTube, too. I'm looking forward to a few games of Scrabble after dinner and to evenings that seem to stretch interminably toward bedtime. And I've written myself a to-do list: Read deeply. Take long walks with my husband and my boys. Listen for loons. Write in my journal. Notice everything. Be amazed by the world.

August 2010

— one good thing —

A young father lay dying. Our sons, then in third grade

together, had been playmates since kindergarten. When word came that Richard was ill, I'd brought soup to the door, then lemon cake. They were small gestures, a way to say, "I'm thinking of you." One day I stayed on to chat with Richard in the quiet house, and later his wife, Jane, called and asked if perhaps I could come again.

"Richard is comfortable with you," she said. "And we are going to need some help here. I think what he'd like most of all is someone to talk to."

So it was that in the midst of my life with two small children, I was invited to pause and draw close to death. Richard's decline was slow. There was time enough for the work of letting go. As the months went by he moved from the sofa in the sun-drenched living room to the darkened master bedroom upstairs. He went from recounting anecdotes of his childhood into a tape recorder for his boys to hear when he was gone to listening while my friend Lisa and I took turns reading the *Tibetan Book of Living and Dying* aloud at this bedside. Festive meals shared at the kitchen table evolved into sips of coffee and bites of cake among the bed pillows. There was nothing to do day after day but show up with an open heart. The lesson, I came to see, was all about being there—allowing, listening, learning to be less afraid of what might come and more accepting of things as they were.

"How are you doing?" I asked him once as the end drew near, not sure at all how to ask my real question: "How can anyone suffer so, and yet go on?"

I think often, still, of Richard's answer, given with a

smile. "As long as there is one good thing in every day," he said, "life is worth living."

One good thing. Most days, I lose count by breakfast time.

August 2010

 toothache

It started on the first day of our vacation at the lake, a little sensitivity on a back molar as I bit into a piece of blueberry pie. I winced, took a sip of coffee, and passed my dessert over to Jack, who was happy to have it. We were thirty minutes from the nearest town and three hours from my dad, the only dentist I've ever had in my life. There wasn't much I could do other than try to distract myself. For three days I managed to do that. I walked and ran, swam, did yoga, participated in each evening's game of Scrabble, read books on the shore, savored mealtimes with my husband and our sons. Except for when I had to actually chew. Suddenly, the simple pleasure of eating together had become a kind of torture. And then came the moment, midway through the week, when I had to give up. I couldn't fake it for one more martyred minute. I was in pain whether I was eating or not. Lots of pain. The blast-through-and-pretend-it-isn't-happening trick didn't work at all once my jaw swelled up and the tears began pricking at the backs of my eyelids.

"Chronic physical pain is one of the harshest teachers

you can have," writes Eckhart Tolle. Amen. Lying in bed, trying to take deep, calming breaths while my jaw throbbed and my temples ached and the pain pulsed in my head with every beat of my heart, I began to get a little panicky.

How much worse could it get? And what was going on anyway? I, the dentist's daughter who'd gone through life without so much as a real cavity, was not supposed to get some random, debilitating toothache. Especially not during the one precious week we all look forward to throughout the other fifty-one weeks of the year, our expensive, idyllic, end-of-summer retreat on a gorgeous lake in Maine.

Steve and Henry and Jack commiserated. They brought me mint tea, melting ice cream, and hot washcloths. Word went out around the campfire, so to speak, and before long, friends in nearby cabins were offering antibiotics and painkillers, acupressure treatments and goldenseal. I walked up the road, called my dad on my cell phone, and read the words on the proffered bottles to him. "Take the antibiotics," he said. "Take the painkillers."

I spent the rest of the week in a haze of pain and woozy stupor. Time slowed down, and I told myself that wasn't such a bad thing. I read a book that I don't remember reading, sat on the porch, slept in the sun, and spent a lot of time curled up in bed listening to the sounds of kids playing on the beach and boats whizzing by.

For a few weeks now, I've been repeating a meditation by Adyashanti that strikes me as radical, simple, and incredibly challenging: "Allow everything to be exactly as it is." Sometimes, sitting cross-legged on my pillow, after a nice long yoga practice, I've actually been able to do it. Having used my body, calmed my mind, gotten back in touch with my own center, it is possible for me to sit in stillness, to breathe, and to allow everything to be exactly as it is.

But I've been humbled by an unexpected sock to the jaw. We're back at home now, and there are lots of things I ought to be doing. Instead, I've been to see my dad three times. He opened a back molar, found a crack in the tooth, put in a bonded filling. The pain, however, isn't going away. X-rays don't show a thing, but the relentless throbbing in my jawbone is real, the jolt when I chew is real, the desperation at 4 am, when the pain extends from ear to chin, is real. I type these words with a couple of cotton rolls stuffed between my upper and lower teeth, to keep them from touching each other.

The pain lesson was not on my to-do list for this week. But here I am, the student who's just been dragged in by her ear and shown to her seat in the classroom. "Resistance is futile" is the theme for the day. Getting on with my life—cleaning house, doing the back-to-school shopping, exercising—isn't an option.

And so I remind myself to go with the program of learning to accept what is. Instead of fighting the pain, I'm trying to bring all those years of yoga practice into this moment. How hard it is, to truly surrender. But that's what I'm up to today. In the grand scheme of things, a sore jaw isn't much, and yet it can feel as if it's everything. (Certainly trying to avoid it, and then fighting it, has taken up most of my attention and energy for the last week.) I know it's time for a different tack. Time to bring some acceptance into my nonacceptance. Time to see what happens when I allow everything to be exactly as it is.

August 2010

——·—— the things we carry ——·——

Tension. Anxiety. Worry. My own load is invisible, but it's definitely been taking a toll. This week I learned that while I've been stretching my spine in downward dog, practicing deep breathing in meditation, walking the back roads of New Hampshire with a grateful heart, I've also been clenching my teeth. Clenching so hard and so fiercely and for so long that I've cracked both of my back molars and pushed my bite out of alignment.

It took my dad the dentist to figure it all out, after I'd called him for the fifth morning in a row to describe my sleepless nights and to confess that I'd begun counting the hours between painkillers.

"Put two rolls of cotton between your teeth so they don't touch, then sit down and completely relax for a half hour, and call me back," he advised. Ever the obedient daughter, I did what he told me, weird as it sounded.

Within moments, I caught myself clamping down on the cotton rolls—clamping down as if they were a couple of bullets I'd been told to bite while undergoing primitive surgery without anesthesia. Except of course, this was not surgery. This was my own everyday life. And apparently, in order to survive it, I've been holding myself in some kind of death grip.

The truth was a bit of a shock. I took a deep breath, *made* myself relax, and then caught myself clamping right down again. For thirty conscious minutes, then, I focused on relaxing my jaw completely. Deliberate, intentional relaxation. And bit-by-bit I felt the pain that's plagued me for a week begin to drain away. Can it really be this simple?

This morning, I watched as my son Jack got ready to head up into the White Mountains for a three-day hike with a friend. It's his first big adventure without an adult along, a test for us parents as well as for him. When he proposed the trip at the beginning of the summer, his dad and I were noncommittal, not wanting to nix the idea yet not at all sure he was ready to take off on his own into the mountains. Back then, August seemed like a long way off. If we said nothing more about his plan, we figured he might forget the whole idea.

Instead, over the course of many phone calls, he and his friend chose a date, got some advice about a route, and finally, with our blessing and my credit card, reserved a couple of AMC huts. The funny thing is that by the time he was actually ready to go, I was ready to let him.

A year ago, this teenaged boy was driving me crazy. I despaired of his ever growing up, wising up, straightening up, *cleaning up*. All of a sudden, though, he is grown up. At six feet tall and 160 pounds, he is a lot bigger and stronger than I am. And finally, it seems that his brain is actually catching up to his body. I send him to the grocery store with a list, and he comes back having made the right purchases. (It was not so long ago that I requested a cucumber and he returned with a zucchini.) He calls home, meets his curfew, texts me when something goes awry and sometimes just to say hi. He asks me how my day was, puts his dishes in the dishwasher, and walks the dog. He usually gets up on time and occasionally goes to bed at a reasonable hour. He reads good books and then wants to talk about them. He still trashes his bedroom, and then just before I open my mouth to say something about how it looks like a bomb went off in there, he turns on some loud music and starts cleaning it up.

It's late now, and Steve and Henry have gone to bed. I was just about to turn off the lights and head upstairs when a text came in from Jack, who is settling into his sleeping bag on the top of a mountain. "Hey mom," he wrote, "random service spot here. Everything is going fine."

I've been thinking a lot today about the things we carry, both literally and emotionally. I watched the seventeen-year-old boys pack their packs, watched them trying to anticipate what they would need, what was worth lugging up into the mountains and back down again. Their enthusiasm was great to see, though I was less impressed by the rations they were taking—Slim Jims, Ritz crackers, Pop-Tarts, and a sausage. They insisted on carrying their own bed pillows from home. I resisted the urge to check to make sure they had toothbrushes and clean underwear. (I did insist on hats and four apples.)

And then it was time for them to shoulder their loads and be on their way. They probably took too much stuff. Their packs looked impossibly heavy to me. But what they have is what they chose to carry.

Me, I'm ready for a lighter load. I've laid down my burden of worry, at least for now. The mouth guard my dad made me will help me remember to relax my jaw in my sleep, to give my poor teeth some rest. And meanwhile, a more conscious part of me is working to let go. I'm sure Jack is fine out there. He'll sleep tonight, and so will I.

August 2010

——·—— walking ——·——

"What are you thinking?" I asked Henry.

We were taking a last hike before he heads back to college tomorrow, climbing up the back side of North Pack on a perfect early autumn morning.

"Oh, nothing much," was his reply. "Sometimes it's nice to just walk in the woods and not think about anything at all."

My own mind, of course, was racing down the trail ahead of my feet, tumbling into the afternoon, considering what we would do for the rest of the day, what I should make for dinner, how we could make this last weekend of family togetherness feel special.

"Henry is already a yogi," my yoga teacher said to me five or six years ago when she first met him. He had never done a downward dog or shown any particular talent for forward bends. What she meant was that he is possessed of the kind of inner quiet that most of us spend years, and lots of time and energy, trying to achieve. When he walks in the woods, he just walks in the woods. Yesterday, as sunlight filtered through the trees, and summer drew to a close, his companionable silence was the gentle reminder I needed to be calm, too. To let the thoughts and plans and voices in my head fall silent for a while and to be fully present right where I was instead, taking a hike with my son.

His plane leaves at 6:30 tomorrow morning. As I type these words, he's upstairs, packing the final load of his clean laundry into his suitcase. Tonight, we'll have an early meal, our last as a family until Christmastime. We'll say what we're feeling grateful for, chat at the table for a while, head to bed early. And in the darkness of 4 am I'll hug him one last time and send him back into his other life. The good-byes are hard for me, still. So I'm grateful for right now, for every moment we are here together. And I'm taking a cue from my son—not thinking about it all too much, just paying attention.

September 2010

—·—— end of summer ——·—

It's September. Summer really is over. But I'm not quite done with it yet myself. You can see it in my half-there-half-here outfit this morning: as I type these words I'm wearing flip-flops and a wool sweater, trying to have it both ways. I keep looking at my bathing suit, tossed on the edge of the bath tub: if I don't put it away, maybe I'll take one more swim in the pond before the water gets too cold. I was tempted by rust-colored chrysanthemums in pots at the farmers' market on Wednesday, but here at home my pink petunias and impatiens are still blooming alongside the fading hydrangeas and spent sunflowers. I keep watering, deadheading, prolonging.

There are local peaches in my refrigerator, a row of Brandywines on the windowsill, the season's first Paula Reds in a bowl: summer and fall all mixed together, gloriously abundant. I savor every bite. Yesterday I sat outside in the sunshine and ate tomatoes from my neighbor's garden for lunch. By evening, we'd cranked the windows shut and were glad to have hot corn chowder for dinner. One son left for school on Tuesday, but one is still sound asleep upstairs on this weekday morning. As long as it's still summer vacation for him, I can pretend it's summer for me, too.

And yet. If I have learned anything at all these last couple of months, it's that I'm still learning how to let go, still caught so often between my wish to stop time in its tracks and my longing to accept with more grace the transience of all things. In New Hampshire, summer's end always catches me off guard, so swiftly do the lush ferns along the stone walls crumple into brittle brown tangles, so suddenly do the evenings turn from balmy to brisk. Next week, Jack, too, will be back in school, and my bathing suit will surely be back in the drawer.

My own days will feel different then: shorter, busier, and—I have to admit this—lonelier. It's still cool now, the temperature hovering right around 60. Too cold for that swim I've been so determined to have. Jack has promised to take a hike with me, though. I'm going to make him some pancakes, give him the car later to go visit a friend, settle in with Steve tonight to watch the semifinals of the U.S. Open. And then tomorrow, I'm going to release my grip and let summer go. It's been good. It's over. It's okay.

September 2010

——·—— anniversary ——·——

Each morning this week, my husband and I have woken early and walked together. With our sons back in school, the daily rhythm of our life has shifted. We've gone from a summer of family schedule-juggling to the quieter intimacy of two.

We take the same route from our house, a loop through the woods and along a quiet bike path, then up the hill toward home. By the time I put coffee on and Steve heads upstairs to shower, the sun is well up and we have said to each other all the things that are on our minds. Already this new ritual feels special, worth protecting and continuing.

Sunday we marked our twenty-third wedding anniversary. I say "marked" instead of "celebrated" because there were no gifts or letters exchanged, no romantic tryst in a hotel, no showy surprises. We shared a bottle of champagne with dinner, and in the morning we put on our sneakers and began the twenty-fourth year of our life together.

A couple of days earlier, I'd had some of our old home videos transferred to DVD, and Steve and Jack and I sat in the kitchen that night and watched the footage of our wedding, September 12, 1987. How odd it was to see my own parents, just about the age I am now. But it was stranger still to see the two of us, not as middle-aged parents but as young lovers. There, too: so many loved ones who have died in these intervening years, but who, on that joyful day, were simply alive, dancing and making toasts and chatting under a white-and-yellow tent. My dad had bought the video camera—a huge, heavy thing—just for the occasion. No one in the family quite knew what to do with it, and so it was casually passed around, from one willing amateur photographer to the next. Someone managed to film our first kiss, a blizzard of rice, my grandmother with her black purse on her arm, Steve leading me out to the dance floor.

My Uncle Chet zeroed in for a while on a college friend of mine who was dancing barefoot in a transparent purple dress. And then, a bit tipsy and unaware he'd failed to press the "off" button, he simply lugged the camera around as he enjoyed the party. So this is what we have: an unwitting, ridiculously precious hour of captured feet and sky and tent top—random and unscripted and oddly revealing. All those legs and pairs of shoes! All those wide, aimless swaths of grass and ground, followed by majestic arcs to cloud and awning and tent pole. The uncensored soundtrack of laughter, clinking glasses, party talk, swing music.

We had a laugh the other day, watching what is arguably the worst wedding video ever recorded. But I can't help but treasure this odd memento, this collage of accidental moments captured for all time. What I realize is that the quality of the picture-taking doesn't matter all that much; meaning is not to be found there anyway. The truth of our lives is not in photographs that freeze time and memory, any more than it is to be found in gift-wrapped boxes or champagne bottles.

And yet each glimpse of that long-ago day, each unplanned kiss and silly dance move, each overheard scrap of conversation and each tapping foot does remind me to pay attention right now. Twenty-three years of marriage is a multitude of moments lived, of gestures made, words spoken. We have not always been kind. Mistakes have been made. Regret, perhaps, is inevitable. And yet what I glimpse in that video—love, optimism, anticipation— endures. How grateful I am for all we've shared, for the two sons who are now nearly men themselves, for the quiet early mornings of this bright autumn.

My heart is full today. A beloved friend is nearing the

end of a long, courageous journey with cancer. Moment by moment, she is being called upon to let go of this physical world and to open to the mysteries beyond it. Watching the sunrise at 6:30 this morning, walking in the woods, touching my husband's arm, I tried to live and love and pay attention enough for both of us, for a friend who is not ready to leave this earth and for myself, so fully occupied here upon it. I wondered whether—if I could only be grateful enough, notice enough, feel deeply enough—I might somehow occupy both realms at once, material and spiritual.

"Write me all the mundane details of your life," she e-mailed the other night from her hospital bed. I try to do that. And each time I pause, and look, and gather up some small bouquet of mundane details, what I see is not ordinariness but evidence: this world in which we are blessed to live is full of meaning, beauty, and holiness.

September 2010

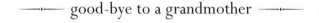 good-bye to a grandmother ———

It is, I'm quite certain, my first real memory: my grandmother washing my hair on the day I was to meet my new baby brother for the first time. I can still see it all in my mind's eye—me sitting in the old claw-foot tub in the bathroom with its windows looking out across an expanse of backyard, the weeping willow tree, the duck pond, the raspberry patch, the mountains beyond. I remember the long rubber hose with a silver sprinkler on the end, the bottle of Johnson's Baby Shampoo, my grandmother's strong, capable fingers. It was August 1961, and I was three. I squeezed my eyes tightly shut, let the warm water pour down over my face, and marveled—I do remember this—at how exciting it all was, and how much I loved feeling my grandmother's hands scrubbing me clean for the most momentous day of my life.

My grandmother died early this morning, just on the cusp of one hundred, and I'm not quite sure how I feel. Relief that her years in a nursing home are over. Guilt that it's been nearly two years since the last time my brother and I drove north to see her. I clipped her fingernails that day, and we brought her a meager plain donut that she thanked us for and didn't eat. We watched her fall asleep in her wheelchair and then we tiptoed away, back into our own busy, distant lives. Sadness, at the passing of my last grandparent and the end of an era, at the realization that it's my own parents now who are on the frontlines between me and mortality. And sadness that my dear grandmother took her last breath after so many years of being almost gone to us already, lost in the fog of dementia and forgetfulness.

"You don't need to visit," my uncle would always say. "If you came, she wouldn't remember you were here." We did come when we could. And then, for too long, we didn't.

I think she would have been pleased to pass from this world to the next on this auspicious night of the full moon, the autumn equinox. Pleased, too, to know that I am sitting alone in my kitchen this evening, the windows open wide, writing a few of my recollections down.

She was a record keeper herself, a faithful recorder of stories from the distant past and from her youth. She once showed me a map she had drawn to perfect scale of the house she'd grown up in, a house that had burned to the ground in a fire when she was still a girl. Having lost everything once, she learned to save and to keep, just in case.

As a child I explored the many closets and cupboards and recesses of her house like an archaeologist searching for clues to a vanished civilization, slipping my feet into the black ice skates my dad had worn as a child, sniffing the contents of the mysterious bottles in the back of the medicine cabinet, poring over the ancient magazines piled up in the vast catchall room known as "the store." (At one time, years earlier, this room attached to the house actually had been a store. By the time I was old enough to rummage around in there, it was stocked with the flotsam and jetsam of my grandparents' lives together—an inexhaustible inventory of memory and artifact and the left-behind possessions of three boys who had long since grown and gone.)

My grandmother tracked the family genealogy, learned to use a computer just to keep it all straight, and then tried in vain to get one of her seven surviving grandchildren to carry on in her stead, to pick up her passion for pursuing the bloodlines. I never could get too excited about my ties to the Green Mountain Boys of Vermont or about finding out whether the Kenistons with a "t" who lived to the south were related to us. And yet, as I sit here tonight, I think I do understand, a bit, my grand-mother's desire to somehow gather up the past, hold onto it all, and make some sense of it. It's what we do as we feel time slipping like sand between our fingers.

My own memories are tumbling all over each other, one giving way to the next. In her honor and in her memory, I offer a few. This is where I'm from, after all, and she is so much a part of who I am.

I am from the front porch stretched across the front of the wide gray house at the foot of Cherry Mountain. Fireflies in a jar, rocking chairs in a row, my grandfather's Camel cigarettes glowing in the darkness. Homemade do-nuts fried in hot oil, melt-in-your-mouth donut holes, crisp and tender, burning the tongue. Day-olds carried out and fed from the palm of my grandmother's hand to the catbird in the bushes. A jar of bacon grease on the back of the cookstove, cereal boxes on top of the fridge, rough soap at the long kitchen sink with its plastic dish drainer and its old rusty pump at one end. A tiny kitchen mirror with a black comb on a shelf. Fresh-baked white bread, slathered with butter and honey. An old pump organ, with heavy carpeted pedals and chipped ivory keys and a row of irresistible, complaining knobs to push and pull. A heavy black telephone, a party line, our own special ring.

Walks to the post office, where I studied the Wanted posters on the wall, shivers crawling up and down my spine, and walks back home again, across the railroad tracks, sucking a jaw-breaker and looking both ways for trains. Tea parties under the weeping willow tree, kittens in the barn, ducks and frogs

in the pond, petunias planted in an old rowboat beached
for all time in the grass. A pile of 1940s' *Boys' Life* magazines
left over from my dad's childhood and every single Hardy
Boys mystery ever written, lined up on a shelf. Cactuses and
African violets in the window, a Bible on the kitchen table,
Billy Graham on the television. A photo gallery of ancestral
family members on the wall up the stairs, black-and-white
portraits of long-dead children in white Victorian blouses,
pushing wicker strollers or posing with stern-looking elders
frozen in history but, somehow, amazingly, related to me.
Pots of Helene Curtis face powder on a tray, on a doily, on
a table, in that bathroom. The tall closet with its medicinal
smell, its nameless brown bottles with black rubber stoppers,
witch hazel and cotton balls, hairnets and Aqua Net and Alka-
Seltzer and Pepto-Bismol and Brylcreem. Crochet hooks
and knitting needles and white socks to be darned. Lamp-
shades protected by plastic, newspaper clippings in a pile on
the Formica table, copies of the *Readers Digest* by the couch,
hard candies in a cut-glass dish, pies baked six at a time. Soft
stretchy pants, cardigan sweaters, and hugs.

These are old memories. The images that keep rising
up, and that still feel so fresh and vivid, are from another
world it seems. My own childhood was nearly half a century
ago. And what's left behind now seems so slight. It's been
quite a few years since my grandmother's house was disman-
tled, the quilt tops and photo albums and teacups scattered to
the winds. What I have left of her is what I can remember—
and what I return to again and again is her hands.

Her beautiful, capable hands, bent a bit from arthritis

and a lifetime of hard work. The fingernails, immaculate and clipped short. These hands could knead bread dough with a few deft strokes, slip a perfect pie crust into a pan, stitch an invisible seam, clean a wound, soothe a brow, coax the tangles out of a rat's nest of hair without a single pull. After her boys grew up, my grandmother went to nursing school and then she took her hands, and all of her maternal energy, out into the world, caring for the old and the ill in their homes, sitting with the dying through long winter nights in the north country, and then driving home on the icy roads of dawn in time to make breakfast for my grandfather. If you were sick or scared or bleeding, she was the person you wanted at your side. One look at those hands, and you knew you were safe. The phrase "you are in good hands" could have originated with her.

My dad has those hands. With them he has performed impeccable dentistry for over fifty years. They are steady still. Healing, fixing, soothing, doing—this is what runs in my family. "Idle hands," my grandmother liked to say, "make devil's work."

There is a stack of afghans, folded and sitting on a chair in our den. Back when her mind was just starting to go but her hands still needed to be busy, my grandmother crocheted afghans. Once she got started it was hard for her to stop. Before long there were afghans for each family member and a few more just because. She gave them to us with a touch of embarrassment. And she gave them with love. At age eighty-five, afghans were what she had to give. Whenever we settle in on the couch to watch a baseball game or a movie, we reach for those afghans and snuggle in. Such small but essential comfort, these four old coverlets made by hand by my grandmother. She would surely like to know they have been of good use here, they are in use still, and that whenever I pull the pink-and-white one across my knees, I pause for just a moment and think of her.

September 2010

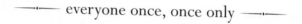 everyone once, once only

Everyone once, once only. Just once and no more. And we also once. Never again. But this having been once, although only once, to have been of the earth, seems irrevocable.
—Rainer Maria Rilke, *Duino Elegies*

These words, the epigraph to Mary Oliver's new collection of poems, pierce my heart. I have read them over and over again and have felt the depth and heaviness and truth of that word *once*. For so it is, every moment of every day, once and only *once*.

Two days ago, I stood in my garden, taking stock after a week away. My neighbor Debbie had protected all my fragile plants from the first two nights of killing frost, spreading black plastic in the entryway, carrying in the heavy pots of geraniums, petunias, chrysanthemums, and ornamental kale, one by one. She had spread bedsheets across my rampant nasturtiums and returned in the early morning, before sunrise, to spray a fine mist of water over everything else, laboring to eke out just a few more days of life and color.

Coming home and standing there, on the most nearly perfect fall day ever, I wanted to grow roots myself, to become still enough to see and absorb everything before me—the mountains ablaze with color; the crystalline sky; the grass, emerald green again after a long, dry summer; the yellow leaves drifting slowly to earth from the maple by the stone wall; the flowers.

Oh, the flowers, these final, brilliant blooms of the season. For weeks I've been cutting things back, getting rid of the spent sunflowers, coneflowers, rudbeckia. And meanwhile, the cosmos and nasturtiums have gone crazy, a riot of glorious, mismatched late-season finery—oranges and pinks side-by-side, wild and beautiful.

I wanted to give myself a moment. A moment in which to simply appreciate the transient beauty and bounty of the day, and then I intended to get right back to the work at hand—the pot of soup on the stove, the load of laundry to fold, the overnight bag to pack so I could head out the door again. Much as I love to be home, I haven't been home much lately.

Steve and I had just returned from a long weekend in Minnesota, where our son Henry was the musical director for the St. Olaf Theater Department's fall musical. Watching him do, at last, the very work he has long aspired to was quite a parenting high. All those hours of "conducting" with a drumstick behind a closed bedroom door, all those years of music lessons, the high-school productions, the accompanist jobs were finally paying off, coalescing into the realization of a dream. We wouldn't have missed it for anything. And yet all mixed up with my feelings of pride and excitement for him was the bittersweet realization that we are visitors in his life out there, the life he lives on his own, far away from us. We dropped in for a while, met his friends and had a meal, and then we said our good-byes to him right on the stage, as the actors began to strike the set around us after the final performance of the show.

The next morning before we headed to the airport, I took a run through a nearby park and found myself alone in an empty playground. Looking at the swings, the slide, the jungle gym, I was overcome with memories of our boys, ages four and seven or so—back when swings and monkey bars offered hours of thrills, back when an ordinary day might include a trip to the park, a snack on the grass, singing along to Raffi on the ride home, a nap, hour upon hour of togetherness. That life I loved so much, that time of close, intense mothering, is so far in the past now that the wave of nostalgia that washed over me, the sudden lump in my throat, caught me off guard. *Once,* and only *once.*

Back at home again, standing in my own yard and wishing I could seize every detail of a gorgeous autumn morning, I felt the same shadow across my heart. I couldn't help but mourn the loss of all that beauty even as I wished I could just hold onto it for a little while longer.

"I've missed the fall," I lamented to myself, thinking

back over these last few too-busy weeks. This, I know by now, is my grasping mind at work, the part of me that is never quite satisfied with the present because I'm so busy regretting what's over (the entire month of September—gone!) or anticipating what's to come (rain in the forecast! no more warm, golden days like this one!).

"This isn't the dress rehearsal," as my husband likes to remind our son Jack. "This is your life." He's nearly eighteen. We can't teach him much anymore. But we can at least keep reminding him that every choice he makes has a consequence, that what he does defines who he is.

The same is true, I realize, of my thoughts. What I think creates the reality I live. I can stand in a deserted playground and feel the loss of my sons' childhoods or I can pause for a moment to remember how blessed we were and to celebrate who they have become. I can wish for more flowers, more warm days, more free time, or I can receive the gift of the present moment—exquisite, fleeting, already vanished.

We die a little every day. With every change, with every loss, with every turn of season or cloud passing before the sun, we lose what was and are asked to respond to what is, again and again. And yet, how easily I can overlook the wonder of my life in my rush to attend to its details or in my dissatisfaction with the way things are.

Seeing my grown son move ever further into adulthood, feeling another season slip away, succumbing to the pressure of a day with too much crammed into it, being with my beloved friend in the final days of the final season of her life, I struggle against what is.

Like a traveler who keeps getting off course and must stop in her tracks and seek out a better route, I find myself rushing headlong down the path of sadness these days, only to realize that I'm going the wrong way. This is a halting journey for sure, full of stops and starts. And so again and again I pause, pull myself together, get turned around, and commit to another direction. I want to choose differently, to replace yearning for what's passed with acceptance of what's offered. Finding something to be grateful for, it seems to me, is a way to honor the fragility of everything and to loosen my grip on what can't be held.

How grateful I am to Debbie, for saving all the flowers for me until I could get home and enjoy them for one last morning. I can be grateful for an autumn day unlike any other. Grateful for bees in the sunshine and wild colors in the garden, for parents who are healthy, sons who have turned into men, a husband who has stood steady through it all, friends who give so much and who allow me to give of myself in return.

I can even be grateful, in this very moment, for gusting winds and the cold rain that has poured down relentlessly all through the night and into this afternoon, pummeling the garden, shredding the last of the flowers and whipping most of the leaves right off the trees. I can be grateful for every quiet hour and every heartfelt conversation my friend and I have shared, grateful for the love she's received, for the grace and courage she's summoned, for the legacy she will leave. There's no rule that says gratitude can't be limned with sadness; indeed, I'm certain it often is.

This has been a difficult fall, with much change and sadness in my life and the lives of those most dear to me. Illness and suffering can seem so random, so pointless—and yet both are a part of every human journey, inevitable. What can we do but meet loss however we're able, knowing that while life itself is a gift, death, too, is deep in the structure of things. Each day offers us a series of endings, losses and transitions that are part and parcel of our daily turn upon this earth, reminders of what it is to be alive. Nothing lasts. And, as we practice dying, over and over, we also learn what it feels like to be fully awake. *Once,* and only *once.*

As I write, the sky grows even darker, the fog settles over the mountains, the garden lies drenched and flattened. In the vase on the table is a bouquet of bright, jewel-toned nasturtiums, picked in the dark last night just before the storm began. They will be the last ones for this year. A long-ago birthday gift from my friend Diane, the vase holds not only flowers but memories, too, of our deep and abiding friendship. I try always to keep it full, full of life and beauty, in honor of a friend who has taught me much about how to live well and whose company I cherish. Finding the blessing in each day, she reminds me by her own quiet example that although we can't resist or refuse the natural course of change, we can allow ourselves to be continually shaped by it. For as long as we are here, the work of soul-making goes on.

And so I say Rilke's words again, to remind myself who I wish to be and how I want to live: with awareness, heart open, grateful for every bit of joy that can be squeezed out of the life I have. "Everyone *once, once* only. Just *once* and no more."

October 2010

—·— so much goodness —·—

I didn't know it would be our last real conversation. I wish now I'd taken note of every word, paid more attention to the sunlight falling across the bed, the single rose in the vase, the light in her eyes, the smile she offered as I kissed her good-bye and promised I would return on Tuesday.

"What are you coming down for?" she asked, as she always did when I told her what day I'd be back. For once—after months of manufacturing haircuts and book-group meetings and pedicures as "legitimate" reasons for me to make the three-hour round-trip from my new town to my old one—I simply told her the truth: "I'm coming to see you."

I do remember this. As I left the room, she told me to go home and have a wonderful weekend with my son Henry, on break from college for three days. "There is so, so much goodness in the world," she said, uncharacteristically insistent. "So much goodness."

Early Saturday morning, my dear friend Diane passed away. (Even typing these words gives me pause. I hear her voice in my head: "Please don't say 'after a long battle with cancer!'" Ok, dear, I won't say that.) I have no words yet for what I feel, for where I've been, for the sadness, the loss, the hole that is left in the place where just a few short days ago a vibrant heart still beat.

A month or so ago, a friend with more experience in these matters said, "You know, when the time comes, everything will be exactly as it is meant to be." I held on to those words all through these last days and found them to be true. Those who were meant to be there were there. Food appeared on the table, friends from near and far appeared at Diane's bedside, the new puppy peed on the floor, the teenagers came and went, poems were read aloud, wine was poured, tears were shed, fires were lit, sheets were changed, and dishes were washed. There was laughter even in the midst of great sadness. Above all, there was love—unconditional, infinite, healing.

Death and life, one inextricable from the other. What I know for sure now is that a heart can accommodate both, a home can accommodate both, a family can accommodate both. Last week, with love and instinct to guide us, Diane's family and friends transformed her upstairs bedroom into a sacred space. And those of us who were present found our own fears transformed as well. We may not know what to expect from death or whether we are truly up to the task we've taken on when we promise to stay near. And then, having made clear our intention to share the journey, come what may, we find that at each step of the way we do know what to do.

Our hearts tell us how to make love visible. Our hands know, without being taught, how to soothe a brow, change a sickbed, tend a body. Dying is hard physical work. And despite the most attentive ministrations, life's final stages are seldom beautiful. To be human, it seems, is to suffer and to pray for an end to suffering. And then, in life's final moments, there is peace, and grace, and even, for one brief instant, a glimpse of the mystery beyond this earthly realm.

Returning from this vigil, taking up residence in my own house again, I'm not quite sure what to do with this new knowledge. I do know, beyond a doubt, that Diane was right: there is so much goodness in the world, so much goodness even in the most wrenching circumstances. But at the moment I'm tired and sad and raw. A bit in awe, still, of what I've seen and lived and learned over the course of this last week. It feels tender yet, this place of grief. So I find my way back into the mundane one step at a time. I am grateful to my husband, for drawing me a hot bath, putting me to bed, folding the laundry and quietly allowing me to find my way back into our life together. I take Tylenol and hot tea to Jack, who is home from school with a cold. I make corn chowder for dinner, search the garden for a few last blossoms to cut, and wonder, What now?

October 2010

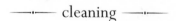 cleaning ——

White vinegar, Citra Solv, and water. This is my cleaning solution of choice. And cleaning, it seems, is about all I can do right now. There are plenty of other things I should be working on, so many tasks left undone over the last few weeks while my heart and hands and attention have been elsewhere. But I've lost a friend. And now I realize I've also lost my own sense of purpose. She needed me. I was there. It was simple. Just over a week since she died, I have no idea how to resume my life. I think I should be able to grieve and keep going, both. Except I can't quite figure out where I'm headed.

I'm home again. But it's hard to focus, hard to care much about the things that usually fill my days. The last autumn leaves have fallen from the trees and the world beyond my kitchen window looks as stark and barren as my own inner landscape. I don't want to go out to lunch with a friend or work on my book proposal or write that speech I have to give next week.

Cleaning, however, feels manageable. And so I dust, I vacuum, I wet mop the floor. Things look fine. But I can't stop myself. I grab a pile of soft rags—Jack's beloved old sky-and-cloud sheets from when he was ten, ripped up now and stuffed into the ragbag—and get down on my hands and knees. The smell of vinegar and orange soothes my senses. It's a relief to do something with a visible outcome, to feel some measure of control somewhere, to transform all this love and heartbreak into a task that supports life in the here and now.

The sun pours in. The floor gleams golden. My tears flow and the soft cloud-sheet rags wipe them away. This is work I can do without thinking, work that satisfies some deep yearning for all that is constant and familiar and necessary. Someone needs to get the crumbs out of the cracks, the smushed raspberries off the counter, the scum out of the sink. It might as well be me.

Life, death, and everything in between—it's all a mystery. The changing light deepens. I sit on the floor, leaning back against the kitchen cabinet. I let the light enter and change me. For today this is enough. I feel all the sadness I can bear to feel. I cry some more. And then I refold my cloud rag and begin once again to clean.

November 2010

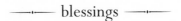 blessings

But listen to me: for one moment, quit being sad.
Hear blessings dropping their blossoms all around you.
—Rumi

There was no need to go, no reason, really, to drive for seven hours in the rain just to say happy birthday. I knew this. Knew the trip was more for me than for my son, who didn't mind at all spending his birthday away from home. We had sent a card, promised a special dinner over Thanksgiving break, planned to call in the evening. But in the end, I baked an orange-and-chocolate cake, put Neil Young's "Prairie Wind" in the CD player, and headed south. Eighteen years ago I gave birth to a boy. Yesterday, it seemed important that I put my arms around him, if only for a moment or two.

On Saturday afternoon, hundreds of people gathered for my friend Diane's memorial service. Diane had chosen the music and readings weeks ago, and then she'd marveled at how strange that felt—both the wrenching process of letting go as well as the opportunity to envision and, to some extent, orchestrate her own good-bye. And yet, once she knew she'd been given a job she never wanted— the task of completing her work here on earth and then figuring out how to leave—she set about that challenge just as she did everything else in her life. Quietly, thoughtfully, with a desire to ease the way for those she loved.

As the first mournful strains of Barber's "Adagio for Strings" poured forth from the choir loft, it seemed that her spirit filled the church, too. Surely, having chosen for us the solace of this familiar music, she was somehow there too, listening. Sitting in the pew holding my husband's hand, I sensed my own grief drawing itself up into a kind of modest intention—to live more consciously, to love more fully, more generously, more joyfully.

Perhaps this is grief's paradox—that in acknowledging the wound in our hearts, in tending with mercy to that which is breaking open within us, we are also given an opportunity to undertake the work of becoming more fully ourselves, committing even more deeply to our own path.

And so I made a trip yesterday that I might not have bothered with even a few months ago, before I watched my friend grapple with her grief over all that she would miss and then make her fragile peace, instead, with gratitude for all that she had had.

"Sounds like a lot of driving," Jack said, when I told him I was coming.

"Well," I admitted, "the truth is, I can't quite let the day pass without seeing your face."

In my mind, November 8 is always bleak and blustery, a day of bare trees, lowering skies, intimations of winter. And it is also a day whose chill is offset by my own happy memories of the day eighteen years ago when our son Jack arrived and made our family complete.

What comfort it brought me, to hand him a birthday card with an "18" on it, a bag of winter hats and socks from home, and a lopsided cake. I took him out for a steak dinner, we talked about school, his college plans, his friends. And then I drove him back to his dorm and kissed him good-bye.

There is no way now for me to be the mother I still wish to be—close by, all-knowing, participating in the minor ups and downs of every day. But neither does my son need or want that kind of mother anymore. He is living a life of his choosing, thriving, finding his own way. So I embrace instead the precious hours when we *are* together. I think I've finally let go of the idea that I'm still preparing him for life's voyage, that I might yet come up with the perfect scrap of advice that will make all the difference and point the way. There's no such thing, of course. What's more, the ship has sailed and he's already on it, charting his own course.

Still, driving home alone late last night, under clear, cold November skies, I felt the opposite of lonely. A little raw still, but not quite so stricken. One thing I've discovered over these last few days is that I can tune right in to what

I'm coming to think of as the "Diane channel" in my mind. I listen for my friend, allow myself to feel her presence, and realize I know exactly what she would have me do—listen to my heart, cherish my family, be grateful.

I'm pretty certain I wouldn't have driven for seven hours just to have dinner and a hug if not for the lessons I've learned from her. And I know, absolutely, that she was with me all the way, that somehow she came along for this ride. Which makes me realize: her legacy is something I'm only beginning to understand. I've had a glimpse of it, though. Already, blessings are dropping their blossoms all around me.

November 2010

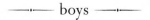

boys

They grow up. They leave home. And then, of course, they come back. They return bearing bags of dirty laundry, stray socks, tee shirts you've never seen before, strange cords for charging various digital devices.

They are different in a way you can't put your finger on. Taller, yes, but that's not quite it. Bigger in some other way; more substantial, with knowledge that won't be shared with you. They are clean shaven because they know you love that. But they also wear their hair short by choice now that you're no longer the one saying, "You need a haircut."

They use words like "fundamentalist" and "metaphorical" and are eager to test your knowledge on constitutional amendments and C. S. Lewis. They want to know your thoughts about original sin and whether you can still scan a line of poetry. They realize that you will be of no help on the paper they have to write analyzing the thematic and rhythmic structure of Gershwin's "An American in Paris."

They are hungry. Really, really hungry. You go through a dozen eggs a day, a gallon of orange juice, a gallon of milk, a pound of cheese. They spend hours on Facebook and YouTube. Their rooms, pristinely vacant these last months, are instantly in shambles. You are not the least bit tempted to pick their jeans up off the floor.

They want you to watch clips of comedians at midnight and you do, even though your bedtime lately has been closer to 10:30 than 12. (Well, admit it, you're often in bed even earlier than that.) They ask for the car keys and you don't think twice about handing them over. When you say, "Be home for dinner," they don't protest. (They *want* dinner. And they don't want to have to pay for it.) When they're running late, they text to let you know. Their friends come over and they seem genuinely happy to see you again—eager to talk, hang around in the kitchen, tell you about their lives as they eat your food. They say thankyou for the meal and put their dishes into the dishwasher without being asked. You hear the thwack of Ping-Pong balls in the basement, cries of victory, deep laughter. You don't tell anyone what time to go to bed or even worry (much) about what they're doing down there in the bowels of the house after you're asleep.

You wake up at 4, in a dark and silent room, and allow

your thoughts to drift. The very thing you once took for granted—two boys asleep in their own beds down the hall—has become rare. You used to think you would never get "your" life back, the one where you got to choose how to spend your own time or what to watch on TV or how loud the music in the car should be. But of course it's been your life all along, and those little boys were always on their way out the door, growing up and growing away from you, even as they were pressing your buttons and driving you nuts and forgetting their home-work and not brushing their teeth.

You wonder if you paid enough attention, if you cher-ished those days enough, if you ever really grasped the fact that your life was a string of irreplaceable moments and that there was no going back to redo any of them.

You don't want to be too hard on your own younger, more impatient, more innocent mothering self. But you are perhaps a little wiser now, more attuned to the moment, how precious it is. And so you don't mind being awake, listening to your husband's gentle breath rising and falling beside you, the dog's soft snore, the wind tossing the bare branches outside the window. Everyone is home and glad to be here. If that's not enough, what is?

November 2010

——·—— the other side of the sweet side ——·——

Checking my e-mail before bed the other night, I found

a note from a fellow mom and writer with whom I've corresponded a bit over the last year.

"I had to tell you that your essay *Boys* was just what I needed today," she wrote. "I so dread the days my kids are off at college, and you showed me the sweet side, the coming-home-and-basking-in-them part."

I thought about the words I'd written in a rush last week. Sometimes I spend all day just getting a few paragraphs to sound right. But that day, with both my sons still asleep upstairs and just an hour at my kitchen table before we needed to be out the door and on our way to an orthodontic appointment, I wrote quickly, a spill of words that captured all I was feeling at that very moment—acceptance of who they are and gratitude that they were home, along with a touch of surprise at how easy things can seem these days, compared to where we were two years ago, deep in the throes of our younger son's adolescent struggles.

My friend went on to say that she had wept into her pillow the night before, mourning the transformation of her sweet seventeen-year-old son, "the treasure of my heart," into "what I hope is a temporarily self-absorbed ogre."

I wrote her back to say something like, "Hang in there, it gets better." And it does. But her letter also made me think about the snapshot of our life I'd shared a few days earlier. Those of us who write memoir know that what finds its way onto the page or into a blog post is never the whole story. It may be true, but it is also, inevitably, a curated version of the truth, a version that's been edited for style and impact, narrated in order to make a point and tell a story, condensed for readability, censored, perhaps, for privacy. I had written about a fleeting moment in time, words straight from the heart for sure, but words that evoked only the tiniest corner of a much bigger picture.

And just as tears soaking a pillow is not my friend's typical response to a hard day of motherhood, neither is rhapsodic domestic harmony an accurate picture of mine. Things just aren't that simple around here. Or anywhere, for that matter.

Again and again and again, I'm reminded that my work as a parent—and as a person—is mostly about letting go of my idea of the way I want things to be so I can work with things as they actually are.

Certainly boarding school was never part of our plan for either of our children, and yet there came a moment when my husband and I both knew that the best thing for our younger son was not another dismal year at the public school in our town—much as he insisted at first that he wanted to stay with his friends and much as I yearned for two more years of a child at home.

Letting go of my idea of what it meant to be a "good" mother (a picture that included a happy, hardworking teenager participating cheerfully in our daily life) was almost easy, compared to the pain of actually letting go of the boy himself. For two months I cried every day as the school bus he used to take drove past our house in the afternoon without stopping. I avoided downtown between three p.m. and four, when the high schoolers could be found hanging out. I skipped over the sports pages in the newspaper, unable to read about his former teammates' exploits on field and court. I mourned the loss of the lovable little boy who had turned into a defiant, depressed adolescent I no longer recognized. And I mourned my inability to live up to my own expectations of myself as a mother who could ride the inevitable ups and downs of adolescence. I wasn't sure if, by allowing him to finish high school in another state, we'd failed him or helped save him.

But slowly the teenager who had claimed not to care about going to college, who had forgotten the joy of sports and the pleasure of a good book, who said he just wanted to be "another brick in the wall," began to get his mojo back. Given a fresh start in a new school, away from home, accountable to adults other than his parents, he ran cross-country again and rekindled his passion for math. He took up squash and figured out how to take notes in class. He began to turn in his homework on time and to go to his teachers for help. He won some awards and made some stupid mistakes and weathered the consequences. He realized how grateful he is for a second chance and how much he loves his new school. He started investing in his future by making better decisions in the present.

And slowly, I eased up on myself. I began to think that being a "good" mom isn't necessarily about preserving an ideal that doesn't exist anyway, but rather about being realistic about what our children actually need from us. Sometimes what they need most of all is for us to let go of our grip on the way things *ought* to be, so that we can accept life as it is, love our children for who they are, and love ourselves simply for doing the best we can.

Last week was far from perfect at our house. There wasn't enough "family" time, in my opinion. There was way too much computer time, too many late nights and late mornings, too much junk food, a few sharp words and hurt feelings. And yet, in our own ways, we were all doing the best we could.

We managed one fire in the fireplace, one board game, a Thanksgiving feast at my parents' old house in the woods, a belated birthday dinner for Jack (the cake came out of the pan in one piece), and an afternoon at the new wing of the MFA in Boston—where, truth be told, the kids texted and threatened to fall asleep standing up. We saw friends and tended to haircuts and dental work, and we debated, among other things, curfews and sleepovers, whether pot should be legalized, how many times I should have to walk into a dirty kitchen on a given day, the fact that someone failed to turn down the heat and turn off the lights at the end of the night. Our days were full of one another, for better and for worse.

I watched Jack make pancakes and listened to Henry play the piano, and I kept reminding myself to focus on what was good. I *reminded* myself to be grateful. And I made a conscious choice, at least once a day, to release my old hold on blame and regret—regret for what never really was anyway, for what isn't now, and for what never will be.

Family life in the real world isn't just one way or

another. It's not good or bad, black or white, peaceful or tense, happy or sad. It just is. It's all of those things and more: messy and complicated and sweet and heart-breaking by turn. There are no charmed lives or perfect children or flawless families. Yet there are good moments in every day. And my own very different, still-struggling kids actually *are* perfect, each in his own very imperfect way. They screw up. As do I. But I wouldn't trade my flawed family for any other family. And I know the pain and unexpected challenges of these hard teenage years have both deepened my compassion, strengthened my spirit, and given me a newfound appreciation for every fleeting, uneventful, ordinary day. Yes, my friend, it does get better. It gets better the very moment we allow ourselves to be ok with things as they are.

December 2010

*Every act of perception, is to some degree an act of creation,
and every act of memory is to some degree
an act of imagination.*
— *Oliver Sacks*

——·—— snow day ——·——

My husband and I were waiting at the gate, eager to see
if a month overseas had changed our son. He had turned
twenty-one in December and then left us just two weeks
later to join a group of his fellow theater and music
majors for an intensive interterm course in London.

All through January we read his blog posts and his daily
theater reviews, and wondered, "When did he become a
critic?" It's a curious experience, to watch your child fly
further and further away from the nest, to see a shy teenager metamorphose first into a capable college student
and then, almost before you know it, into a young man
ready to make his way in the world.

"This trip has given me a taste of what it's like to be
completely responsible for myself," Henry wrote on his
last day in London. "As I near the end of my junior year

of college, my mind frequently turns to what life will be like 'in the real world' without the consistent foundation that I have come to expect from school, home, and family. While I was still under the wing of St. Olaf here in London, having money, tickets, and accommodations provided for me, the reality that I'll have to come up with these sorts of things on my own in a year and a half is starting to hit me."

Reading those words while my son was making his way back across the Atlantic, the reality started to hit me, too. Another chapter is almost over. It feels as if his senior year of high school is still close enough to touch yet his senior year of college is just months away. How did we get here so fast?

When Henry appeared in the terminal, tired, rumpled, dragging his bag, my heart leapt at the sight of him. There is some irrepressible maternal instinct that surges through me even now, urging, "hold on tight and don't let go." The three of us went out to dinner, Steve and I mindful of the fact that it was well after midnight London time, but unable to stop our flow of questions. And yet, even though Henry was happy to supply some details, describing the food, the plays, the people, even his drinking exploits at various pubs, it was clear that the real experience, the real growth, was invisible and inexpressible. The trip was his, not ours, no matter how vivid his travelogue. Travel transforms us. Age changes us. Distance is distance and children grow up and leave the nest for lives of their own, away from their parents.

This week, though, Henry is at home. For a few days,

he's back in his bedroom upstairs, eating breakfast with us in the morning, watching reruns of the *Daily Show* with me in the middle of the day, sprawling on the couch with a book. He's also busy applying for summer jobs and practicing the piano, preparing pieces for a solo concert in the spring. There is not a moment that I don't want to seize, prolong, capture, and save.

Today, I'm delighted by snow. Snow means we can skip the errands and the haircut and stay put instead. The houseguest who was supposed to arrive tonight isn't going to make it; all flights are canceled. Good. We'll eat leftovers from the fridge, light a fire, watch a movie before bed. When Henry sits down at the piano to play a suite of Spanish dances, I stop what I'm doing, stand still, and listen.

I'm so aware that these visits now really are just that— visits. More and more his life will occur elsewhere, in places determined by love, luck, career, destiny. Proofreading his cover letter for a summer job in St. Louis, I'm a little astonished at how much he's already accomplished in his short life, how much he has to offer a potential employer, how clear he is about his career goals. I'm excited for him and conscious, too, that a job at a theater far from home will be one more step in his journey away from childhood and into adulthood, a journey that began years ago with kisses and good-byes at classroom doors and is simply continuing now into more distant territory, just as it's supposed to.

And so I remind myself—not for the first time!—of the futility of trying to hold on to any of these moments. Why be sad? How much easier life is when I remember to keep things simple in my heart. Why not just enjoy this wintry week of togetherness without mourning its passing at the same time?

"Think of mindfulness," writes Buddhist teacher Sylvia Boorstein, "as hanging out happily." That, I think, is a good instruction for a snow day with a grown-up child at home. A good instruction for life, too.

February 2011

 —•— presence —•—

It's been a week of snow and ice and the kids at home. Henry left early yesterday morning to fly back to Minnesota. Jack and I are about to start packing the car, in the hope we can get out ahead of the latest snowstorm—a couple more inches predicted for today—and get him back to school before dark.

As always, there's a little bit of a letdown as the house goes from full to empty again. You'd think I'd be used to it by now, and I guess, in a way, I am. I know at least that silence has its own sound, that the scent of aftershave lingers for a long time in empty bedrooms, that a damp towel left on the bathroom floor won't hang itself back up—but that it can somehow tug at my heart. I know I might as well dump the rest of the whole milk and toss out the half bag of tortilla chips rather than wait for them to get stale sitting in the drawer. I know to wait a few days before changing the sheets on their beds, that it will be easier then.

I also know how lucky I am. The other day Henry and I struck a deal: he'd climb up Pack Monadnock with me if I'd make his favorite ridiculously rich Ina Garten pasta dish for dinner. The snow was deeper on the mountain than we expected, the going was slow, and although he didn't complain (much), there was no question my son would have preferred to be home chatting with his friends on Facebook than slogging up the trail with his mom. He went hiking for me. That night, with pleasure, I cooked for him.

Last night, we hosted a Super Bowl party here for five of Jack's friends and their parents. Jack sat at the kitchen island in the morning, chopping peppers for the chili. He played sous chef, opening the cans, rinsing beans, taste-testing for spice and heat. Cooking is definitely not his first choice of activity for a Sunday morning but he knows that his help—and his company—means a lot to me.

"I'll do any mother-son activity you want this morning," he'd offered when he got up, "just, please, don't ask me to go hiking!"

Whenever our boys are home these days, it feels as if the time is too short and the demands are too many. How to balance their eagerness to see friends with our eagerness to see them? How to stay on top of work that needs to get done and still make space for the kind of hanging out that gives rise to connection and conversation? I can't tie the kids down and insist that they talk to us. And there's not much we can say, at this point, that will affect the choices they make or the things they do. I ask for details about their lives, and they tell me what they want me to know.

And yet more and more it seems that the ties that bind us—stretched to the snapping point at times during adolescence—are being rewoven and reinforced as our sons come and go, and as we create new ways of being together as a family. Home, once the only place to be, assumes a different significance now, a brief resting place where nourishment, acceptance, and embrace are always available. When the four of us sit down to dinner, we still pause for a moment as we always have. We hold hands and say the grace we've always said.

For quite a few years it seemed to me that the gratitude at our dinner table was rote, not felt. As teenagers, the kids endured the ritual, went through the motions, their minds elsewhere. Now, though, I sense a return to feeling. Perhaps they had to leave home and return again to begin to appreciate the comfort of continuity, our moments of togetherness and the traditions that have always shaped us as a family.

For so many years my husband and I have expressed our love mainly by trying to be present—as if, somehow, the very gift of our attention might be enough to carry us through the roughest patches of parenthood. Sometimes, paying attention means hanging in there through unpleasant moments. It means not shying away from intensity but confronting it. It means addressing trouble head on, insisting on the truth, ensuring consequences, holding feet to the fire. Sometimes being present is almost unbearably painful. Parenting an adolescent is not sweetness and light.

This morning, though, as I look back at the last few days, the word that comes to my mind is "presence." It seems to me that my sons have been present, too—present in a way neither of them could have been even a short time ago. It's as if the self-absorption of their teenaged years is yielding to a new, more-adult awareness, to kindness, and to a willingness to reconnect.

I wonder if one essential part of growing up is coming to see that happiness isn't necessarily derived from doing exactly as we please. Often, we find happiness when we choose to please someone else. Giving of ourselves, we receive something intangible but precious in return. We parents, of course, live and breathe the truth of this. But it can take a long time for children to mature enough to acquire such wisdom. This week, I've seen glimpses of it.

A hike in the snow, sharing the cooking tasks, saying our blessing—these are small kindnesses in the grand scheme of things. But to me they feel like love coming full circle. Sometimes, still, I doubt my mothering. Certainly in the thick of some family crisis or conflict, I wonder if attention is really enough to save us. Receiving my children's attention in return, I begin to suspect it's the very thing that will.

February 2011

—·—— first day of school ——·—

I've had it only a few times: a sudden sense of arriving at my own front door, of being home without even knowing I'd been away. I felt it twelve years ago when I first unrolled a yoga mat in the back corner of a power yoga studio in Cambridge. Never mind that the room was heated to 102 degrees and I'd dressed, unwittingly, in sweatpants and a heavy long-sleeved shirt. Never mind that I couldn't bend over and come anywhere close to touching my toes, that I had no idea what a downward dog was, that my body felt so ungainly and awkward and disconnected from my brain (not to mention my heart) that I spent most of the class sweating desperately and watching everyone else flow through a series of poses that looked at once impossible, and impossibly lovely, to me. I did what I could, which wasn't much, and knew, the way we sometimes do know these things, that I'd finally arrived at a place I'd been seeking all my life.

There was a part of me even then that dreamed of full immersion. Sometimes, I fantasized about what it might be like to study deeply, to practice for more than an hour and a half a couple of times a week, perhaps even to one day teach this practice I love so much to others. And always the ever-ready critic in my brain responded with all the reasons why that would never happen.

It was too late. I already had a job. My kids and husband needed me. I've never been athletic and never will be. No matter how many years I spend on a yoga mat, I won't ever have a "yoga body." I can't do a handstand. I'm too shy. I'm too uncoordinated. I'm too old.

Twelve years later, I'm even older than I was then. But I'm also sensing it's time to attend more closely to my soul's longings rather than to the nattering, negative voice that tells me what I'm not and can never be.

The truth is, my children no longer need me day in and day out, the way they once did, and my husband is quite able to take care of himself. I don't get paid to edit books on someone else's schedule anymore. And a yoga body is not the goal or the point of what I do on my yoga mat, although I certainly appreciate every little bit of core strength I manage to acquire. The reasons I practice, the reasons I keep a mat spread on the floor between my kitchen and living room, have more to do with learning than with doing, more to do with curiosity than mastery.

Yoga, as I've slowly come to understand, isn't for the flexible. It's for the willing. I practice yoga because I clench my jaw till my teeth ache, and tuning in to my breath is a gentle, necessary daily reminder to let go. I practice because so often I fail at being the wife, the mother, the friend I yearn to be, and learning to accept myself as I am on my yoga mat helps me accept who I am in the world. I practice because I tend toward judgment, and yoga softens my rough edges. I practice because I get so easily lost in worry or regret or plans that I miss the beauty right under my nose, and yoga is a lovely wake-up call. I practice to quiet my mind and to open my heart and to honor the moment–by–moment experience of being alive.

Early this morning, I threw all of my doubts and fears and nerves and excitement into the car, along with my yoga mat and duffel bag, and drove to the Kripalu Center for Yoga and Health in Western Massachusetts. For the next month, I'll live in a dorm room here with four other women and practice yoga five to eight hours a day with a bunch of other would-be teachers. There will be no place to hide.

All afternoon yesterday, as I vacuumed and dusted, watered plants and changed the beds, I fought back tears, wondering if I'd been nuts to think I could do this. I wondered how I could possibly have imagined that being away from home for such a long time was a good idea. Every insecurity that's ever plagued me came roaring back: the embarrassment of showing up for the first day of first grade with a lunch box that was horribly wrong; third grade—the wrong stockings; eighth grade—the wrong friends; tenth grade—the wrong everything. It's been years since I've endured the butterflies in my stomach that always marked the first day of school, but today is the first day of school all over again, and those butterflies knew just where to find me.

Funny, how I almost had myself convinced that I'd constructed a solid, reasonably confident grown-up self—and then all it took was the anticipation of a single step out of my well-established comfort zone to bring me right back in touch with the uncertain child I once was.

"Nervous?" my son Jack asked me at breakfast this morning. "Very," I admitted, "but in a good way. And grateful, too." As a girl, I took refuge in books and the world of my imagination. Since I didn't quite fit in, I mostly opted out, choosing solitude and stories over socializing and physical activity, both of which were too scary to deal with. So much easier to disappear than to negotiate the complicated social hierarchy of my more with-it peers or to risk embarrassment in gym class.

I was the master of the independent study, the sick note, the excused absence. Given that I also managed to get through four years of college without spending a single night with a roommate, setting foot in the gym, or donning a pair of sneakers, what I'm about to do now does seem a little radical. Or, maybe I'm just finally ready to show up—not only on my yoga mat, not only for my family and my friends, but also for the beautiful, challenging privilege of finding out who I am and who I might, even yet, turn out to be.

February 2011

 never a dull moment

Unfortunately, there is still snow on the ground, even though it's April. Fortunately, a robin convention is under way in my front yard, and there are crocuses blooming alongside the stone wall.

Unfortunately, I thought I'd been left off the guest list to a friend's surprise birthday party. Fortunately, it turned out the hostess had an old e-mail address and was wondering why she hadn't heard from me—just as I was wondering why I hadn't heard from her.

Unfortunately, I'd already made plans for that evening, but fortunately, I was able to stop by the party long enough to be part of the surprise, have a glass of champagne, and wish my friend a happy fiftieth.

Unfortunately, my son Jack and I had a horrible conversation on Friday that kept me awake, tossing and turning all night. Fortunately, he called the next day to set things right, and we both felt much better.

Unfortunately, a good friend is facing a frightening biopsy this week. Fortunately, he sat at our dinner table on Saturday night and was reminded how much love and support surround him as he takes the first step on this journey into the unknown.

Unfortunately, none of my son Henry's many applications have resulted in a summer internship or job offer. Fortunately, he decided yesterday to take a leap and attend a meditation retreat for pianists—a big step outside the box that may take him right where he needs to go.

Unfortunately, the huge brush pile my husband and I were burning yesterday sent a wild spark into the field. Fortunately, friends and neighbors came quickly to our aid, and together we were able to stamp out the fire before damage was done.

Unfortunately, I was so sore and exhausted after a long day of hauling brush and tending raging fires that I could barely move my body off the couch last night. Fortunately, Steve made his own dinner and emptied the dishwasher and said, "Let's go to bed early."

Friends keep asking me: "What is it like, coming back to the 'real' world, after a whole month away?" So far, I have no good answer to that question. Life is what it is, what it's always been. I am who I am, the same person I was before I had the lovely opportunity to practice yoga and meditation for eight hours a day. And yet, there is something going on here that feels a little different.

I think of a book our family adored when Henry and Jack were small, a book by Remy Charlip called *Fortunately,* that we read aloud over and over again.

"Fortunately," it begins, "Ned was invited to a surprise party. Unfortunately, the party was a thousand miles away. Fortunately, a friend loaned Ned an airplane. Unfortunately, the motor exploded. Fortunately, there was a parachute in the airplane. Unfortunately, there was a hole in the parachute."

The charm and appeal of this playful picture book is the speed with which Ned's luck turns from good to bad to good again. He's up, he's down, he's up, he's down—until, of course, we realize right along with him that there's no point at all in judging any of the crazy things that happen to him as either "good" or "bad." They just are. And at the end of the day, at the end of the book, he wouldn't have had it any other way.

And that, I think, is one thing I learned in my time away. I can continue to go through my life keeping a tally sheet of the "good" stuff and the "bad" stuff, or I can let go of that kind of judging and comparing.

As I practice being present in the moment that is right now, I come into closer relationship with an inner self that is not at the mercy of every thought or fear or perception that passes through my busy mind. It's an awareness, a curious self that somehow stands apart, watching, abiding, and holding faith that everything will turn out fine in the end.

My "witness consciousness" is still a toddler, which is to say that this non-judging, non-reacting aspect of me is not terribly reliable yet. (That awful phone conversation did send me into a tailspin of worry and frustration, after all.) Yet, I'm growing fond of this quiet, less-reactive entity. I want to know her better, trust her more, and encourage her presence. Sitting on my yoga mat, allowing my breath to be a doorway into the moment, I realize how good it feels just to be here, alive.

"The seed of suffering in you may be strong," wrote Buddhist monk Thich Nhat Hanh, "but don't wait until you have no more suffering before allowing yourself to be happy."

What a radical idea: allowing myself to be happy. I don't have to put happiness off until some future day when everything is as I want it to be. In fact, I can be content now, just by accepting what is—the whole messy, imperfect ball of wax. Instead of being buffeted about by a swirl of emotions, self-doubts, or fears, I can watch life unfold with a curious eye and a grateful heart.

The other day I had tea with my friend Pam. It was the first of April, and we were watching it snow—hard. "Never a dull moment," she said, smiling. So true. So obvious. So profound. As soon as I stop worrying, complaining, comparing, I become a participant in the swirl of life itself, with all its close calls and wacky surprises and twists and turns.

Unfortunately, things never really go as planned. Fortunately, they do have a way of working out. Meanwhile, there's never a dull moment.

April 2011

—•— perfect —•—

I began writing my first book, *Mitten Strings for God,* the year Henry and Jack were five and eight. My husband and I were right in the thick of it, parenting two small children. We were busy, exhausted, finding our way, certain everyone else must be better at this than we were. I remember struggling to accommodate and care for our two boys—so very different from each of us and, miraculously, complete opposites of each other as well—and wishing these two single-edition models had arrived with instruction manuals, so we wouldn't have to flail about day after day, trying to figure out what they each needed and how to give it to them.

Looking back, I wish I hadn't been so afraid. I wish I'd trusted myself more. I wish I'd believed I already had what it takes to be a good mother, rather than so often berating myself for not being creative enough or patient enough or wise enough or loving enough.

I wish I'd had more faith in my kids. Faith that they could survive their bumpy, perilous journeys to young adulthood and be stronger for the bruises endured along the way. Faith that, no matter how crazy or irrational or clingy or tearful or restless or angry or oversensitive or afraid they seemed at two or five or eight, they would eventually get it sorted out and grow up and be fine.

I wish I had laughed with them more and worried about them less. I wish I'd forgiven myself and my kids more easily, rather than tossing and turning through so many sleepless nights, reliving the day's mistakes. I wish I'd known, really known then, what I think I do know now: that every moment is precious, that life is short, and that it's all good, even when it's not.

Writing was a way for me to remind myself, day after day, what mattered. In order to write, I had to gaze at my children with clear eyes. When I did, I was stunned by their goodness. In order to write, I had to become quiet and still. When I did, I was amazed by the beauty that was my life. In order to write, I had to look into the truth of things as they actually were. When I did, my heart cracked wide open. What I saw, again and again, was the miracle of our existence together: two children held in the sturdy embrace of two parents who loved them with a depth I never did find adequate words to express.

A couple of months ago, when the boys were both home for a weekend, we watched some old home movies of the two of them cutting up in the backyard, playing catch, impersonating their favorite umpires, goofing off and being funny and adorable and heart-wrenchingly young. There was footage of Jack at five or so, plucking herbs from the garden in the backyard and eating them straight out of his hand. A serious young Henry at the piano, painstakingly playing his first songs. I put my arm around Jack as the video screen went blank and jokingly said something like, "You see, you guys did have a good childhood."

"Mom," he said back, with uncharacteristic seriousness, "we had a perfect childhood."

And that's what I am thinking about now, as I consider a batch of fresh challenges, the challenges that come with the territory of being eighteen and twenty-one. Or, perhaps I should say, with being the parents of an eighteen and a twenty-one-year-old. Maybe, years from now, we'll look back on this early spring and recall not the worries about the lack of summer jobs, the hazy plans, the shortage of cars and money, but rather, goodness. Maybe we'll look back and remember the taste of the sweetness of life, even when it's not as simple a dish as we might prefer. Maybe we'll even say what none of us would say right now: "It was perfect."

April 2011

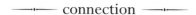 connection

Given the pace of our lives, the needs of our loved ones, the demands on our days, it's hard to give ourselves the time it takes to sit still and go deep. Yet carving out even a few moments of quiet time means we're attending to our thirst for contemplation, creativity, and solitude—a thirst that's all too easy to ignore when there seem to be so many other hungers and priorities competing for our time.

More often than not, when the choice comes down to writing or some concrete task on my list, I choose to do what seems truly "productive": pay the bill, vacuum the floor, clean the fridge, answer the letter. But I am learning to heed the call of quiet. Without much of a plan (and I would feel much more comfortable *with* a plan), I sit and allow my fingers to begin moving.

Writing, staring out the window, writing some more, as the hours roll by and the dishes sit on the counter and the weeds multiply in the garden. Writing because it is the best, the only way I know to investigate myself, to figure out what I think and how I feel and what matters right now. Writing because I do need to connect with some inner "me" and, even more, because I also need to reach out a hand and tug at something ineffable, something "out there" beyond my own orbit of thoughts and feelings and perceptions. Writing in order to remember that I'm part of something mysterious and huge and eternal. Writing to remind myself that, yes, I'm connected to everything else in the universe.

You and I may not ever meet face-to-face. We most likely would fail to recognize each other on the street. And yet I'm convinced that in certain ways that matter, we know each other. Our lives are intertwined, our journeys shared, thanks in part to the power of words. Somewhere out there, you sit with this book in your hands—at a desk in a crowded office, perhaps; or on the sofa while a baby naps nearby; or hunched over a table in a coffee shop, waiting till your latte is cool enough to drink; or propped up on bed pillows for a stolen moment before sleep—and you read a few paragraphs written by me, a stranger who perhaps feels almost like a friend.

You, too, are reminded now that we're all in this together. We both know this to be so: much as the details of our everyday lives may differ, when it comes right down to what resides in our hearts, we have so much more in common than not. "We read," says C. S. Lewis, "to know that we are not alone." I write for the same reason.

April 2011

—·— letting go again —·—

The lilacs bloomed this week, and tulips appeared like magic all through the front garden. (It was a surprise to see the purple ones come up, as if part of some carefully orchestrated color scheme. Did I really plant them?) Summer is nearly at hand, and it seems that the shape of things has begun to emerge. I've been cleaning closets, reorganizing rooms, preparing myself for a full house again. After a long winter, I'm more than ready to trade the quiet of two for the high energy of four.

Having sent out résumés, gathered references, and completed many job applications over the winter, our son Henry found himself a month ago facing the grim realities of the economy and the tough job market for budding musicians. For the first time since he was in high school, it looked as if he'd actually be home for the summer. So, he shifted from plan A (a job playing piano somewhere) to plan B (an opportunity to do anything else). He got busy and applied to become a full-time volunteer for the Obama reelection campaign, one of fifty-five young people who would be trained to start setting up infrastructure in New Hampshire. A phone interview later, he was hired.

My son, the self-proclaimed homebody, goes to college in Minnesota, spent January term in London, and has been under this roof for all of about eight weeks out of the last two years. So it was easy to look at the fact that he didn't get the piano job in Maine, or the paid musical-theater internship in St. Louis, or the teaching job at the summer camp as a blessing in disguise.

In the Mother's Day letter he sent me last Sunday, Henry wrote about how much he was looking forward to family dinners, hikes up Pack Monadnock, concerts at Apple Hill, taking runs with me, and having weekends off to spend hanging out at home. He thought there might be time to take an online music class and go to a Red Sox game or two. I loved getting that letter, for of course I'd been looking forward to the exact same things. Hard as it seemed to believe, he'd be home in two weeks—sleeping in his own bed every night till the end of August.

And then Tuesday came, and a call from Henry. He'd gotten an offer, he said, to play piano and be the assistant to a musical director in Maine. It was the summer job he'd had his heart set on and hadn't gotten, but now something has shifted, and they can use him after all.

"I'm not sure what do," my son said. "I've already committed to the volunteer job. And I've been so excited about finally just getting to be at home with you guys. But it sounds as if they really want me to come up there. And I'll get to play a lot. I know I'll learn a lot. And the money's good."

Sometimes the hardest part of being the parent of a grown-up child is remembering that my job is still to be somewhat more grown up than he is. Which, in this case, meant finding the self-restraint to listen and ask questions and listen some more. Could he weigh the commitment he'd made to work for free against the opportunity to pursue his career in the job he'd hoped for all along? Could he give up the attractions of home and some time off in favor of a contract that ends four days before school starts in the fall? Could he work this all through and make a decision that would feel right to him? I had to trust that he could.

Meanwhile, Steve and I had our own conversation. We confessed to each other how disappointed we were that the family summer we'd been envisioning might not happen after all. We pulled the plug on the family vacation we were in the midst of planning. We discussed the fact that our son really is an adult now, and that being an adult means earning a living and creating a life that is separate from ours. We reminded ourselves, not for the first time, that there is love in letting go.

Next week, I have to be in New York to serve on a

panel. Henry will fly in after his last final exam and meet me and Steve in the city. We'll have dinner, see a show, cram into one hotel room for a night, and make the long drive home with all his stuff. A few days later Jack will be home, too, and then we'll have four days of being together before Henry packs his trunk and leaves for Maine.

"Live your own life," Tao scholar William Martin advises parents, "with all your heart, and with all your mind, and with all your soul. There is no need to live theirs. They will do that wonderfully for themselves."

May 2011

—·— New York memories —·—

I was up at 6:30 the last two mornings, running in Central Park—the same route I used to follow most weekend mornings back in 1985, when I lived in a one-room studio on the Upper West Side.

Being in the park this week felt a bit like time travel. There, as always, were the dogs, cavorting in an exhilarated frenzy of sociability, their bleary-eyed, solitary owners sipping cups of takeout coffee. There were the serious runners, buff men and lean women in coordinated spandex, speeding by as I loped along in my tee shirt and yoga pants. There were the bikers, usually in pairs, hunched over their handlebars, slicing through space. There were the old folks, sitting on benches with the Times folded into thirds and their breakfasts in brown paper bags.

My feet knew just where to go, each turn giving rise to a view that was at once surprising and familiar. I've always loved running in the park. Now, the early morning city vibe coupled with my passion for people-watching, carries me further than any sense of determination I ever manage to muster on the quiet back roads of New Hampshire. Put me down at the corner of 60th and 5th as the city's waking up, and I can run easily for an hour.

But it's been nearly twenty-five years since I could call myself a New Yorker, and as the years roll by I find it harder and harder to believe this was once my life, this city my home, and that I used to be one of those striving young twenty-somethings making my way and trying to figure out where I fit in the grand scheme of things.

"She's ambitious," a senior editor once said, warning my boss, I think, that he should watch his heels. The comment stung at the time. I thought of myself as hardworking, eager to please, dedicated—but not ambitious. That word connoted cold-blooded calculation, a willingness to do anything to get ahead. It made me cringe. A small-town girl with no connections, I'd already concluded that the only way I could survive in the world of New York publishing—and still like myself—was to do it on my own terms.

I knew I wasn't the smartest young editor in midtown or the most brilliant manuscript doctor, the best dealmaker or the most desirable party guest. But I was thrilled to have landed in the big city, I was in love with my job, and I was willing to give it my all. At the same time, I was determined to still be a nice person. In a town that could be tough and a business that was often more about who you knew than what you knew, I hoped there might be some like-minded souls. Other young people who cared about the written word and who felt grateful, as I did, for the opportunity to work with authors to make good books even better and then bring them into the world. As it turned out, there were, and we found one another.

I was earning $11,500 a year and just barely managing to get by: an English muffin and a grapefruit half for breakfast, an expense account lunch (those were the days when even a junior editor was expected to be wining and dining somebody between the hours of 12 and 2), a cup of soup for dinner. My good friend Jamie was in the same boat, trying to pay the rent and have a life on an editor's salary that afforded no extras.

One Saturday we agreed we'd both had it with trying to iron skirts on our kitchenette counters. We went to the hardware store together and treated ourselves to two tiny, apartment-size ironing boards. I remember this purchase vividly because it seemed, at the time, both a splurge and a step into adulthood.

I thought of those years as I ran through the park this week. Looking back, I realize now that the older editor who called me ambitious wasn't entirely wrong. But what she didn't know was that my yearnings were not so much for a place at the top as they were for a life that would one day be connected to a place and a deep sense of purpose. I didn't want to succeed in business nearly as much as I wanted to succeed in creating a life that felt like a fit, a life in which the outside matched up with my insides. A life in which I would feel at home.

I knew even then that New York was an experience, a special chapter, an important part of my coming-of-age story. And I also knew I would never really put down roots there, that my deepest, truest ambitions would ultimately call me elsewhere—to a husband and children, to a slower pace, a quieter way of being, a connection to nature, solitude, a world far from the fast lane.

The wonderful thing is that the very path that led me away from New York all those years ago has now circled round and brought me back as a regular visitor. My friend Jamie, who counted pennies with me back in the early eighties and who set the standard for decency and kindness and intelligence in publishing, stayed the course and is now running the publishing company that publishes my books. If there is such a thing as a publishing family, Jamie has created one, and I'm a lucky relative.

Yesterday morning I had breakfast with my editor, who has also become a good friend in the years since we first talked about motherhood, the passage of time, and the joys and sorrows of children growing up and leaving home. Karen and I are exactly the same age. Our sons are the same ages. And our lives, which seem at first glance so very different (she represents, most certainly, the road not taken) turn out to be, in the ways that count, remarkably similar.

I may not be attending editorial meetings, negotiating contracts, or racing for a train; she's not shooing turkeys out of the yard, facing a blank page, or taking long week-day walks at dawn with her dog. But we understand and empathize deeply with the challenges of each other's days. And we share the even more visceral challenges of age, empty nests, grown children, shifting expectations, and new priorities.

It's my spot on a literature panel that brings me to New York every few months now. What's different, of course, is that I come as a visitor, do my work, savor all the city has to offer, and leave again. It's a gift, this opportunity to move so easily after all these years between two worlds, and to renew an old love affair with the city without questioning the choices I made long ago.

New York has never looked better. I cherish every high-intensity moment I spend there, and then I sigh with relief as I walk through my own back door and drop my suitcase to the floor —exhausted, sated, full of images and impressions and ideas, grateful to have gone, grateful to be home again, grateful to have a life that allows for such contrasts.

"I am rooted," wrote Virginia Woolf, "but I flow." Yes, I think that sounds exactly right.

May 2011

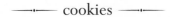 cookies

A lot has been going on here: the school year ending, boys returning home and leaving again, family dinners, loads of laundry, staggered breakfasts that go on for hours,

houseguests and arriving and departing, forsythia and lilacs
and irises and peonies blooming and passing in their turn,
hot days and cold ones, walks in the woods and runs on
the bike path. We've put almost a thousand miles on the
car, driving to New York, to the Berkshires, to Maine, to
Boston—picking up kids, bringing kids home, delivering
kids to the next places they need to be.

It seems that no matter how early I get up in the morning or how late I stay up at night, I can't quite manage
to place a comfortable margin around these days. And I
haven't written about any of it. It feels as if nearly every
minute has been spoken for, busy, packed.

I've loved this time of family comings and goings, have
loved having both our sons at home for a few days. They
seem at once completely known to me and at the same
time almost like strangers, these young men still not quite
formed, "each fate," as Sharon Olds has written, "like a
vein of abiding mineral not discovered yet." I've loved
being fully engaged right where I am as wife and mother
and aunt and friend and host and gardener. I've savored
each and every one of these spectacular, lengthening days
of June.

At the same time I find myself a bit in awe of the writers
I know who feel as if they aren't fully living unless they're
writing. I think of them as the "real" writers, the ones
who manage to weave their writing right into the fabric
of their days no matter what else is going on around them.
"Real" writers, as I imagine them, are those souls who are
fed and sustained by the daily process of turning the raw

stuff of life into shapely, meaningful prose. I wish I was one of them—faster, more disciplined, more determined, more productive, more—and this is the one that's really hard to admit—courageous.

When it comes right down to it, I know I could find or make the time to write more than I do. It's not really hours I lack so much as the confidence to clear the space necessary to sit down and come face-to-face with myself every day. To commit my thoughts to an empty page and then to say, "This is ok, this is worth doing, this is more important than everything else right now." Sometimes, I simply don't have what it takes to wrestle with my own swirling emotions, emotions I can barely put into words, let alone words I might share.

In these last weeks I've sipped tea with a friend who is facing major surgery, prognosis unknown. I've watched my older son sit down at a piano in front of a hundred people and play a gorgeous Rachmaninoff prelude from memory. I've taken early morning walks with my husband and gathered around a table at my parents' house with our entire extended family. I've listened in while Henry read a book to his four-year-old cousin and while Jack sang to himself in the shower.

There have been sights that stopped me in my tracks: a bluebird perched on the edge of the birdbath, a hummingbird trembling at the lip of a petunia, an alabaster peony's unfurling petals in the heat of an afternoon. And there have been moments that have made my heart swell: watching Jack walk through the door of his old high school (the one he left after sophomore year) to take the SAT IIs last weekend, sitting down to dinner on the porch and holding hands with my husband and two sons to say grace before dinner, listening to Jack play his guitar, saying good-bye to Henry for the summer.

In the midst of all these comings and goings, all these meals cooked and cleaned up after, all this being and doing and celebrating, a letter arrived on Monday from a reader whose twelve-year-old son died in an accident two weeks ago. She wrote to let me know that at his memorial service last weekend she asked her best friend to read a passage from a book of mine, a paragraph about missing, most of all, the perfectly ordinary days.

All week, her letter has haunted me. This mother's unfathomable loss runs like a hot, quiet undercurrent through my own busyness.

"Your words are helping me heal," she wrote, "and I wanted to thank you. The memories are all I have now and I thank you for showing me how to look at life a little differently."

The lesson, the great, overarching truth that I keep repeating even as I learn it again and again myself, is that the sacred *is* in the ordinary. It is to be found right here, right now, in our own daily lives. It is here in our most inconsequential yet most holy connections with our children, our loved ones, our neighbors, our colleagues, our friends. It is in the kitchen, the bedroom, the office, our own backyards.

I do know this. Nearly everything I write is some variation on the same theme: paying attention, being grateful. Sometimes I wonder if I'm the only one who needs to keep hearing it or if others need to be reminded just as I do. This week, a heartbreaking, generous letter from a grieving mother returned me to this simple, essential truth all over again. It made me think that perhaps the most important lessons do bear repeating after all. And that there are as many ways to be attentive to our lives as there are ways to pray, to grieve, to celebrate.

I am still hoping for courage. I have a contract for a new book and one for a small essay due next week. And instead of getting down to that work, I find myself in the kitchen grating chocolate, chopping apricots, baking batch after batch of cookies to share. To my husband and sons, who know little of my inner dialogue, these few weeks have become known in our house as The Time of Those Amazing Cookies. Baking, feeding the people I love, I grant myself a reprieve from the struggle to find the right words, words that might begin to respond to another family's tragedy or that could possibly do justice to the preciousness, the pain, the fragility, the wonder of life as it is.

When I'm floundering, when I lose my way on the page or in my thoughts, I retreat to the safe haven of my kitchen. I'm not always disciplined enough to write. But I can always cook. And once I began making these not-too-sweet but delectable ginger cookies a few weeks ago, I didn't stop. It feels almost as if the cookies have expressed everything I haven't managed to write about: love, empathy, joy, gratitude, pride, hope. I make batch after batch of the dough, pop it into the refrigerator, and bake more as needed.

I took ginger cookies to a friend facing her first round of radiation for breast cancer, to a special dinner where they complemented the earliest strawberries and rhubarb of the season, to my parents' house where my little nephew definitively pronounced them "the best." I served them to my writing students and to friends who dropped by for a spur-of-the-moment supper. I made over two hundred cookies for Henry's concert and a dozen to console Jack while he watched his favored basketball team, the Mavericks, go down in defeat to the Miami Heat. If you have seen me in the last month, chances are I've handed you a warm cookie.

"Let the beauty we love be what we do," Rumi reminds us. "There are hundreds of ways to kneel and kiss the ground." Loving this life, cherishing these perfectly ordinary, quietly beautiful summer days, I do aspire to be attentive, thankful for all that is. Sometimes I kneel and kiss the ground by sitting at my desk, fingers hovering over the keyboard. Sometimes, I just bake cookies.

June 2011

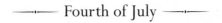 Fourth of July

The newest citizen in this morning's Fourth of July parade was less than three weeks old. The oldest arrived on the planet more than one hundred years ago. The span of years between the tiny, swaddled infant riding in his mother's arms and the frail old man waving to the crowd from a vintage Chevy was astonishing—a century's worth of Independence Days come and gone for one, a first public outing for the other.

The fact that they were both on hand to be honored on this steamy summer day seemed cause enough for holiday spirit. The sight of these two, the innocent baby and the proud centurion, put everything else into perspective: the down-home joy of a small town's annual celebration, the comfort of tried-and-true traditions, the preciousness of this particular, never-to-be-repeated morning, the inevitable passage of time.

I tried to take it all in: my own parents, cheering for their two youngest grandchildren on their decorated bicycles; my brother and his wife, gamely marching alongside the trikes and training wheels; my husband snapping pictures; the multigenerational crowd gathered along Main Street; the antique tractors; the Shriners in their absurd little cars; the kids with water balloons and squirt guns; the bagpipers, boy scouts, and baton twirlers; the fire trucks and vintage cars.

The Fourth of July always feels poignant to me. It's a day when my heart lifts and, at the same time, feels heavy in my chest. It is the too-soon turn of summer, the moment when this brief season suddenly starts to feel over instead of still beginning. We go from one first after another—the first dinner on the porch, the first day it's still light at nine, the first ripe strawberries, the first hummingbird at the feeder, the first nasturtium blossoms in the garden—to a glimpse of endings. The baby robins leave the nest, the foxgloves drop their blossoms, the furled goldenrod appears alongside the road, the school forms arrive in the mail, the sun sets a little earlier.

I'm greedy. There is never enough summer for my liking, never a long enough day, never an afternoon that fully satisfies my yearning for more. "The strange part about being human," writes essayist Verlyn Klinkenborg, "is that 'life' so easily comes to mean a quantity of time, an allotment of experience. We note that we are alive, without recognizing that we are, for a time, indomitable organisms sharing a planet with indomitable organisms of every other kind."

I've thought about those words all week. They acknowledge not only the mystery that delivers us into existence and the luck-of-the-draw allotment of time, but also the very fact of our own insignificance in the large scheme of things. And yet, because we are indeed human, we do need to invest our time on this earth with meaning. More and more it seems to me that the real meaning is not in the big moments, but in the chain of interconnected small ones, the ones we might miss altogether, so eager are we to get on to the next thing.

A parade is a pretty good time to slow down, take a look around, and remember the blessing of our being here. What we tend to forget, unless we are the awestruck parents of a newborn or the venerable holder of the Oldest Citizen cane, is that every moment in life is big.

July 2011

—·— trading kids —·—

He didn't need training wheels anymore, but there was no way our cautious little boy was going to let us take them off. Although my husband didn't say it, I knew what he was thinking: "The kid will be twenty and he still won't know how to ride a two-wheeler."

Up and down the driveway they went, Steve patiently urging him on, a hand at his back, seven-year-old Henry earnestly pedaling. It was past time for this bird to fly. But he was afraid to test his wings.

So, we did what we always did in our old neighborhood: we turned to "the village" for help. Henry needed a push, and he needed to get it from a dad who wasn't his own flesh and blood. Which is how it happened that our next-door neighbor Bob loaded Henry and his little bike into their van one summer afternoon and took off, with a promise that they wouldn't return until our son was ready to arrive on his own two wheels.

Within an hour we were standing out in the backyard to see our boy come sailing down the driveway, a mile-wide grin plastered across his face. Bob was modest, as always, but clearly pleased: another child launched. It didn't matter that it wasn't one of his. My husband ached, just a little; he'd wanted for himself the satisfaction of teaching his firstborn son how to ride a bike. But he was also wise enough to know that what we had was even better—a web of parents looking out for one another and sharing the joys and challenges of raising our children together.

Our sons grew up knowing all the nooks and crannies, the refrigerator contents, and the house rules of the neighbors' homes as well as they knew their own. We had the yard for baseball games and the overflowing basket of dress-up clothes and puppets for theatrical productions. The Wickerhams were the go-to family for backyard bonfires, sleep-outs on the deck, and a reliable bagel supply. The Cashions had the best house for hide-and-seek, dance music, and Slip 'n' Slide on a hot summer day.

They were a pack of seven children thrown together by age and proximity, and they forged fortuitous, enduring friendships, just as we parents did. Somehow we all agreed, without ever having to discuss it, that we would be there for each other. We traded kids and meals and driving duties, hand-me-down clothes and hard-won wisdom. There were laughter and tears, lots and lots of listening, plenty of advice both sought and unsought. Traditions, celebrations, and memories.

The kids range in age now from fourteen to twenty-one and are separated by geography, different schools, different life experiences. We left our old green house on the cul-de-sac seven years ago, certain we were leaving as well our accidental, fortuitous village, the extra moms and dads who had contributed so much to our sons' lives just by being there, by loving them enough to keep their homes and their hearts open to the two little boys who happened to live next door.

If someone could have flashed me forward then, from the day we pulled out of the shared driveway for the last time to this summer of 2011, I might not have shed quite so many tears about moving away. I would have seen that friendships can be nurtured and deepened from a distance, that children turn as naturally toward love as plants turn toward the sun, and that the closeness our families created back when we were all just learning how to be families is stronger than the pull of either time or distance.

This summer, Jack is once again working in Boston, an hour and a half from our house in New Hampshire. It's possible only because the Cashions' back door is still open for him. Monday through Thursday he sleeps at their house, where he is fed and loved and driven to the train station each morning by my friend Carol, his "other mother."

I'll always remember how we learned that Lia had arrived in the neighborhood, nineteen years ago last week: over our baby monitor, tuned to the same frequency as the Wicker-hams', only a few yards away: "I'll change her," we heard her dad say on the night they brought her home from the hospital. "I might as well learn how right now."

Born between Henry and Jack, Lia was friend and play-mate to both. So when she came home the other day after nearly two weeks in the hospital, still struggling with some mysterious digestive illness, it seemed only natural to offer her a few days of R&R at our house in the country, to give both Lia and her exhausted, worried mom a break.

Yesterday morning, Jack and Lia and I took a walk through the woods. The kids reminisced about old times, their childhood memories astonishingly vivid and fresh.

What they clearly cherished most of all was the very fact of their long history together, the intimacy of these friendships that began at birth and have managed to survive all the twists and turns in the road to young adulthood. And there was something else too. "We all had three moms," Lia said. "That was so cool."

Sometimes I still miss being the 24/7 mother of two little boys and the on-call mom for whatever combination of children happened to be playing on our swing set on any given afternoon. But I wouldn't have traded any of those long-gone days for the pleasure of yesterday, walking through a sunlit July morning and listening to the conversation of these two thoughtful young people who trust each other enough to share not only their memories of the past (Barney underwear and backyard circuses) but also the challenges and questions they face in the present.

This may be one of the greatest lessons we can pass on to our children—that in this complicated world, neither nations nor individuals can resolve their problems by themselves. Our lives, our destinies, are interconnected. We do better when we ask for help. And we're lucky if we're in a position to offer it, whether we are fifteen or fifty-two, for someday the tables will be turned. Cultivating a sense of shared responsibility, we move toward a better life for all.

Perhaps I wasn't fully conscious of that, back in the days when our sons felt perfectly comfortable grabbing an apple out of the next-door neighbor's fridge or wearing a best friend's outgrown winter jacket, but I know it now. We are meant to share this journey. There are plenty of children to go around, always someone to nurture, always a child who could use a sympathetic ear, a bed to sleep in, or a meal prepared with love. Being a mother means taking care not only of our own families, but of our neighbors and our global family as well. We need each other.

July 2011

———•——— wilderness ———•———

For years my friend Maude has been saying we should go to her little cabin in Maine. Somehow, although we talk about it every summer, we've never actually managed to set aside the time to make the trip. Leaving home means finding someone to water the garden and feed the dog and bring in the mail. It means tidying up the desk, answering the e-mails, making sure the appointments are rescheduled, and that there's food in the fridge for the family left behind. Easier to sigh and say, "Some day, yes, we must go," and then put the adventure off for another year.

I'm so glad that this time, when she asked, I just said yes. It's a five-hour drive door-to-door, a journey from civilization into remote wilderness—dirt roads, moose, rugged mountains, vast lakes. Maude warned me we'd be roughing it—no plumbing, no phone service, no Internet, no "amenities." But she couldn't really prepare me for what we got instead of an indoor toilet and Wi-Fi: the wild beauty, the stillness, the sensuous pleasure of a wood-fired sauna, skinny-dipping under the stars, drinking hot tea in bed together late at night, sharing stories.

"Everybody needs beauty as well as bread," naturalist John Muir wrote, "places to play in and pray in, where nature may heal and give strength to body and soul." I'm just back from the woods, still assimilating the memories of this sacred, rugged place. But already I find myself yearning to return. A taste of wilderness has whet my appetite for beauty as well as bread.

Stripped down to bare essentials—food, fire, water, air—we remember what it means to be open, unbounded, receptive to all kinds of knowing and seeing. Leaving conveniences and technology behind, it's easier to remember what we lose sight of in the midst of our daily lives: our own vulnerable, wild souls and our membership in the infinite web of creation. In the timeless dance of sunlight and shadow, earth and sky, water and mountain, we find ourselves. The ghostly cry of a loon, the gift of friendship, the sweet pleasure of a hammock strung between trees, simple food, good conversation, a sound sleep in a bed at water's edge—this is happiness.

Home again, I find myself cranky and out of sorts, feeling hemmed in and burdened by the "stuff" of my life. I wonder if I can find a way, even here, to stay in touch with the silence inside? How disciplined would I have to be to reduce the distractions in my life, to begin to honor and protect my connection with my own hungry spirit?

July 2011

————•—— summer memories ——•————

When our sons were young we had a tradition of spending a summer week on Monhegan Island, eleven miles off the coast of Maine. For quite a few years we managed to get there right after school let out. Carrying coolers packed with food and bags full of books and sketchpads and crayons, we'd arrive on the ferry and then find our way on foot to some bare-bones rented cottage, a place I'd secured sight unseen the moment the year's rental properties were offered at 9 am on New Year's Day. Sitting at my desk in the midst of winter, waiting for the phone line to clear, it was a thrill to make that leap of faith into our future, conjuring boat rides and summer days on an island.

We went with another family, good friends who loved Monhegan as much we did. In later years, we would all pile into one rambling house for the week, having realized that what we lacked in privacy was more than made up for by the fun of sharing the cooking, eating together, staying up late playing raucous games of slap and spoons, lounging over coffee in the morning, and watching five happy children roll out of their sleeping bags to begin another day. The routine was minimal: long hikes around the island in the morning and lazy hours with books on the porch all afternoon.

It was the perfect vacation for children still too young to be independent at home but eager to assert themselves and longing for some space in which to roam. There are no cars on Monhegan, hardly any commerce. Short of falling off a cliff, there really isn't much opportunity for a an unsupervised child to get into trouble. And so, to their delight, we turned ours loose and left them to their own devices. They read, played ball, explored, made up games, and scrounged for change to spend on ice cream at the store.

It didn't take long, that first year, for the slow, unscheduled days to inspire an entrepreneurial spirit. The kids watched boatloads of day hikers come and go and quickly realized that all of the travelers and cottage dwellers passed at one time or another through the main corner—a dirt-path intersection where the small grocery store and art gallery are located. People arrive on this quiet, idyllic outcropping of rock and forest and quickly shed their real-world defenses. There is not much to do, other than inhale the fresh air, wander along the footpaths, admire the flowers and the weathered seaside cottages, most of them faded to a soft silvery gray. It is hard not to smile. It is easy to imagine staying for weeks. It is lovely to realize that such special places still exist in the world, places where children and dogs and chickens are free to do as they please, donuts are baked fresh each morning, and the leisurely journey from point A to point B is always more important than the destination itself.

Our children spent a morning that first year scavenging the beach for smooth rocks and bits of beach glass. By the afternoon, they'd spotted a potential market for their wares, had priced their treasures, lugged a card table and a blanket down the trail, and set up shop under a shade tree near the general store. The beach-glass venture expanded over the years, growing to include lemonade, homemade Rice Krispie treats, watercolor paintings, painted rocks. The kids negotiated with one another, learned to make change, and realized that, when the baking supplies ran out, they had little choice but to invest a portion of their earnings back into the business. They made a little money but most of all they had a wonderful time painting, cooking, shop-tending, and keeping themselves entertained for hours each day on an island far from all the electronic devices that exert a pull at home. Now, years later, they look back on our Monhegan holidays as some of the best times of their lives.

I feel the same way. The island cast its spell on us all, became a touchstone, our idea of "the good life." I'm not sure why we stopped going, but that's how life is: a boy signs up for summer baseball, a girl commits to cleaning stalls at a barn, a work deadline looms, priorities shift, and suddenly a tradition becomes the stuff of reminiscence.

This week, after a hiatus of seven years, my husband and I took some visiting Midwestern friends out to Monhegan for two nights at the inn. It was a relief, getting off the ferry and looking around, to see how little has changed in the years since we last visited. Even the long-haired collie Jack fell in love with as a little boy was still there, an old dog now, lounging in the sunshine outside the coffee shop as always. We bought lattes from Pam, who remembered our names, and visited the lighthouse, with its serene, timeless view of the village below. Every turn brought back a memory. Wonderful as it was to introduce friends to one of our favorite places, it was bittersweet, too—a reminder of how much time has passed since the days of Harry Potter books, beach glass, and Rice Krispie treats.

On our second morning, we got an early start for our long hike around the perimeter. It was early afternoon when we made our way back to the village. There, beneath the old shade tree, a group of children was selling painted shells, necklaces, and signed watercolors. They had a card table set up in the very same spot our own kids had once claimed, and they were eager to give us their sales pitch. We bought necklaces and oyster shells, snapped photos, and chatted up the affable merchants, delighted to see that this lucrative location was bringing good fortune to a new generation of entrepreneurs. For 25 cents more I purchased a drawing of a pirate that bore an uncanny resemblance to my son Jack's early work—how could I resist?

Meanwhile, our own boys are off living their own independent lives. Once back on the mainland, I called them both to check in. It was nearly 9:30 pm when I reached Jack, who is housesitting for our former neighbors this week and taking the train into Boston each morning for his job. He was at Stop & Shop when I reached him, tired, hungry, and mulling his options for dinner. He had a few questions.

"I couldn't afford to go to Whole Foods," he said, "and I'm not sure what to buy." He told me he had a box of pasta and six eggs in his cart and was debating some chicken; at 79 cents a pound, he was worried that the chicken probably hadn't had a very good life. He decided to pass and to make zucchini instead.

"The stuff they have here looks exactly like zucchini," he reported from the vegetable aisle, "but they are calling it green squash. Do you think it's the same thing?" I said it probably was and wished him luck with his dinner preparations. It was a sweet, rite-of-passage kind of conversation—my son on his own, trying to figure out how to make his money stretch at the grocery store. But I hung up the phone feeling a little melancholic.

It seemed, once upon a time, that those childhood days would go on and on, that we would always board a ferry for Monhegan to celebrate summer, that our boys would be ten and seven forever, selling beach glass and lemonade and then falling into bed in an adjoining room instead of negotiating the world miles away from us. I don't even remember our last time on Monhegan. In memory the years all blend together—the card games, the fireflies, the solstice cake with yellow icing, the seagull with the broken wing, the hikes to the cliffs, the candlelit dinners with all the kids and adults crammed around the table, holding hands and saying grace.

"No one knew that ordinary breakfast would be their last," writes Annie Dillard in her novel *The Maytrees*. "Why not memorize everything, just in case?" I read that line this morning and put the book down, to let it soak in. How I wish it were always possible to know. Because of course no one knew, the last time we all did the dinner dishes in our shared summer cottage, that our two families would not return the next year, or indeed, ever again. If I had it to do over again, I'd have memorized it.

My sons are doing what they should be doing at eighteen and twenty-one. Working, learning about life, figuring out what to cook for dinner. I'm proud of them, so it's hard to admit how much I also miss them. But I do. What I wouldn't give right now for a Rice Krispie treat, a bag filled with smooth glass treasures, and a beach house full of happy, tired kids counting quarters into piles.

July 2011

 rain swim

This is the week we look forward to all summer—the rented lake cabin, the family together, the comforting routines of idleness. It is August, and the lake is northerly, nestled at the foot of mountains, and so we pack sweaters and jeans and socks as well as bathing suits and sunscreen and flip-flops. We come prepared, carrying more rainy-day books than anyone could possibly read in a week, and then we pray for sun.

Yesterday morning I woke early to gentle mist, cool air, clouds blanketing the peaks across the water. As summer draws to its inevitable close, each day feels edged with a scrim of sadness; I'm always hungry for just a little more. Or, if not exactly hungry, at least aware that these golden days are numbered. A month from now, back at home and yoked into fall schedules, these summer swims will already be a memory. And so without thinking it over, I slipped out of the warm bed and into my still-damp bathing suit, left my sleeping family, and walked down to the water.

I wonder if there is any place more solitary than the middle of a lake in the rain at dawn. Alone in that chill, dark water, shrouded by mist and suspended in a dance of raindrops, I disappeared from myself. What a relief it is, to leave the mind and all its small preoccupations behind, and to swim far from shore, out into the middle of the big picture. Lake, mountains, sky, rain—and me, one small human body treading water within this great universe. I watched my pale arms moving before me, allowed my breath to carry me along on its rhythmic journey, felt the water's buoyant embrace, and offered up a prayer of gratitude: thank you for allowing me to be here.

The dense, civilized smells of bacon and coffee came drifting across the water, summoning me back to land. My skin pricked with cold. The rain, by then, was falling in sheets. Yet it was with some reluctance that I finally turned around and began stroking toward shore.

"Without a big perspective, we are only half awake to our life," writes Buddhist teacher Jack Kornfield. "Lost in a thousand errands, and our small self, we are not truly free."

It's easy, when lost in our small errands, to lose sight of the world's magnificence. But nature's beauty is always available, if we're willing to take the first step toward intimacy, to stop what we're doing and thinking long enough to quiet our minds and open our hearts and immerse ourselves.

I didn't go swimming in the rain in search of anything but one more sweet taste of this waning summer. And so the moment's poignancy, its splendor, caught me by surprise. The world spoke to me in a whisper, easy enough to hear once I was out there in the midst of it: Remember your connection to all things. Rejoice in the mystery. Be free.

August 2011

—·— running —·—

All through August I've been out the door each morning at 6:15 to run two and a half miles to town in time for a 7 am yoga class. It lasts for only a month, this early class, but I'm hoping after it ends I'll continue with some variation on the new routine. My daily run began as something I was making myself do, but with each day it's come to feel more and more like a privilege, a gift, a challenge I look forward to meeting.

There's something liberating about moving through space at your own speed on your own two strong legs. I love being out in the world before anyone else is up. I love running right down the center of the empty road. And I love the fact that, after four weeks, I've shaved a few minutes off my time.

As summer draws to a close, I find myself, as usual, regretting all the things I didn't do. I'm sorry I didn't read poetry in the hammock or set up the tent in the backyard. I wish we'd had more dinners on the porch, more swims, more fires on the hilltop, at least one picnic, or campout, or barbeque. Next week both boys will head back to school, and already I feel the small pricks of sorrow that arrive with every Labor Day, as predictable as the first cool mornings, the grapes alongside the road ripening from green to dusky purple, the intensifying chorus of crickets. The change of season is definitely bittersweet for me, the shorter days a reminder that this very existence of ours is as transient as a summer cloud.

"The spiritual path," writes Pema Chodron, "has always been learning how to die. That involves not just death at the end of this particular life, but all the falling apart that happens continually." At fifty-two, I am constantly butting up against the fact that I can never hold on to anything, that nothing lasts quite as long as I want it to, and that no matter how old I get or how "grown up" I should be by now, the letting go doesn't get much easier.

Heading out in the morning just as the sun appears from behind the mountains, the dawn light illuminating the mist as it drifts up from the valley, I always stop to watch. How beautiful it all is: another day's beginnings, this cosmic of-fering that is mine for the taking 365 days a year. Not a day goes by when I'm not pierced by some awareness of loss and time passing. But I'm learning to linger, too, here in this place of contentment and gratitude. I think growing more comfortable in the good moments really is the answer: we can live all curled up in our self-made dark holes of regret, or we can rise up and stretch our limbs out into the beauty that is all around us. We can claim it as our own.

There are lots of reasons to wake up early. For me, the best reason is simply the opportunity to be present for a little longer, to glimpse the sun coming up, to notice how it appears just a bit later each morning, rises ever so slightly further to the north, alters the quality of the light, turns the season almost imperceptibly toward fall.

These changes, these small deaths, are part of nature's choreography of impermanence. Gratitude is an awakened heart's response to this eternal dance of change. And so I'm choosing to focus on what is and to be glad for all the things I *did* manage to do this summer. For one thing, I've racked up many miles on foot. I've grown stronger, healthier, and faster. I've learned to run for the joy of it. And I give thanks that I still can. Someday, this too will change.

August 2011

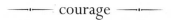 courage

Toward the end of my month of yoga-teacher training at Kripalu last spring, each person in my class was handed a sheet of paper and a pen and asked to write the words "What I want to tell you is . . ."

The assignment was to write a letter. A letter from the radiant, wide-open, yoga-saturated, heart-full self of that moment to some beleaguered, tired and doubting future self who might one day be in need of a little bucking up. These letters, we were assured, would arrive in our mail-boxes at the right time.

There were so many wild and wonderful experiences crammed into those thirty intense days of teacher training that I didn't even remember writing a letter to myself. When a hand-addressed envelope arrived in my mailbox a week ago, I didn't recognize the writing, which was more graceful than my typical, hasty, printing-cursive hybrid. It seemed odd that the return address was my own. I sat down outside, opened the envelope, and read words I had no memory of putting to paper.

It felt as if I'd suddenly received a handout from the universe. And, at the same time, as if the familiar voice on the page was that of some long-lost best friend from ages ago, a soul mate whose memory I cherish but whom I haven't seen or even thought about for a long time. To get such a letter, out of the blue, was an unexpected gift. And to realize that this distant, nearly forgotten person seemed to know exactly how I'd been feeling lately, and could say just what I needed to hear, was like having my own unspoken prayer answered.

"When it's a choice between love and fear," my wiser self told my struggling self, "choose love." Tears rolled down my cheeks. Sometimes, when things are really awful and not the way I want them to be at all, choosing love over fear seems crazy and impossible. But of course, love really is the only good choice. It's just that choosing it can sometimes require so much more courage than I think I have.

In two days, both of my sons will head back to school. At our house right now, the bedrooms look like they've been ransacked, full of clothes and twisted bedding and backpacks and shoes and notebooks. (Both boys claim that what's going on up there is a "deep clean." To me it looks more like a deep shuffle.)

The TV is tuned to the U.S. Open. The kitchen has been turned into Poster Rolling Central—Jack is working for his dad, earning money by stuffing hundreds of posters into mailing tubes. Steve is affixing labels. Henry is deleting two thousand songs from his iPod. The washing machine is running nonstop. The food is getting eaten as fast as I can cook it. As I sit here typing on the porch, I can hear the three guys laughing in the other room, commenting on the tennis, enjoying this last full day of summer vacation. Tonight we'll go out for our ritual meal at Chili's (democracy prevails on this front; alas, the vote for Chili's is always 3 to 1) and to see the new Steve Carell movie. It's all good.

Except for the moments in the past week that have been hellish. The ones that have pushed me to the outer limits of my patience, my compassion, and my abilities as a parent. There have been some of those, too. If you've shared your life with teenagers, you can easily supply your own details. And you probably also know that giving an adolescent the space he/she needs in order to grow up is as necessary as it is terrifying. Kids make mistakes, and one of our hardest jobs as parents is to step back and allow them to fall—and then to make sure, too, that they actually experience what it's like to hit the ground.

"I feel completely lost," my son Jack said to me the other afternoon. I knew what he meant. The truth was, I was feeling pretty lost myself. But then I suddenly realized that I did have something to offer him.

"You know," I said, "you don't have to figure everything out now. All you need to do is make the next good choice for this moment. You can certainly do that." And then I left him there to figure it out. I put on my sneakers and went out for a run.

Choosing fear in that moment would have kept me in my chair, talking, trying to repair the damage and make things right for him. Choosing love means allowing him to own the struggle that rightfully belongs to him. It means having faith that this, too, shall pass.

"Parenting requires courage," my friend Bruce wrote in an essay this week. "Courage to set limits and bear anger; courage to let go and tolerate fear that our kids may come to harm; courage to trust that we and our children are enough."

That pretty much says everything I need to hold on to during the final days of this summer. I could hope for all sorts of things as my children make their way out into the world, but I doubt that even my most fervent appeals for their safety, health, and well-being would do a single bit of good. Those pleas are born of fear, of my own sense of helplessness in the face of dangers and environments and situations that aren't mine to control.

And so, I pray instead for the only thing I can really ask for: courage. Because courage, of course, is love in action, love in the face of fear. Somehow, after a month of yoga and meditation, a soft, vulnerable part of me knew that very well. Back in the world, faced with problems I can't solve and children I can't protect, I forgot.

Put two parents and two nearly grown young men in a house together at the end of a long summer spent apart, and it's probably inevitable that everyone involved will do or say something they will later regret. On this peaceful, companionable Sunday morning, I can now cut us all at least that much slack. The good news is that choosing love over fear brings us back to one another. As soon as I stop giving in to my fear of the dark stuff, I'm free to savor the pleasure of these few moments of light. To feel the fear, acknowledge it, and then move beyond it—maybe that's courage.

September 2011

 touch

As summer gives way to fall, the change of season reminds me that the first anniversary of my friend Diane's death is looming. The boys have gone back to school, I have a birthday around the corner, a book deadline to meet, commitments made long ago that are now upon me.

A week ago, I could feel my own personal dark autumn cloud settling across my shoulders like a cloak. And then, almost on a whim, I enrolled in a two-day course on Reiki healing.

Last fall, spending time with Diane, sipping tea on the couch and chatting through the early September afternoons, I often found myself wanting to put my hands on her—as if my touch might somehow bring some small solace to us both. Sometimes, I rubbed her feet with lotion or held her ankles in my hands as we talked. Small gestures that felt somehow important. Necessary but always a little awkward, too.

Ours is a hands-off culture. To reach out and touch another person, human to human, hands to body, almost always means crossing some kind of barrier. We may feel free to *talk* about anything, but sustained physical contact outside of romance is not something most of us experience regularly or casually. For me, the impulse to offer comfort through touch has always been there. What I lacked was a belief that my touch might actually be helpful or welcomed.

Two days of hands-on Reiki and I still don't know if my hands are of much use to anyone but me. But I have learned this: simply settling into a quiet space with another person and allowing our hands to speak for us is a beautiful way to say, "You matter to me." Touch invites a sense of well-being. There is nothing quite like the gift of time and a loving hand gently placed to communicate caring and compassion.

As I took my turn upon the table on Sunday, my fellow students laid their hands on my body and invited their Reiki energy to serve the highest healing good. That's all there was to it. It was so quiet. So practical. So. . . *good*. And you know what? The elegiac case of "the blues" that visits me like clockwork every September has pretty much lifted. I'm not certain I'm cured, but it feels as if some sort of quiet emotional healing has been going on here—and touch seems to have been part of it.

Out for a run, I inhale the soft scents of the late-summer woods and give thanks for the fleeting beauty of the season. Each time I pause and put a hand upon my own heart, I'm pleased to feel it in there, beating steadily away. Laying Gracie out on the bed and resting my hands on her old arthritic haunches, I'm grateful for all the years of walks we've shared, for all the mornings she got me up out of bed and out the door. She thumps her tail upon the mattress: could it be that she's grateful, too?

Sliding my palms against my husband's sore back and breathing with him, I think how lucky we are to have known and loved and shared one another's bodies for a quarter century now. "That was nice," he says, "thank-you." His back may not be that much better, but *we* are, reconnected by touch. Out in the garden, my hands resting lightly on my neighbor Debbie's shoulders, I watch a hummingbird hovering over a petunia and am struck by the way this tiny, vibrating being embodies the words we heard in class: "An invisible but palpable life-force energy infuses and permeates all living forms. This energy is infinite, limitless, and pure."

Visiting a sick friend, I can tell she has no energy for conversation. But we can still spend time together in companionable silence as she reclines on her porch, my hands gently cradling her aching head.

I am a beginner, with just a few days of Reiki experience under my belt. Sitting with my hands cupped in my lap, drawing Japanese symbols in the air in my imagination, whispering strange words to myself, envisioning the highest healing good, I'm not quite sure whether I'm praying, or meditating, or just opening myself up to forces already at work around me. Maybe it doesn't matter. Maybe what's important is simply to live in a state of awareness, and to give ourselves and others the opportunity to take a few moments each day to move back into balance and harmony with our souls, our bodies, our environment, each other.

September 2011

———·——— the treasure of an ordinary day ———·———

It was the softest of dawns, the quietest of sunrises, the sweetest morning to step out into. I love these September days—the silky air, the damp, honeyed scent of summer succumbing to fall. I walked across the wet grass, sat on a rock, and watched the mists drift across the valley, the sky brighten, a single bird soaring high, silhouetted against the sky. Never do I appreciate the beauty of home more than on a day when I have to leave it.

I write these words in an airport terminal, waiting for my delayed flight to Atlanta, where I'm giving a talk tomorrow on "the treasure of an ordinary day." These invitations still catch me off guard. I'm not used to the idea that someone would think of me as a person with enough to say that my appearance is worth organizing an event around. But I'm learning to trust the people who ask, to gather some thoughts, and to show up where I'm wanted.

Of course, I have nothing to offer that every one of us doesn't know already. The themes are plain and simple: That life is precious. That we already have everything we need. That we can choose to be grateful. That to live well is to be present in the here and now. That we always discover something good when we opt to slow down, rather than racing so fast through our own lives that we miss them.

I also know how hard it is to remember what we already know. If you're like me, you probably have to remind yourself, over and over again to notice where you are, to accept what is, and to love that. Sitting still always helps. Coming to a stop and allowing my busy mind to be at rest is the only way I've found to be truly mindful. It's why, after years of not meditating, I finally do. Walking helps, too. It's why, although I love to run, I also spend hours each week walking alone on the empty roads near my house, allowing my thoughts to drift and noticing everything there is to notice.

Last week, I spent a few days alone at a friend's small secluded cabin. There was no Internet, no opportunity to toggle back and forth, as I tend to do at home, from e-mail to a friend's latest blog post to my own stop-and-go writing to the most e-mailed stories in the *New York Times*. With nothing to do but sit and write, I sat and wrote. With no company to keep but my own, I got back in touch with a deeper, quieter part of myself. With no to-do list to whittle away at or schedule to keep, I felt the expansiveness of an hour, an afternoon, a day. Time became generous with me.

I tried to carry some of that spaciousness home, of course. I want to stay in closer touch with my own capacity for quiet, focused attention, whether I'm alone in a cabin or standing at a podium in front of a room full of strangers. I can react to events, get carried away by stress, allow myself to be distracted and distractible. Or I can simply do the next thing that needs to be done, with care and commitment and faith in the rightness of things as they are. Without making a fuss. This really is the way I want to live. And yes, I do need to keep reminding myself.

Now, held captive in an over-air-conditioned terminal, with CNN blasting away, boarding announcements crackling over the loudspeaker, and the smell of pizza in the air, such presence is a little more challenging to practice. But living mindfully isn't just about sitting and meditating or about appreciating a beautiful sunrise. The real practice comes when we are called to keep going even when things aren't exactly to our liking. It's acknowledging whatever's at hand and working with that. And so, shifting my attitude, I can see that time might be generous here, too. I have hours and hours to myself, with no place to go and nothing to do but wait for my delayed plane to arrive at the gate.

Annoyance or grace. The choice is mine. The treasure of an ordinary day is right in front of my nose. All I have to do is decide to see it.

September 2011

—·— a birthday —·—

I've already received what I asked for for my birthday tomorrow. I gave my sons plenty of advance warning and then I was clear about my wishes: handwritten letters, please. Not e-mails. Not hastily signed store-bought cards. Not presents. Just letters from each of them to me.

Somewhat to my surprise they both came through—early, in fact. There are two sealed, handwritten envelopes sitting on the kitchen table at our house. But there are many other gifts, invisible ones, that I find myself thinking about today as well.

The gift of friendship, offered me daily in so many guises and gratefully received. The gift of good health, so easily taken for granted until it's taken away. The gift of mindfulness, always elusive for me yet always worth cultivating. The gift of gratitude, a choice I can make right now.

The gift of the present moment, renewed over and over again without ceasing. The gift of breath—where would I be without it? The gift of marriage, constantly transforming and evolving, challenging me to become a better version of myself. The gift of motherhood, which has shaped every response I've had to life for the last twenty-one years.

The gift of beauty, worth organizing a life around. The gift of memory, filling in all the empty spaces left by loved ones no longer here. The gift of presence, and the realization that there are so many ways to be present if I'm willing to stay with what is. The gift of imagination, ready to take flight at a moment's notice. The gift of dreams, especially the ones worth sacrificing for. The gift of silence—expansive, rich, and deep. The gift of touch, love made manifest.

The gift of spirit, infusing all creation. The gift of wonder, mine whenever I take time to attune myself to mystery. The gift of kindness, which I aspire to offer generously and to accept with humility. The gift of joy, that most precious and precarious of blessings. The gift of sadness, the inevitable measure of darkness that lends meaning to happiness. The gift of connection, which I experience with every word and thought and good wish shared with others.

I have been reading Mary Oliver's poetry this morning, her slender volume called *Evidence*. As always, I marvel at her wisdom, generosity, and grace. Each poem is a small, contained hymn of gratitude, a summons to my own heart. This one, especially, speaks to me today as I contemplate my own dreams and aspirations here at the beginning of my fifty-third year.

I Want to Write Something So Simply
I want to write something
so simply
about love
or about pain
that even
as you are reading
you feel it
and though it be my story
it will be common,

though it be singular
it will be known to you
so that by the end you will think—
no you will realize—
that it was all the while
yourself arranging the words,
that it was all the time
words that you yourself,
out of your own heart,
had been saying.
—Mary Oliver
October 2011

—·— playing hooky —·—

This life. There's always something that needs doing. But there are never enough days like yesterday, days when the trees don brilliant robes and stand tall, rustling softly in their finery. When the sky melts into azure infinity, when the air is as soft as breath and nasturtiums bloom like crown jewels scattered upon a tumbled carpet of fallen leaves. The oscillations of insects, the call of a crow, the gossamer light, the almost voluptuous warmth—it was too fine an October afternoon to miss. It was a day that whispered, "Play hooky."

The dictionary defines hooky thus: "an unjustifiable absence." It seemed to me that the leaves and the flowers, the golden afternoon, the unseasonable temperatures, were justification enough. Summer was offering an unexpected encore, free for the taking. My husband, Steve, and our friend Nance met me on the trail, and with the dogs bounding ahead, we climbed up to a quiet clearing with a view of mountains, a place we call "the meditation chairs." Over many years, visitors to this spot have assembled hundreds of stones large and small into an arrangement of artful cairns and comfortable seats that invite reverie and repose and reflection. It was a perfect place to sit for a while, savoring an uncommonly balmy autumn afternoon.

Nance and I looked at each other as we headed back down the trail. We both had the same thought at the same time: would it be crazy to go swimming? We went from the mountain straight to the pond, smooth as glass in the waning light. There was nothing to do but peel off our clothes and plunge. The stinging cold was small price to pay for the exhilaration of stroking through that icy water, straight out to the middle of the lake, and then turning around, gasping with the cold, to look back at hills soaked in color, the empty beach, the stillness. We swam to shore and ran out shivering, exultant, silly with happiness.

When our boys were young, a full moon on a clear, mild night was always a good excuse for sleeping outdoors, but it has been years now since I've done it. Perhaps I haven't been quite ready to return, alone or even with my husband, to some of those sweet traditions that were so much a part of our family life. My greatest joy as a mother was to introduce my children to the world, to lead them gently into wonder, to provide an abundant harvest of experiences that would stir their senses and quicken their imaginations—walks in the woods, nights under the stars, stories told by firelight, hushed sunrises, and barefoot walks through dew-soaked grass.

Now that they're grown, I miss those times more than I like to admit. I miss my sons as the little boys they were, much as I love the young men they've become. And I miss the joy of our shared play, the small adventures woven through our days and nights, the fun of dragging air mattresses and sleeping bags out into the backyard on a moment's notice and cuddling up together beneath a canopy of stars. I miss seeing the world through a child's eyes.

I'm also realizing that herein lies one of the challenges of this new phase of my life as a person whose child-raising days have ended. I need to learn all over again to see the world through my *own* eyes. I want to look and feel as deeply now as I did as a child—not for my sons' sake any longer, but for myself. For isn't this our task as adults, too? To stand still in the middle of this unexplained, inexplicable world, breathing in and out, quietly listening to whatever is just beyond the field of our knowing, calling us to wonder, to devotion?

To live well on the earth means to inhabit gently its fields and streams and wild places, to praise its abundance and variety, to protect its treasures, to celebrate its beauty even as we honor our own playful spirits, no matter how old or how young we are. Now that I have no little boys to take by the hand and lead out into a wonderful morning, it's easy for me to get so caught up in the doings of my "grown-up" life that I miss the soft curve of a day, the tender approach of evening, the first wink of stars at twilight. I forget to pause long enough to savor the day's small miracles.

But it's time for me to pay attention to the stars' far-off fires, to the wind turning in the trees, to the dark invitations of the dirt at my feet. I want to do this now for my own soul's sake, just as I once offered these gifts to my children. It's such a simple thing—to sit, to look, to see, to cherish.

And so, I pitched my own little tent on the crest of our hill last night and unrolled my old sleeping bag. I lit a fire in the darkness and sat very still beside it for a long time. A distant bird called. The harvest moon inscribed her graceful arc through the night sky. When I awoke this morning, my hair damp with dew, the first streaks of pale pink light were just appearing on the horizon. I lay alone in my tiny green shelter, looking out across the mountains. "What joy was it," as poet Mary Oliver asks, "that almost found me? What amiable peace?" Just gratitude, my heart replies. Gratitude for the perfect beauty of everything. For this world. This day. This life.

October 2011

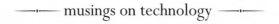

—·—— musings on technology ——·—

My son Jack and I spent most of last Sunday in the kitchen together. Although he has a desk upstairs in his bedroom and I have one in my office, the kitchen is the place in this house where most of the creative work gets done, whether it's putting together a pot of soup, writing a blog post, reading a manuscript, or composing a college-application essay.

Jack sat on the sofa, wrestling with one short essay after another on the Common App and various college supplements, while I perched at the table, reading online submissions for a panel I'm on next week. Between essays, he chatted with me about possible angles he might take, and then he'd go outside to shoot hoops in the driveway for ten minutes and think things through.

Essentially, Jack's challenge was the same one every high-school senior we know is wrestling with at the moment: how to present himself in words to complete strangers who will all-too-briefly compare him to thousands of other kids competing for the same spots in next year's incoming freshman class. Of course, I have no one with whom to compare my son; I'm reading just one college application, not a thousand. And, as his mother, I'm about as far from an objective judge as I could be. But I was struck by the depth of his thinking and the range of experiences that have contributed to the construction of his eighteen-year-old self.

By late Sunday night he'd answered one question with a sonnet, written an honest essay about the difficult but valuable lessons he learned from getting suspended from high school, tried to compress two summers of work he's passionate about into a thousand characters, and described how his environment growing up has influenced the person he is today.

As Jack emailed his essays from his computer across the room to mine, and we zapped updated versions back and forth, I couldn't help but marvel at the efficiency of the process. Thanks to the wonders of the digital age, we could work independently yet side-by-side in the coziest room in the house. At the same time, I found myself thinking of the role that technology has—and has not—played in shaping the multifaceted picture of my son that emerged from his day of writing and reflection.

The next day, a newspaper article titled "Trying to Gauge the Effects of Growing up Digital" caught my eye. "A few clicks, a couple of swipes," it begins, "and Bridget Colvin's four-and-a half year old son, August, was tapping away on an iPad smudged with tiny fingerprints." Author Michael B. Farrell goes on to point out that "there is little doubt we are seeing only the early stages of a hyper-connected world that is changing childhood."

The images brought the point home: toddlers swiping fingers across board books, expecting the characters to come to "life"; parents handing their iPhones to fussy babies to quiet them; one-year-olds adeptly playing Baby Birds, a version of Angry Birds for the pre-K set; three-year-olds skillfully surfing for videos on YouTube; a description of Fisher-Price's hot new toy, the $15 Laugh & Learn Apptivity Case: an "oversize iPhone case that doubles as a baby rattle."

My son never was never an "easy" child; active, curious, sensitive, bright, he struggled to find his place in a world that often seemed too overwhelming. Learning how to be at ease physically and emotionally, and how to live comfortably in his own skin, has always been his greatest challenge. It still is. Confronting that challenge through all the years of his childhood and adolescence, he has suffered, matured, and confronted some hard truths about who he is, lessons that will surely continue to test and humble him.

I can't help but wonder what kind of young adult Jack would be today had he been offered an early escape route from his complicated, uncomfortable feelings. How would he have developed had he been able to lose himself in an app at age three or four, instead of having to negotiate the complex emotional and tactile stimulation that life continually threw at him?

Would he have learned resilience if he'd been able to tune out the intensity of real experience by tuning in to an animated wonderland instead? What would feel important to him now, if he had spent the hours of his early childhood having interactive adventures in front of computer screens instead of getting into mischief and experiencing the painful consequences? Who would he be, if he hadn't been a boy who grew up playing in the backyard with his friends, lying on the couch under an afghan sounding out the words to *Frog and Toad,* learning to do math by collecting a hundred acorns during an autumn walk, and then adding and subtracting them into piles?

I got a disturbing glimpse of the answer to some of those questions a couple of years ago, when Jack became so enamored of video games—and then so good at them—that he rejected the real world of relationships and heartache and expectations for a virtual one that he could create and control at will. At first, it seemed to him like the perfect escape. His quick brain and extraordinary hand-eye coordination made him really, really good at video games. But the more hours he put in in front of the screen, progressing through increasingly difficult levels of complicated games, the more his ability and willingness to engage in the challenges of the real world atrophied. He lost the concentration necessary to read deeply. He lost interest in homework and he quit sports. He pulled back from school and friends and he shut the door on family life as well.

Was it depression? Addiction? Both? All we knew was that our son was lost, helpless to stop the downward spiral. And our efforts to reach him, to pull him back, were useless. For the better part of a difficult year, he was physically home but emotionally absent. Intervention took the form of an intense wilderness therapy program that thrust him into direct confrontation with himself, with the natural world, with the very struggle for survival.

For Jack, making the hard choice to endure the emotional ups and downs of reality rather than escape into an alluring alternative universe has turned out to be a formative, life-altering experience. He is still figuring out how to use technology constructively, as a tool with which to work, rather than as a substitute for life. He's still relearning how to be alone with himself rather than withdrawing into a fantasy world online.

But fortunately he did have some firsthand experience from childhood to draw on. At eleven, Jack had to figure out how to build a sustaining, meaningful friendship with himself—at the very moment of dawning awareness, early adolescence, when we humans are often most desperate to escape from ourselves. Because we'd moved away from the suburbs, where he was surrounded by friends and neighbors, to the relative isolation of the country, that new friendship with himself had to sustain him through many long, solitary hours.

"Life in rural New Hampshire was as lonely as I predicted," Jack wrote in one essay. *"The driveway was dirt and undribble-able and while the lawn was big enough for a complete baseball diamond, there weren't any players around. Being alone with my thoughts was uncomfortable. I'd never had to be alone in my life. But in the midst of my sadness, I began to grow up. I became more creative with the ways that I entertained myself. I spent time drawing, reading, inventing card games and playing the guitar, as well as just sitting and thinking.*

"In my pensive misery as a twelve-year-old it dawned on me that I would never become the self-sufficient, creative person I wanted to be if I couldn't even enjoy my own company. I would continue to distract myself with all of the problems around me and never face my own. Although I'm a social person by nature and love spending time with good friends, I owe the security I have in myself to learning how to become my own friend, in the silent, lonely countryside of New Hampshire."

Jack and I talked about all this as I drove him back to school last week, where he's taking a demanding senior-year course load and has decided to try out for the varsity basketball team—despite the fact that he's spent the last two winter seasons playing squash and his chances are slim. He's been playing basketball for hours a day all fall, just for the fun of it. He's also started working out, lifting weights, running, and practicing his jump shot. Whether or not he actually makes the team, he says, is less important to him than the pleasure he's found in the discipline of trying.

As Jack would be the first to admit, a couple of years ago, in the midst of his video-game obsession, he wouldn't have taken on the challenge of making any team, nor would he have risked the disappointment of rejection. Now, having come to understand himself a little better, he knows that it's by actively engaging in the physical world that he connects with his own best self. Fortunately, when he realized he needed to abstain from video games for a while, he *had* a "self" to return to, a work-in-progress self to be sure, but one that had been shaped by an early child-hood without much access to TV or movies or computers.

Having spent those years with no choice but to learn to live in his own body and be entertained by his own imagination, he had plenty of experiences and skills to build on. He had some familiarity with the satisfactions of making things, getting lost in a book, or climbing a mountain. Thinking about this, putting it into words on a form on his computer, he couldn't help but wonder what life, and adolescence, might be like for a boy of his temperament coming of age in this next generation.

Having watched Jack's journey these last eighteen years, I wonder, too. If you grow up with a gadget in the palm of your hand, do you ever develop an inner life? If large portions of your first years on earth are spent online, will you ever make contact with that sacred entity within that guides you toward your full potential as a human being? If you're an expert at surfing the Web by age three, will you ever discover the pleasure of crocheting a hat, building a snow fort, or lying on the grass and staring up at the sky? If there is no silence in your mind, no quiet place in your heart, no true solitude in your soul, will you ever hear the small, quiet voice within, the one that tells you who you are and who you might yet become?

No one has the answers to these questions yet. But they will be revealed by the next generation of children, the ones who are now tapping away at iPhones in their car seats. Still, I think it's interesting that my eighteen-year-old son, who has battled his own addiction to video games, is worried about those kids. And I'm glad to hear him say he's actually grateful now for the low-tech early childhood he had—even the loneliness, even the boredom, even the hard parts.

Jack has one more essay to write, and he's chosen the topic "mastery for the sake of mastery." In it he wants to write about the pleasure he's found over the years in teaching himself all kinds of random, mostly useless, but deeply satisfying skills: how to do the Rubik's cube, how to skip stones across a pond, flip an omelet in the air, climb rocks, hit a wicket shot in tennis, recite Hamlet's soliloquy, juggle five balls at a time, play "Purple Haze" on the guitar. Like I said, I'm not a very objective judge, but I think he's ready for college.

October 2011

—·— a wish —·—

He turns nineteen tomorrow.

Last week we were in Boston for a college interview. It was an opportunity for him to tell his story in person, this young man who attended three different high schools, spent nine winter weeks living in the woods and sleeping under a tarp, got into his share of trouble, and has not always seen the point of homework.

"If your fifteen-year-old self were sitting here in the room right now," the college admissions person asked, "what would you have to say to him?"

"Well," the about-to-be-nineteen-year-old replied, "I'd have a lot of advice for him. But he wouldn't listen to any of it."

And then he thought for a moment, and added, "And actually, although I would really want to save him from some pain and trouble, I'm glad he'd blow me off, because those were all lessons he really had to learn for himself, the hard way, by living through them."

Jack told me this as we drove out the Mass Pike, back toward his school. He wouldn't want to change anything about these last few years, he said, hard as they were and miserable as he'd been. As he sees it, the mistakes he's made and the consequences he's endured have made him who he is today and brought him to the place he is now—a place he's grateful to be.

I remember the first time I ever laid eyes on my younger child, nineteen years ago tomorrow. He arrived wide awake, curious, and hungry. He looked, to my husband and me, a bit like a tiny, startled Jack Nicholson, with his spray of fine dark hair pointing northeast and a quizzical little scrunch at the eyes. I remember gazing into that brand-new face and making a wish for the future, a wish that this life would be one of ease and health and happiness.

Tonight, I send my son a different, perhaps more realistic wish: that he will always find something to be grateful for. Much as I might long to protect him from struggle and pain, what I wish even more is that he might learn to ride out the hard times knowing that each heartache offers its lesson, each day its own blessing. I want him to understand that who he is is who he's meant to be: flawed and striving and human. I hope he realizes that he doesn't need things to be easy or perfect in order to be content. That life is both beautiful and perilous, that screwing up is inevitable, that love trumps fear, that secrets do harm and that truth can heal, and that loss and disappointment are always part of the equation.

Listening to him talk about his interview, I was somewhat reassured. I know better than to take anything for granted. But it seems to me that my son, whose path through life so far has been neither easy nor particularly happy, has already figured some of this out. And that's reassuring to me. As David Steindl-Rast writes, "Happiness is not what makes us grateful. It is gratefulness that makes us happy." Let my son learn, then, to be grateful. That in itself is an education that will take him far.

I baked Jack a cake, the same cake he liked most as a kid,

with M&Ms and walnuts and chocolate chips on the top. I packed it up in a box, along with plates and napkins and forks and even a few party hats, and mailed it to arrive tomorrow, in time for him to gather some dorm mates around to help eat it. And I hope that sometime during the day, between class and basketball practice and dinner and study hall and hanging out with friends, he pauses for a moment to regard his own young life as the unpredictable journey it is. May he continue to grow up knowing that the boredom and pain of life are as essential as the excitement and the fun. May he come to understand that every choice he makes matters. As does every minute of every irretrievable day. And may his feelings in the years to come tilt further and further away from regret and more and more toward gratitude.

November 2011

——·—— reclaiming peace ——·——

Ultimately, we have just one moral duty: to reclaim large areas of peace in ourselves, more and more peace, and to reflect it toward others. And the more peace there is in us, the more peace there will also be in our troubled world.
—Etty Hillesum

I find myself returning lately to Etty Hillesum's words, hoping they will take root and live in me during this holiday season.

As I sit in my kitchen on this gray December morning, so aware of time passing and wishing to make the most of each shared family moment, the idea of cultivating peace at home and in my heart seems particularly apt.

These are short, dark days. Much of the world is in turmoil. Our country feels divided, split by cynicism and anger and falsehood. In my own life, I'm feeling the weight of having too much to do and not enough time to do it all. No matter how early I get up or how late I go to bed, I don't seem to get enough accomplished. There are no Christmas cookies this year, no handmade gifts, no special things to place under the tree. My writing is stalled, my concentration jagged. I keep thinking of all the loose ends I've left dangling, keep wondering where, exactly, I'm meant to be and what I'm meant to be doing. No place feels quite right. I "should" be working on my book manuscript, and I "should" be creating Christmas for my family, but instead I'm spinning my wheels somewhere in the middle, feeling as if I'm failing at both.

Yesterday, my son Henry turned twenty-two, a fact that fills me with both pride and wonder: how did we get here so fast? Wasn't it just a few years ago that he was a week old and we dressed him up in a tiny velour Santa suit and posed for our first family portrait? Wasn't it only yesterday that he spent the days before Christmas sitting upstairs at his desk writing college applications? Now, he's just months away from graduation, months away from having to find a job, a home, an adult life of his own. The years fly by, gathering speed, and I struggle to keep up, never entirely comfortable with the too-swift passage of time.

This week Jack was accepted early at the school of his choice for college. I'm thrilled he'll be in Boston next year, close to us, but stunned to realize he's actually old enough to *go* to college. Over the weekend, my husband pulled out a pile of old photographs of our boys when they were little: all fat cheeks and cuddles, innocence and giggles. Tiny beings that live now only in pictures and in our memories. Amazing to think that our lives have already had such breadth and span, that we've lived through our child-rearing years, raised sons to young adulthood, watched them leave home, and then awaited their return knowing how soon they'll leave again.

Tomorrow night, Henry will arrive, and our family will have two short weeks together. Today, I'm preparing for his homecoming by clearing all of my own books and papers out of his bedroom, where I've installed myself to write during these last few months. But I'm also taking some time to prepare *myself*. Instead of getting started on a new book chapter or running around doing last-minute shopping, I've decided to stay home and just sit in stillness for a while. Today, I need to cast my lot with "being" rather than with "doing," and to trust that being is enough. To believe that reclaiming large areas of peace in myself is perhaps the most urgent, most necessary work I could do.

I feel inspired by a moment on Saturday afternoon at my brother and sister-in-law's house. Jack and Steve and I had attended their four-year-old's Christmas pageant, an epic musical production performed by sixteen nursery schoolers in full costume. Afterward, as the extended family sat around in the living room enjoying a late lunch of chili and corn-bread, little Gabriel accidentally whacked his grandfather's full dish from his hand. Food flew everywhere—an entire bowl's worth of chili spattered on the beige wall-to-wall carpet. There was a moment of stunned silence in the face of the disaster. Gabriel's eyes filled with tears. And in that instant, as chili seeped into the rug and everyone leapt into action, an unspoken choice was also made for peace. No one shouted. No one scolded. No one got upset or delivered a lecture about little boys who ought to be more careful.

"It's all right," Gabe's mom said, as she went for the Resolve and paper towels. "It's all right," my brother reassured his son, as he got down on his knees and simply began to clean up the mess.

You could feel the tension in the room dissipate as quickly as it had come. Peace reclaimed and reflected back into the world. Peace as moral duty. Peace as the true lesson of the day. Peace because Gabriel, too, will be all grown up in the blink of an eye, and soon enough his own parents will be looking back at his vanished childhood, wondering if they've taught him well, if they've prepared him to bring peace into this troubled world. Small moments. Big, lasting impressions. I like to think that, as the big sister with the grown-up kids, I'm the one who can teach my younger sibling a few things about being a parent. But just as often, he teaches me.

I know that what matters most this week is not how much I manage to get done, how many words I write, or how many presents I wrap, but how I choose to be. I know that what brings our own sons home to this house, my parents to our hearth on Christmas morning, our family and friends to our table for dinner, is surely not just a sense of duty and tradition but a universal longing for connection and love, acceptance and peace.

Peace is what we all yearn for, and peace is the gift we can offer one another—in a word of forgiveness, in a smile, a hug, a kindness done, a gratitude expressed. Even in the ease with which a huge mess of chili gets cleaned off a rug.

Reading the newspaper each morning, it's easy to despair, easy to see how readily seeds of hatred and fear grow into crops of violence and cruelty. But I'm taking a cue from my brother and sister-in-law's loving patience with their children, and I'm finding solace in the faith of a young Dutch woman who could envision the possibility of peace even as she awaited her own certain death at Auschwitz in 1943. This is the holiday spirit I aspire to embody, the truth I will try to remember as we light the candles, serve the meals, play the music, and celebrate this time together: peace begins here, right now, right where we are. And peace is always possible.

December 2011

Whatever happens to you belongs to you. Make it yours.
Feed it to yourself even if it feels impossible to swallow.
Let it nurture you, because it will.
— *Cheryl Strayed*

——·—— unimaginable ——·——

We sat around the kitchen table after dinner last night—
my son Henry; my husband, Steve; and two of our dearest
friends in the world, Lisa and Kerby.

I met Lisa eighteen years ago, when Henry visited her
kindergarten classroom for the first time as a small, shy
four-year-old. He already had an Individual Education
Plan, or IEP, from the public school system and a medical
file that was two inches thick. He'd been diagnosed with
asthma at three months, sensory integration dysfunction
and low muscle tone at two, and various other physical
and developmental delays and concerns ever since. He saw
an occupational therapist, a speech therapist, and a physical therapist every week—to learn how to do the things
other children his age could do without being taught,
things like moving his tongue from side to side, skipping,

or jumping up and down. To say we were worried about him would have been an understatement. It seemed every expert we talked to was quick to point out something else that was wrong with our son.

Lisa, quiet and gentle and observant, watched him in her classroom for two mornings. And then she did what no one else had ever done: she told us what was right with him—how carefully he listened, that he was clearly drawn to music, that he was emotionally aware, empathetic beyond his years, and kind.

She became Henry's teacher and, soon, my friend. Our sensitive son thrived in Lisa's rose-colored classroom. "I don't know what you guys are doing," said the occupational therapist after six months, "but it's working. Henry doesn't need to come anymore." Soon, the others concurred. Meanwhile, Lisa and I clicked. We ran together, hiked, shared books, laughed and talked over countless cups of coffee. Steve and I met her future husband, and the four of us grew as close as two couples can be. Three years after Henry left her class, Lisa became Jack's kindergarten teacher as well.

Our families spent time together, her three older boys much admired and emulated by our two younger ones. The memories piled up: New Year's Eve feasts, camping out at their New Hampshire cottage, weekends in Maine, ferry rides to Monhegan Island, wonderful meals cooked over campfires, long walks, and epic swims. Years of affection and laughter and good times.

When I turned forty, we celebrated at their cabin in the woods, watching the October sunset from a high hilltop, and then hiking down in the darkness to light a fire, share champagne and hot soup at the hearth, and then pile on hats and mittens for sleeping in the crisp fall air. It is still my favorite birthday ever.

Ten years ago next month, my friend's older son was killed just a few months shy of his college graduation. My own memory of that horrific day is still so fresh it's hard to believe it's been a decade. I remember Lisa asking, a few days after the funeral, "How will I live without him?" I remember not knowing how to answer her. I remember wondering, day after day and month after month, how I could help and what I could do. And I remember realizing there was no way to help and nothing anyone could do—except keep showing up.

Ten years ago, I couldn't imagine what it would be like to lose a child. I still can't, although being Lisa's friend through these difficult years has helped me to understand. But ten years ago, I couldn't imagine a lot of things. Back then, I couldn't imagine how my friend would ever heal or how the rest of her family would keep going, or even how the two of us could ever possibly laugh again over nothing, the way we always used to do. I couldn't imagine my own sons all grown up. How would I ever release them to the world and all its dangers, or bear witness to their loss of innocence?

Maybe a certain lack of imagination is what saves us from being paralyzed with fear for our children as they make their way in the world. Certainly what seemed unimaginable when my own sons were nine and twelve, the year that Morgan died, has slowly, inevitably, become the reality I've learned to take in stride as the years rolled by.

Right under my eyes, my children have done the un-imaginable: they've grown up. They drive cars and stay out late and have friends I don't know and drink beer and pay bills and make mistakes and hold down jobs and put money in the bank and learn things I can't begin to understand and have lives that belong to them, lives they live away from me.

I couldn't imagine any of this when they were children and now I am living it. And, you know what? It's okay. In fact, it is unimaginably good. In four months, I will be the mother of a college graduate myself. The boy who had to be taught how to send a message from his brain to his tongue is an accomplished pianist, an A student, a young man whose talents far exceed anything I could have imagined on that day when I crossed my fingers and prayed that he could hold his own for a morning of kindergarten.

The other day, as the two of us sat during intermission at the Boston Symphony, he patiently explained to me the mathematical theory behind post-tonal music. At this moment, Jack is in Montreal for winter break with thirty friends from his senior class and no adults. Even a year ago, I couldn't have imagined granting permission for an unchaperoned roadtrip to a city five hours away where the drinking age is basically moot. And yet, after many conversations and agreements about how often he needed to check in with us, my husband and I found ourselves on the same page about this: ready to say yes.

There comes a time when our job is no longer to keep our children protected under our care but to entrust them to themselves. They are going to leave us anyway. But I think perhaps we give them a special gift if we can summon the courage to let them go with our blessings and our faith.

"Keep some room in your heart for the unimaginable," writes Mary Oliver. This strikes me as profound parenting advice, a reminder that there is so much more to this life than we can possibly see or touch or understand. Our children's paths are revealed slowly and in time, their true gifts perhaps obscured for years, their destinies not ours to write. We will love them no matter what. But we can't keep them safe. And somehow, we must make our fragile peace with both of these truths. Keeping some room in my heart for the unimaginable makes it a little easier. For what can any of us do, but work our way toward surrender, surrender to reality in all its beauty and unknowable ways?

A lot happens in ten years. What I've learned from sharing my friend's journey is that grief doesn't go away, but like everything else, it changes over time. The empty place in your heart is never filled up, but it changes, too. You get a little more used to the hole being there, and you learn to feel your way around it. Your sadness slowly becomes a bit more bearable for being familiar. You begin to realize that the world is full of people with broken hearts, and that what you thought was unique and singular to you is in fact part of being human. You are surprised when, for the very first time, you laugh again. And then you discover that, even in the midst of unimaginable sorrow, there are also moments shot through with grace and, yes, happiness.

Which brings me back to last night and our dinner table. We lit the candles and ate chowder and cornbread. We talked about the ten-year anniversary of Morgan's death, a few weeks away, and how the girl he had planned to marry is a mother now herself. She and Lisa stay in close touch, bound still by their love for a young man who died too soon. After dinner, Henry gave Kerby a piano lesson, helping him work through a song while the rest of us did dishes. Then we all sat around the table and played Balderdash. Before we knew it, it was 11 pm and we'd been laughing for hours. Eighteen years ago, when a kindly kindergarten teacher put her hand on my son's small, vulnerable head and said, "I think he'll be fine," I couldn't have possibly imagined a day when that boy would be a man, sitting at a piano teaching a complicated jazz riff to that teacher's husband. Ten years ago, as my friend tried to get used to the world without her oldest son in it, I felt as if I'd lost her, too. I couldn't imagine a future lit by her laughter. But here we are.

February 2012

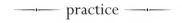

—·— practice —·—

The theme of my life this winter can be summed up in a word: practice. Two-thirds of the way through a memoir, with another four chapters to go and a deadline less than two months away, I have made a commitment to writing practice.

But I am a slow writer, never certain of the way forward, and so I have no choice but to practice patience.

Waiting for words to come, trusting that if I sit in one place long enough, the next sentence will find its way home to me, requires a certain kind of faith. Faith in mystery and faith in the process—and so I practice faith, too. Faith, it turns out, takes quite a lot of practice.

Yoga practice makes my writing practice possible. In order to be at my keyboard for hours on end, I must first get up and really move.

Breathing practice fuels the yoga practice. Without the union of breath and movement, yoga is just exercise, and I need a little more sustenance from my practice these days than a few leg lifts would provide.

Meditation practice guides me back into my writing, for before I can write so much as a line, I must listen. And in order to listen, I must practice stillness.

Stillness is a challenge, possible only when I practice discipline, for stillness is so not my nature. Discipline practice returns me to my yoga mat day after day, and then it hustles me right back upstairs, to my spot against the bed pillows, and my laptop balanced on my knees, and the words on the page, and the view out the window.

I look at the dark curve of mountains against the winter sky, hear the whoosh of wind curling around the corner of the house, the ticking clock, the soft, steady breath of my dog asleep on the rug, and I practice gratitude, for really, what could be better than this—this life, this moment, this practice of pausing and noticing and saying thank-you?

I used to think of my life in terms of the various roles and responsibilities that made me me: there was motherhood, housework and editing work and writing work, marriage, exercise, spirituality, friendship. Lots of expectations to juggle and jobs to tackle and experiences to either embrace or endure or reject. And never, ever enough time to fit it all in or get it all done.

Writing was always the first thing to go. How could I sit alone in a room typing words on a screen when there were so many more "important" things I should be doing instead? But with only a slight shift in imagination, things have changed. I've come to see my life for what it is—not some tired old "I'm-too-busy" story I've told myself a thousand times, but simply this: an opportunity to practice.

And suddenly there is plenty of room and all the time in the world for me to do the only thing I need to do—keep practicing.

February 2012

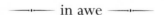 in awe

"You have to admit, this is an indulgence," my husband says as we walk across the windswept campus to meet our son. We've traveled from New Hampshire to Minnesota, just to watch the last performance of a college production of "A Chorus Line."

Here's the way I see it. Going out to dinner is an indulgence. Buying jewelry or lingerie or a new pair of boots is definitely an indulgence. Raspberries in February, yes. But taking a couple of days off and flying halfway across the country to watch our son realize his lifelong dream of being a musical director—to me this feels as important as anything else I've done as his mother.

There is not an empty seat in the theater. The houselights dim. Henry, dressed in black, walks out and takes his place in front of the keyboard at the rear of the stage. For a moment, the spotlight falls on him as, his back to the audience, he lifts a hand to cue the band and begin the show.

How does anyone become who they are meant to be? How are life stories written, paths revealed, passions ignited? By what alchemy of genes and temperament and serendipity are gifts bestowed, talents honed, and then offered to the world?

I remember this: We have flown to Orlando on the afternoon of December 25, with two-year-old Henry, to spend the second half of the day with Steve's parents. We are still newlyweds, and every holiday feels like a game of tug-o-war between our two families; having bestowed a grandchild, we are much in demand. It is Sunday morning, the day after Christmas, and we have just finished brunch with Steve's family at a glittery Disney World hotel.

There, in the sun-drenched lobby, an enormous grand piano gleams. Our quiet, cautious toddler walks toward it as if drawn by a magnet. His dad follows, on the job, not about to let his kid start banging the keys in this very public place. But Henry is not a key-banger. He stands with a hand on the piano as if mesmerized. He's never seen one before, has no idea what it's for or what it does. He knows only that he needs to know. Steve lifts him up onto the bench and sits down beside him.

My two guys are dressed in the matching teal and purple flannel shirts I've given them for Christmas—a little corny and out of place among the red-and-silver holiday décor of the Hilton. But to me they are adorable. They spend a few minutes there, meeting the first piano of Henry's life. Tentatively, he plunks a couple of notes. I snap photos, mostly because of the matching shirts. I am not thinking, "Maybe he'll be a musician." In fact, I'm probably not aware of much other than that Steve's folks want to get on the road and that I've eaten too much. We still have the pictures I took that morning. And, looking at them now, I do know: something began right then, in that moment twenty years ago when a little boy first touched a finger to an ivory key and heard music of his own making.

In one hundred days he will graduate from college. He is sending out resumes, putting together recordings, doing interviews with theater directors by phone, trying to figure out the next step of his journey toward his Broadway dream. But this weekend, sitting in the audience and watching our son play piano and conduct the pit orchestra he'd been rehearsing and coaching for weeks, we had a glimpse both of his past and his future. Being there wasn't an indulgence. It was an opportunity to pause and give thanks for every moment that led to this one: our son doing what he loves most and offering the best of all he's worked so hard to be.

And what is our job as parents, if not first to nurture the beings entrusted to our care, to have faith in their inchoate processes of growing and becoming, and then to show up, again and again, for as long as we are able, to bear grateful witness to their unfolding destinies?

February 2012

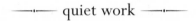 quiet work

Remember that poster in your high-school guidance counselor's office? The one with an airbrushed photo of some generic sunrise and a caption that read, "Today is the first day of the rest of your life"? At seventeen, I really did not want to hear that.

This morning at dawn I stepped outside. The sunrise was spectacular. The first words that popped into my head were, "Today is the first day of the rest of your life." The birds were singing like crazy. Steve was already down in the field, throwing a tennis ball for Gracie. And my heart was full with the sweetness of the moment. The first day of the rest of my life seemed like a good reason to stand in one place for a while, watch the sun climb up into the sky, listen to the songbird symphony going on in the yard, and give thanks for everything.

Yesterday at 2:08 in the afternoon, I hit the SEND button and e-mailed the final chapter of the manuscript I've been working on for over a year to my editor. It took a little while for the fact of that to sink in: I did it. I walked downstairs in a daze, went outside and sat down in a lawn chair next to Steve, who was innocently reading the paper in the spring sunshine. And then I burst into tears. The transition from writing to suddenly being done with writing pretty much undid me. There was the relief of making my deadline (barely, barely), but it was inextricably intertwined with the despair of knowing that the finished product is so much less than the beautiful creation I envisioned all those months ago, before I actually got down to the business of trying to translate my lived experience into words.

While I've been sequestered upstairs in Henry's bedroom, surrounded by his old Red Sox posters and various drafts and file cards, the seasons changed. I missed most of winter and barely noticed the arrival of spring. Yesterday, with the finish line in sight, I sat on Henry's bed with my laptop in front of me for seven hours without even looking up. When I finally ventured out into my own front yard yesterday afternoon, it felt as if I was returning home from an extended trip or just recovering from a debilitating illness. I've been gone a long time. Now, suddenly, with one tap of the keys, I'm back. Reentry has been a little rocky. I keep thinking, "I'm done and I did it but I failed."

My husband wiped my tears away yesterday and then he gave me a sweet letter he'd written me in the morning, when he could see the end was near. He gave me Wendell Berry's *Collected Poems,* a perfect gift for that tumultuous moment. I sat down in the chair next to his and opened the book. And the first poem I came to was this one, called "Like Snow."

Like Snow
Suppose we did our work
Like the snow, quietly, quietly,
Leaving nothing out.

Such simple words. Such a fine thing to aspire to. I wonder why we humans suffer so with our fears of not being enough. We do the best we can, give all we have to give, and then turn a harsh eye on the beauty of our efforts. Today, on this first day of the rest of my life, I want only to do my work like the snow. Quietly, quietly.
April 2012

—·—— mystery ——·—

A memory from about ten years ago, my birthday. I am visiting my friend Lisa in New Hampshire. It is unseasonably cold for early October; already, less than two hours north of our Boston suburb, frost has ravaged gardens, stolen life from the flowers in the big planters downtown. While my friend is at work, I spend the day wandering through her town. For the last few years, ever since she taught both Henry and then Jack in kindergarten, we have been every-day friends. Now she's moved here to join the man she plans to marry, and sustaining our friendship means planning and traveling.

Peterborough is just half an hour away from where I grew up, but it feels farther, thanks in part to the mountain in between, the harsher climate over here on the other side. When I was a child, we rarely came west; "civilization" lay to the south and to the east, toward Boston, not up and over Temple Mountain in the direction of Vermont. Yet our occasional family trips—for summer-evening ice-cream cones at Silver Ranch or to prowl antique stores with my mother—made lasting impressions. The town seemed special even then.

On this day, my forty-second birthday, my eye catches a sign propped up on the sidewalk in the middle of town: Tibetan Monks from the Drepung Gomang Monastery Create Sand Mandala. Each day this week, 9–5. I have no idea what a sand mandala is, but the door of the old brick building, a former Baptist church from the colonial era, is open, and I have an empty afternoon stretching out before me. It seems unlikely that a New England town with a population of five thousand could support a multicultural museum, but that is what the Mariposa appears to be: an arts center devoted to bringing world culture to one small community in New Hampshire. I drop a donation in the jar and walk through a gallery stuffed with vibrant artwork, handmade dolls, puppets, and wall hangings.

Upstairs, the soaring main hall has been transformed into a sacred space. At one end of the room, an altar has been created, adorned with apples and oranges, small bowls of rice, flowers, candles, and a statue of the Buddha. On a large blue board on the floor, an intricate design is taking shape, made entirely of colored grains of sand. I slip off my shoes, take a seat, and watch the monks silently bending to their work.

There are several monks, dressed in crimson robes, sitting quietly, meditating. Two others are down on their knees on the hard wooden floor, hunched over, noses inches from the ground as they "paint" with what look like narrow metal funnels and small sticks. There is no sound but for the rhythmic tapping of metal on metal, as they painstakingly fill in their exquisitely detailed design with grains of colored sand.

Afternoon sun streams through the high windows. People come and go. A young mother arrives to watch with her little boy, who solemnly eats an apple, never taking his eyes from the monks, who look up every now and again, stretch, and smile at us, nodding hello. The mandala increases in complexity, each intricate design element appearing as if by magic from the thin streams of sand. Not a grain falls out of place. The slightest breeze or sneeze or misstep would destroy its geometric perfection. Yet the monks move easily around their creation, barefoot, their robes flowing, seemingly heedless of the danger, yet as mindful of each movement as they would be if performing a dance. Unhurried, graceful, lighthearted. Peace pervades the room.

A thought arrives, alights like a bird upon my shoulder: I want to live here.

That night, back at home in Massachusetts, my husband is waiting for me; he and our sons have made a chocolate cake and a birthday dinner. But there is something going on in the backyard. The people who recently bought the house right next to ours have decided to cut down all the trees between our two houses. The chainsaws are still roaring. The landscape has changed. But it suddenly feels as if everything has changed. Where, just yesterday, there were golden leaves shimmering in the sunlight, a thick, leafy canopy of protection and privacy surrounding our home, there is suddenly devastation. Our familiar treehouse view is gone, replaced by a stark, unfiltered view into someone else's brightly lit TV room. Tears fill my eyes.

"I think we need to move," I say, as surprised by the words coming out of my mouth as Steve is.

Sometimes we recognize the pivotal moments of our lives as they're happening. But not always. It was a long time after that emotional October evening before my husband and I finally decided that yes, in fact, we were going to move. And longer still before we finally settled into a house of our own on a hilltop in the town of Peterborough. But looking back now, I know: for me, the journey to the place we now call home began in the presence of a group of exiled Tibetan monks from India, who came to spend a week creating a mandala for peace in a small town in New England.

This week, the monks returned to the Mariposa. They are traveling in the United States now at the request of the Dalai Lama, re-creating a new sand mandala designed to inspire world harmony and to honor all beliefs and all religions. Early on Friday morning, Jack and Steve and I sat for a while and watched them put the finishing touches on their week's work. The monks welcomed us warmly, in silence, eyes twinkling. The mandala was breathtaking—intricate, finely textured, each minute detail meticulously rendered. A half hour passed. Jack needed to get to school, but none of us could quite bring ourselves to leave.

According to Buddhist scripture, sand mandalas transmit positive energies to the environment and to all who view them. They are believed to effect purification and healing. On this beautiful April day, there was no doubt — we were in the presence of peace, enveloped in love, steeped in goodness. And, it occurred to me, we were also exactly where we were meant to be.

Funny how ten years go by, and while you're busy living your life, that life is slowly, without your even quite realizing it, turning into something else altogether. Funny, too, how destiny is revealed, and how it's only by pausing and looking back that we can truly discern the gifts given us by grace—the moments that have shown us who we are, that have briefly illuminated the dark path, revealing just where we're meant to put our feet and the direction in which we are meant to go.

Lately, I've been thinking about intuition. Was it just a random thought or some kind of inner knowing that brushed against my awareness all those years ago, on my forty-second birthday, loosening my grip on things as they were and whispering in my ear that change was already in the wind?

I can't say. But I'm coming to believe that we are in fact being guided all the time. And that support and direction are right there for us if we take time to pause and listen to the quiet inner voice that whispers, go here, or, do that. Perhaps the way forward can only be revealed in those empty spaces in between moments, when we are sitting still, so still that gentle breezes from another realm can be heard to murmur.

This spring, coming to the end of an intense time of writing, I find myself at loose ends, dogged by uncertainty. Our two sons are about to graduate, one from high school and the other from college. Life is full of unknowns. But one thing I've learned over these last years of change and transition is that there are energies at work in all our lives that can be trusted. Our job may simply be to ask the questions, to open ourselves to possibility without presuming to nail down the answers. Perhaps there is no right answer anyway, other than the rightness of trusting that things will unfold as they are meant to—as long as we're willing to make room for our many ways of knowing, even the ones that seem beyond reason, the ones that dwell in the invisible precincts of soul, instinct, faith, mystery.

On Sunday, I returned alone for the monks' closing ceremony. The room I entered for the first time as a visitor more than ten years ago was filled now with my neighbors and friends. It seemed that nearly everyone I know in town had come out on this rainy afternoon to view the completed mandala and to bid it farewell. For, within hours of completing their masterpiece, the monks destroy it. In a deep bow to the impermanence of all things, the monks chanted, prayed, and then, using two ordinary paintbrushes from the hardware store, they swept the beautiful offering they had spent the entire week making into a small rainbow-hued pile.

I came home with a little packet of sacred sand. And later today, when the sun comes out again, I will sprinkle it in the garden outside our kitchen door, in this place that we have come to call home.

April 2012

———•——— commencement ———•———

It's an iconic photo in our family album: Henry, age seven, and I are standing face to face in a deserted Times Square. It is about 8 am on a summer Sunday morning. Bits of trash, empty soda cups, and old newspapers lie at our feet. His face wears a rare, uncharacteristic pout. I am bending over, leaning in toward my small son, and in a rare, uncharacteristic gesture, I'm waggling my finger at him, trying without much success to make a point: Broadway shows are not like videos. The fact that seeing *Beauty and the Beast* yesterday had been the high point of his entire life to date did not mean that we could wake up the next day and go see it again.

What neither my amused husband, snapping the picture for posterity, nor I, engaged in an effort to put Broadway ticket prices into some sort of perspective for a second grader, knew at the time was that, in fact, seeing a Disney production featuring dancing teapots and singing candlesticks had indeed changed our son's life. One Broadway musical matinee and a shy, quiet boy was not only hooked, he suddenly had a vision, a sense of a road opening at his feet, even if the destination wasn't yet something he could quite articulate. Someday he would be part of such a show. He would get to go back again and again, night after night, until this music that made his heart crack open had become a part of who he was and of what he knew. A passion to be carried in his bones and in his blood. In other words, a vocation. A calling whose faint summons he was just beginning to hear for the first time. There was a big musical life out there, and it was just waiting for him to grow up and grow into it.

The thing about turning points is that we rarely recognize them until we're much further down the road. Then, one day, we turn around to look back at where we've been and see that the future was in fact written long ago—if only we'd known how to read the writing on the wall. That fifteen-year-old photograph and the cascade of memories it releases seem particularly significant—and poignant—now, as Henry begins his new life as a college graduate.

A week ago, my husband and my parents and I sat in the bleachers under a hot Minnesota sun, waiting to hear one name among the 763 being read into the microphone. "A graduation ceremony should not be rushed," the president of St. Olaf had said in his remarks to the sweltering crowd. And, hot and sweaty as we were, I found myself in agreement.

There was a kind of beauty in just being there, allowing time to slow down, taking this opportunity to consider that behind each and every name called from the podium that afternoon there was a unique life story to be told, a path that had led to this particular moment and to an unknown future still waiting to unfurl. For every graduating student, there was also a community of connection and caring, a whole group of relations who had worried and cheered and laughed and cried all along the road to young adulthood, friends who had shared the ups and downs of growing up, teachers who had given of themselves in order to make a difference in a young person's life.

And for each of those graduates there was, too, a complicated, private history of epiphanies and obstacles no more or less challenging and meaningful than our own. There were memories of triumphs and heartbreaks, and just as much infinite potential in each of these young lives as we discerned in our son—all of it intertwined with the unfathomable mysteries of determination and destiny, fate and luck, choices and the consequences of those choices.

How amazing it was, simply to pause and contemplate the fact that 763 different life paths—paths that had had their various beginnings just over twenty years ago in countries that spanned the globe—China and Vietnam and England and South America, as well as in each of the fifty United States—had somehow, finally, briefly, converged right here, at this Midwestern college, on this football field under a cloudless blue sky in May, in an age-old ritual marking the culmination of one journey and the beginning of another.

Soon enough, the solemn procession of students to the

stage would come to an end. The caps would fly into the air, the cameras would be tucked away, last loads of laundry carried out of empty dorm rooms, final hugs tendered and tears shed, car doors slammed shut. The class of 2012 would scatter into the world, never again to gather together in one place nor to turn their collective eyes to the future even as they bid farewell to their shared past. No, commencement exercises should not be rushed.

Last week, two days after his graduation, Henry and I returned to Times Square. I had a day of work in the city and we had tickets to three Broadway shows—his graduation gift. For a kid who grew up far from Manhattan, he has racked up an impressive Broadway attendance record over the years—testament, in part, to the passion born on that very first visit, and to the singular nature of his desires. So it seemed fitting that we return together to the place where it all began. This time it was *The Book of Mormon* that had us laughing along and still singing in the morning. And the next night, at *Once,* it was my son who pointed out to me the subtle complexities of the lovely orchestration and staging.

He is a knowledgeable theater date, this young Bachelor of Music who has put in his time at the keyboard and in the classroom, doing the hard, necessary work that dream fulfillment demands. I still remember his first recital at age six, in which he plunked out the notes to "Blue Jello" on a tiny guitar. Last month, for his senior project, he created, produced, directed, and played piano for an original Broadway revue with a cast of ten and a combo. I wonder if someday I will look back and remember sitting in *that* audience, and think to myself that it, too, proffered a glimpse of what was to come.

Meanwhile, the road at his feet twists yet again: on Friday, after a few days at home spent unpacking and repacking, our son will leave for his first postcollege job, as accompanist at the College Light Opera Company, on Cape Cod. It's a career move that the seven-year-old Henry surely would have approved of, if he'd known back then that such opportunities existed—nine musicals produced in eleven weeks, a summer comprised of rehearsals all day and tuxedoed evenings in the orchestra pit.

As I type these words, Henry's putting winter clothes away in his closet, packing summer clothes into a trunk. The soundtrack to *Smash* is playing through his iPod speakers. He is singing. In a few days his room will be empty again; he'll be setting up housekeeping with a bunch of young actors and musicians in an old Victorian house near the beach. The partings are still a little hard, but after four years of college and summer jobs away from home, I've grown used to them. His life is meant to be elsewhere. I wouldn't have it any other way.

And I've also realized this: when our children were small, our job as parents was to introduce the world to them, to expose them to a wide range of experiences that might begin to give shape to their aspirations. Now, the tables are turned. Growing up, finding his way into adulthood, independence, and the first steps of a career doing what he loves, our son is providing us with some new experiences in return. Steve and I have already made reservations at a B&B on the Cape. We're looking forward to heading down there later this month to see the first musical of the summer season at the College Light Opera. I suspect I'll be tempted, when I wake up the next morning, by the same impulse that moved Henry all those years ago. Maybe I'll even put in a call to him, to see if he can possibly score us a couple more tickets, so we can go back and see the show one more time.

June 2012

 berries

As a child I lived next door to an elderly couple who spent their golden years cultivating roses, raising chickens, growing strawberries, and nurturing a special friendship with my little brother and me.

Each year the last day of school seemed to coincide with the beginning of strawberry season. For every two quarts we picked for Dike to sell for 50 cents from his side porch, we were allowed to take one home for ourselves, which seemed to my brother and me like gainful summer employment. Once we'd picked our quota, we were rewarded by the pleasure of returning to the shady swing set in our own backyard, payment carefully balanced in hand: a soggy, juice-stained, balsa-wood box tip-top full of warm, sweet berries.

By the time I grew up and had children myself, Dike

and his wife had died, and his lovingly tended strawberry fields had long since been subdivided into condominiums. It wasn't until twelve years ago, when I found myself alone in a rented cabin with my own two little boys, that I rediscovered the joy of berry picking.

I had rented the place on a whim, over the phone and sight unseen, envisioning swims in the lake, games of Old Maid on the screened porch, hot dogs cooked on sticks over a fire. I wanted time alone with Henry and Jack, away from the easy comforts of home and the distractions of our suburban neighborhood. Ever since my own parents had rented a small, plain cabin on the shore of Lake Winnipesaukee when I was a little girl, I'd been in love with cottage life. Some of my fondest childhood memories coalesce around that first passion and that unadorned place: the scent of pine carried on a breeze through an open window; the baptismal shock of lake water on my face just moments after waking up in the morning; hours whiled away on a lumpy daybed on a screened porch, reading *The Borrowers* from cover to cover. I was hoping my sons would love what I had loved as a child, that they too would be enchanted by old books and long days spent in damp bathing suits.

But this was June in Maine. And my sons were used to a little more structure than I had in mind. The cabin was remote and charmless. The lake water, inky black and freezing cold. We read for a while, huddled in blankets by the woodstove. They laid out a game of Strat-O-Matic on the kitchen table. There were ants everywhere, and so we came up with ingenious ways to protect our food supply. By the morning of the third day I was wondering what on earth we would do with ourselves for an entire week.

"Let's go exploring," I suggested after breakfast, hustling the kids into the car. "Let's just go home," Jack, who was seven, replied.

Strawberries saved us. Driving down the country road toward town, I spotted a sign: "U-Pick." We pulled over, and within minutes the three of us were plopped down in the middle of a fragrant, abundant row, the sun warm at our backs, the long, empty day salvaged by a new sense of purpose. My children, having come of age eating pale, juiceless berries, industrially grown and shipped to our grocery store from afar, were amazed. Who knew that a strawberry could taste so good?

We picked two heaping flats that morning and feasted on strawberry shortcake with freshly whipped cream, and hot chocolate, for dinner that night. I think we ate strawberries and chocolate at every meal that week. We slept together in one bed to stay warm and never did go swimming even once, though I nearly drowned us all when a sudden, violent storm swept our tipsy canoe all the way across the lake and I found myself unable to paddle against the wind back to shore. (Later, Henry managed to eke three school essays out of that near disaster, one of which he entitled, "The Worst Day of My Life.")

Now that my sons are grown, our week in that isolated cabin is just one more bit of childhood nostalgia—though amazingly enough it's a memory they now seem to cherish

just as much as I do my own youthful recollections of endless cabin afternoons and quiet pleasures. In recent years,
though, we created a new berry-picking tradition here in
New Hampshire at a nearby farm that opens its fields to
the public for as long as the crop lasts.

Strawberry season—like childhood, like marriage, like life
itself—is fleeting. Fail to pay attention, get too distracted by
other things, and you'll miss it. Steve and I could usually co-
erce our teenaged boys to put in a couple of hours of picking
on a Saturday morning as long as there was a promise of
shortcake for dinner. The effort was always worth it, more
than worth it, and any initial grumbling would soon give
way to the elemental satisfaction of harvesting sweet perfection. Who could be grumpy while picking strawberries on a
glorious morning in June?

This year, though, it was just two of us on our knees in
the strawberry field. Again and again, these days, I find
myself brought to this threshold between acceptance of
what is and awareness of what's over. Henry is already
gone for the summer, playing piano at a musical theater
on the Cape. Jack, who graduated from high school last
week, is sharing an apartment in Cambridge for the summer, working at the studio where he's been an intern for
the last two years. He'll come and go from home; but
slowly, over the last couple of weeks, he's been moving
stuff out of here to there: his guitar, his speakers, a set of
dresser drawers.

And so, carrying on our old tradition but in a new
way, Steve and I got up early yesterday and headed to the

farm alone. We played Cat Stevens on the car stereo and planned out the rest of the day—a few hours of hulling and slicing, the French Open finals on TV, an afternoon in the garden, omelets for dinner, strawberry shortcake for dessert. I thought about how grateful I am to have a partner with whom to share the doings of an ordinary Sunday, and at the same time, I found myself wondering if I'll ever get used to the reality of our new, downsized family.

In years past, the four of us could pick thirty or forty pounds of strawberries in an hour. By late winter, they would all be gone. Yesterday, Steve and I agreed: twenty pounds would be plenty. There are, after all, only two of us. And yet, what a treat it will be, some winter's night, to thaw out a generous heap of our own strawberries, sprinkle them with sugar, and ladle them over bowls of vanilla ice cream, each bite a redolent reminder of summers past and a promise of summer's eventual return.

June 2012

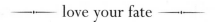 love your fate

Some true stories.

On a tennis training trip to Florida last March, two months before his high school graduation, my son Jack felt something snap and spasm in his back. He'd played tennis through chronic pain for over a year, but this was different. The sudden jolt stopped him cold. He didn't know in that moment that he'd just suffered two stress fractures in his L5 vertebrae. What he did know was that his final high-school tennis season had just ended before it had even begun. His dream of being named captain of his team senior year would not come to pass.

Later that night, in pain but not yet diagnosed, he sat in a hotel room with some of his teammates. Drinks were poured and consumed. Jack and a friend put the empty liquor bottles into a knapsack and set out to carry them to a Dumpster at a gas station up the road. On the way, they were intercepted by their coaches. By seven the next morning, Jack was on a plane home. One minute he had been president of his senior class, a varsity athlete with an early decision acceptance to his first-choice college. A day later, he was expelled from high school, at home, and in bed with two cracked vertebrae. His college acceptance was rescinded a few weeks after that.

My neighbor Debbie has managed the challenges of living with an ileostomy for over twelve years, despite nearly constant blood loss and pain. When the oozing gets to be too severe she undergoes a bowel cauterization, an uncomfortable procedure that has always been worth the result—a few months with less blood leaving her body, which means more energy and strength for her. In May, however, the cauterizing procedure that had worked well in the past had the opposite effect. Home from the hospital, Debbie bled continuously into her pouch for nearly a day. A friend and I drove her to the emergency room. Halfway there, we realized she was losing consciousness and called an ambulance to meet us on the road. Debbie spent a couple of days in the ICU, stunned to realize just how close she had come to death's door, just how fragile her condition really was. Back at home, she was weak, thin, exhausted—and still bleeding, uncertain whether her ravaged bowels were healing or finally giving way altogether.

Up the road, just two miles from where we live, a young couple took over the farm where we have been CSA members for the past few years. The plan was for the elderly owner and his wife to slowly hand the farm over to Frank and Stacey, who have been working tirelessly since early last spring, reclaiming and planting fields, building greenhouses, raising goats and pigs and chickens. We spent a day earlier this summer with our new neighbors at the farm, admiring the fruits of their labors—bountiful vegetable gardens, happy animals, a lovely farm store well stocked with fresh, organic produce.

A few weeks ago, when I stopped to buy kale from Stacey at the farmer's market, I could tell she was upset. "We have to get rid of all the animals," she explained, fighting back tears, "and as soon as we do, we have to leave the farm." It turned out that the owner's wife had decided she didn't want animals being raised for meat on the property, and that was that. The deal was off.

"We've done the numbers every which way," Stacey said sadly. "And we just can't make a go of that property without the income from the animals." Yesterday was Frank and Stacey's final day at our local farmer's market. They have found homes for all their animals, except for a few rabbits, which they are keeping. On Saturday the remainder of the garden's harvest will go to the handful of CSA members and be offered for free at their roadside stand. Just as all the hard work of these last months is resulting in plentiful crops at this beautiful old farm, the owner is meeting with real-estate agents and developers. And Frank and Stacey are packing up to leave the place where they had hoped to sink their roots and stay.

On the early summer day that Steve and I spent touring the fields and barns with Frank, he explained the origins of the new name he and Stacey had bestowed on the farm: "Amor Fati." "It means 'love your fate' in Latin," Frank said.

"We named the farm in memory of our best friend," he continued, "who was planning to move here with us to farm this land. His motto was Amor fati. And that's the way he lived his life, open to the world and loving his fate. He was killed in a car crash just before we moved to New Hampshire. But he would be here, farming with us if he could. And so it seemed right that our farm, and our work here, should honor his memory and his great love of life."

Amor fati. I have carried this resonant Latin phrase in my heart all summer. Love your fate. What a challenge that is, when what fate has to offer is not your dream come true but rather broken bones, stupid mistakes, dashed hopes, eviction notices, loss and pain and heartache. And yet, surely we are shaped as much by dashed hopes as by those that come to pass. We are strengthened not by the easy stuff, but by what brings us to our knees. And we realize our full potential as human beings as much by losing at the game of life as by winning.

To love your fate is to believe that the way things are right now is the way they're supposed to be—even if nothing is the way we wanted or expected. We can either go down swinging, or we can die to the way things were and begin instead to live into them as they are.

Jack has spent the summer in Boston, packing cards and rolling posters for his dad to earn money, and doing intensive stretching and physical therapy to heal his back. Every day has been a struggle. He has had to give up all the activities he loves and remain pretty much immobile, in the hope that with enough care and rest, his bones will begin to knit back together. The most recent scan, a few weeks ago, showed just the slightest bit of new growth, a dim shadow of healing. Enough progress for his doctor to say, "Just keep doing what you're doing, and stay quiet for another six months, and then we'll see."

Last night, just as I was falling asleep, Jack called, wanting to talk about reapplying to college for next year, something he's been hesitant to even discuss. "I think getting thrown out of school and then having college taken away was probably for the best," he said. "And having these broken vertebrae, the most horrible thing that's ever happened in my whole life, has also made me a stronger person in some ways."

I listened, phone to my ear in the dark bedroom, as my son acknowledged that the worst thing that had ever happened to him—a possibly incurable back injury—had led him to territory he might not have explored otherwise.

"I've had to change everything about the way I live," Jack went on. "I've gone from being someone who was living totally for sports and for pleasure, to someone who realizes that there are other ways to live and be happy, and that's huge."

I agreed that it is, indeed, huge. "And so I'm pretty sure I do want to apply to college again," Jack said. "But I also think I'm a better candidate now than I was a year ago. I've learned a lot. I feel as if I actually might have something to offer." Amor fati.

As I write these words, Debbie is outside, clipping faded stalks of coneflower and rudbeckia from my tangled August garden. "I worked hard for this little life of mine," she said the other day, as she sipped the high-protein breakfast smoothie I make her each morning. "To be able to spend time in your garden, go to the pond with the dogs, and take a walk in the woods. It's all I want. And every day that I'm here, able to do what I love, I just look up and say thank-you, thank-you, thank-you." Amor fati.

Stacey smiled yesterday when I told her how grateful we've been for their beautiful food all summer. "We want to come back and look for another place," she said, as she weighed my potatoes and filled a bag with arugula. "Everyone has been so kind and supportive to us. All the other farmers have been great. And this town has come to feel like home, where we belong."

For now, Frank and Stacey will move in with her aunt in Massachusetts. She will return to her old job, working with autistic children, while Frank begins to search for another farm, a small piece of land they can buy outright, where they can start all over again from scratch, dreaming and planting and living close to the earth. Amor fati.

The pain of life isn't ever going to disappear. But perhaps it is in our efforts to accept and work with what life hands us that we grow our souls. Day by day, as we struggle to carry on in the face of grief and disappointment, we begin to see that even a great setback may contain a gift: the opportunity to discover, through practice, what lies behind sorrow. "How can we reconcile this feast of losses?" asks poet Stanley Kunitz. Maybe the answer is this simple, this beautiful, this all-encompassing: Amor fati.

August 2012

————•—— a wedding anniversary ——•————

Twenty-five years ago last week, my husband and I were married in a small church in Maine before fifty friends and family members. When I was in my twenties and living in New York, and Steve was in Boston, my parents' house on Bailey Island was our favorite getaway, a patch of wind-swept neutral territory where we could walk and talk for hours. There, we learned how to be together, how to share a bed and a kitchen, how to live as a couple before returning to our separate lives in separate cities. It seemed fitting that we marry in this place that meant so much to both of us, a place where we had already begun to create a history of shared memories.

All through the summer of 1987 we worked to get ready. Our wedding was to be a do-it-yourself affair, simple and modest and of our own making. We asked the elderly couple who ran the seasonal Driftwood Inn if they'd be willing to stay open the weekend after Labor Day for us. "No kitchen, though!" Mrs. Conrad said, wagging a finger at me. I assured her we'd be happy to feed everyone ourselves.

I remember all the weekends Steve and my brother and my dad spent painting the house that summer. My mom and I gathered yard-sale vases for flowers, scoped out sources for hydrangeas around the island, asked a woman down the road if she'd take the pictures and the firemen's wives if they'd be willing to put on a fish chowder rehearsal dinner at the library the night before.

I bought my wedding dress off the rack at Filenes while on my lunch break from work one day, and then came back to the editorial offices at Houghton Mifflin and proudly announced to my fiancé that it was in the bag—a plain ivory lace tea dress that I adored all the more for the fact that it fit me perfectly, cost only $200, and had taken fewer than forty-five minutes to choose. We picked up a couple of cases of champagne at Marty's Liquors in Newton and drove them to Maine in the trunk of our car. The morning before the wedding, Steve and a few other guys put up our rented yellow-and-white-striped tent and laid down a dance floor. My mom made fruit salad and cheese strata. While my husband-to-be hit tennis balls with his friends, I took a long run, from one end of the island to the other, taking care so as not to cross paths with my groom before we met at the altar. And then I sat down on a rock on the beach and stared up at the sky, wondering what the life we were about to embark upon held in store for us.

My memories of that day a quarter century ago are all good. I loved our wedding—loved the way my family worked with us to realize our vision; loved having all the people we cared about, from all the disparate parts of our lives, gathered together in one place to bear witness to our vows; loved the fact that our married life began at the intersection of sea and sky; loved the long walk my new husband and I made from the church to the reception, strolling along alone, hand in hand, while all our guests drove by, honking and waving.

Last Wednesday, on our anniversary, Steve pulled the photo album off the shelf. He had taken the day off from work to celebrate with me, but our plans were thwarted. Laid flat by a stomach flu, I was too sick even to look at the pictures, let alone go out to dinner or rouse myself for a meaningful conversation with my husband of twenty-five years. While Steve waxed nostalgic, I lay curled up on the couch under a blanket, nauseous, dehydrated, exhausted. And bearing little resemblance to his radiant bride of yore.

Every once in a while, I'd make my way to the bathroom for a few sips of water and cringe at my own pasty reflection in the mirror. Meanwhile, my husband gave up all hope of enjoying a fun day off with me and tackled a few household projects. Lying on the couch, watching him push the lawn mower around the backyard, I tried to conjure in my mind the guy I was once so enamored of— the lean, handsome publishing executive with dark curly hair and an athlete's build. Time was, my heart would go wild just looking at him.

What happens now is different, of course. The bright fireworks of first love settle over time into a long, slow burn, both darker and richer. The years have humbled us, but they've also added up to something: a marriage. We no longer believe, as we did on our wedding day, that we can do a better job of being married than everyone else. We've had our share of pain and fury, misery and misunderstanding, resentment and mercy.

I once read that in marriages that last, each partner can still see in the other the same person they fell in love with all those years ago. Even the physical diminishments of age or illness can't obliterate the ever-present memory of youthful beauty or extinguish the recollected spark of first passion. And even as bodies grow old and frail, there remains a powerful spiritual connection, an unwavering belief in the power of this union, a profound sense that each partner is far greater together than either could be alone.

That makes sense to me now. When I look at my husband these days, I see a sixty-three-year-old father of two grown sons, but I can also conjure the tender young groom who slipped a ring on my finger half a lifetime ago. Still, I had to laugh, thinking that if I could have had a glimpse on my wedding day of the two of us on our twenty-fifth anniversary, I would have been seriously underwhelmed: an aging guy in a sweaty tee shirt mowing the lawn; a pale, wrinkled woman with a severe case of bed-head, sprawled on the sofa.

And yet, the thing that surprised me on our anniversary was realizing just how content I felt with the way things were, even though the day itself was hardly what we'd hoped for. The celebratory dinner out can wait. And we already have the thing that really matters: twenty-five shared years, testament enough that ours is a love that will go the distance, for as many more years as time and fate will grant us.

Steve and the boys went out for pizza on our anniversary, and I stayed behind and sipped a cup of mint tea. When they got home, Steve sat down next to me in the kitchen, put his arm around me, and called me his "bride." And so it is that, in the best possible way, love truly is blind.

September 2012

——•—— I want to remember ——•——

I want to remember waking from the soft flannel nest of sleep beside my husband, pulling on warm clothes and stepping outside in the dark in time to see the day begin.

I want to remember the holy hush just before dawn, the mists rising out of the valley, the sharp, clear sky still pricked by the bright eye of Venus. I want to remember the way light returns slowly to the earth, taking its time. How it arrives at last from behind a curtain of rose and purple clouds. How glad I am to be here.

I want to remember the sudden up-rise of Canada geese bursting through the silence, honking and flapping and lifting into to the sky, oblivious to our astonishment. I want to remember their wild call as they jockeyed into a ragged V before shearing off through the clear veil of morning. The way my husband and I smiled at each other, silent, as we watched them go.

I want to remember the cold smell of my dog's coat when I bury my face in her neck, her silky hair so dry it fairly crackles. She is twelve. I want to remember everything.

I want to remember the September woods. The rich, smoky, earthy smells of nature concluding a season's business. I want to remember the great buttery clumps of mushrooms, such fecund, untouchable bounty. And when, exactly, did the pliant maple leaves grow brittle and thin enough to see through? How subtle was the moment when summer's green palette was exchanged for the golden hues of fall? I want to remember the exquisite turning of this page, as the blue-green hills I've gazed upon all summer begin now to glow with color. I want to remember the way, every hour, the scene repaints itself. We are heading toward brilliance, fleeting and irrepressible.

I want to remember the nasturtiums, how they came up everywhere this year, tumbling through the garden like handfuls of jewels, tossed and scattered with abandon. I want to remember the shy orange poppies, how all summer they held back, only to bloom now at the end of September, long after I'd given up all hope of them. I want to remember the greedy, glorious, rampant pink and violet petunias, spilling out of their pots, cascading over the steps, pushing forth through every barren crack in the walkway. I want to remember the hummingbird that comes each afternoon to drink their depths. I want to remember these days before frost lays claim to every fragile blossom.

I want to remember the industriousness of bees, the hum in the garden. I want to remember the slow undulation of a monarch's wings as it sips from a pink zinnia. I want to remember the robin splashing like a hedonist in the birdbath beneath a stand of exhausted sunflowers, their drooping, heavy heads plucked clean of seed. (I should cut them down, haul those useless stalks to the compost pile.) I want to remember how reluctant I am to see anything come to an end and how even now I leave the dead flowers standing there, patiently waiting for me to summon my resolve.

I want to remember the last breakfast on the screened porch, the penultimate bouquets, the hydrangeas drying on their curved stems, the end of peaches, the first Macouns from the trees up the road, the puckery sweetness of a Concord grape splitting on the tongue.

I want to remember Henry's oatmeal cookies and the rich buttery smells in the kitchen, Diana Krall singing "*Love Me or Leave Me*" as he washes dishes at the sink. I want to remember how good it is to have a son come home.

I want to remember my favorite sandwiches, made without bread: sliced Brandywine tomatoes and white mozzarella ovals and basil leaves still warm from the sun. I want to remember the briny grit of sea salt, and juice dripping off my elbows, and not minding.

I want to remember dozing in the lawn chair with a book in my lap as the first yellow leaves spin through the air. I want to remember days with windows wide open and the way cold seeps through the house as soon as the sun disappears behind the trees. I want to remember Henry practicing Rachmaninoff. I want to remember lighting candles at dinner again and how it feels to live in one place for five years, to feel one's own roots sinking into the earth. I want to remember that change is part of being alive. I want to remember to take time to sit in silence, to breathe into the still point, where past and future are invisibly gathered. I want to remember some lines by T. S. Eliot:

Neither movement from nor towards,
Neither ascent nor decline.
Except for the point, the still point,
there would be no dance,
and there is only the dance.

I want to remember that in the week before I turn fifty-four, I am vexed by a private catalog of imponderables. I want to remember that even these nearly perfect days and nights have been limned with sadness, punctuated by sleepless hours, a host of worries, questions without answers. I want to remember that sometimes I can set my troubles aside and choose instead to see my life as a blessing. I want to remember that surrender is always possible and that I can be sad and grateful at the same time. Filled up and emptied out, both. Even a heavy heart can overflow with contentment. I want to remember to keep my eyes open, to pay attention. Life is short. I want to

remember: this is it. There is only the dance.
September 2012

 —·— hard lessons —·—

I'm probably not the only person who abandons her good habits when life speeds up, or who fails to practice when practice is the only thing that might actually save me from myself. My guess is there are others like me, who get so frazzled and caught up in the stresses of events and obligations and misunderstandings that we don't even see the plain truth staring us in the face: there is another way. A small shift in perception, a different attitude, a quieter approach.

And yet, knowing I'm not alone and that failure is part of being human doesn't make it easier to confront my own shortcomings.

Writing this morning as the sky lightens, waiting quietly for words to come rather than rushing to get something down on paper, I realize what I'm really waiting for here is a glimpse of the thread that might lead me back to a better me. Or at least back to the person I still hope to be: reflective, aware, moving slowly and attentively in the world rather than racing through it, all sharp elbows and jangled nerves and oblivious hustle.

The dawn sky is peach and turquoise beyond the thinning canopy of golden leaves outside my bedroom window. The clock ticks steadily on the nightstand. Gracie sighs and stretches and goes back to sleep on the floor. My husband, away on a business trip, isn't here to see how quickly in his absence the other side of our bed becomes strewn with notebooks and pens, a wicker basket full of paperwork, a pile of books and pillows and half-done projects.

The day ahead is already pressing in—the housework I've postponed, a daunting list of book tasks and family tasks and outdoor tasks needing attention. A long drive to reconnect with a cherished college friend after a gap of nearly twenty years. It's tempting to leap out of bed and get started, to go tearing into the day, as if by moving faster I might actually come out ahead, might win the big race to some invisible, constantly shifting finish line. Or better yet, I might magically transform this scattered, over-committed schedule I've created into the artful, deliberate, simpler life I keep straining to achieve.

But looking back over the last week or so—a week of moving ever faster only to feel things slipping more and more out of control—I do at least know this: the best thing I can do, both for myself and for those I love, is to remain here propped among the bed pillows for a while longer. I can choose to start this day, at least, in stillness. And so I sit and look out the window, patiently allowing my heart its own slow refueling. Gratitude for things as they are seeps in slowly. It takes some patience to refill a soul, patience and a certain faith, too. Faith that the blessing I hunger for is already mine. I need only breathe in to receive it, exhale to offer it forth. Faith that grace isn't a prize to be earned or claimed but rather the gift of being alive, here, now, in this moment, no matter how many challenges await. Faith that who I am—this flawed and wanting human self—is enough. Faith that my life as it is—a little chaotic at the moment—is my life as it is meant to be. Faith that paying attention is my true spiritual practice. Kindness, my real work, invisible though it may be. And love, still the most creative and demanding path of all.

Practice, I know now, doesn't make perfect. The inescapable truth is that to live in this world is to both harm and heal. So is it really any wonder that we can sometimes bring the greatest pain to those we care about the most? This week, I deeply hurt a friend. The injury I caused was unintentional, but no less damaging for that. Tending to these wounds, flinching at the raw and tender places in a relationship that means the world to me, I wonder how to make amends. There's nothing to be gained by dissecting the errors of my ways all over again. That list is both painful and mundane. My own petty failings are nothing special. And, as poet Mary Oliver reminds us, "You want to cry aloud for your mistakes. But to tell the truth the world doesn't need any more of that sound."

What can I do but say, "I'm sorry"? And then it's up to me to bow low and accept forgiveness in whatever form it takes. To set down the heavy, awkward burden of shame and take up in its place the worthy work of paying closer attention. I am constantly humbled before all that I don't know. But I can at least move forward more gently, taking even greater care. I can commit all over again to love, to kindness, to the inestimable gifts of friendship, to this practice called being human.

What have I learned? Only to keep trying. And to be grateful for every second chance. Grateful for every opportunity to become more skillful in the demanding arts of living and accepting and loving.

October 2012

—·— carrying on —·—

It was little more than a fleeting inconvenience here, the mighty autumn storm that stole the homes and lives and livelihoods of so many others. Standing in my kitchen on Monday afternoon, the phone pressed to my ear, I watched as a brazen gust of wind lifted our storage shed right up from the ground and away, lodging it amid some roadside trees. Steve and Henry and I put on boots and raincoats and headed out into the gale, but there wasn't much at stake—a lawn mower, some flowerpots, bikes and gas cans and gardening tools. A neighbor stopped by and gave us a hand, and an hour later we had filled the basement and garage with our stuff, thrown our sopping clothes into the dryer, and settled down to listen to the wind and rain lashing the windows.

We ate soup at 5 on that wild, windy night, and by the time the power went out at 6, the dishes were already done. In the morning, with the lights back on and the clocks reset, we turned to the TV to see what was happening beyond our horizons. All week, the images of nature's devastation have scrolled across our screens. Having ascertained that friends and loved ones are alive and safe, we watch the news with a combination of horror and disbelief and grim fascination. How could this be happening? The heartbreaking scenes of fire, flooding, destruction, and loss are almost too much to assimilate here in the comfort of my own business–as–usual life.

The coffee drips and the heat kicks on and the laptop pings the arrival of e-mail, while not far from here, in homes and neighborhoods no different from this one, thousands of people still wait for the basics to be restored: water, lights, gasoline, phone lines.

"Overwhelmed emotionally," a friend typed at dawn this morning. Although she is fine, the city she called home for decades is not. How to make sense of that?

I'm not the only one who's lain awake this week in the grip of vague fear and nameless anxiety, safe and yet unsettled by the knowledge that while I snuggle into flannel sheets in a warm house, others go without.

"It seems almost like a betrayal," I said to Steve at breakfast this morning as we ate cereal and read the *New York Times,* "to have it so easy while so many others are suffering. I'm not even sure how to feel, other than helpless and lucky and sad all at once."This afternoon, another e-mail from a friend: "I just want to return those baby boys to their mother and the photographs to those who lost them and life to the man who was crushed by the tree. I want to do what can't be done."

That is surely the crux of it. Wanting to do what can't

be done, we're reminded that all life is fleeting, security an illusion, and suffering is part of the human condition.

Perhaps the only way to move beyond fear and helplessness is to cultivate a different response. Aware that we are, all of us, participants in this great ongoing dance of both living and dying, we can gently transform sorrow for all that's lost into gratitude for all that is. Awakened to the fragility of our own existence, we can't help but see things through fresh eyes: each moment is a new moment, life itself a gift. And any act of kindness, no matter how small, shines a bit more light into the darkness.

Compassion, it turns out, is a powerful antidote to help-lessness. And so I remind myself to simply stop and look around. There is always some way to be useful, someone nearby who could use a hand, a hug, a listening ear, some kind of sustenance, be it physical or spiritual or emotional.

"Anything you do from the soulful self," says activist and writer Clarissa Pinkola Estes, "will help lighten the burdens of the world. Anything. You have no idea what the smallest word, the tiniest generosity can cause to be set in motion."

She goes on to offer an assignment particularly suited for these chaotic and confusing times, one that just may be worth ordering an entire life around: "Mend the parts of the world that are within your reach. To strive to live this way is the most dramatic gift you can ever give the world." Slowly then, day by day and bit by bit, what is broken will surely be healed. Each and every part of the world is within someone's reach. Sometimes, our arms are even longer than we know. Meanwhile, with full hearts, we carry on. We do what we can to be of use. We work with what we have, from where we are.

November 2012

—·—— this life, here, now ——·—

Tomorrow night, for the first time in months, both our boys will be home, everyone sleeping in their own beds under one roof. And on Thursday afternoon we will gather round the table at my parents' house for Thanksgiving dinner with the whole extended family.

For well over forty years, with barely a miss, I've spent Thanksgiving in that same familiar kitchen, have eaten my dad's grilled turkey and homemade ice cream, my mom's pumpkin pie and peas and mashed potatoes. The cast of characters around the table has changed over time, of course. Various cousins and aunts and uncles and significant others and spouses have made entrances and exits. Dear loved ones have passed on and dear little ones have been born and grown up. And along the way each one of us has created our own enduring memories: walks in the woods between dinner and dessert; skating on the pond (long, long ago, when there was ice in November); a fiancé's first appearance at the table; a grandfather's final one; a grandmother's last apple pie; a baby who is suddenly grownup enough to sit with the adults; a sullen teenager miraculously transformed into a mature and engaging young man; an aunt and uncle determined to make a trip all the way from Florida so as not to miss the homemade gravy.

What's been constant through all those decades, through all those comings and goings and births and deaths, is the house itself. A house that somehow contains us all, not only the people who show up and the memories of people who are no longer with us, but also the stories that get retold year after year as the plates are passed. Of course, this house is also, to me, a symbol of our family and of my parents themselves, who even as they round the corner toward eighty, still manage to make a Thanksgiving feast with all the trimmings look effortless.

Each year, when my mom gets out her old gravy-stained notebook and begins her Thanksgiving countdown (pretty much the same to-do list, whether there are going to be eight of us at the table or thirty-eight, as there occasionally were in the old days), she pulls out the crayoned drawing my cousin Paul made thirty-five years ago, when he was seven; the one that says: "I love going to the Thanksgiving house." My mom adores that faded picture. She always sticks it up on the refrigerator, where she can see it as she cooks. And then, three days before we all show up for dinner, she gets busy, shopping for groceries, making stock, setting the table, brining the bird.

My parents are the keepers of the sugar-and-creamer set shaped like turkeys (which always grossed out my Uncle Chet, who didn't like to see milk pouring out of a ceramic gobbler). They have the ice-cream maker, the pie servers, the turkey platter, the covered dishes, the baster and twine, the big cutting board and carving set, plenty of dishes and silverware to go around. The tried-and-true recipes, annotated for crowds. The notes my mom has kept, religiously, about who came to dinner and what was said and who was missed this year. Thanksgiving, to her, isn't just a holiday. It's an archive. And it's a gift.

Even after all this time, my mother and father are happy to put the meal on the table for the rest of us—grown children, spouses, grandchildren, and assorted invited guests. All we have to do is show up and appreciate the day they gladly create for us—not only the food but, even more important, a spacious circle of togetherness. And so it happens that once again this week, my family will come together in the house that has been home base for all of us for decades. At the same time I can't help but think: it will not always be so.

At fifty-four years of age, I have yet to cook a turkey myself. Somehow, thanks to my mom's dedicated service in the Thanksgiving house year after year, this is one rite of passage I've managed to avoid. But the day will arrive when the baster will need to be passed. I think I'm going to take myself out of the running. Henry is going over to his grandmother's house tomorrow afternoon to give her a hand with the potatoes and the squash. He knows the drill, and I have a feeling he would be honored to inherit my mom's Thanksgiving notebook when the time comes.

For now, though, I don't want to contemplate the future, but to fully immerse myself in the present. Two grown sons both at home tomorrow night. A couple of too-short days.

Time set aside to slow down and take stock of all that is good. If I've taught my children anything about living well, I hope its an awareness that gratitude is not a given but rather a way of being, an attitude to be cultivated. It doesn't come packaged like the Stouffer's stuffing mix nor is it ensured by the name of the holiday. No, real "thanksgiving" requires us to pause long enough to feel the earth beneath our feet; to gaze up into the spaciousness of the sky above; and to stop and take a good, long, loving look at the precious faces sitting across from us at the dinner table.

Life can turn on a dime. Not one of us knows, ever, what fate has in store or what challenges loom just around the bend. But I do know that my own life is an interplay of light and shadow, blessings and losses, moments to be endured, and moments I would give anything to live again. I will never get them back, of course, can never redo the moments I missed or the ones I still regret, any more than I can recapture the moments I desperately wanted to hold onto forever. I can only remind myself to pay attention, and to say my prayer of thanks for the only thing that really matters: this life, here, now.

November 2012

—·— blessing —·—

Blessings. What happens when we begin to count them? The counting becomes a practice, the day becomes a poem, the list a prayer, life itself a gift.

sunrise
flannel sheets
spooning
bare skin on bare skin
cold water
hot water
peppermint soap
oatmeal
long underwear
iTunes
sturdy legs
running shoes
dogs
silence
online friends
close-by friends
new friends
forever friends
traditions
sons with jobs
nephews and nieces
oranges in a bowl
peppermint tea
tech support
hardcover books
1.50 reading glasses
a good haircut
a good partner
cardinals

clouds
stone walls
old trees
pink geraniums
piano music
faith
photos
grandmothers
grown children
little kids
handwritten notes
child pose
a new kitchen sponge
Mary Oliver
parents
laughter
magazines
folded towels
matched socks
candlelight
cloth napkins
soup
resilience
forgiveness
foot rubs
wrinkle cream
peppermint ice cream
chocolate sauce
sunset

stars
the moon
the sky
space
wonder
the words "good night"
flannel sheets
spooning
bare skin on bare skin
dreams
breath
today
tomorrow
this
now

Make a list of your own blessings. Feel the quiet pulse of gratitude.

November 2012

———•—— light, dark ——•———

Light. Last Sunday afternoon. The brief, brilliant sun bedazzling through the high window in the town-hall auditorium. The audience arriving, shedding coats, searching for friends. The musicians warming up on stage. Henry in his tux, a quick smile (just for me) as he files past to take his place on the risers, preparing to sing. My

neighbor Debbie sitting beside me, sharing her chocolate-chip cookies. Familiar faces in the crowd. Christmas
trees festooned with white lights, men in holiday sweaters
and red neckties, the lady selling homemade baked goods
at the table in the back, the rustle of programs, the golden
light, the expectant hush that hovers just before the first
note of song bursts through the silence and takes flight.

My son, who will turn twenty-three this week, standing
onstage before a packed house in our hometown. His deep,
sure tenor filling the room, filling my heart till it pushes
against my chest and overflows and I am brushing away
happy, astonished tears. All these years, and I've never once
heard this most private child of mine sing out loud—till
now, as he performs this deeply felt solo in a room packed
with people who have paid money to come.

Dark. The night before, crowding into the small room
at the funeral home, surrounded by family from near and
far. The photograph of my uncle as a young man himself,
crew-cut earnest and just out of school, gazing toward
an unknown future that would hold more than its share
of heartbreak. The small urn full of ashes, a fishing scene
etched onto the side, and above it that photo I've known
all my life, the same photo that hung on the parlor wall of
my grandmother's house alongside two more, a triptych
of brothers framed in gold and presiding silently there
through the long quiet afternoons of my childhood, when
I would study every ancestral image, every picture in the
crowded gallery of family likenesses.

Reassembling those memories to meet the present: the

familiar faces of aunts and uncles and cousins, each one softened and creased by age and time. It has been too long since I last saw them. My cousin's children, suddenly grown and confronting a new truth: even larger-than-life grandfathers die. (Wasn't it just yesterday that they were children running wild with my own boys through the frozen November field behind my parents' house?)

Anecdotes gathered up and shared haltingly. The unaccustomed effort of giving voice to what's hard and sad and lost. The three brothers who have suddenly become two, oldest and youngest, the one in between gone at seventy-one. An image in my mind from years ago: my big, brawny uncle with his sideburns and beard and aviator glasses, his inexhaustible supply of stories, holding forth at Thanksgiving dinner, spinning tales from events he remembered that everyone else had long since forgotten.

And then, later, the long trip home after the funeral, the stories, the meal, the farewell hugs and tears. Fighting to stay awake as my father drives down the empty highway. The odd sensation of being both a fifty-four-year-old mother of two grown sons and, at the same time, a child again myself, sitting alone in the back seat of my parents' car as if I were still ten years old, the backs of their heads, grayed now, yet as familiar to me as my own two hands.

Light. It is dusk. The only lamp on in the silent house is here, beside the sofa where I sit surrounded by evening shadows. I type these words slowly, from within a small, golden patch of brightness.

Dark. The paragraphs above, written early yesterday

morning, so trivial today, as the news of a mass elementary school shooting in a small town in Connecticut settles upon our shoulders like a heavy, black cloak of brutal knowing. Innocent children dead, families ripped apart, the nation shaken once again by violence beyond reason or comprehension. Grief and anger, the deep sense of failure and helplessness. Gratitude for a life that is intact intermingled with mourning for lives lost and for lives ruined.

Sun and shadow. Joy and heartache. Life and death. To be human is to become intimate with both darkness and light. It has always been so. Yet on this somber December day, we are asked to do even more: somehow we must carry on with our lives as they are—and, too, we must stop in our tracks, and look with clear gaze into the ruins.

How to respond to such a random, meaningless act of hatred? How to open ourselves to the grief caused by this rampage of mindless destruction? How to accommodate and embrace both the darkness and the light of today?

Perhaps there is no good answer, other than to honor the sanctity of life by loving more and loving better, whatever that means for each of us. Compassion is the thread that binds us to one another. Compassion is the balm that heals the soul. Compassion is the offering we carry to the altar of regret and anger and grief. Compassion is what clears our vision, so we may begin to see, even in the midst of the darkest and most unspeakable horror, the light of something larger than our own understanding at work. Compassion is what allows us to seek redemption in the midst of tragedy—to reach out a hand and step toward rather than away from, to act rather than to wait for others to act in our stead. Compassion is, perhaps, the point of the journey, both our purpose and our calling, the place where healing and hope for tomorrow resides. A reminder that in all its shadow and its light, this fragile, fleeting life is full of beauty and meaning nonetheless.

December 2012

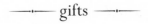

——— gifts ———

It is still dark as I write these words, though I've been awake for hours on this snow-hushed morning of the year's shortest day. Soon, I will turn lights on, make some coffee, let the dog out, confront the pile of unwrapped Christmas gifts in the basement. But here in the shadowed quiet before dawn, I'm thinking of gifts that aren't wrapped and placed under a tree. Gifts that are hidden within each of us, waiting to be brought forth and shared with the world.

This week, to celebrate Henry's birthday, our family went to see the dark, dazzling revival of *Pippin* at the American Repertory Theatre in Harvard Square. "How far will you go to be extraordinary?" the show's narrator asks Pippin, an aimless young man with oversized hopes and dreams who's desperate to find his "corner of the sky." Will he choose a life that's mundane and ordinary, or sacrifice all in exchange for one blazing moment of glory?

Last night we went to another production, right here in our

hometown: an abridged version of the medieval *Shepherds'* *Play*, performed in a plain church hall by members of our local life-sharing communities, men and women whose mental and physical challenges require special care in special homes devoted to their well-being.

On the surface, these two productions could not be more different. And yet, I'm thinking of the ways they are alike. Rehearsals for each began months ago. All fall, the actors in each committed themselves to the work of learning lines and music, preparing for their roles. And then, when the moment came to shine, every one of them got up on stage, took a long deep breath, and offered everything they had to give.

In the case of *Pippin:* death-defying, gasp-inducing acrobatics, soaring interpretations of the timeless Stephen Schwartz score, and a faithful re-creation of Bob Fosse's dazzling original choreography. Thrilling moments of pure, over-the-top theatrical magic and stripped-bare moments of aching, human vulnerability.

And at *The Shepherds' Play:* simple lines painstakingly re-cited (with some unobtrusive support from unflappable volunteers and patient staff members), age-old songs and foolproof comic bits, a few inevitable stumbles, and a few unexpected onstage tears. And, yes, here too, thrilling moments of theatrical magic and stripped-bare moments of aching, human vulnerability.

In the plush urban theater, my eyes filled as a young Broadway star sang an exquisite love song to the older woman who finally cracks open his heart. And in the dusty church hall, I wept again, as a stout, shy, young Mary hesitantly lifted her arms in silent rapture to receive the divine touch of an awkward, determined angel Gabriel, a Gabriel whose hair stuck up and whose mouth was a little odd and whose words were a little garbled, and whose white tunic didn't quite fit his gawky frame.

At the end of both of these plays, the audiences leapt to their feet. The ovations were long and heartfelt and joy-filled—our grateful human response to gifts shared openly, offered in good faith and with nothing held back.

There is, of course, no way to compare these two productions, the extravagant Broadway–bound musical and the humble, small-town pageant. One is not "better" than the other. They are both special, both worthy, both performed with all the love and courage their players had to offer. I wouldn't have missed either of them.

And side-by-side, they have set me to thinking. All year, I've been squirreling away presents in closets; yesterday, I was out in the stores, buying yet a few more. But today, as I wrap these gifts and put them under the tree, I realize how quick I am to judge my own gifts and find them wanting.

I love finding the perfect something for a friend, surprising a loved one with just the "right" treasure, taking time to spend with those near and dear, answering letters from strangers. I take deep satisfaction in sharing the books I love, the food I prepare, the seats at our dinner table, the hours in my day, the freshly made bed in the guest room.

Yet, I am much less sure when it comes to sharing the gift of myself. Looking at my book publication schedule of bookstore visits and library talks and public appearances in January and February, my stomach clenches into a tight little knot. Can I really go out and do all that? Will I sell enough books to make my publishers' efforts worth it? Will I disappoint readers who expect more than I can possibly deliver? Will people understand that just because I've written a book about growing older, I don't actually have all that much figured out? That I'm still grappling myself with losses and changes and questions that leave me at a loss for answers?

At the end of his two-and-a-half-hour search for fulfillment, Pippin discovers that his own "corner of the sky" isn't fame or fortune after all, but the place in his heart that's filled with love for others. His search ends not with a blaze of glory, but with acceptance of his own ordinary, unglorious and imperfect but truly compassionate self. He chooses a life that's authentic and meaningful to him, rather than a flashy trick to impress an audience.

The message hit home. As I watch my own two sons at twenty and twenty-three, each struggling in his own way to make sense of inchoate hopes and dreams, each wondering what mark he'll leave on the world, I do know what they cannot possibly have learned yet: it's the journey itself, not the destination, that matters most.

Only time and hard-won experience can teach them this lesson—that the more truth they are willing to risk along the way, the more courageously they are willing to give of themselves, the more they will have to offer. And, of course, each time they do step forward and bring their own humble gifts into the world, the more they will receive in return.

Perhaps that's exactly the reminder I need myself at this vulnerable moment before my new book arrives in bookstores. And perhaps this is my task for now: to remember that my job over these next few months isn't to judge the worthiness of my gift, but to find the courage to show up and offer it.

For what, after all, do any of us really want from one another? Certainly it is not more stuff. Nor is it perfection or foolproof answers or secondhand wisdom. We want more presence, not more presents. And the most valuable gift we have to give is, always, the unvarnished, unadorned truth of who we really are. Joy comes when we are both courageous and generous—brave enough to be who we are, and as generous with the gift of our own flawed, vulnerable, unique selves as we are with the gifts we wrap up in pretty paper and ribbons and bows.

December 2012

Time offers this gift in its millions of ways,
turning the world, moving the air, calling, every morning,
"Here, take it, it's yours."
— William Stafford

—·— pub date reflections —·—

We were an unlikely pair, Olive Ann Burns and I.

She was sixty, a gentle, charming, Southern housewife with dreams of finally publishing the enormously long novel she'd spent years writing—years when cancer and chemotherapy and its complications had kept her confined to her house, and the joy of creating characters she loved had kept her going.

I was twenty-five, an earnest, aspiring New York editor who was certain I'd just discovered my first prize in the slush pile. "Cold Sassy Tree *could become a classic,*" I confidently predicted in my typewritten manuscript report. *"It needs some cutting, but we MUST publish it."*

Not quite ready to trust my eager enthusiasm, my boss had his wife read the manuscript, too. She agreed with me. And so it was that Olive Ann became a first-time author and, in doing so, allowed me to become a first-time editor.

In the process, we became friends. In those more leisurely, pre-Internet days (this was 1983), she typed long,
chatty letters to me, full of anecdotes about her family
and friends in Atlanta. Thrilled to be engaged in an actual
"literary correspondence," I answered every one. We spoke
on the phone, too, nearly daily for months, as she revised
and as I cut pages, both of us trying to whittle her 640-page
novel down to a more manageable size. (I wanted to excise
what I called "the dying stories," long, rambling, invari-
ably funny accounts of the demises and funerals and burials
of various minor characters and their relatives. Olive Ann
insisted that every Southerner appreciated a good dying
story, and that my failure to do so was just evidence of my
constrained Yankee heritage. We compromised.)

Olive Ann's book was a hit, and it did become something
of a minor classic, assigned in schools all over the South,
featured on Oprah long before the advent of her first book
club, and made into a movie starring Faye Dunaway. Sales
were brisk. And Olive Ann was in demand everywhere.
After all those years of being confined to her sickbed, she
was thrilled to be in remission from cancer and delighted
to clip on her dangly earrings, put on a sparkly scarf, and
go forth to meet her fans.

"I'm a ham!" she would proudly announce to her adoring
audiences. And then she would entertain them for an hour,
telling wildly improbable yet, she swore, absolutely true
stories in her soft Southern drawl.

I was thinking of Olive Ann this morning, as I sponged

down the kitchen counter and swept the sand off the mud-room floor. Although she died in 1990, I can summon the sound of her voice still, that musical intonation, her way of turning everything into a story you wanted to hear.

Houghton Mifflin hosted an elegant party in Atlanta on the day *Cold Sassy Tree* was published, and I got to fly down from our New York office for the big event. Rosalynn Carter was there, and various other luminaries and sophisticates. I finally met "my" author for the first time in person and was startled by how beautiful she was. (She admitted to being a little surprised by the looks of me, too. "Why, I thought you would be chubby," she said. "You have a chubby voice.")

But what I remember most vividly was Olive Ann's admission that night that, even though she was all dressed up and the star of her own glamorous party, with people lining up to get her to sign their books, there was still no escaping the ordinariness of her real life.

"I thought that when I became an au-u-u-thor," she said, drawing out the word, "it would be like in a fairy tale, and I would turn into, well, a princess. So I was kind of surprised this morning when I looked down at my feet and realized I still had to cut my toenails!"

Indeed. My book *Magical Journey* is officially published today. I've been on the radio since 7 am this morning and I'll be in my car driving north to a bookstore luncheon tomorrow. There's a party on Saturday night, and the next day I'll fly to Nashville to give a reading at Ann Patchett's bookstore. My calendar for the next two months is full of travel and appointments and appearances. Exciting, nervous-making, exhausting. And to me right now it's all a little unreal.

At the moment, however, I'm sitting on the couch, looking at my own toenails. I should absolutely give them a trim. Meanwhile, there are few other things on my plate as well: Jack's college essay needs another read, the dog's butt is stinky, there's something wrong with the printer, and the car is due for an oil change. The kitchen floor needs vacuuming. We are out of milk. This is my day. This is my life—pub day or not. Thank goodness. And thank-you Olive Ann, wherever you are, for reminding me to keep my feet on the ground and my toenails looking nice.
January 2013

—·— magic —·—

Just over a year ago, I hit the wall. I'd been writing for months, throwing away more pages than I kept, feeling less sure of myself and what I was doing with every passing day. I had a deadline, the end of March. But I wasn't at all sure I had a book.

Two days after New Year's, with both sons back at school, I flew to Florida and set up camp in the guest bedroom of my parents' house there. My mom, keeping her promise not to tempt me with distractions, went about her care-free retiree's life. Meanwhile, I holed up in my self-created bunker, sitting cross-legged on the bed for hours on end, bent over my laptop, pretending no one would ever read what I was writing. My immediate goal was not to send words out into the world, but to be quiet and disciplined and attentive enough to find out if I actually had anything to say.

Now, twelve months later, the book that finally began to take shape during those weeks is in the bookstores. The irony of the title *Magical Journey,* of course, is that I didn't actually go much of anywhere, except in search of a bit of solitude and silence. Sometimes the most challenging journeys aren't the ones that require backpacks and sturdy shoes, but rather a willingness to turn inward, to seek something deep and as yet unknown within ourselves. And sometimes, as the last two weeks have revealed to me, it is the work done in lonely isolation that ultimately forges and affirms our most essential human connections out in the world.

This morning, home again after a flurry of travel and bookstore appearances, I paged through the journal I kept last winter. Every day, I attempted to clear my mind and face my fears by writing longhand in a notebook before turning on my laptop and confronting my manuscript. A few excerpts from those uncertain days exactly a year ago:

I am so slow. What I've written is probably not terrible. I'm trying to convince myself that it is at least good enough. Yet moving forward feels really hard. What is the right attitude? Maybe just to try to keep on writing without judging, to think my thoughts and feel my feelings, and get something down on the page, and then decide later whether it's any good or not.

And this:

The slowness, the uncertainty. What am I learning from this process? That in my writing, first and foremost, I must put my faith in the truth. That the truth is mundane, embarrassing at times, difficult to distill clearly, yet still worth reaching for. That the only way through is through. That writing doesn't get easier, at least not for me. That living wholeheartedly can mean going within rather than without. Not fun, exactly, but wholehearted nonetheless.

And also:

So strange to be in a time of life, a place, where Steve and Henry and Jack can all be living separate lives in different places. They are doing just fine away from me. I'm the one who feels the loss of all that used to be. All I used to be. Guess that's what it's been like for my own mom for years now. Perhaps I'll get used to it. I feel alive in different ways—alive when I'm needed at the center of my family, making dinner or having a heart-to-heart with one of the boys, keeping all the balls in the air. And alive in a totally different way now, in solitude, when all the structure and to-dos fall away and I'm left with my own thoughts, my own demons and dreams, my own not-so-pretty inner landscape. Time slows way, way down. There is nothing to do right now but honor my commitment to keep at this, uncomfortable and hard as it is. But I wonder: to write from this vulnerable place, to be who I really am on the page—can even this be some kind of path or calling? Perhaps, for now anyway, it is. And perhaps, if I can just stick it out, it will at least lead me back out of myself, with some sense of where I'm meant to go next.

Yesterday, my friend Dani Shapiro, wrote a thoughtful piece about the difference between taking risks in life and on the page. Most of us, as she points out, will go to any length to keep our loved ones safe. Learning how to assess risk is part of growing up. Making prudent calls is at the heart of every mother's job description. And yet, says Dani, "When it comes to the writer's life, risk is what it's all about."

She's right. We have to step out on that high wire again and again, even though we teeter with every step, even though we're dogged by insecurity: "Maybe it won't work. . . . Maybe it will be really awful. Maybe I'll waste my time and all this energy pointlessly, on work that will be dead on arrival."

I don't suppose there's any way to avoid the inexorable loneliness of the process, the feelings of frustration and powerlessness that come at the end of a day in which the only thing you really accomplished was staying put in your chair. Still, I wish that when I was sitting alone in that Florida bedroom, I could have flashed myself forward a year, just for a glimpse of the joyous scene last week in a hotel room in Nashville.

All the women from my book group had flown in earlier in the afternoon to celebrate the launch of *Magical Journey* with me and to attend my reading at Ann Patchett's beautiful bookstore, Parnassus. On that first evening, we were all gathered together, toasting our trip, our thirteen years of books and lives shared, and the publication of this new memoir of mine—despite the fact that the work of writing it had kept me from attending a single one of our meetings last year.

The conversation soon turned to vulnerability and risk and the importance of sharing our stories, even the painful ones. After all these years together, we trust one another completely and hold little back, knowing that we can close the door and bare our souls in safety. And yet, as my friends began to share their own first reactions to my book, we found ourselves talking as well about taking risks in public and on the page. And how, perhaps, in taking some risks myself, I've cleared a space in which other women might be more willing to share their own stories, or at least come to feel a little less alone.

This, it seems to me, is the reason any writer undertakes the speculative work of memoir. Not so much to tell "what happened," as to illuminate the slow, halting process by which we learn to make our peace with what happened. And in that vulnerable revealing, in the stumbling, wayward truth of that story, lies something worth offering: not the gift of what we've accomplished or survived or learned, but rather the gift of who we really are.

To be vulnerable on the page is indeed a risk—hang yourself out on the line and anyone can come along and take a swing at you. Yet my own experience over these last two weeks has been the opposite. People are kind. And words build bridges between us. As I've met and talked with readers in Connecticut and Nashville and Washington, DC, and as I've read and responded to the letters and Facebook messages and e-mails from strangers, I've been moved deeply by the stories women have shared with me, joyful stories of change and growth, but also intimate stories of loss and hardship, suffering and grief. Stories told in confidence within this safe space, a space created by kinship and kindness and courage.

Publishing a book, any book, is an act of faith—in oneself, yes, but in one's readers even more. How humbling and gratifying it is to have that faith returned a thousandfold.

I would not want to relive last January, all those days spent, as Dani so aptly puts it, "in the teeming, writhing darkness," trying to beat back my own self-doubt long enough to make something lasting and sturdy out of words. But I'm glad now that I did it. What I'm learning, I think, is something one of my favorite writers, Anne Morrow Lindbergh, knew all too well.

"I do not believe that sheer suffering teaches," she writes in *Gift from the Sea*. "If suffering alone taught, all the world would be wise, since everyone suffers. To suffering must be added mourning, understanding, patience, love, openness, and the willingness to remain vulnerable."

This, it seems to me, is the central work of any writer: finding something of value to add to the suffering. Sometimes, yes, it is isolating, to dwell in that place of risk and revelation. And yet what we find on the other side is so worth the effort: community, connection, kinship, healing. Nothing less than the road back to grace.

January 2013

———·—— guideposts ——·———

Before the first winter snow flies here in New Hampshire, some of us pound bright orange stakes into the ground alongside our driveways to remind us later, after the landscape is blanketed in white, of exactly where the pavement ends and the lawn begins. Nothing fancy, just a few metal rods, perhaps with a reflector at the top, to keep the plow or the snowblower from straying off track. They are, quite literally, guideposts.

As I sit in my bedroom today making notes for a talk I'll give to a group of parents on the West Coast on Tuesday, I realize that some of the words of wisdom that have shaped me as a mother are really the spiritual equivalents of those guideposts poking up through the snow: truths that keep me on track when the familiar landscape of our family life is suddenly altered by some challenge or unexpected turn in the emotional weather.

It's so easy, when things get stormy around here, to lose my way. But if being the mother of two sons has taught me anything, it's that weather passes and that control is an illusion anyway. Still, it helps to have some markers pounded into the earth, words that remind me of where I want to put my feet, of the solid ground I know is there for me, just beneath the blinding swirl of whatever's coming down.

Attachment to outcome has probably been my own biggest challenge on the parenting path. Little wonder then that my central task as a mother seems to be learning to let go of my expectations about the way I think life *ought* to be. I can get quite caught up in really, really wanting things to be a certain way for my children. Or in wanting my children to behave in certain ways that would make life more comfortable for *me*.

When I catch myself trying to control things that aren't mine to control or wishing that reality would just match up with my own idealized image, I always have to pause, regroup, and remind myself that this is another opportunity to practice the art of nonattachment. At the heart of it, attachment is all about refusing to accept the cards in my hand at any given moment. It's about wanting something different, something *better*. And when my mind is clinging tightly, it's hard to let go. Hard to believe there's actually a certain beauty in surrender. Hard to believe that things will work out or that, indeed, they already have.

And so I look to the wisdom of others to remind me of what I already know but tend to forget when the emotional weather turns tumultuous: I can love and care for my children, but I can't possess them. I can lend a compassionate ear when they ask for one, but I mustn't try to draw a roadmap for the lives I want them to lead. I can support them and pray for them and wish them well, but in the end their happiness and suffering will depend on their choices and their destinies, not on my wishes.

Paradoxically, as I remind myself to let go of attachment, I'm met with a deeper sense of the ways we are all interconnected—both in our suffering and in our longing for peace. I become a better mother—a more curious, more resilient mother—every time I release my grip on my own narrow little story of how things should be and open up instead to reality, in all its flawed, glorious, challenging beauty.

It surprises me a little to notice that none of the quotes that help keep me on track as a parent actually come from books about parenting. But perhaps that's as it should be. For the most important lesson this journey of motherhood has taught me is that my children are not extensions of me, and my real work isn't about changing them or shaping them into the people I think they ought to be. It's about changing *myself*—learning to soften, learning to trust, learning to accept myself as I am and my children as they are. And buried deep within that surrender is a jewel I've had to dig deep to find: the faith I need to let them go.

So, here are the guideposts I've placed along my own path, to keep me moving in the direction I aspire to travel. What words serve as *your* guideposts on this journey?

some words for the journey

To bow to the fact of our life's sorrows and betrayals is to accept them; and from this deep gesture we discover that all life is workable. As we learn to bow, we discover that the heart holds more freedom and compassion than we could imagine.
—Jack Kornfield

A feeling of aversion or attachment toward something is your clue that there's work to be done.
—Ram Dass

I try to remind myself that we are never promised anything, and that what control we can exert is not over the events that befall us but how we address ourselves to them.
—Jeanne DuPrau

It has something to do with submitting rather than dominating. Surrender, submit. Have faith, trust in the mystery. That's not easy. Surrendering one's life to living in, and serving, the beauty of a mysterious world is a big step. The purpose of the journey is compassion.
—Joseph Campbell

What we need, and what we love, what consoles and what redeems us, is here each moment, already within us. It waits for us to recognize its presence. We have only to give ourselves up to it, and our one life, and all life, welcomes us into its arms.
—John Tarrant

The only path to forgiveness is learning to see the world through different eyes. The world will not change; we must change. We must find a way to replace yearning for what life has withheld with gratitude for what we have been given.
—Kent Nerburn

We must love our children for themselves, and not for the best of ourselves in them, and that is a great deal harder to do. Loving our own children is an exercise in imagination.
—Andrew Solomon

February 2013

—·—— free empathy ——·—

Perhaps it was his eyes, the kindness there, the depth of his gaze. Or maybe it was the quality of his listening, the way he seemed to hear with his whole body, leaning in to catch every word.

His lined face held no judgment, no impatience or tension or hint of boredom. Nothing but love. Waves of people surged by on the busy sidewalk, laughing and chatting, but his attention never wavered from the young woman who sat across the table from him, pouring out her tale. I'm pretty sure he didn't even notice me when I paused, and then hesitated before snapping a photo, uncertain about intruding on this very public and yet strangely intimate exchange.

Home at last from two weeks on the West Coast, I find myself still thinking abut this man who sits at a card table on the bustling, hippest street in Santa Cruz and openheartedly gives himself away. "Free Empathy" his sign says. And, indeed, there is not so much as a cup or a hat or a money box in sight, no way to pay for his compassion even if someone wanted to.

Free empathy. I wonder if there is any greater gift, any exchange between two people, that could be more valuable than this?

Free empathy. Nothing less than an offer of refuge, of rest, of acceptance: you are safe here, your story matters to me, and you are ok, just as you are.

Free empathy. A promise to bear loving witness to another's struggle.

Free empathy. A reminder that we won't save the world with big gestures or grand schemes, but by becoming better listeners. By asking how someone else is doing, and then taking time enough to put ourselves in that person's shoes, to see the world through that person's eyes.

Free empathy. One precious natural resource that is in short supply and yet endlessly renewable.

February 2013

———·——— waiting ———·———

You could say, we are waiting here.

Waiting to find out which colleges will accept Jack for next fall. (So far, one yes, one no, one wait list.) Waiting to see what choices he'll have and which choice he'll make for this second time around. Waiting—after a year of his working and living on his own—for him to decide once and for all that he actually does need to continue his education. Waiting to see if the next round of x-rays will show further healing in his two broken vertebrae. Waiting in the hope that his lingering, chronic pain will someday, finally, disappear altogether. Waiting to find out if he'll be able to play tennis again or have to content himself with being a passionate fan. Waiting to learn which doors have closed in his young life and which have yet to open before him.

We're waiting to hear if the job Henry has his heart set on will pan out. Waiting for the musical he's codirecting to be performed. Waiting to know where he'll be working for the summer. Waiting to find out where he'll be living next year. Waiting to see if he's going to need a car. Waiting for him to decide whether grad school is still part of the picture. Waiting to see if the pull of a someday-maybe Broadway dream turns out to be as powerfully alluring as the illusion of security conferred by a paycheck and a plan.

We are waiting for two young adults' ever-shifting and unknowable futures to become the nailed-down and predictable present tense, for dreams to become reality, hopes to be realized, expectations fulfilled, applications accepted or denied, next steps executed, job offers revealed, life to turn this way or tha———t. It feels like a challenge, all this waiting— until the moment when I suddenly see it as the privilege it is.

A letter arrives from a reader who has lost a child. I turn the calendar to March and realize it's been ten years since my dear friend Lisa's son was killed three months before his college graduation. I open the newspaper and read a headline: "BU student dies at party." A new friend on Facebook posts that, had her daughter lived, she would be turning twelve today. I find myself in tears as I read Emily Rapp's fiercely moving memoir of parenting her son Ronan, who died of Tay-Sachs disease last month, just shy of his third birthday.

"Life is long," I like to tell myself. But of course, that isn't always true. Everything will turn out for the best, we assure our children and ourselves. But that's not always the case either. Sometimes life is cut short. And sometimes the most beautiful, worthy dreams are derailed by tragedy. Sometimes children get sick or hurt and sometimes they leave us. How foolish and naive, to think we think we can skim along on the surface of life without cultivating, at the same time, an intimate relationship with its dark and unknown depths. And how much we sacrifice when we trade the quiet, unobtrusive pulse of the moment that is right here, right now, for the false promise of some brightly imagined future.

Last night, while Henry and his dad watched the Celtics game on TV, I climbed into bed with Emily Rapp's memoir, *Still Point of the Turning World.* Ronan's brief life was never about making progress or racking up achievements. He was only nine months old when his parents were told their baby boy was going to die. Emily's task, then, wasn't ever to prepare her son to succeed in the world, but to love him just as he was for as long as he was here. Somehow, every moment of her mothering had to contain multitudes: both the joy of being Ronan's mom and the grief of letting him go.

Perhaps there is no one better suited to speak to us distracted, harried, future-oriented parents than a mother who has had no choice but to live in the "now" and to embrace her child in the moment because he will not live long enough to have a "someday."

"How does the knowledge that nothing lasts forever and that all of our time is limited change the way we approach the world?" Emily asks.

And then, like the best spiritual mentors, she answers her own unanswerable question with more questions: "Will we be fearless in our pursuit to live a life we consider big and beautiful, no matter what other people might think of our choices and no matter what difficult changes we might have to make? How does this knowledge affect the way we parent? Not knowing what tomorrow will bring, would we be so concerned with our children's 'progress' and perhaps more interested in activities that simply make them happy?"

The sun is rising as I type these words, pouring light into the sky after two days of snow. In a few minutes, I'll shut down my computer, take a shower, go out for blueberry pancakes with my husband and older son. Later today, I'll do a reading at the bookstore in the town where I grew up. I'll hold up the twelve-foot-long piece of blue finger-knitting that Jack did when he was five, giving me the title for my first book, *Mitten Strings for God,* which contained everything I knew as a young mother about slowing down and paying attention. And then I'll drive to the bus stop and pick up my twenty-year-old son and bring him back to the house for dinner. We'll light the candles, hold hands for a moment before we start to eat, say "Blessings on the meal and each other."

I will mention, as I always do when we're all home together, how happy I am to have everyone at the table. My husband will agree, and our sons, who have yet to fully comprehend that each human life is a progression of farewells, will roll their eyes and remind me that I always say that.

And then I'll remind *myself:* there is nothing to wait for. All we need, we have.

March 2013

———·——— quiet days ———·———

You have traveled too fast over false ground;
Now your soul has come to take you back.
Take refuge in your senses, open up
To all the small miracles you rushed through.
Become inclined to watch the way of rain
When it falls slow and free.
Imitate the habit of twilight,
Taking time to open the well of color
That fostered the brightness of day.
Draw alongside the silence of stone
Until its calmness can claim you.
—*John O'Donohue,* from "A Blessing for One Who Is Exhausted"

Hard as it is for my mom to be away from her elderly, beloved cocker spaniel for a few hours, let alone three days, she couldn't bear the thought of not being present for her sister's grandson's wedding up north this weekend.

My Aunt Gloria's been gone for three years. But this winter, my mother says, has been harder than the first one without her. She is missing her big sister more these days, not less. Being with her extended family, staying in a hotel with my dad in Newport, watching the first grandson take a bride—none of that would fill in the hole carved by loss, but it would make her feel a bit closer to her sister and remind her she wasn't alone in missing her. Of course, she was torn between going and staying home with her dog.

"I'll come down there and take care of Justin, so you

can go to the wedding," I promised her weeks ago, happy to fill in some empty March days on my calendar with a trip to Florida and grateful for any excuse to have a visit with my mom.

"Words Justin knows (but can't hear)," she wrote in the extensive care-and-feeding manual she left for me. "Sit. Stay. Off." Justin is sweet-natured, half blind, deaf, and above all else, a creature of routine: up to pee at 5 am, breakfast at 5:03, back to bed till 7, dinner at 4:30, a walk at dusk, playtime, bed. During the day, between periodic call-of-nature visits to a small circle of bleached crabgrass in the backyard, he sleeps.

"I'm looking forward to this," I assured my mother as she packed her suitcase on Friday. "I've been going non-stop since December. Three days alone, with no human being who needs me for anything, will be a luxury."

I meant it. It feels as if the only conversation I *haven't* had lately is one with myself. So, coming to the end of a couple of months of book-tour events, I had my own plans for the weekend: disconnect totally and do nothing. I would read, think, write in my journal. I liked the idea of hanging out with myself, of allowing my soul to welcome me back.

And what a relief it would be, I was certain, to just close up shop on my own busy life for a couple of days. I vowed to take a technology holiday—leave my laptop asleep in its case, my phone on vibrate, my e-mails unread, incoming texts unanswered, my Facebook status unchanged, my Amazon sales figures unchecked.

Yesterday, all alone in my mother's house, I erected my

cathedral of quiet.

And then, moment by moment, I struggled to live inside it. All day long, I fought against the uneasy, unfamiliar discomfort of keeping company with my own silent, non-doing self. It's pretty humbling to realize I've grown so accustomed to distraction and busyness that it's a challenge to simply stop in one place and be, to inhabit an empty space in time without giving in to the impulse to fill it up with something.

For some time now, I've been in high gear, doing not only my normal everyday stuff (shopping, cooking, cleaning, mothering) but also the adrenaline-rush stuff of traveling, giving readings and talks, connecting, and promoting—what I've come to think of as the job of being a person who's written a book. It's been a privilege to visit bookstores all over the country and a joy to hear from readers, to receive so many thoughtful letters, to meet new friends and reconnect with old ones. At the same time, I have to wonder: have I become so used to being connected somewhere, to something, all the time, that making a deliberate choice to unplug and shut up, even for a day or two, has become difficult?

"Stop," I kept reminding myself yesterday, each time I reflexively reached for my phone, "just to check my e-mail," until at last I did force myself to hide it out of sight in a drawer.

Pausing just to *be* sounds simple enough in theory, but it can be surprisingly hard. Making a choice to inhabit a windswept interior emptiness rather than trying to stuff it full of mental furniture feels awkward, even a little scary.

"Is this all there is?" my busy mind kept demanding,

casting about for something, anything, to do or to worry about or to click or fixate upon.

Having grown used to velocity as my automatic response to complexity, I've become pretty efficient when it comes to getting things done, but somewhat less graceful, apparently, in repose. Give me a to-do list and I know how to power through to the bottom line. But even competence comes at a cost. Give me a day without an Internet connection or a deadline or a self-imposed goal to be met or a finish line to cross, and all my self-doubts come rushing out to meet me, jostling for position, demanding to be seen and heard.

I floundered around for a while, at odds with myself, rubbed raw by the rough edges of my own solitude. It was hard to sit still, hard even to focus deeply and completely on the pages of the book I very much wanted to read. I did some yoga and tried to match slow steady breaths to slow steady movements. I took the dog for a walk, frittered the hours away, spoke to no one. I didn't try to get Justin to read my lips, as my mom does, or engage in doggie small talk he couldn't hear, just to break the silence. I resisted the urge to e-mail a friend, to text my sons, call my husband, or turn on the TV and catch up on *Downton Abbey*.

In the end, I stretched out in a lawn chair, put down my book, and gazed up into the turquoise expanse of sky. Finally, time slowed down. Finally, I felt something inside me begin to soften and settle.

This morning, I've been reading a memoir called *Until I Say Good-bye,* by Susan Spencer-Wendell, who was diagnosed with ALS two years ago, at the age of forty-four.

Knowing she had, at best, one good year of life left, Susan made a deliberate choice: to plant a garden of memories for her beloved husband and their three young children, and to cultivate joy in whatever time remained for her.

She wrote her book in three months, painstakingly using her one good finger to type into the Notes function on her iPhone. By the time she was finished, she had lost her mobility, her voice, nearly everything except her courage, her consciousness, and her conviction that although she had no control over her illness, she could control the attitude she brought to her approaching death.

Certain the greatest gift she can give her family is her own acceptance of her fate, Susan is facing the end head on. As her book makes its way in the world, she is preparing, with little fanfare, to leave it. "I am not gone," she writes. "I have today."

Last week, following up an earlier NPR interview conducted a few months ago when she could still speak, Scott Simon asked Susan how she is doing. Her written reply to him was simple, straightforward, and moving: "As well as can be expected. My body and voice become weaker every single day, but my mind becomes mightier and more quiet. You do indeed hear more in silence."

She is right, of course. And so, with gratitude now, and a good bit more ease than I felt yesterday, I sit outside at my mother's quiet house, beneath the rustling palms, and watch the sun go down. I receive John O'Donohue's words of blessing into my being and feel what it means to imitate the habit of twilight. I wonder whether, if I abide here long enough, a well of color might somehow open within me, too, just as the evening sky itself grows diaphanous at last light, the clouds translucent veils of rose and gold and mauve.

March 2013

————•—— full house, full heart ——•————

I've sometimes wondered if I'll spend the rest of my life missing my sons as the little boys they used to be. Even now, though it's been years since I reminded anyone to look both ways, the sight of a mom crossing the street hand-in-hand with a little guy with sleep-tufted hair and rolled-up jeans fills my eyes with sudden tears.

Arriving at an elementary school to give a talk one morning not long ago, watching parents bending low to kiss their children good-bye, observing the sea of bobbing backpacks, the bright art on the walls, the exuberance of six-year-olds beginning their day, I was so overcome with emotion that I had to slip back out to my car for a few minutes and compose myself. Still, standing up at the podium in that room full of young mothers, I wasn't quite sure I could trust my voice.

"Do you *know*," I wanted to say to them, "how quickly this will all be over? Do you realize just how sweet and rich your lives are right now? How fleeting?"

Of course, this is what older people have been saying to younger ones since time began. And no one wants to hear it.

Busy, distracted, wondering how to schlep the kids from point A to point B and pick up some food for dinner and get the homework done without too much of a fuss, an overstretched, overtired parent isn't worrying about the end of childhood so much as how to survive the hours between three in the afternoon and bedtime. I know that. I've been that mom, too.

But it's been a while since we had two boys still living at home full time, and what I'm most aware of now is not how endlessly long those days could be, but how quickly those years flew by. Adjusting to my new empty-nest reality, after over two decades of 24/7 mothering, has been a painstaking, bittersweet process.

At times my nostalgia for our family life as it used to be—for our own imperfect, cherished, irretrievable past—is overwhelming. The life my husband and children and I had together, cast now in the golden light of memory, seems unbearably precious; what lies ahead, darker and lonelier and less certain.

When I wrote those words just two years ago, I couldn't imagine ever feeling differently. Even as my days slowly filled with new joys and occupations, I felt as if I also lived in the shadow of that darker, lonelier future. With both my sons grown and away at school, I wondered if any as-yet-unwritten life chapter could ever feel quite as *right,* quite as challenging and fulfilling, as those years of intense, day-in-day-out togetherness.

It is such a raw and relentless business, motherhood. There is the constant physical engagement, at once exhilarating and exhausting. But there is also the vehement, insistent emotion: the frightening, thrilling ferocity of our love for these souls we've delivered into the world. How many times was I brought to my knees by the visceral intimacy of tears and blood and poop, fevers and sweats and strange skin rashes, sibling battles and wild nightmares and crazy, irrational fears? And then, within the same hour sometimes, I would be lifted right up again, exalted and turned inside out by the accidental, extravagant grace of wild laughter or a whoop of glee, a whispered confession, a cuddle, an imponderable question, a kiss delivered to an elbow or a knee (why *there??*), some random joke without a punch line that made us all giggle anyway. When all of that ended, when first one son and then the other had the audacity to grow up and leave the nest, I was sure our family life would never again be quite as good.

Last weekend, both our boys were home. We had about three feet of snow on the ground and not much of an agenda—a lot of March Madness basketball on the TV, a couple of family dinners, unplanned hours. I made chicken potpie from scratch. Jack (a pretty skilled body worker after three years of interning at a studio in Boston) offered to get me up on the massage table and work on my stiff muscles. For an hour he patiently stretched and manipulated my arms, neck, and shoulders, with assurance and attentiveness.

On Sunday morning we went to church and listened to Henry play the organ—an intermittent job when he's at home. As the light poured in through the tall windows, as the choir sang the Palm Sunday anthem he'd chosen and rehearsed with them, I was flooded with memories of our son as a little boy straining to reach the foot pedals, practicing hymns on our old upright piano in the living room. But the tears that sprang to my eyes then weren't tears of longing for what was, but of gratitude for all that's come to be.

The journey between dreaming and becoming, between childhood and adulthood, doesn't end, of course, when the kids head off for school or leave home or embark on careers or marriages. It is ongoing, full of twists and turns, detours and disappointments, surprises and sudden revelations. Who knew that what seemed like a catastrophic loss for one son—expulsion from school, freshman year of college missed, two broken vertebrae and constant, chronic pain—would inspire this impulsive teenager who once fantasized about being a tennis star to become a compassionate healer instead? And how could we have ever imagined that the shy, dreamy child who seemed almost too frail for this world at times, would one day grow up to be a competent, self-assured music director, perfectly at ease performing in front of a congregation and coaching singers four times his age? We couldn't imagine or foresee it, not any of it. We just had to live it.

In the afternoon last Sunday, between basketball games and my marathon in the kitchen, Steve and the boys and I put on our boots and took a walk, our favorite loop through the woods. Gracie trotted ahead, glancing back every few steps as if she couldn't quite believe her good fortune. For a border collie, heaven is having your entire herd in the same place at the same time—ideally, out in the woods and sticking close together. I knew how she felt. I was happy, too.

In fact, as we tramped along the path it suddenly occurred to me that I wouldn't turn the clock back now even if I could. Not for one hour, not for one day, not for one year or ten. Not for anything. It hit me with the power of epiphany: this sudden, unexpected end to the nostalgic longing I've carried like a bruise upon my heart for so long that I'd nearly forgotten what true ease in the here and now feels like.

Who we are, what we are, where we are at this moment is different from what was, absolutely. But it is in no way less than. And the surprising truth is, I seem to be done with looking longingly in the rearview mirror. I wouldn't trade our family's good, complicated, ever-shifting present for any simpler, golden-hued yesterday. I'm grateful for who we are in this moment: four still-growing human beings, each of us irrevocably, mysteriously connected. Each of us finding our own unique way to be in the world, and at the same time, each of us returning to this hallowed place of our own creation: this piece of earth, this house, this dinner table, this history, this tangled web of us-ness. Yes, we are each still and always unfinished parts of some greater, unknowable whole. And yes, we are still and always something else, too. We're a family.

March 2013

———·——— inhabiting a moment ———·———

Life passes into pages if it passes into anything.
—James Salter

On the bed where I sit cross-legged, leaning against the headboard: eyeglasses; a couple of paperbacks; a new but already much-loved hardcover novel, half read, its pages folded over, the margins scattered with lightly penciled exclamations, each one a silent, emphatic *yes*. Two pens, gray and black, a notebook with a dark brown cover and magnetic clasp. A pile of down pillows pushed aside, the familiar quilt, softened by age and use, sun-faded. The folded comforter.

Beyond the tall triptych of windows, the view that is the backdrop of all my days and nights. Sloping fields still patched with snow, the stone walls that define our edges here, meandering tendrils of wood smoke curling skyward, the final exhalations of a slow-burning brush pile. The maple tree that's almost close enough to touch, its dark limbs silhouetted against a twilight sky: rose, transparent blue, violet, and gold. The fading palette of an April dusk. Tiny, tight-fisted buds where just yesterday there were none.

A platoon of robins that descends as if summoned to the yard. They work away at the newly bared patches of earth, eyes cocked like surveyors taking measure of the land. The mushy, receding snow. The flat, matted grass. A lone yellow crocus still clenched shut, withholding its bloom. The distant mountains drenched for one singular instant in the day's last light, already slipping into shadow as the sky drains of color. The ticking clock on the bedside table. The quiet way evening settles in.

One son on his way tonight to New York City—hopeful, off to answer a call, a long-shot opportunity to take one small step closer to his Broadway dream. The odds aren't good. He knows that but he goes anyway. This is what it is be twenty-three and wishing for something, anything, to happen—you say yes and figure out the details later. The brief heart-tug when he left an hour ago, fresh shaven, clothes shoved into a backpack, one eye on the clock, car keys jangling in his hand. Imagining him tomorrow morning at ten, climbing the stairs of some building in Times Square, giving his name at the door, slipping into a reserved seat at a pre–Broadway workshop where, just maybe, he can convince somebody he'd be a useful guy to have around.

From the kitchen below, the muffled sound of a basketball game on TV. The rise and fall of my younger son's voice and his dad's responses, their staccato, companionable conversation punctuated by alternating cheers and cries of despair. The pleasurable stillness of the house in the hour after dinner when the dishes are done. The slow, unwinding hours before bed. The sense of embrace.

I concur with James Salter's observation that "everything that is not written down disappears, except for certain imperishable moments." By imperishable, I assume he means the big ones—the birth of a child, a phone call bringing good tidings or bad news, a vow spoken, a declaration of love, of betrayal. We don't need to preserve those moments that instantly engrave themselves upon our hearts. For better and for worse, they become part of who we are, our own indelible, unwritten, enduring history.

But everyday life—the life we fumble through and take for granted and get distracted by—this ordinary life is comprised of little else *but* perishable moments, random strings of details, most of them barely worthy of our notice: the slant of sun across the breakfast table, the coffee steaming in the mug, the brush of a hand across a brow, the dog's head in your lap, a son's casual, quick embrace, a handful of stars flung across an empty night sky, a few notes worked out on the piano. The flotsam and jetsam that add up to days lived, days forgotten.

It takes a kind of determined willingness to pay attention, an eye deliberately refreshed and attuned to nuance. And it takes time, time I rarely spare of late, to pause long enough to truly see. To sit in silence and slowly, haltingly, put what is fleeting and ephemeral into words. The inescapable truth of the present moment: it's already gone by the time I manage to set it down upon a page.

And yet, I do believe there's something to be said for trying. Something to be said for inhabiting stillness and then looking out at everything as if for the first time. For me, it is always the same lesson, one I learn by lingering in one place for a while and softening my gaze. Making myself at home in the moment means allowing time and space for each thing to become wholly itself, distinct and beautiful in its own way, each bearing its own secret revelation.

What I'm noticing as I sit in bed this evening and take stock of the fading, golden light, the muffled sounds of home, the unimportant particulars of here and now, is this: the simple act of recalibrating my attention calls me back into relationship with my life.

Perhaps a day will come when I will be grateful even for this humble record, this snapshot of an unremarkable twilight. I still believe with all my heart in the gift of an ordinary day. But I also have to remind myself, again and again, to accept that gift for what it is: proof that every moment offers another quiet opportunity to be amazed.

So, why not try this? Close your eyes. Draw a deep breath in and then exhale a long, deep breath out. Step gently through that opening, into *now*. Allow your eyelids to lift quietly, as if you are drawing back a curtain. See whatever is at hand. This is where you are. Before the moment sheds its skin and assumes a new shape, weave a skein of words around it. Write down what you see. Say "thank-you" out loud and feel the texture of those words on your tongue. See how the very act of noticing is something akin to wonder.

April 2013

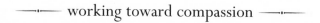

——·—— working toward compassion ——·——

I try, pretty much every morning, to catch a glimpse of dawn. Sometimes it's just a sleepy glance through the windows at the foot of our bed, but many mornings I'm up, standing outdoors shivering in my flip–flops and pajamas, gazing eastward. Once in a while I snap a photo as the sun makes its entrance, although no picture can do justice to the silent miracle: the arrival of another day.

Although I tend to wake up with all sorts of emotions already swirling through my consciousness, indifference is never one of them. Instead—and I don't think I'm alone in this—I'm often as not overcome with a wild brew of feelings as I stand on my small patch of earth and try to contemplate the much larger world out beyond my view and understanding.

Early yesterday morning, unguarded and unsettled, ears attuned to birdsong and wind, watching the sky brighten and the landscape glow with golden light, I struggled to comprehend how life can be both so beautiful and so horrific. How, I wondered, am I to hold in my small, imperfect human heart both the tragedy that unfolded at the Boston Marathon on Monday and, at the same time, gratitude that no one I know was hurt? How do we process the unimaginable?

On Monday afternoon, I drove a friend to the doctor and then we stopped for ice cream downtown. We sat outside in the mild sunshine eating peppermint stick and choco-late, happy in our innocence, our only worry the fact that we were filling our bellies way too close to dinner time. At home a few minutes later, slipping on my sneakers to take a walk, I had no idea what to make of a text that arrived from Jack saying, "I'm safe." My first, innocent response was, "Well of course you are."

Only when I opened my computer a moment later, and saw the scrolling news on the *Boston Globe* website, did I realize how lucky I was that the very first news I heard of the bombings came in the form of assurance from my younger son that he was all right. And yet, alongside my own relief was the realization that thousands of others were still awaiting news of loved ones, and that when it finally did come, not all the news would be good.

When tragedy strikes, it feels as if the entire world should stop and reassemble itself into some new pattern. Given the way grief, loss, and violence rip through our own precious complacency, we look around for some corresponding external shift, half expecting the moon and sun and stars to change course, too; wanting the entire universe to register and accommodate our human loss and somehow render it fathomable.

It doesn't happen.

The sun rises in the morning, unperturbed. The sky turns bright and sheer as a veil and slowly, imperceptibly, the last rim of snow vanishes under the eaves on the north side of the house. Out front, as they do each spring, the sturdy pansies tip their tiny purple faces toward the warmth. The birds take up their song, regardless. Overhead, a pair of great blue herons glide silently toward the pond, reminding me of the steadiness of their return, year after year. The world spins on, abiding. How we choose to live in it, and where we look for meaning, is up to us.

Standing outside in the early morning—open, attentive, reverent—I allow myself to be filled with the solace of nature's eternal rhythms. Here, in the gentle breeze upon my cheek, in the joy of watching my dog run at full tilt across the field, in the squish of mud beneath my boots, I am nourished and restored even as the weight of sadness sits heavily in my heart. Reminded that I'm never far removed from the source and mystery of things, I'm reminded, too, of all that is beyond my comprehension and control.

Two days later, as the investigations into who and why and how grind on, the best response to the violence I can come up with is this: to reaffirm my faith in kindness and to commit myself even more deeply to a practice of living and speaking with compassion.

If I can remember that versions of what happened on Boylston Street on Monday afternoon are occurring each day, all over the world, then I'm reminded that we are all connected, and that there will be no lasting peace for me until there is peace for you, too, no matter who *you* are.

If I stop to consider that the attack that feels singular and incomprehensible to us—an assault on *our* home, on *our* marathon, on *our* innocent people—is not unique at all, but the opposite, then I remember that until all people are safe, no one is safe.

If I can dissolve my own barriers and assumptions enough to taste the experience of life from inside someone else's skin, then I take a small step out of the numbness and daze which keeps me separate from the mistakes and miseries of our own messy human creation, and a step into empathy.

Last night, Jack called, and we talked on the phone for a while. "It didn't really sink in until today," he said, "how close I was to what happened. How it could so easily have been me, or anyone I know, there at the finish line." "Yes," I said. "It took me a while to grasp that, too."

Now I'm coming to think it is our task—as citizens of Boston, of America, and of the earth itself—to hold the truth in our hearts and minds: we are all one, and it is only through our willingness to reach out and touch the pain of others that the world will change.

April 2013

————•———— mending the parts of the world ————•————

I suspect I'm not the only one feeling a little wary and vulnerable in my skin these days. A week after the Boston Marathon bombings, as people across the nation paused yesterday afternoon to observe a moment of silence at 2:50, I stood alone in my own quiet kitchen, sad and somewhat at a loss for what to do next.

There is so much in my life to be grateful for. No one I know was injured last week. All my loved ones are fine. Nothing visible in my world has changed. And yet, I find myself blinking back tears at the slightest provocation or criticism or harsh word. *There is too much violence in the world. Please, help me to not add to it, not even with one more negative word or gesture.* Is this a prayer, a promise, or a wish? It doesn't matter; these are the words that best express what I've been feeling. Perhaps you have your own variation on this theme, your own yearning for peace amidst the chaos.

The headlines in the newspaper are both an accounting and a measure of our collective sorrow: the suffering that spills across the pages in articles and images, the anger and confusion still searching for an outlet, the grief still so fresh and raw. Looking at the photos of two brothers accused of the attacks, one dead and one facing death or life imprisonment, I search in vain for some clue that would explain such calculated, senseless evil. And then, because I am myself a mother of two boys, I can't help but think: these boys are also someone's sons.

At the same time, photos from the funerals remind us of all the other parents who are mourning. The losses, and the ripples from those losses, are unfathomable. Yet in the midst of loss, there is always some kind of grace, too, and resilience. On TV, a composed young dancer's face lights up as she tells Anderson Cooper how glad she is to be alive, even as she envisions her new life without her left foot. She will dance again, she insists, leaning into her husband's arms and gazing down at the bright pink bandage that wraps her stump. And then she makes a promise: somehow, though she's never been a runner herself, she intends to return to the marathon next year—as a participant, even if it means she walks or is wheeled across the finish line.

There is more than one path toward healing, no one right way to grieve or to recover. But after a week of monitoring the unfolding developments in Boston, after listening to this courageous young woman try to articulate why she is choosing not to look back in anger but to move forward with hope, I sense it's time for a break from the relentless onslaught of news. Time to find my own still center and embrace the texture of life as it is—not an easy task in the best of times, perhaps even more challenging today.

The sight of my welcoming house at the end of a long car ride Sunday night filled my heart. Hugging my husband and son after a weekend on the road, receiving a sweet text just now from a friend, bending down to the floor to snuggle my aging dog, reading a poem I love, watching the sun slip behind a cloud, just *being*—alive and aware and present in my own ordinary life—feels more intense than usual. It's as if everything has become heightened, both the fragility of my own brief time here, and the exquisite, complicated beauty of our interconnected existence on this earth.

Maybe, for a while at least, we are meant to be this raw and tender. Forced to acknowledge the dark shadow side of human nature and to feel the full brunt of that knowing, we have to face the truth: people hurt each other. Violence and suffering are intertwined, one giving rise to the other. And somehow, it is up to each one of us to do better, to soften our hearts, to sing our songs even in the midst of sorrow, to take better care of ourselves and of one another.

I think of how many opportunities I have each day to be brave and vulnerable, to offer a hand, to be kind—and how many of those opportunities I squander because I'm too annoyed to be expansive, too scared to reach out, too distracted to notice, or too busy to bother. And then I'm reminded of words by Clarissa Pinkola Estes that have been a touchstone for me for years now, words that guide me home when I stray away from the person I aspire to be:

Be brave…
"Anything you do from the soulful self will help lighten the burdens of the world. Anything. You have no idea what the smallest word, the tiniest generosity can cause to be set in motion. Be outrageous in forgiving. Be dramatic in reconciling. Mistakes? Back up and make them as right as you can, then move on. Be off the charts in kindness. In whatever you are called to, strive to be devoted to it in all aspects large and small. Fall short? Try again. Mastery is made in increments, not in leaps. Be brave, be fierce, be visionary. Mend the parts of the world that are within your reach. To strive to live this way is the most dramatic gift you can ever give to the world."

April 2013

—·— the gift of ordinary days —·—

An odd thing happened last weekend. I turned on my computer to check e-mail, and there were a dozen letters from Australia, each bearing kind Happy Mother's Day wishes from down under. There were even more messages for me on Facebook. I was puzzled at first, but the fifth note I read explained what was going on: "Your *Gift of an Ordinary Day* video is going viral in Australia," a mom of two wrote to me.

Sure enough. I paid a visit to the YouTube link: 200,000

more clicks in just a couple of days—and suddenly my three-year-old video was inching toward two million views. (When I told this to my friend Ann Patchett, she promptly pointed out that *Fifty Shades of Grey* first went viral in Australia, too, which is probably not relevant, but who can say? I'm pretty certain her e-mail is the only time the titles *Fifty Shades of Grey* and *The Gift of an Ordinary Day* have appeared in the same sentence, and that alone gave me delighted pause.)

"But where can I find the words to your poem?" my Australian correspondent asked. "What I really want is the coffee table version of this video so I can read the words again and again."

I wrote her back, but I couldn't give her what she wanted. The fact is, I didn't envision the video script as a poem, but it isn't a direct excerpt from my book either. To write it, I did take a few sentences from my memoir. But then I also began to muse about my children and about all the things I lost sleep over and loved and missed, and I added some more sentences in order to create a piece that could stand on its own. Then I tried reading the whole thing out loud to a friend. There were two problems.

Given that I was still smack in the middle of that raw and tender place of having sent one son off to college and knowing his brother would soon be gone, too, I couldn't get through it without tears. And it took me over seven minutes to read out loud.

"I know it's way too long for a video. No one will watch," I said to my friend. (The whole point of doing the video was to spread the word about my *book*—and everyone had told me that three minutes was the maximum amount of time anyone would pay attention to anything.) But try as I might, I couldn't find a line to cut.

In the end, I went with it. I practiced a few times, so I could read about my boys growing up without choking up myself, and then we filmed it. To my surprise, people did watch. And they shared it with their friends, who shared it with *their* friends, which is how a reading I did three years ago in my living room for my book group and my neighbors came to be seen by thousands of moms in Australia last weekend.

Over the last couple of years, I've received many requests for the written words to the video, especially in the springtime, with the end of the school year approaching, graduations looming, and big life transitions right around the corner. For a long time, I held off (I was hoping people would buy the *book,* after all), but since there will never be a coffee-table version, I decided the best way to answer the demand would be to just print the words here, for anyone to read and use.

Three years later, and I haven't changed my mind: the gift I still cherish above all else is the gift of a perfectly ordinary day. It seems that mothers and fathers everywhere feel exactly the same.

The Gift of an Ordinary Day
You think the life you have right now is the only life there is, the one that's going to last forever. And so it's easy to take it all for granted—the uneventful days that begin

with pancakes for breakfast and end with snuggles and made-up stories in the dark. In between, there might be a walk to the creek, a dandelion bouquet, caterpillars in a jar. Countless peanut-butter sandwiches, baking-soda volcanoes, and impassioned renditions of "The Wheels on the Bus." Winter's lopsided snowmen and summer trips to town for cookie-dough ice-cream cones. Cheerios poured into bowls, fingernails clipped, cowlicks pasted down with warm water. Nose kisses and eyelash kisses and pinky swears.

Of course, I worried. I thought if I didn't carry my four-year-old back to his own room after a bad dream, he would sleep with us forever. I thought, when one son refused to share his favorite puppet, it meant he'd never play well with others. When my firstborn cried as I left him at the nursery-school door, I believed he would always have trouble separating. Sometimes, out in the parking lot, I cried too, and wondered why saying good-bye has to be so hard, and if maybe I was the one with the problem.

"All the flowers bloom in their own time," my eighty-five-year-old grandmother said when I confided my fears. Of course, she was right.

There were disappointments—teams not made, best friends who turned mean for no reason, earaches and strep throats and poison ivy. A cat that died too soon, fish after fish gone belly up in the tank. But mostly, the world we lived in, the family we'd made, childhood itself, felt solid, certain, enduring.

What I loved most of all was a boy on my lap, the Johnsons baby shampoo smell of just-washed hair. I loved my sons' kissable cheeks and round bellies, their unanswerable questions, their innocent faith in Santa Claus and birthday wishes and heaven as a real place. I loved their sudden tears and wild, infectious giggles, even the smell of their morning breath, when they would leap, upon waking, from their own warm beds directly into ours.

For most of us, the end comes in stages. Baseballs stop flying in the backyard. Board games gather dust on the shelves. Baths give way to showers, long ones, at the oddest times of day. A bedroom door that's always been open quietly closes. And then, one day, crossing the street, you reach out to take a hand that's always been there—and find you're grasping at air instead, and that your twelve-year-old is deliberately walking two steps behind, pretending he doesn't know who you are.

It hits you then: you've entered a strange new territory, a place known as adolescence. Arriving on these foreign shores, you feel the ground shift beneath your feet. The child you've loved and held and sacrificed for has been transformed, en route, into a sullen, alien creature hunched over a cereal bowl.

And you wonder where you went wrong.

The thing is, you can't go back and do one single minute of it over. All you can do is figure out how to get through the rest of the day, or the midnight hour when your mind keeps replaying the last argument you had with your tenth grader, and wondering: how can I do this better?

Slowly, you begin to get the lay of this unfamiliar landscape, just as it dawns on you—the life that once seemed like forever has already slipped away. The old routines don't work anymore. Instead, every day now, it's like you're learning to dance all over again, with strangers, spinning faster and faster. Holding on, letting go.

You do what you can to keep up. You fill the refrigerator, drive, supervise, proofread, and fill the refrigerator again. You negotiate curfews and car privileges, fill the refrigerator, confiscate the keys, set new limits. You celebrate a part in the school play, a three-pointer, a hard-earned A minus. You fill the refrigerator, and you fill in every bit of white space on your calendar: SATs and ACTs and SAT IIs, playoffs and performances and proms.

You ignore a bedroom that looks as if it's been bombed, write lots of checks, try not to ask so many questions. You fill the refrigerator, count the beer bottles in the door. You willingly give up the last ice-cream sandwich in the freezer, buy pizzas when their friends come over, keep the dog quiet on Saturday morning till you hear feet hit the floor upstairs. You text and you trust and you pray.

There are many nights when you trade sleep for vigilance. You become an expert in reading the rise and fall of a phone conversation muffled behind a door, the look in their eyes as they walk through the room, the meaning of a sigh, the smell of a jacket, the unspoken message behind the innocuous, "Hey mom." "Hey," you say. "Hey, hon."

Before you know it, you're in the homestretch of high school—and face to face with a truth you should have known all along: this time of parents and children, all living together under one roof, isn't the whole story after all; it's just one chapter. Hard as it is to live with teenagers, you can't quite imagine life without them. And yet this time of 24/7, zip-your-jacket-here's-your-sandwich mothering by which you've defined yourself for so long, is coming to an end.

So, you remind yourself: learn the art of letting go by practicing it in the present. Instead of regretting what's over and done with, savor every minute of the life you have right now. A family dinner. You and the kids, all squeezed onto the couch to watch a movie. A cup of tea in the kitchen before bed. Saying goodnight in person. If motherhood teaches us anything, it's that we can't change our children, we can only change ourselves.

And so, instead of wishing that the kids could be different somehow, you try to see, every day, what is already good in each of them, and to love that. Because any moment now, you're going to be hugging a daughter who's turned into a woman. Or standing on tiptoe, saying good-bye to a son who's suddenly six feet tall and heading off to a college halfway across the country.

They leave in a blur—packing, chatting, blasting music, tearing the closets apart in a desperate last-minute search for the gray sweatshirt or the Timberland boots. And then, too soon, they really are gone, and the house rings with a new kind of silence. The gallon of whole milk turns sour in the fridge, because no one's home to drink it. The last ice-cream sandwich is all yours. Nobody needs the car.

You look at your husband across the dinner table, which

suddenly feels way too big for two, and wonder, *How did it all end so fast?*

The bookshelf in my own living room is full of photo albums, nearly twenty years' worth of well-documented birthday cakes and holidays, piano recitals and Little League games. But the memories I find myself sifting through the past to find, the ones that I'd give anything now to relive, are the ones that no one ever thought to photograph, the ones that came and went as softly as a breeze on a summer afternoon.

It has taken a while, but I certainly do know it now—the most wonderful gift I had, the gift I've finally learned to cherish above all else, was the gift of all those perfectly ordinary days.

May 2013

—·— writing the truth —·—

"Wow. Really? That's not the way I remember it at all," my husband said, shaking his head in disbelief after reading a chapter in which I untangled the complex reasoning behind our decision to sell our house in the suburbs, uproot our children, and move to the country.

"Mom! I can't believe you put my black sweatshirt in your book! Now everyone's going to think I was a Goth in seventh grade!" my son Jack protested when he discovered I'd written about a particular oversized garment with long, dangling sleeves and a capacious hood that he'd insisted on wearing to school every day for six months.

"That wasn't the World Series; it was actually the postseason play-offs," my son Henry informed me, upon reading a passing reference in my manuscript to a baseball game on TV.

"You *never* put chocolate-chip eyes into bear-shaped pancakes," both of my sons pointed out after attending a reading during which I referred to an old Saturday morning tradition in our family. "*Raisin* eyes, but not chocolate chips."

"I just don't want everyone to hate you," my friend Carol said in response to some pages about the death of a close mutual friend. "And I'm afraid if you write about her, it will feel too much like you're trying to own her, when in fact *we* all loved her, too."

Welcome to the world of the memoir writer. A world in which everyone has their own version of the truth, but you are the one who happens to be choosing to sit alone in a room day after day, crafting *your* version of the truth into a story.

I wasn't surprised my husband's memories didn't exactly match mine; we don't pay attention to the same things. The two of us can sit across the table from each other at breakfast and each have a completely different experience of the meal: he's tunneling through a bowl of oatmeal, lost in the *New York Times;* I'm eating a banana and noticing that the kitchen windows need washing. It's not that one version of breakfast is true and one isn't. What's true is that we are each having different experiences.

As for my younger son, he'd had his chance to censor

me. I'd asked him if he wanted to read my manuscript before I sent it to the publisher, but he didn't bother. A year later, when he finally took a look at the chapter about him, the black sweatshirt was both preserved in print and ancient history. *The Gift of an Ordinary Day* was published, and he'd long since moved on to fitted tee shirts in bright primary colors. But Jack made a request that day—no more writing about him without his permission. And since I value my relationship with my son more than any book contract, I agreed.

Henry's minor baseball correction, I made. Gratefully.

Chocolate chips vs. raisins was a little more complicated. I often did make bear-shaped pancakes. And sometimes, under pressure, I stirred in some chocolate chips. I think the kids are probably right though; the eyes *were* raisins. But the cadence of my sentence worked better with two words instead of one. I went with chocolate chips simply for the rhythm. Reason enough to nudge the facts just a little? I think so. My sons, however, are sticklers when it comes to the details of their childhoods.

And what to do about my friend's concern that if I wrote about the death of someone dear to us both, I would be resented for it, as if I were somehow stealing everyone else's grief and claiming it for my own? I took a long deep breath. I thanked her. And then I took the risk.

Writing about my own life means that I must also write about the people who are *in* my life, the very people I love most in the world—my family, my neighbors, my friends. Every memoir is, to some degree, a story of relationships. But to write memoir is also to stand alone, shouldering the burden of truth. Truth not as arrived at by consensus, but truth as I know it and experience it myself. And the truth, as I've learned the hard way, is rarely simple or black and white.

I am honest in my writing about my own inner struggles, self-doubts, mistakes, and shortcomings. If a narrative is strengthened by my willingness to be vulnerable, then I gather up my courage and step naked onto the page. But just because I'm baring my own soul doesn't give me a free pass to expose someone else's in the process. This is where truth hits up against trust.

I write what's true for me in a way I hope also honors the experience of those I'm writing about. When in doubt, I err on the side of kindness. If I'm telling someone else's story, I give my subject the pages to read well in advance of publication, and I ask for, if not exactly approval, consent. I willingly change names. I correct factual errors. I remove words that cause pain or embarrassment or even discomfort. I acknowledge, right up front, that our individual memories and experiences are almost certainly different, and that that's okay—this is simply one version of reality.

And yet, I also know there's a grain of validity in what my friend said. Putting words to an experience is also a way of owning it: This is what happened, as I remember it. This is how I felt. This is what I thought. This is what I've learned. And, for better or worse, this is one rendition of the truth that will survive if only because it happens to be the one that got written down.

I have a responsibility to my reader to tell it like it was and a responsibility to myself to get it right. But I feel an even greater responsibility to the innocent bystanders who, simply by virtue of being part of my life, run the risk of becoming characters in my writing as well: to do no harm. So, I draw a big, invisible circle of protection around my loved ones, and I then do my best to write right up to the edge of it, but not to overstep. Most of the time, I think I do get it right. But not always. Writing about the living (or the dead, for that matter) is always a risky business, no matter how pure one's intentions. We venture into the territory of memoir, and we wrestle with the truth, at our own peril.

And so, I remind myself: Write on. Proceed with caution. Err on the side of discretion. And of kindness.

May 2013

——·—— housework, soulwork ——·——

Shall I strip the sheets off the bed?" I asked my friend Ann, a writer who happens at the moment to be between books.

"No, no, leave them," she insisted. "I'll change the sheets. I love having an excuse to interact with my house."

An acclaimed novelist whose books settle onto best-seller lists for months at a time, Ann is also, in her heart of hearts, the happiest of housewives.

When I visited her a few weeks ago, the two of us stayed

up way too late talking about other writers we know, ideas for new projects, the books we were in the midst of reading, the ones we'd set down before finishing. And then, in the morning, we made breakfast smoothies, hauled out a stack of cookbooks and her notebook full of clipped and saved recipes, and perched on stools in the kitchen, comparing notes on our favorite vegetarian dishes.

We took time to admire the brief, sudden bloom of the climbing rosebush in the backyard, to take her dog for a long walk around the neighborhood, to check on the herbs growing in pots on the porch. I loved interacting with my friend's house, too. It is a well-loved home, not grand or flashy or huge, but warm and nurturing and soulful, tended with care and deeply inhabited.

I've thought of Ann's response often over the last few days. What's stayed with me about our visit, I realize, is not only the beauty of the life she's created but also the simple joy she allows herself in each day's doings—joy she experiences fully and without second-guessing her efforts, whether she's sitting at her desk and crafting a paragraph, or taking an elderly friend to the grocery store, or spending twenty minutes at the stove caramelizing onions, or (as she always insists on doing) driving me to the airport, even if it's rush hour.

What freedom there is in such joy: the freedom of not judging our work but choosing instead to see the value and the meaning in all of it. There is, after all—as my wise friend has figured out—no hierarchy, other than the one we impose on ourselves.

Who says that an op-ed in the *Times* is more important or meaningful than an arrangement of fresh flowers in the guest room or a pizza made from scratch? And yet, how tempting it is to draw that line, and then to start right in analyzing and evaluating. How reverently we place the "creative" work above the line *(this matters!)* and consign everything else a lesser status—the dishes in the sink, the recycling to be sorted, the vegetables to be chopped, the dried mud to be swept from the floor.

I do the dishes and sort the bottles and chop the veggies. I stay on top of the routine household chores. But I often catch myself rushing, too, distracted and contrite, as if the keeper of some invisible Writer's Time Clock is frowning down upon my domestic labors and finding me wanting, failing to live up to larger expectations. *"What, you spent two hours putzing around in the garden this afternoon, and you didn't get a single word written?"*

Perhaps it's because writing doesn't come easily for me that I always feel as if everything else I do, even the most essential domestic task, is really just some slightly disguised version of playing hooky from my "real" work. A choice between a mountain of laundry to fold and a blank page? No contest. Give me the dirty clothes! I actually love the beginning, the middle, and the end of laundry duty—from the physical exercise of lugging the heavy baskets down two flights of stairs to the washing machine in the basement, right through that moment when everything is neatly stacked and sorted back upstairs on my bed, socks matched and rolled the way my husband likes them, tee shirts folded into squares, towels in thirds, dishcloths ready to go back in the drawer. But it's a guilty satisfaction. I know that writing is harder, that I've chosen the easy way out.

"You should be doing something more meaningful, more productive with your life, than folding pillow cases," my inner taskmaster chides. "You haven't written anything for a week," she reminds me. *What kind of writer are you, anyway?*

The answer, at the moment, is: I am a writer who isn't writing much.

But my house! Finally, the screens are in, the kitchen floor is washed, the outdoor pots are spilling with blooms. There are fuchsia rhododendrons in the vases. Tender sunflower seedlings are growing by the stone wall, spinach and arugula and lettuce from the garden will fill the salad bowl tonight. My closet is clean. I bought a new tablecloth for the dining-room table, got the spots out of the old placemats, ironed all the napkins. For the first time since before Christmas, we've had friends over for dinner.

It felt so good to sit around the table, catching up with loved ones and watching the candles drip down that, two nights later, we did it again. I've been pulling out my cookbooks, trying new dishes. Stuffed peppers on gorgonzola polenta, roasted eggplant with buttermilk sauce, kale pesto, haddock Florentine. Perhaps the subtle creative forces haven't abandoned me after all. It could be they are just assuming a different form, recharging in the kitchen amid the makings of dinner.

In a couple of days, Henry will leave for his summer

job on the Cape. This week, every meal and shared moment feels like an occasion. Soon we will be two here again, readjusting to silence and solitude. Last night, while Steve mowed the lawn and Henry practiced the music for *Die Fledermaus* (he's determined to know the scores for all nine summer musicals by Friday), I made pasta and roasted vegetables and marinated steaks for the guys. The windows were open, the scent of fresh-cut grass wafting through the kitchen, the sound of the lawnmower a steady comfort. My husband and son and I were all absorbed in our labors, busy and peaceful and content.

The Keeper of the Time Clock was silent. Perhaps she's finally gotten the message: there is no line. There is nothing to judge. No one else cares how many words I write or how clean my floor is. And the only thing that really matters is the attitude I bring to the task at hand, whatever it may be. What I aspire to this summer, then, is this: to do my work, all of it, with conscious intention. With love, not judgment. And with gratitude for the gift of this life, with its countless blessings and small miracles. May I take up willingly the daily actions of living that create a home for the soul, a place where both joy and effort can flourish.

As poet Maya Stein observes, "one must never ignore the instinct to create"—be it scones or novels, a poem or a terra-cotta pot overflowing with pale petunias. There is no line. There is just our own beautiful offering, our song, in whatever form it arrives.

Irreverent Baking
I should be upstairs with the others, drumming up ways
to heal the world, save the animals, pray for water
in a far-off continent, devote the remainder of my days
to a catalog of restorations. But this morning it was the matter
of scones that drew my gaze, and my feet remained
planted in the kitchen. One must never ignore the instinct
to create, is what I told myself, and soon the counter was stained
with flour, my hands sticky with dough, the house inked
with the smell of blueberry possibility, and I knew I was not
wrong.
This was my prayer, my act of healing, my offering, my song.
—Maya Stein
June 2013

—·—— peonies ——·—

The peonies at our house bloomed this week, bursting onto the scene with the fanfare of a chorus line. A hundred or more voluptuous beauties, as fragile as they are flamboyant, the impermanence of life embodied in all shades of cream and palest pink and scarlet. Each fleeting blossom is worthy of its own lipstick shade or perfume label. For a day or two they hold their heavy heads up high, and I snap photo after photo—trying, in vain of course, to somehow capture their brief moment of perfection.

And then, too soon, *always* too soon, the heavy heads bow toward the ground, brought low by the sheer weight of their own extravagance. Yesterday, beneath a gathering of storm clouds, I walked through the damp grass, bending down to gaze into one fragrant, implausible peony heart after another. And then I cut them all.

Already, here in the bittersweet beginning of summer I anticipate the pathos of its ending. I wait all year for the peonies' burst of glory and then mourn the moment's passing even as it arrives. I know exactly how this languid season will bend overnight to fall; how the water in the lake I have yet to swim in will turn suddenly cold; how the spikes of goldenrod will appear by the roadside as I run down the hill toward town on an August afternoon; how we will walk through the house to close windows at dusk, speaking wistfully of how short the days have grown, marveling at the early darkness and wishing we'd had more dinners on the screened porch when we still had the chance.

My family has been teasing me for days: "It's only the first of June, and Mom's already sad because summer's going by too fast!" It's true. I want so badly for it all to last that I miss it before it's begun. Which means, if I'm not careful, that I might just miss it altogether.

Last night the rain came down in torrents, keeping me awake. I didn't mind, really, for the hours of a sleepless night slip by slowly, offering time and space for thoughts to drift. (I'm learning through these menopausal years that "trying" to sleep is always an exercise in frustration, that allowing for wakefulness can actually be less stressful than willing sleep to come.) And, in fact, I love lying in bed in the darkness, listening to the steady thrum of rain on the roof while I'm curled up warm and snug within, waiting it out. As the storm intensified toward dawn, I thought of the peonies, glad I'd had the foresight to save them from this ruinous lashing of wind and water.

I know they won't last long in the house, either. But my rescue mission has afforded them a few more days at least. Every vase I own is full, as if we're preparing to host a wedding here, or a funeral. The air is sweet, every silken petal a work of art demanding admiration, right here, right now: within a week, they really will be gone.

It occurs to me as I sit typing just inches away from the pitcher full of pink blooms on the kitchen table, that perhaps I cherish my favorite flowers as much for their impermanence as for their beauty. If I lived always amid such spectacle, how soon would it be before I'd take it for granted or fail to notice it at all?

Finally, a weak, intermittent sun peeks through the clouds, and I'm lured away from the computer, ready for a break. I pour a second cup of coffee and take the time to drink it slowly, sitting outside on the granite step by the kitchen door. The swallows are more determined in their work this morning than I am, swooping in and out of the birdhouses, taking food to their babies. Fat bees bounce from blossom to blossom in the salvia and a steady procession of swallowtail butterflies hover over the poppies. A dragonfly glistens, emerald green, on the walkway and then lifts off, coming to light briefly at the edge of the birdbath. A chipmunk, cheeks stuffed like a cartoon character's, pauses, quivering at my feet, before scampering off with his stash to a hole in the stone wall. It's a busy world out here.

I linger in my spot, watching, for a long time. Everything, it seems, is in harmony with everything else. The insects, flowers, birds, all have given themselves completely to the luxuries of this early summer day. Slowly, it dawns on me: these creatures, each industriously tending to the urgent work of *being,* count their brief lives not in months but in moments. And yet they have time enough. So do I.

Eventually, everything ends. Time isn't ours to own, to measure and mete out in portions of our liking. It just is. Instead of wishing for my flowers, or this June day, or summer, or life itself, to last longer, I am simply meant to be here. My only task: to live into this fleeting, immutable time. And just as lying awake feels easier when I don't struggle to achieve sleep, accepting the truth of impermanence again and again brings me gently back into alignment with reality. There is joy to be found both in seizing the day *and* in letting it go.

On Sunday my parents will come over for dinner. We'll eat out on the porch and celebrate Father's Day. Our own sons won't be with us, and I'll miss them, but absence is part of the fabric of our lives now, their comings and goings woven into this larger, more complex and forgiving family tapestry. So, I'll set the table for four instead of six, light candles, put on music, write a card for my dad. If the peonies have all gone by, there will be daisies to pick. Perhaps I'll find strawberries at the market, prepare the first shortcake of the season for dessert. Whatever the day brings, I'll welcome it.

It's so obvious, really, and at the same time such a challenge to let go of my own battles, large and small. I keep reminding myself that this is what we're all here to do as we engage in this ongoing spiritual practice called being alive: notice, give thanks, and pour ourselves wholly into life as it is.

June 2013

—·—— summer afternoon ——·—

Summer afternoon, summer afternoon; to me those have always been the two most beautiful words in the English language.
—Henry James

I took a long walk yesterday, listening on my headphones to poet David Whyte talking about "what to remember when waking." And I confess: I was two miles down the road and completely under the spell of Whyte's romantic Yorkshire accent before it occurred to me that he is not referring to waking up *literally,* as in what to remember as you roll out of bed in the morning, but rather to waking up in a larger sense—as in, waking up to your life.

Suddenly, in the heat of the day, trudging back up the hill toward home and dripping with sweat, I got it.

Each day offers me a choice. I can keep my head down, my heart locked up, my soul tethered to my to-do list, my feet on the same old well-worn path.

Or, I can wake up. I can pay attention to the subtle

currents of my life and allow them to carry me in a new direction. I can feel my feelings rather than sidestep them. I can be fully present rather than half here. I can wake up to the challenges of the journey, the conversation I don't want to have, my fears about where I'm headed, the truth of who I am, the gifts and losses of my life as it is.

Today is as good a day as any other to wake up. It is a summer afternoon. Why not luxuriate in its fullness? Succumb to the brief beauty of June. Allow your tender heart to open, both to grief for all that's over and gladness for what remains. Eat strawberries. Watch a robin splash in the birdbath. Blow bubbles with your kids. Go for a swim or a bike ride or a walk around the block. Watch the clouds drift past. Pick daisies for your table. Snap some peas. Hang your damp sheets on the line. Sit in a lawn chair. Feel the air on your face. Read a book. Close your eyes. Take a nap. Wake up.

June 2013

———·—— a healing journey ——·———

Nothing ever goes away until it has taught us what we need to learn.

—Pema Chodron

We looked at the x-rays together, Jack and I. "This is last August," the orthopedist said, pointing to the image on the left, showing two clear lines in Jack's L5 vertebra, one on each side—fractures that, after six months, were showing no signs of healing on the left and only a minimal feathering of bone growth on the right.

"And this is now," he said, indicating the scan from last week. "Completely healed.

"I can tell you," he said turning to Jack and raising his hand for a high five, "this hardly ever happens."

I remember my very first glimpse of my younger son. The dark, cool room. The ultrasound wand sliding through the goop on my swollen stomach. My husband peering over me to get a look at the shadowy little curlicue of a person floating deep within my belly. It was twenty-one years ago this summer—my son's entire lifetime ago—and yet still fresh and vivid in my mind's eye. The technician asked if we wanted to know the sex of our baby. Steve and I looked at each other, but he waited for me to say yes.

"It's a boy," she said, sliding the cursor over, showing us. I can admit it now: one brief tear slid out of one eye, for the daughter we would never have. And then, in that same moment, we began to imagine our future as the parents of two sons, a family of four. By the time we'd walked back to our car, we were thrilled with our baby boy and Jack had a name.

A couple of weeks ago, on the Fourth of July, I sat in my brother's living room watching *his* little boy do his six-year-old version of a hip-hop dance. Gabriel knows the words to "Stronger" (though not what most of the lyrics mean), and he has some pretty impressive moves. "What doesn't kill you makes you stronger, stand a little taaaaa–ller," he sang along with Kelly Clarkson, dropping down to the floor, swinging his legs around, happy to have an audience.

It's an old saying, but only sometimes true. "What doesn't kill you makes you stronger." Character can be built by adversity. And yet, as my nephew and his younger sister danced with abandon, all I could think was how beautiful they are in their perfect, tender innocence. And how hard it will be for all of us who love these two children to stand by and watch when, inevitably, life starts roughing them up a bit.

Perhaps it's human nature: we want to protect our off-spring from pain and struggle for as long as possible. We want their lessons to be painless, the road to be smooth, the waters calm, the sky clear. When the challenges begin, we want to do everything in our power to take the sting out, to ease our children's way.

How many times did I field calls of distress? "I left my math homework at home." "I forgot my lunch." "I lost my sweatshirt." "Mr. D. was mean to me in class." My natural inclination, always, was to rush to the rescue—to jump in the car with the forgotten homework, to deliver the lunch, to replace the missing sweatshirt, to make the phone call that would make things better.

Did I do my boys any favors by helping them avoid some of the bumps and bruises of childhood? I'm not sure. Perhaps I made things too easy for them, delayed their understanding that every action has a consequence, that people aren't always kind, and that sweatshirts don't grow on trees.

On the other hand, perhaps there's something to be said for knowing, when you're young and impulsive and distracted and forgetful, that there's a safety net in place, ready to catch you if you fall.

Eventually, though, life delivers its hard lessons anyway. Kids do stupid things and then have to pay the price for their mistakes. Bad stuff happens, and they must summon enough resilience to pick up the pieces, dust themselves off, carry on. Our children reach, and fall short. They try, and fail. They hope, and have their hopes dashed.

And somehow we parents must learn to step back and allow them to absorb the hard knocks of growing up. Slowly, and with more than a little heartache, we figure out what our job really is: not to prepare the world to meet our children, but to prepare our children to meet the world—in its splendor, but also in its dark places.

Letting go means putting our trust in the rightness of their journeys and putting our faith in their resilience. It means remembering that there are larger forces at work in our children's lives, carrying them to the places they need to go. Watching my athletic, active, competitive son live with chronic pain over the last eighteen months has taught me a lot about letting go. It was hard to see him suffer. It was just as hard to accept my own helplessness in the face of that suffering. I could make him dinner when he was home, give him some Reiki touch, love him, encourage him. We could pay the medical bills, the physical therapy bills, help out with expenses when he couldn't work. But whether he recovered fully or not wasn't up to us.

Jack has spent much of the last year, while his friends were off at college, on the floor, stretching his hamstrings and his quads—the only way to bring the broken bones into proper alignment so they could have a chance to mend. At one point, discouraged and wondering if he would ever again be able to move through a day without pain, he pointed out that at least if he had a broken arm in a cast, people would be able to see his injury. They wouldn't expect him to lift heavy boxes or carry groceries or shoot hoops. Jack *looked* fine. He was worried that, to rest of the world, he also looked lazy.

In fact, there was a lot of invisible work going on, and not just in the hamstrings and L5 vertebra. Much as I might have wished my son to have traveled a different path, much as my heart hurt right along with him during the hardest times, I've also come to see that many of the lessons he learned this year are ones that only a dark night of the soul can teach.

He learned he can do hard things. He learned that pain is often invisible. He learned that empathy begins with the understanding that there is always more going on than meets the eye. He learned that even when dreams shatter and plans go awry, life continues. He learned *(a lot)* about anatomy. He learned that the rocky road he's on has its own beauty, its own logic and shifting landscape, its own rightness for him.

Last week, when he was home, Jack spent hours outside in the driveway shooting baskets. He played before breakfast in the morning and under the lights before he went to bed—happy, sweaty, grateful, moving slowly, finding his way back into a body that can once again do his bidding. Nothing like a year of not moving to make every dunk or rebound cause for minor celebration. He is twenty, and I'm pretty sure he will never again take feeling fine for granted. In the meantime, his plans have changed once again. In the fall, he's going to Atlanta, to major in exercise science in a pre-chiropractic program at Life University. "I like the idea of helping people," he says. "When someone comes to me in pain, I'll know how they feel."

How little I knew twenty-one summers ago, as I gazed at that first hazy gray picture of my baby floating in amniotic fluid. All I could do then, as he grew deep inside me, was say yes to him, to the mystery of this unknown being, to my necessary faith that things would work out. They have. They do. In ways I never could have anticipated, never would have chosen, yet wouldn't change.

What doesn't kill you makes you stronger, stand a little taller. Yes, sometimes it does.

July 2013

 words fail

Early last Sunday morning, came the news of a death. A nineteen-year-old boy, a motorcycle failing to make a curve, a crash.

He was a boy I've known since the day his mom joyfully

revealed her pregnancy by announcing to a group of us women friends, "I did it again!" A boy I've loved and cheered for and prayed for since he arrived on this earth. A boy who grew, right alongside my own younger son, from a chubby blond toddler into a handsome, thoughtful, athletic teenager with a passion for music and motorcycles. A boy whose young life was both touched by early tragedy and full of hope and promise. A boy whose childhood was inextricably intertwined, day in and day out, with two other boys I love with all my heart.

In the backyard that our three families shared, it was always Jack and Nick and Will. Three pals, born within a year of each other and living within a stone's throw of each other. Boys who never had to arrange a playdate because there was always a best friend right next door, ready to throw a baseball or play a game of hide and seek or go in search of an adventure.

There is a part of me that yearns to write more about the loss of this beautiful young man, because writing is the way I work my way toward peace. But there is also a part of me that must acknowledge at this moment the failure of words.

I can't quite imagine sharing either this grief or the memories behind it. I can't do a Facebook post or tweet about loss or even wrestle an essay into shape in an attempt to make some kind of sense of things. When a young person dies, words fail, and peace is a long time coming, and there isn't any sense to be made. Perhaps "peace" isn't ever achieved. He was only nineteen and he is gone. There is no peace in that. It may be that the most we can hope for is a slow, painful comprehension of one of the hardest truths of all for a parent to bear: we can love our children but love doesn't keep them safe. And that is simply all the more reason to love them as they are, with all we have, while we can.

July 2013

——·—— hard, beautiful ——·——

I was outside at dawn this morning, as I've been most days this summer. Standing in the wet grass, watching the molten red sun slide from behind the mountain into a rose-colored sky, two thoughts occurred to me at exactly the same time: Life is hard. And it's more beautiful than ever.

The hard things are easy to list. They've been running on an endless loop in my head through every sleepless night this week: An ongoing conversation with my younger son that keeps ending badly. The helplessness of not knowing how to make things better. Worries about the other son as he wraps up a summer job he's loved and embarks on a new life chapter. A slightly frayed, unraveling edge in my marriage—and not knowing how to mend that, either. Grief for a young man gone too soon from this earth. The piles of things around the house that I should have cleared away by now and the to-do list that doesn't ever seem to get any smaller. The familiar, nagging sense that

I'm spread too thin, letting too many people down, not doing quite enough or being enough or giving enough.

Wakefulness takes its own toll, as if exhaustion has peeled off a protective layer, leaving me a little more raw and vulnerable than usual. I am less resilient, more prone to sudden, brief tears; frustration; anxiety. I do an interview over the phone, make a birthday dinner for my dad, handwrite a few overdue letters, pay the bills, read a bound galley that needs a blurb, call to congratulate a friend who's just finished writing her book, sort the laundry, sweep the floor. I try again with my son. Reach for my husband's hand. Pick flowers for the table and bake scones from scratch. Take a deep breath, and then another. Take a run. Smile at a stranger on the street. These are all good things to do. And yet. My mind feels not quite all here. I'm tired. Life is still hard. And beautiful.

There was, for starters, that sunrise. The silent spectacle of it, with a just-past-full moon fading away in the west as, for one brief moment, night and morning shared the sky. There was my phone vibrating in my hand even as I snapped a picture, a cherished friend's early morning greeting arriving with the sun to lift my heart. There was the sleek beaver swimming silently upstream as I ran along the river toward town. There were my own two feet standing on my yoga mat, the stillness of mountain pose. There was the sound of forty voices chanting, "Peace, Peace, Peace."

There is the quiet day unfurling as I sit here allowing thoughts to come and go, the steady accumulation of hours, the pulse of time passing. There is this house, this hilltop, this place we call home and the people who pass through the door. The memories layered over the course of years, the joy and sadness that have already been accommodated beneath this roof. The knowledge that there will surely be more of each in all our futures.

There was dinner on the porch last night, the clatter of dishes, the deepening shadows, the white lights strung around the windows, the first stars. Good, strong coffee this morning in a smooth blue mug that fits my hand just so. Ripe peaches in a wooden bowl, a row of tomatoes on the kitchen sill, gazpacho already made and in the refrigerator for tonight.

There is our beloved border collie who turned thirteen this week and still begins each day with a wild dash through the fields, the white flag of her tail wagging in enthusiasm. There are the lessons she teaches all of us, free of charge: roll in the grass, savor the moment, run while you can. And of course, this, a dog's essential truth: it's enough to offer love, no matter how imperfectly received or given.

There are the bronze-faced sunflowers blooming every-where this year, taller than I am and still growing an inch a day, and creamy hydrangeas, their heavy heads bowing gracefully to the ground. There is the woodpecker upside down at the feeder, the dragonflies cruising open-mouthed above the shaded potted plants. There is the softness of this August afternoon, the gentle touch of wind on skin, the bees thrumming in the flower garden, the constancy of crickets, the wide, pale expanse of sky, the arc of a swallow's flight.

There is a sentence written by a stranger that takes my breath away. A letter from a reader in Ireland that erases miles and cultures and differences. There is the slow reaching out for connection, as my son wanders into the kitchen to make a sandwich and pauses to ask what I'm writing about. There is the relief, at last of, simply speaking a few words of kindness in return. There is the sound of the basketball thwacking the driveway and there is the knowledge that soon enough the ball will sit, silently deflating in the closet, when he goes away to school. There is my husband, e-mailing from his desk at his office twenty miles away, making plans for next week and the week after that— the moving truck secured, the airline tickets bought, the rental cars, the dates on the calendar, the reminder that, come what may, we will get both of these sons of ours moved once again—one to Atlanta, one to Minnesota— and launched into the next phases of their newly grown-up lives. There is his steadiness and my gratitude for who he is and what he does.

There is, for now, this solitary hour on the screened porch. The laundry waiting to be folded. The few, final days we will all spend together in this house. The sense of summer's ending. The first red leaf on the maple tree. All that is unknown and unknowable. The densely woven tapestry of our lives. The words that come. The feelings that need to be felt. Remembering, all over again, that this is the way life is. Hard. Beautiful. Both.

August 2013

———·——— small moments ———·———

"Ok," I said to my family, "I have a question."

We were halfway through dinner at my parents' house in Maine. The sun was setting, casting the room in amber light. The table was littered with lobster shells and corncobs and wadded-up napkins: the perfect ending to a perfect end-of-summer day.

No one could remember the last time we'd all been gathered together in this place we love, a place layered with memories and history and hallowed artifacts. Twenty-six years ago this week my husband and I were married in the church at the head of the cove. We began our life together in the bedroom off the kitchen (repainted by my mom and dad in honor of the occasion)—the room where we still sleep when we visit and where my wedding dress still hangs in the back of the closet. Our sons spent all the best vacations of their childhoods at "Nana and Bapa's Maine house."

Even now, the books they read as little boys are stacked on the bedside table between the twin beds upstairs. My own old threadbare Winnie the Pooh sits in silent meditation upon a pillow, awaiting a third generation of children who might want a snuggle with an accommodating stuffed animal. The board games are piled neatly on the shelf, most of their pieces intact. The sea glass and smooth stones collected over many years line the windowsills. There is a special kind of beauty in a place where nothing changes but the pages on the calendar.

And yet, time and summer jobs and new interests and horizons have their way with all of us. Life doesn't always carry young adults back to their best-loved places. But over Labor Day weekend, with both boys home, we seized our chance. And for one night, my parents and the four of us were under one roof.

Everyone knew what was coming: as is my wont on such occasions, I was going to ask the family to *reflect*. My dad rolled his eyes. "It's a nice meal," he said, only half-joking. "Do we *have* to make it meaningful?"

The kids laughed. Steve said, "You can't stop her, you know." And in fact, no one really tried. What I wanted to know was simply this: what moment from the summer are you especially grateful for?

Through all the years of our sons growing up we asked "the gratitude question" at the dinner table once a week or so, usually on a Friday night. Passing was always an option, but I don't remember a time that any of us actually chose to opt out. There were plenty of "terrible, horrible, no good, very bad days," as we used to call them, after Judith Viorst's beloved children's book. But even at the end of one those days, it was usually possible to dredge up some small moment worthy of a smidgen of gratitude. (A Jack classic: "I saw a toad.")

But last Saturday, as the golden light faded from the sky, we were all feeling expansive. Gratitude was easy. Jack talked about an August afternoon he'd spent at the beach with a best friend from childhood, the week after their beloved mutual friend had died. The two boys couldn't hold each other and cry, that is not their way. But they managed to share their grief nonetheless, and some laughs, too, whacking rocks into the ocean with a stick. They did it for hours, this impromptu home-run derby, till they couldn't lift their arms anymore or swing the stick one more time. Nothing special, really—except that of course it was.

Henry told us about the final night of his summer job on the Cape, sitting at the piano with a friend at 1 in the morning, the two of them playing and singing their favorite Bruce Hornsby songs together one last time before going their separate ways. Not a big deal, perhaps, at the end of a summer full of opening nights and parties and performances and drama. Except that it was.

Steve, who has never had any interest in joining me for my chilly early-morning swims, decided this year that if I was going to start every morning of our August vacation by jumping out of bed and into the lake, he would do it too. His favorite moment? Swimming through the dark cold shadows, all the way out to the place where the rising sun is just hitting the water at dawn. I'm with him on this. There is nothing quite like greeting the day by diving into it and swimming toward the light. A small ritual, yes, but precious now to both of us.

My dad, who spent all of last summer wondering if he would ever recover from a debilitating slipped disc in his back, is so relieved to be able to move around again that he had a hard time choosing just one pain-free moment to be grateful for. At seventy-eight, he wasn't sure he'd ever regain the ground he'd lost. Little wonder that fixing the roof in Maine made him so happy. "I was up and down that ladder fifty times today," he said. "I couldn't have done that a year ago." Not a big deal, perhaps. Except that, of course, it is.

"Well, my life isn't very dramatic at all," my mom began. "But here's a moment that meant a lot to me." She had been watering her garden with the hose, she said, when a hummingbird appeared—so close she could have touched it—and then hovered there, thrumming its wings just at the outer edge of the spray, receiving a little shower. She didn't move; the hummingbird didn't leave—it was the two of them, suspended in time, eyeing each other. Just a flash of connection, really; nothing dramatic at all. But, as my mom said, "It meant a lot."

It probably doesn't surprise you that what struck me most as we went around the table was how simple each of these memories is. A moment shared with a friend. A swim at dawn. A day of work without pain. An encounter with nature. The kinds of moments available to most of us all the time. But also the very moments that are so easy to miss in our busy, wired, distracted lives.

At my parents' house last weekend, there wasn't a lot to do. We read books, took walks, made meals, cleaned up after them. I spent time at the water's edge with each of my sons and we did exactly what we've always done there—climbed on rocks, played with rocks, made piles of rocks, collected rocks, skipped rocks. We talked about everything and nothing. We watched the sky and felt our hearts grow calmed by the sea.

On Monday, we cleaned the house, changed the beds, and loaded our stuff into the cars, Steve and Henry in one, me and Jack in the other. I drove home in an epic traffic jam through pouring rain, stopped at the farm stand for some groceries five minutes before it closed, threw all our dirty clothes into the wash, and made some vegetable soup for dinner. Four of us at the kitchen table, just as we were for years and years—and as we are so rarely now.

All week, with summer officially over and yet with both sons still home for a little while more, I've been thinking about what I most want them to take away when they leave again—Henry on Friday for a job in Minnesota; Jack, at the end of the month, for school in Atlanta. I'd hoped for this "togetherness" time to be special, of course. And I've looked forward all summer to these days in early September, when I knew we would finally have some unscheduled time just to enjoy each other.

Things haven't gone quite as I planned. Last Wednesday morning I woke up with a toothache that quickly went from uncomfortable to painful to excruciating. For me it's been a week of dental visits, curling up on the couch under a blanket, counting the hours between painkillers, sipping liquids through a straw, and going to bed hours before anyone else. Not the memorable "togetherness" I'd envisioned.

But it's also been a week of moments I want to remember: Henry doing the grocery shopping and making dinner, including a killer blackberry hazelnut cobbler, the last solid food I was able to eat. Steve and the boys gathered round the TV in the kitchen, switching channels from the Red Sox to the U.S. Open. Jack preparing ice packs for me and tucking them around my cheek. The guys doing the dishes together, meal after meal. My sons have taken care of me over the last few days with all the tenderness I could wish for. In the meantime, they've gone about their lives here—taking runs, playing basketball, going for bike rides, seeing friends, feeding the dog, working for their dad to earn some extra cash. And no one really needed me to do anything to make it "special."

What do I want my young adult children to take away with them into their own next chapters? Maybe just this, the simple instructions that, when heeded, make for a good life: Be kind. Pay attention. Do what needs to be done. And remember that the little things, the small moments, actually matter quite a lot. They are the texture and the truth of who we are and what we care about.

September 2013

———·—— time in a bottle ——·———

I spent most of yesterday morning in the kitchen with my son Jack, windows open to the September air. In ten days he will move to Atlanta to begin his new life there as a student. But for now, the two of us find ourselves home alone together. Henry left last week to return to his alma mater, where he's helping out with the fall musical. Steve is away for a few days on business. And so, it's just two of us here, a rare mother-son combination that hasn't happened for years and may not recur any time soon.

All summer, as usual, I've mourned the end of summer. Back in June, my family laughed at me for regretting the passing of time before the time I'd been anticipating had even arrived. (Yes, I know, it's crazy.) The days were still getting longer, they pointed out, and already I was imagining how I would feel when they began to grow shorter. The lake water was perfect for swimming, and I was wondering how many more swims we would have. A piercing awareness of the preciousness, the transience, of everything is both the blessing and the burden of my temperament. It is also the price my family has to pay for living with me. I'm always reminding them (*myself!*) to notice, to appreciate, to be aware of all that is and of all that's in flux.

Honestly, I'm sure I write so much about inhabiting the moment just to help myself remember that it's where I really want to be: present. But my own particular consciousness comes at a cost; I have a tendency, always, to live with a lump in my throat. I experience the pain of endings even as I cherish the tenderness of beginnings. I allow every joy to be shot through with a slender thread of sadness. And I see in all that lives all that has passed. In all that is, all that one day will no longer be.

And so I sit in my garden amid the wildly blooming nasturtiums and feel the fleetingness of their splendor. I adore our thirteen-year-old dog all the more for knowing her days are numbered. (When she placed her head on the bed this morning at 6 am and pleaded for a walk, I swung right into action—because, of course, I can so easily imagine the future, when there will be no need to be out taking a hike at dawn.) I fill our basement freezer with strawberries and blueberries and raspberries picked at the height of the season because I'm always aware of the season's inexorable turning.

Hanging out with my soon to be twenty-one-year-old son yesterday, I reminded myself to just enjoy the moment, without layering on the fact that in a few weeks he'll be in his own new place a few thousand miles away, and we'll be texting instead of talking.

Being present, without regret for the past or anticipation of the future, feels to me like a lifelong practice. It's a lesson I keep on learning, one I need to take up again each day. But Jack has always been good at keeping me in my place: here, now. He is nothing if not practical.

"Do you want me to write out some recipes for you?" I asked him, envisioning the notebook I could create, with printed recipes slipped into plastic sleeves, complete with shopping lists—chili, chicken soup, corn chowder. "Grandma did that for Dad when he moved away to live on his own," I said, "so he would have a few things he could cook for himself." My son declined. "If I want to make chili, Mom, I'll go online." Right.

So, I'll resist the urge to send him to Atlanta with my recipes. Instead, yesterday, we just made some food together. I had twenty pounds of heirloom apples, gathered up from the ground around my friend Margaret's hundred-year-old tree. The gentle, deeply resonant voice of Bhava Ram, my current favorite singer, filled the house. Jack sat at the table and cut the knobby, homely apples into quarters. I stirred them down over low heat, adding cinnamon, anise, lemon. Good smells bubbled up. We talked about this and that, nothing special. It was just a day. I didn't need to shape it or mourn it or grip it—or do anything at all, other than live it.

And yet, as I ladled the thick sauce into jars, the refrain from an old Jim Croce song kept running through my head: "If I could save time in a bottle . . ."

It felt as if that's just what I was doing. Bottling not only the apples, but also time itself. The quiet of the day, the sunlight pouring through the windows, the togetherness with my son, the easy pleasure of making something good to eat. We have had our struggles, he and I. We still do. Let's be honest: he is twenty, and we are different, and nothing is easy. And yet, our bond is close.

Perhaps, as we haltingly find our way into a new relationship with each other as two adults, we are closer than we've been in years. The more space I'm able to give him, it seems, the more comfortable we are with each other. I don't know what thoughts went through his mind yesterday. I didn't ask. And for once I didn't feel the need to tell him what was in mine, either. No matter what mistakes we've made with each other in the past or what trials we may face in the future, there is beauty in the now—and now is enough.

Can I bottle that wisdom, too? No. But perhaps, some winter night, I'll take a jar of our applesauce out of the freezer, warm it on the stove, and allow good memories of being with my son to mingle with the goodness of learning how to let him go. Again.

September 2013

———·—— a threshold ——·———

A Saturday afternoon in September, the last of them. Where the air leaves off and my skin begins, I can't quite tell. They are the same temperature, the same softness, the same. There's no need for a sweater or shoes. I sit in the lawn chair by the garden, eyes half closed, listening to the low, incessant churring of crickets, the intermittent hammer taps of a woodpecker in the maple tree overhead, the chatter of birds, their wing beats as they come and go from the feeder, the acoustic hum of bees burrowing into the orange and yellow nasturtiums.

It is that gentle, golden, in-between moment, no longer summer but not fully fall, either. The sun, already sliding down the sky, casts long purple shadows across the grass and, elsewhere, creates translucent pools of light. It feels nearly holy, this luminous glimmer shafting through the trees. Everything is softening, crumpling, fading. And yet, on this mild, sun-kissed afternoon, it isn't an ending I feel, but an urgent, insistent turning toward life and change.

Any day, the hummingbirds will depart our New Hampshire yard for warmer climes, but for now they are here still, a busy iridescent blur vibrating in and out of the purple petunias, intent upon visiting each cascading blossom.

The sunflowers are spent, their heavy heads drooping upon slender necks. But I'm in no hurry to cut them down, not till the finches and squirrels have finished feasting on the seed heads. Today, they are like a crowd at a banquet—eager, gathering around, intent on the work at hand. A neighbor's rooster crows, heedless of the fact that dawn was hours ago. A red squirrel perches on the stone wall, chittering loudly to no one.

On the other side of the house, I can hear my son laughing with his friend, the thwack of the basketball in the driveway, occasional cheers for shots made or missed. Another day, and he and I will be on a plane heading south, delivering him to his new life at school. What I feel—hearing him play as he always has, seeing his suitcases open on the bed upstairs, making our shopping list for Target in Atlanta—is not the sadness of an imminent good-bye, but readiness. He is ready, too.

It's not his first leave-taking. Four years ago this fall he went away to boarding school. That time, the house rang with silence, as if a door had abruptly slammed shut on both his childhood and on my day-in-day-out job as his mom. That departure, a new beginning for him, marked the end of an era for me. I wasn't sure if, by allowing him to finish high school three hours away from home, we'd saved him or failed him. But I could hardly bear the sight of his empty room, his chair, the shoes he'd left by the back door. A year ago this month, Steve, Jack, and I caravanned to Boston in my dad's borrowed pickup truck, our old van, and the car, all packed to the brim, and moved him into an apartment in Boston for a gap year of back healing, working, growing up, figuring some things out. Time well spent, despite the hard realities that led to Plan B. And now, with two broken vertebrae mended and a year's experience of living on his own under his belt while most of his friends were enjoying freshman year of college, our younger son is about to step into the long-envisioned future that has finally become the present.

I came outside an hour ago with a stack of mail to open, a bound galley to read, my phone in my hand, my mind buzzing with its own plans and busyness. But all I've done is sit. Listening. Feeling. Being.

The quieter I am, the more I hear. The longer I can be still, the more I see. The more my heart opens, the more it fills. Doing nothing, I am perhaps doing the only thing that really matters in this moment. To be here now, just feeling these feelings and thinking these thoughts, is not only a gift but a practice. And I'm a little rusty.

Remember this, I tell myself: the rise and fall of boys' voices, a ball keeping time on pavement, birdsong, the bees' tuneless canticle, the time-addled rooster's piercing call. No need to hold on or to mourn. Nothing to regret or anticipate. Just life having its way with all of us.

The pliant, golden leaves rustle overhead, like the whisper of a curtain being drawn slowly back. The sun slips out from behind a cloud. The day gives up its meaning slowly. Silence becomes its own kind of language. And this language without words yields its own kind of understanding. There is a secret key that unlocks the world: attention.

In attention there is presence. In presence there is grace. And then, into that grace arrives a small revelation: it is enough, more than enough, simply to be here. To be quiet. To do nothing but sit in a chair in my front yard and receive what the world has to offer—the afternoon turning toward dusk, a finch poised on a sunflower, my sweet old dog sprawled in the grass beside me, a son turning the next page of his life, radiance everywhere—just now, just here, just for this moment.

Already the light is draining away. A flash of red and a cardinal disappears into the pines, his graying mate bobbing along in his wake. The basketball falls silent. The back door opens, closes. A car engine turns over. Tires crunch down the gravel drive. The air grows cool. I gather my sweater, my flip-flops, my untouched pile of work and head indoors to flick on lights, shuck corn, make dinner for my husband and our son.

September 2013

———·—— this is fifty-five ——·———

I've been fifty-five for a little over a week now. Rounding this corner, finding myself squarely in the long-shadowed afternoon of my own life, has given me pause.

I've spent a lot of time lately gazing out the window

in my kitchen, watching the sunlit leaves float from tree to ground. The days, the hours, even the moments, feel ripe and full—time to be cherished rather than rushed through. And so, on this autumn afternoon I close my laptop. For the first time in ages, I pick up a pad of paper and a pen instead. I grab a sweater and head outside to write. Perhaps what I'm yearning for is a different kind of knowing—words that come from the still, silent place in my soul, a glimpse of my own depths, some intimation of my rightful place in the world, now that I've crested the arc of life and begun my descent down the other side.

Fifty-five. How strange it feels to write that pair of fives, to associate them with me. Have I really been alive that long, half a century plus five? And what exactly am I, now that I'm no longer technically middle-aged but not exactly old yet, either?

I turn to a fresh page, brush a stray leaf from my hair, and allow myself to write whatever comes.

This is fifty-five. . .

Fifty-five is being aware there are fewer years left ahead of me than I've lived already. It is understanding, in a way I couldn't have at twenty-five or even forty-five, the bitter-sweet truth of impermanence. It is knowing that tomorrow isn't a guarantee, that every plan is provisional, that life isn't a promise.

Fifty-five is dreaming less of the future, dwelling less in the past, and learning (yes, *still* learning) to be *here,* in the now.

Fifty-five is realizing that being present is my choice to make, again and again and again—not always the easiest choice for me, but always the best.

Fifty-five is asking the same "What next?" question I was struggling with when I graduated from college. It is knowing there are an infinite number of answers. And that none of them is wrong.

Fifty-five is two sons in their twenties. It is still-fresh memories of motherhood as it used to be: intensely physical, all consuming, endlessly challenging, viscerally satisfying. And it is finding my way, day by day, into this new, arm's-length role of mother to young adults. Fifty-five is holding on to faith in their best selves and letting go of fears for their well-being. It is holding on to all I love in each of them and letting go of my need to have them under my roof. It is holding on to a vision of their destinies and letting go of my ideas about how they should get there.

Fifty-five is not knowing where my children are, who they're with, what they're doing, what they ate for dinner, or what's on their minds. It is resisting most of my impulses to text or call. Fifty-five is learning to worry less and to trust more.

Fifty-five is pride and delight in the two young men who come home to visit us. It is laughter around the dinner table and help with the dishes and crowding together on the couch to watch *The Daily Show*. It is honest, heartfelt conversations and easier partings. It is growing used to empty bedrooms. It is being in the homestretch of paying for college.

Fifty-five is being a couple again. It is having the central task of our marriage—raising a family—completed. It is reinvention, renegotiation, and renewal. It is a different kind of commitment. Fifty-five is looking at my husband's nearly sixty-five-year-old face and seeing, even now, the same kindly eyes I fell in love with all those years ago as a young woman of twenty-five.

Fifty-five is twenty-six years of marriage. It is routines and rituals, family traditions and jokes told a thousand times. Fifty-five is knowing my husband so well that his story has become my story. It is a mountain of family photographs, moments preserved for posterity. It is realizing how many more moments have passed, unrecorded and forgotten. It's realizing I've lived more of my life alongside this man than I lived before I knew him.

Fifty-five is not sweating the small stuff (the ice-cream scoop left on the counter, the toilet seat left up, his tendency to talk too loud) and being grateful for the big stuff (loyalty, forgiveness, humor, love).

Fifty-five is feeling the ten-year age difference between us in the slowing pace of our morning walks and not feeling it at all when his arms are around me. It is less about trying to change the man I married and more about loving him as he is for as long as I can. It is knowing the words "till death do us part" will one day come true.

Fifty-five is passion transformed into tenderness. It is the end of "the quickie." It is love that's long and slow and unguarded. Fifty-five is less often but with more feeling. Fifty-five is less self-conscious and more trusting. It is less awkward but more exposed. Fifty-five is still good. Fifty-five, my husband says, is better than ever.

Fifty-five is discovering that my heart has no notion of time or propriety. It is admitting that love can still surprise me. Fifty-five is my pulse quickening at the touch of a hand; the blood rushing to my cheeks at the sight of a smile; a funny flip-flop in the pit of my stomach at a sentence in a novel that puts into words something I've never dared to say out loud. Fifty-five is being invisible when I'm walking down the street. Inside, fifty-five is as chaotic and as confusing as fifteen.

Fifty-five is tears and laughter every day. Sometimes, it's both at once. It is joy and sorrow intertwined. It is shadow and light. It is admitting I've learned as much from my losses and failures as from the gifts that have been laid at my feet.

Fifty-five is going to bed in pajamas and fleece and socks. It is being stark naked at 3 am. It is my husband knowing better than to mistake this for an invitation. Fifty-five is hot flashes and night sweats and Swiss cheese for a brain. It is bedclothes off and on and off again. It is sleepless nights and staring at the ceiling and Tylenol PM and earplugs. Fifty-five is getting by on fewer hours of sleep than I ever thought possible. Fifty-five is standing outside in the wet grass, watching the sun come up. Fifty-five is being astonished, still, by the resurrection of morning.

Fifty-five is jeans that stretch, bras that lift, shirts that cover, and shoes that don't pinch. It is knowing I'm too old for the Gap and not tall enough or rich enough for Eileen Fisher. It is throwing the Victoria's Secret catalog in the trash on my way back from the mailbox. It is lingering over the earrings and the peasant blouses in the Sundance catalog and then throwing that away, too. It is one pair of good black boots.

Fifty-five is making peace with my habits: a cup of dark roast coffee every morning laced with half and half, a glass of wine with dinner. It is saying yes to champagne and no to mixed drinks. It is cooking meat for my family without being tempted to eat it myself. It is drinking extra glasses of water, taking "Wiser Woman" vitamins, thinking about bone density, skipping dessert more often than not. It is a private stash of dark chocolate not meant for sharing.

Fifty-five is standing in front of the mirror and drawing the sagging skin of my neck up and back. It is glimpsing the possibility of looking a decade younger. It is considering getting a little "work" done. It is turning away from the face that looks too old to be mine and getting on with the day.

Fifty-five is accepting there are some things I used to do that I will never do again: downhill skiing, rollerblading, galloping across a beach on a horse, hot yoga. It is realizing how much I long to do some other things before it's too late: sleep outside under the stars, swim naked in the dark, sit by a campfire, hike the White Mountains, visit my best friend from college in Santa Fe, wear a cocktail dress and heels, take a trip with my mom.

Fifty-five is knowing that some of my secret, youthful fantasies aren't going to come true: living in a cabin by a lake, spending a month in Paris and learning French, writing a best-seller, owning a book store. Fifty-five is realizing I've outgrown those fantasies anyway.

Fifty-five is talking less and listening more. It is choosing less screen time and more real time. It is saying no to things I don't want to do. It is craving solitude. At the same time, it is a willingness to be more open, more intimate, more vulnerable with the small handful of people to whom I've entrusted my soul.

Fifty-five is knowing what makes me happy: time alone, time in nature, time with dear friends, time with my family, time with a book.

Fifty-five is reading glasses and wrinkle creams and con-cealer for the dark circles under my eyes. It is a root canal. It is a basal cell removed and a new, worrisome place on my forehead. It is a groin pull. It is a stomach growing softer and shoulders growing rounder. It is a pair of tweezers kept in the glove compartment for plucking the stray black hair that sprouts from my chin, which I discover (always) while sitting at an intersection waiting for the light to change.

Fifty-five is also twenty-six miles walked with friends to raise money for cancer research. It is a three-minute plank pose. It is breathing deeply in headstand. It is running just for the fun of it. It is two strong legs and a strong will and an undiminished sense of adventure. Fifty-five is still going strong. It is knowing that someday, it will be otherwise.

Fifty-five is finding out what it is to lose a friend. It is being there right till the end. It is death growing more familiar and hitting closer to home. It is grieving with a mother who's just lost her son, a boy I've known since the day he was born. It is an e-mail bearing news of a diagnosis. It is a loved one calling from the hospital. It is a new understanding of the word "random." It is learning that finding meaning where there appears to be no meaning is part of our spiritual work.

Fifty-five is two parents just shy of eighty. It is the joy of still allowing them to parent me. It is awareness that one day I will be the one caring for them. It is a whispered "thank-you" for every family gathering, for my dad's grilled turkey on Thanksgiving, for my mom's handmade cards, for their voices on the other end of the phone. For all that was and all that still is and all that someday will be no more.

Fifty-five is finding my sense of purpose in unexpected places. It is teaching yoga after years of thinking I could never be a yoga teacher. It is writing for the joy of writing rather than to be recognized as a writer. It is sitting on the floor, feeding our old dog by hand. It is helping my son hang a shower curtain in his new apartment. It is proofreading another's son's job application and not changing a word.

Fifty-five is sitting quietly with someone in pain and it is celebrating another's joy as if it were my own. It is driving a neighbor to the doctor, making dinner for the millionth time, answering a letter on the day it arrives, cutting sunflowers and putting them in a vase. It is holding hands with my dearest friend, heart brimming, no words needed.

Fifty-five is ordinary. It is the relief of not being exceptional. It is recognizing what is precious and beautiful in someone else. It is choosing not to live in drama but in harmony. It is less ambition and more appreciation. It is gratitude for things as they are rather than grasping for something just out of reach. It is seeing the futility of comparing and judging and craving. It is a deepening sense of compassion. It is gratitude. It is plain and simple. It is less clutter. Less talk. More love.

Fifty-five is learning to approach each day as a blessing, each word as a benediction, daily life as my practice. It is being open to what comes, offering prayers of hope and healing for the universe, trusting there are forces at work here that are larger than I am.

Fifty-five is the joy of waking up each day and taking part in the great, ongoing human conversation. It is mystery. It is me for just this little while.

October 2013

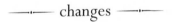

—·— changes —·—

I've been paying close attention to the weather lately. Over the last few days, frost has claimed the last of the nasturtiums outside the kitchen door. The maple tree, as of yesterday, is bare, save for two golden leaves stubbornly clinging.

"The leaves fell so much earlier than usual this year," I've been saying to my husband, as if we've been deprived of something, an extra week of gazing at them perhaps. "It's gotten colder sooner." He doesn't believe me but I'm pretty sure I'm right. And then it occurs to me: I have a record.

It was just a year ago that two young filmmakers from Boston drove up to our house in New Hampshire to shoot the book trailer for *Magical Journey*. I was watching the weather closely that week, too, worried it would be freezing by the time we finally had a shot list together and that late October would prove too stark and wintry to allow for the photogenic, carefree outdoor moments I'd been envisioning.

I haven't watched the video myself for a year, not since the day I okayed the final cut and sent it off to my publisher to post on YouTube, with fingers crossed that it might inspire a few book sales. Perhaps some movie stars get used to seeing themselves on film or hearing the sound of their own recorded voices but I doubt I ever will. It's easier not to look.

A year ago, making a book trailer was just another item on my prepublication to-do list, one more thing to worry about getting right and submitting by the deadline. This morning though, aware of all that's changed since we spent a day filming footage for a four-minute movie, I clicked on the YouTube link and allowed myself a short trip back in time.

I have no idea if this brief video actually moved potential readers to buy my book. But I have to admit: sales or not, I'm grateful now for one October day in my life that was not only lived but captured for eternity.

Watching the four-minute film that resulted from that day of shooting, I'm reminded all over again that it really is the ordinary stuff of life that's the most lovely—the light through the kitchen window, a walk in the woods with a friend, tossing a ball for a dog to catch, raking leaves into a fragrant pile, a chat over a cup of tea, a son's quick kiss on his way out the door.

As I type these words, I can't help but marvel yet again at how relentless change is. How inevitable, how eternal, how unpredictable. I think of our two sons, each living now in distant states and following paths none of us could have foreseen a year ago. They check in, have been texting with their dad during the World Series games, ask us to send a few things from home. But the ties that bind are lengthening, stretching, and growing thinner all the time. Change propels us forward, urging us to stretch, to grow, to risk. Change separates us, too, demanding that we release our hold on what's over.

And, at the same time, change challenges us to surrender, to accept, to soften into what is. Bright fall days give way to gray winter afternoons. The last leaves finally do drift from the trees. The ground hardens over, the sky darkens, a season ends.

Our dog, Gracie, so eager to show off her fielding skills a year ago, tearing across the yard to snatch a ball out of the air, is thirteen and battling a sudden, advanced cancer. A week ago, we almost lost her. And then to everyone's astonishment, she rallied, responding to good care, a barrage of drugs, and an enormous gush of love. (I always said I'd never cook for a dog. Last night, Gracie had beef stew for dinner, which she lapped—delicately, out of a spoon—while lying down on the dining-room rug.)

"We have to take it day by day," the kindly veterinarian warned last week as I took notes about her chemo treatments and wrote down what side effects to watch for and the schedule for her pills at home.

For the time being, she is doing well enough, holding her own. But as I sit next to her on the floor, kissing her nose and feeling with my fingertips to see if the lymph nodes on her neck are shrinking, the words "day by day" assume their own resonance. This, after all, is the way each one of us must approach our lives, appreciating all that we have for as long as we can. Day by day. Hour by hour. Precious moment by precious moment.

Knowing now that our time with Gracie is coming to an end, I'm glad the need to make a book trailer last fall prompted us to catch our dear, fleet-footed girl on film when she was still healthy and in her prime. And I'm grateful, too, for every quiet, pain-free day she is granted here. Precious moment by precious moment, we are allowed to love her, to care for her, to celebrate the joy she's brought into our lives for thirteen years.

Last week a fellow dog lover assured me, "She will let you know when it's time to say good-bye." I will trust in the truth of that and hope, for her sake and for ours, that we are wise and gracious enough then to let her go.

Meanwhile, for the record, it's Steve who's right. The hard frost came and the last of the autumn leaves fell this month just as they did one year ago. It happened the very same week, in fact, while the October Hunter's moon waned in a cold, clear, star-strewn night sky. It is only in my own imagination, faulty and greedy as it is, that I've been shortchanged—yearning as always for a few more mild hours, another golden day, a bit more sweetness, a little more time.

October 2013

 mean mail

I will call her Mary. Of course, even all these months later, I do remember her real name. I remember it as clearly as I do the words she used to describe me: "sham," "self-absorbed," "selfish," and "failure." I remember reading those words with my heart pounding, my hands shaking, my mouth going dry.

I remember how deeply they cut, how defenseless and ashamed they made me feel, how brutally close to the mark they came. I remember that, alone in my kitchen on a bright winter's day, I read a letter from a total stranger and crumpled into a ball on the sofa, as if shielding myself from another blow.

And yet, the first thing I do when I turn on my computer this morning is retrieve Mary's long-ago e-mail from my inbox. If my task here is to write about mean mail from readers, I figure I must begin by putting Exhibit A out on the table.

I take a deep breath. And then I read it again, this silent, perfectly aimed strike from a woman who read the first chapters of my most recent book and felt compelled to pause and let me know that although she considers me a "wonderful writer," who "gets to the heart and soul of a woman's thinking," she now realizes that I'm a failure as a mother, as a person, and as a role model.

If memoir is a slice of curated reality in which not everything that happens shows up on the page, but in which everything that does appear there must be faithfully rendered, then failure probably has to be part of the deal.

We go to self-help books in search of answers. We turn to memoir, I suspect, to engage in a conversation about the questions themselves. Perhaps what we want most of all is both to find ourselves and lose ourselves in the pages of another's story. We read memoir not to fix our lives, but to see how this person or that one manages to heal his or her own broken places. We long to know how others play the hand they got dealt, how the path twists and turns beneath another's feet, whether someone else has survived the wrong turn, the crack-up, the heartbreak. We may arrive at memoir's door hoping for inspiration, but we enter into its rooms to be reminded of the painful truth we already know: life is both precious and painful, things rarely go as planned, and no one comes through unscathed.

Which does not make confessing my own shortcomings any easier. The temptation is always there: to offer up a smarter, tidier, more impressive version of myself. How much easier it would be to show up on the page with some answers, some hard-won wisdom, a handful of foolproof tips about life and parenting and growing older—good, solid advice gleaned from deep reflection and personal experience, neatly packaged and ready for public consumption. How great it would be to have things

all figured out and to write about *that*. Sometimes I write
to express and share the simple joys of ordinary life, aware
that both the life itself and the quiet time to reflect upon
it are gifts.

But just as often, my writing process goes something
like this: I procrastinate for a few hours. I get the dishes
done, make sure every crumb is swept from the counter,
from the floor. I water the houseplants, throw in a load
of laundry, pay a bill. And then, when I can put it off no
longer, I sit down on a stool at the kitchen table. I force
myself to stay. I swear off checking e-mail or reviewing
the weather forecast online. I watch the shadows lengthen
on the wall, feel the hours slide slowly by.

Eventually, if I'm patient and sit there long enough, I
drop down into the inchoate, confusing place that gives
rise to all my own unanswered questions, the messy, trou-
bling stuff that remains unresolved in my heart and that
gnaws at my soul in the dark of night.

Slowly, something inside me begins to open, to accept
that this feeling of discomfort is indeed my starting place.
It isn't a place of certainty, but rather one of hunger and
longing and not knowing. And my job, as I continually
remind myself, isn't to come up with tidy answers, but to
find words that might convey the disheveled, imperfect
truth of who I really am and how I really feel—the confusion and the fleeting clarity, the despair and the hope,
the joy and the heartbreak of being a human being who is
wrong about things every bit as often as she's right.

Perhaps it is in our very nature to fear being found out.

Don't we all get up each morning determined to do the best we can at being the person we aspire to become? And don't we worry, too, that any minute now we'll be called out, have our most embarrassing failings exposed, our unsuitability for the job revealed? Try as we might to put the best face forward, there is, deep inside, that persistent, unshakeable, uniquely human fear that we aren't really all we claim to be, that we are and will always be somehow "less than."

For a memoir writer, the stakes can feel even a bit higher than that. Consider: there is the person I feel myself to be inside. There is the (better!) person I aspire to become. There is the highly fallible person my closest friends and family know and love in spite of everything. There is the somewhat more presentable person who chats with the grocery-store clerk and shows up at yoga class. And then, in addition to all those "me's," there is another, even more public and considerably less together person who appears on the page. A character who comprises, perhaps, bits and pieces of all these beings.

She is me, but she is also my creation, my own vulnerable, narrated self; the "me" who lives between the covers of a book and who carries my story of how I stumbled from "there" to "here" out into the world. She is at once me and not me.

Take a swing at her, though, and I am, without a doubt, the one who feels the punch.

"I'm a very private person," I once said to my neighbor, in an attempt to explain why I spend so many hours at

home alone, why I cherish a day when I don't have anywhere to go or anything to do but putz around my house
in a pair of old sweatpants and a ratty fleece and a pair of
flip-flops.

"A private person?" She laughed, incredulous. "How
could you be? You write about yourself!"

She's right. I do. And yet to do that, I first have to construct and inhabit that illusion of privacy. Sitting alone in
my kitchen, dropping down into the dark, difficult place
from which truth flows, it is easy—and necessary—to pretend that no one will ever read the pages that accumulate
beneath my finger tips.

I can't write honestly if I'm also anticipating the possibly
averse reaction of some unknown reader. No. My challenge
as a writer is to be acutely present in *this* moment, to put
down upon the page both what I know and what I don't
know, and to have faith that there is value even in the
not knowing. To have faith, too, in this paradoxical process by which the personal becomes universal, individual
experience becomes shared experience, one life expresses
the unwritten truth of many lives, and words conjured
in solitude make their way out into the world to forge
connections that didn't exist before.

Last night, over dinner, I told a friend I was going to
write a piece about mean mail from readers. "I said I'd
do this months ago," I confessed, "and now I'm wishing
I hadn't."

I had thought, back when the wound was fresh and
writing about it seemed like a sly way to respond to the

hurt, that I would quote Mary's entire letter, perhaps even drum up a bit of sympathy for myself. But as I reread her letter this morning, I realize there is no need to share it, any more than there is reason for me to defend myself against its accusations. The desire to strike back, to make my case, or even to have the last word, is gone.

All I can do—all any of us can do—is write what we know right now from where we are today. I can't claim to have it all figured out, neither the writing nor the living. To tell one's own story is to step into vulnerability, to open oneself to judgment and criticism. But to write a memoir is also to believe that any human presence, imperfect and undefended, is in itself an offering.

In sharing our innermost struggles, our joys, our sorrows, we invite others to consider their own fumbling steps in the dark with a bit more tenderness. In cultivating empathy for ourselves, for our mistakes and shortcomings, we also clear a space for the stories of others who struggle. That seems to me work worth doing. It is the conversation we long to have, the exchange between reader and writer we are all here for, the reason I'm willing to dwell for hours in an uncomfortable place waiting for the words to come.

That sharp-edged essay about mean mail I thought I'd write? It turns out I don't really have it in me. Sitting with Mary's letter today has reminded me what a blessing it is to soften and what a relief it is to forgive. For better and for worse, the words we write form bridges between us, connecting us soul to soul, heart to heart. The communion isn't always easy or comfortable—how could it be? Perhaps it's the connection itself that matters, though, and not the approval. And perhaps the best response to a reader like Mary is to understand that she isn't hurting me because I'm who *I* am, but because she's who *she* is. Which means there's nothing I need to defend after all.

And so, all these months later, I drag Exhibit A over to the tiny trashcan in the corner of my screen. I click the icon and let it go.

"Thank God there's only one of her," I said to my friend last night, after reciting Mary's list of accusations from memory. But perhaps what I really want to say is, "Thank God there *was* one of her"—a sad, angry woman who reached out through the ether to remind me that my challenge, both as a writer and as a person, isn't to make people like me but to become a little better at loving and accepting myself.

A version of this essay first appeared in the online journal Compose, *October 2013*

—·—— Gracie, 8/20/00–11/18/13 ——·—

Everyone we know who's ever loved and lost a dog told us the same thing: she would let us know when it was time to say good-bye. And, of course, she did. Yesterday morning we let Gracie go, with sad hearts but also feeling certain it was her day to leave us.

Since she was diagnosed with cancer just a month ago, Gracie rose to the challenge of treatment just the way she did everything else in her life: willingly, without fuss or fanfare, and with complete trust in her humans to do what was best for her. We took a big swing at it, with three rounds of chemo, and were amazed and thrilled as she gained back weight and strength and her zest for life.

A week ago, she was like her old self—up at dawn, taking us for long morning walks, playing in the leaves, chasing balls and sticks. There were no bad days. These past few weeks have been about massages and Reiki and hand-feeding, lots of special, home-cooked food, visits with all her friends, treats and walks and togetherness. We had the great gift of getting her back for a little while, knowing as well that things could turn at any moment. When they did, we took our cues from her.

Yesterday morning Steve and Debbie and I had breakfast together, while Gracie dozed on her bed beside us in the sunshine. After a long, difficult night, she was breathing peacefully. She was "present" and, at the same time, so clearly ready to go. We played the Brandenburg concertos on the stereo, the Saturday-morning pancake music of her puppyhood. We loved her and kissed her and held her. I told her the story of her life, all thirteen wonderful years of it. And then I read her poems from Mary Oliver's collection *Dog Songs.* She had a lovely, pain-free morning, which felt like another gift. And then one last ride in the car, to the vet who has been so kind and helpful through this journey.

Gracie passed at 11:25, with her sweet head in my hands and Debbie holding her body. She leaves a great hole in all our lives. I know we will find tennis balls on every walk we take in the woods for years. And we will miss her and remember her always, the companion of our lives.

Tonight, sitting here in a quiet house without her in it, I am almost unbearably sad and raw and lonely. Every spot here speaks her name. Each time I think I'm done with crying, the tears flow again. I want her back. It is as simple, and as impossible, as that.

Instead I turn again to the words of Mary Oliver, who knows as much as anyone about loving and letting go of dogs:

"And it is exceedingly short, this galloping life. Dogs die so soon. I have my stories of that grief, no doubt many of you do also. It is almost a failure of will, a failure of love, to let them grow old—or so it feels. We would do anything to keep them with us, and to keep them young. The one gift we cannot give."

November 2013

the soul of solstice

One December when our sons were little, I hung a piece of paper painted a deep dark blue in our kitchen. "A sky," I told them. I painted another piece of paper gold, cut out about a hundred small stars and put them in a basket, along with a glue stick. "Every star represents a good deed," I said. "Let's fill the sky with kindness."

My hope was to distract the boys a bit from the idea of "getting" things for Christmas, and to shift the emphasis instead to the kinds of simple acts of charity that actually make us feel good inside ourselves.

I knew I wouldn't have much luck telling them that the shortest route to happiness isn't paved with possessions. (Try explaining that to a six-year-old who has been trying to prioritize his Christmas list.) They wouldn't believe me if I suggested that more stuff doesn't equal a better life. Or that a surefire antidote to restlessness and craving is to do something nice for someone else. I wanted them to discover for themselves the joy of giving, the deeper meaning of the season.

And so, for every random, unsolicited act of kindness anyone in the family did during the day, we placed a star into the sky. Each night at dinnertime, we turned off the kitchen lights, lit candles in an Advent wreath on our table, held hands and said grace. And then we talked about the opportunities we'd each found during the day to do good deeds.

The December of Good Deeds was a long time ago. For some unknown reason, we did it only that once. And yet this is one of my favorite holiday memories ever.

Last night, Henry and Steve and I grabbed the afghans and lined up on the couch together to watch a couple of recorded episodes of *The Daily Show*. The clips of shoppers mauling each other in a race to claim discounted printers, dollar DVDs, and Rachel Ray cookware on Black Friday were more horrifying than funny. Jon Stewart didn't need to say much about the stabbing in Virginia over a parking space, the shooting at Kohl's, or the mayhem at Wal-Mart. There was no need to comment on Sarah Palin's claim last week that she loves the commercialization of Christmas because it reminds us all that this is the "most cheerful holiday on the calendar." All he had to do was play the footage.

This morning, I woke up early, still haunted and disturbed by those scenes. We are warm and dry and safe and well fed here. There is nothing anyone in my family needs or wants so badly that we'd line up outside a store at 6 am to get it. None of us went shopping the day after Thanksgiving.

But I also realize what a luxury our comfort is. I don't want to take any of what I have for granted—not the food in our refrigerator, not the heat rising from the grates on the floor, not the laptop on which I type these words, nor the fact that, at 6:30 in the morning, I am privileged enough to be sitting on the couch in my pajamas writing a blog post rather than driving through darkness to get to work on time. I can't even begin to know what it's like to live in a constant state of worry or hunger or not-enough.

And yet, I'm certainly not immune to the pressures of the season. I may not agree with those who extol the commercialization of Christmas but I can't always resist it, either. In this season of short days and long, cold nights there is, perhaps, a nearly universal impulse to dispel the darkness. And what better way to escape the discomfort of our own dark places, anxious thoughts, and fears of scarcity than by rushing forth—out into the bright lights and cheerful music and super sales at the shopping mall?

The winter solstice is a time when the natural world is still and dormant. Outside my own window this morning, the ground is frozen solid, the trees lightly coated with a scrim of ice. The only lights to be seen are the neighbor's holiday decorations, left aglow all night. The truth is, I would prefer complete darkness. I realize that my own desire as the winter solstice approaches is to unplug, to fully experience the shortest days, the longest nights, the deepest shadows.

Sitting here while the rest of my family sleeps, I'm reminded how healing it feels when I can take my cues not from the culture but from nature. Each day this month, I want to make that choice. To slow down, to sit quietly, to turn inward. Instead of banishing or fleeing from the silent darkness, I can welcome it. Instead of trying to escape my complicated, pre-holiday feelings of sadness for times past and anxiety about the days to come, I can simply acknowledge them: my annual desire for things to be just so, my annual worry that they won't be.

Later today Henry and I will decorate the Christmas tree he and Steve have already set up in the living room. We'll put on our favorite music, bring the decorations up from the basement, test out last year's strings of lights. My December to-do list is long—there are meals to plan, presents to buy and make and wrap and send, cards to write. Jack will come home. We will visit friends and uphold as many traditions we can. As always, the whole family will gather here on Christmas day for gifts and a brunch that lasts for hours. I love and cherish every moment of it. But I can also get a little overwhelmed thinking about all I have set myself to orchestrate and plan and do.

The other day, feeling my old, familiar December panic setting in, I confided to a friend that part of me would like to skip this month altogether.

But that's not really true. What I want is to fully embrace it instead—in my own way and at my own pace. Instead of thinking about "producing" Christmas, I want to align my heart with the soul of solstice. Here in the predawn darkness, I'm seeing more clearly just what I wish to cultivate and bring into the light this season. Such simple things: love, laughter, ease, togetherness, gratitude, hospitality, joy.It doesn't have to be hard and it doesn't have to be expensive. Perhaps all I need to do is re-create, in my own mind at least, that long-ago piece of blue paper taped to the refrigerator. And then fill it up with stars of goodness.

December 2013

*You will find as you look back upon your life
that the moments that stand out, the moments
when you have really lived, are the moments when you
have done things in a spirit of love.*
— *Henry Drummond*

——·—— walking the labyrinth ——·——

Each New Year's Eve morning, volunteers in our town painstakingly tape a labyrinth onto the floor of the Town Hall, creating an exact replica of the famous thirteenth-century labyrinth at Chartres Cathedral. In silence, townspeople arrive throughout the afternoon, New Year's Eve, and New Year's Day to walk the path and reflect. It has become a special tradition in our family. Yesterday, as I traveled through the labyrinth with my husband and son, I was surprised by the emotions that came up. Such a simple ritual. And yet, so much mystery. So much beauty. So much.

Coming home, contemplating this new year, wondering what lies in store, I sat down in the kitchen and wrote these lines quickly, trying to capture the experience before it slipped away:

You take a step forward, and another, still not sure you're on the right road. And yet, there is something deep inside you that seems to be urging *this way.* The child in you is afraid. You look around for confirmation, for some wiser, older "adult" kind of person to nod "yes." If only someone else would fall into step beside you, someone who could take your hand and tell you who you really are and where you're meant to go. Instead, every morning you wake up and set out once again, a fumbling beginner on the path of awakening.

The road is full of travelers. (You wonder: Does everyone else have this all figured out? Am I the only one who's lost?) You can—and do—follow in another's footsteps for a while. But ultimately, you have to find your own way. This life, this trail through the wilderness, is a creative journey: your own. And it's full of unknowns. No map or guide or friend can tell you what's around the next corner. All you know for sure is that the view isn't ever quite what you expected. The plans you make? No guarantees, no promises.

You have no choice but to proceed on faith. Little by little you learn to trust: the murmurings of your own heart, the wisdom in your own two feet, the forces at work in the world that are larger than you. What you need, you have. What you want changes moment to moment.

Road-weary, you begin to shed the heavy baggage of wanting and craving and worry. There is a kind of freedom in letting go. You move more slowly, more quietly—taking time to listen, to look, to marvel. Befriending the silence, you turn away from the chattering voices in your head.

You see into the depths of things. And what you come to understand, as your pace slows and your heart opens, is that not all desires need to be met. That there is a kind of mercy in accepting yourself as you are, your life as it is, the path you are already on.

Once you slip through the net of your own fears, you begin to appreciate the beauty that is yours for the seeing. Out here, in the open space between the yes and the no of judgment, you discover the treasure that's been yours all along: your life is filled with grace. You stand still for a moment, overcome by the shock of it. You look around, through new eyes, and are suddenly filled with compassion for all those who are walking ahead of you, behind you, beside you. There is nothing to do but love them all. There is no other place to be but here. There is nothing to feel but gratitude.

January 2014

 full circle

I've written about this particular photo of me and Henry before: Times Square, New York City, early on a Sunday summer morning in 1996. The day before, Steve and I had taken our seven-year-old son to see his first musical, *Beauty and the Beast,* on Broadway. A friend working on the show had reserved our seats, front and center, and had arranged a backstage tour after the final curtain. Henry had been allowed to walk around on the set. He'd touched the teacups and candlesticks and glimpsed the piano gleaming in the orchestra pit. He'd shaken hands with the Beast himself, who had been kind and friendly to this scrawny little kid who knew every song in the show by heart. And now, the next morning, all Henry wanted was to go back and do it all over again.

My husband snapped the photo because it was so not like our shy, mild-mannered son to be demanding. And it was so not like me to speak sternly to him. And yet, there we were, facing off in the first and pretty much the only real argument we've ever had.

I think the whole scene cracked Steve up—while the rest of Manhattan slept, the three of us were out on a street corner trying to explain to our star-struck child that Broadway shows aren't like videos and that you can't just wander in and watch them whenever you want to.

What we didn't quite realize, as Henry stood his ground, insisting he would go back to Broadway, was that a dream was taking shape in his young mind. Now that he knew this magical place existed, where musicals came to life every night in darkened theaters, he suddenly had an answer to the question, "What do you want to be when you grow up?"

The dream stuck. He's twenty-four now, and he's stayed the course. Played a lot of piano. Applied for a lot of jobs. Gotten a few. Come in second too many times. But late on Monday night, the call he's been imagining nearly all his life finally came. And since I'm his mom, and therefore have never doubted, I wasn't all that surprised. But I am incredibly proud to say our son has come full circle. Next job: music production assistant for the forthcoming Disney production of *Aladdin* on Broadway.

Tonight, as I was making dinner, Henry sat at the piano in our living room playing Gershwin. It's been snowing all day, and the snow is still coming down, closing us in here with one another. Jack, recovering from the removal of two wisdom teeth first thing this morning, has been stretched out on the couch all afternoon, applying ice, reading a Stephen King novel. We watched a movie earlier, drank tea, looked at some old photo albums, hung out, and let the hours pass. As I type these words, the guys are watching basketball in the other room, eating ice cream and making a racket. Soon both our sons will leave, and it will be just the two of us here again. Although I'm used to the empty nest by now, I'll still miss the noise when they're gone, the crowd around the dinner table, the sense of security and connectedness I feel when we are all safely gathered together under one roof.

And yet, knowing the house will soon be quiet again, I also think of a line I've always loved: "There are two lasting bequests we can give our children: one is roots; the other, wings." And I am here to say, there is nothing more thrilling than bearing witness to their flight.

January 2014

re-enchantment

The first thing I did when I found out I was pregnant,

twenty-five years ago this winter, was get in my car and drive to Harvard Square to buy a copy of *What to Expect When You're Expecting.* I am a book person, a lifelong reader. And so my first response to anything new or challenging in my life has always been the same: go find a book on the subject.

For a few years, as I became a mother to first one son and then another, I read my way through an entire shelf of parenting titles. I read books about every age and every stage, about attachment and achievement, discipline and diet.

But the book that finally set me on my own path, both as a mother and as a person, wasn't a parenting book at all. It was a book called *The Re-Enchantment of Everyday Life* by a writer named Thomas Moore. Most of us have a handful of books we consider seminal, books that make such profound, deep, and lasting impressions that we remember, even years later, exactly where we were and how we felt as the words landed in our hearts.

I was in a lawn chair at my parents' house in Florida, savoring quiet. Our boys, about seven and four at the time, were off somewhere with their dad. So I found myself in that relaxed, open, on-vacation state of mind that's particularly receptive to new ideas.

And, although I probably didn't know it then, I was very much in need of a new idea. With each passing year, as our sons grew out of infancy, through toddlerhood and into early childhood, it seemed our life was moving faster. The stresses of working and parenting and marriage intensified. More and more, I felt as if my old idea wasn't working all that well.

The idea I'd begun with, the one that had led me to read all those books in the first place, was that if I worked really hard at being a mom, and did everything right, and signed our kids up for enough enriching activities, and somehow achieved a perfect balance between my work life and our family life, our two sons would grow up to have the successful, well-adjusted, happy, high-achieving lives we envisioned for them.

We were in the thick of all that—juggling school schedules, doctors' appointments, play dates, lessons, and work and birthday parties. The calendar was full. Everyone was busy. I was managing. We were fine. We were also exhausted. So this title, *The Re-Enchantment of Everyday Life,* captivated me. "Re-Enchantment" sounded lovely. It was exactly what I wanted.

In the book's opening pages, the author suggests that to "re-enchant" our ordinary, mundane adult lives, we simply need to reconnect with the magical, "enchanted" world most of us knew as children. As we grow up, he says, we get sophisticated out of enchantment. We get too busy, too practical, and too smart about the things that cause children to wonder. It made sense to me.

When I thought of my own leisurely, uneventful childhood in a small New Hampshire town in the early 1960s, the memories were still vivid. I could conjure a musty basement nook under our house, where I once placed a Concord grape on a cobwebbed windowsill and watched, day by day, until it turned into a raisin. Wonder! I remembered the scary excitement of sleeping outside in a tent in the backyard, the thrill of skinny-dipping in the middle of the night with my best friend. I recalled reading *Gone With the Wind* and crying my way through the last pages of the book—and how, every day for a week, until I had to return the book to the library, I picked it up and re-read the ending again, weeping every time, marveling that words on a page could exert such power over me.

There were so many long, empty summer days spent reading books, which always meant entering a world of enchantment. There were aimless bike rides to the sandpit and, once there, secret games and rituals and stories to share with my friends. There were orange popsicles that cost a dime for the long ride home.

I remembered spending a long, hot summer afternoon sitting outside a neighbor's chicken coop watching a sick chicken die. The mystery of life and death! I remembered almost believing in ghosts and fairies and haunted places out in the woods. I even recalled a day when I had so little to do that I sat down in the yard and told myself I wouldn't get up again till I'd found a four-leaf clover. I stared into the grass for hours, until I'd found three, proof enough for me that the world was a magical place. (I've never found another one since, although I continue to search, and to believe my efforts will one day yield another.)

So, no, it wouldn't be too hard for me to conjure that childlike sense of wonder. But it also occurred to me that my own sons, perhaps someday reading this same book as adults themselves, might not have any idea what

Thomas Moore was talking about. It seemed possible they wouldn't have a store of such private, indelible memories to draw upon. And that unless we made some changes in the way we were living, my own children might grow up with very little experience of either boredom or enchantment. Sitting in my mom's lawn chair that day, reading this quietly revolutionary book, I got a glimpse of a different path. It's not an overstatement to say it changed my life.

Of course, as Moore points out, change begins in silence, in the private realm of the imagination. And suddenly I had a new vision—of a different kind of pace for our family and a different approach to my own task as a parent. I hadn't ever thought of motherhood as a spiritual practice before, but now I saw that, for me anyway, it could be. A practice that would be more about deepening my faith in my own path than following the experts' advice, and more about being than about doing.

The biggest shift was indeed invisible. It was my dawning awareness that my real challenge as a mother wasn't just to meet my children's physical needs, but to nurture their inner lives as well. And that to do that, I'd need to carve out time to simply let my children be children. Instead of finding things for them to do and creating experiences for them to have, I could create empty spaces in our days. Instead of trying to hustle us all toward some kind of future happiness, I could trust that, left a bit more to their own devices, each of our sons would bloom in his own way and in his own time.

And instead of striving to do more and to be better, I

could practice simply relaxing into the here and now. I could remind myself that the enchanted world of childhood is not a place to be rushed through, but rather a garden of innocence, a sacred time and space that will not last for long and that is to be appreciated and fiercely protected for as long as possible.

The re-enchantment of our family life, the care of our souls, began right there, right then, with the realization that this work of mothering wasn't all about my children, but about me, too. Because, in order to care for my children's souls, I would also have to learn to care for my own.

I didn't know Tom Moore when I began to read his work. But I'm quite certain that were it not for his writing, I wouldn't have become a writer myself. Approaching my ordinary life as a practice worthy of mindfulness and attention changed the way I did almost everything.

Letting go of my need to be right, of my desire to understand and control, meant deepening my faith in the rightness of things as they were. It meant loosening my grip, quieting my inner critic, and trusting my children's destinies to unfold according to a plan greater than my own. It meant resting more and accomplishing less, exchanging some of my ambition for acceptance, tuning in to my intuition, making beauty a priority, creating rituals around everyday activities like mealtime and bedtime and story time. It meant seeing each moment of the day as an opportunity for reverence. It meant cultivating gratitude.

Bringing that kind of attention to my everyday tasks, I began to see our family and our life together in a new light. And the more awareness I brought to this life, the more deeply meaningful and precious it became. And so I found not only a spiritual path but also my subject as a writer. The gift of an ordinary day. It never ceases to amaze me.

January 2014

—·— how to savor a winter morning —·—

"If your daily life seems of no account, don't blame it; blame yourself that you are not poet enough to call forth its treasures."
—Rilke

Open your eyes in darkness.
Listen to the heat kick on.
Snuggle more deeply into flannel sheets.
Say a prayer of thanks for the roof over your head,
for your warm house, for the hot shower that awaits.
Turn your gaze toward the feathery frost on the
windowpane.
Allow moonlight to wash away sleep.
Watch stars wink out, the sky lighten, a scrim
of rose etch itself across the mountain.
Rise with the sun.

Check the weather on your phone: minus 8 degrees on your New Hampshire hilltop, 7 for the son working in New York City, a balmy 22 for the one in school in Atlanta, negative 15 for your husband visiting his sister in Minnesota.

Realize: everyone in your family is waking up in a cold place.

Send each one a "Brrr-good-morning-I-love-you" text signed with x's and o's.

Brew your coffee with two extra scoops, the way you like it.

Drink slowly from the small blue mug that fits your hand just right, while the silent kitchen floods with sunlight.

Eat your oatmeal with everything on it: sea salt, brown sugar, raisins, walnuts, a sliced pear, a handful of half-thawed blueberries you picked last August, yogurt from the farm on the other side of the mountain.

Read from the book that arrived in the mail yesterday, a gift from your friend Margaret, who knows the workings of your heart. Allow the words, written over sixty winters ago between two other dear friends, both long dead now, to wend their way into your own here and now, startling your imagination to life:

"Yes, there is something to be said for living in this climate. Don't you notice a special kind of warmth between the folks who stick it out? Who wants to go pick oranges and grapefruit, we ask? A winter sunset is worth all the gold in the Indies. And shoveling tons of snow is fine exercise, just as good as water skiing!"

Wash your bowl, spoon, mug by hand. Turn up the music till it fills the rafters. Dance in the kitchen. Notice how gratitude gives rise to joy. Dash outside with a scoop of sunflower seeds for the hungry chickadees.

Dress for the weather: wool socks, long underwear, polar

fleece pants, down coat, hat, the scarf Margaret sent you made from patched-together old sweaters, the Christmas mittens from your sister-in-law, also stitched from old sweaters.

Smile at your reflection as you pass by the hall mirror: you are an anti–fashion statement swathed in polar fleece and sweater scraps, reclaimed pieces of other lives, other mornings, other peoples' old warm clothes. Lace up your boots, zip your L. L. Bean coat, buckle on your snow-shoes. Go.

Enter the cathedral of silence. Carve a fresh trail through the woods. Feel your heart pound in your chest, your own legs carrying you forward, the whoosh of powder in your wake. Stop and take in everything: the sounds of ice cracking, brook water running, a drift of sparkling powder cascading from a bough, the creak of tall pine, a cardinal's sharp call, your own breath rising in plumes around your face.

Study the tracks at your feet and know: you aren't alone here. Widen your circle of compassion to embrace these silent winter neighbors: turkey, deer, hare, coyote, bobcat, shrew.

Lie down in a place no one as been before. Watch the clouds drift by.

Move your arms, your legs. Remember what it felt like to be a child leaving the imprint of an angel in the snow, making your own private magic, at one with the world.

Remember that you are blessed. Remember that we are *here* to bless, to see, and to be blessed by one another.

May you awaken to the mystery of being here.
May you have joy and peace in the temple of your senses.
May you respond to the call of your gift and find the courage to
follow its path.
May you take time to celebrate the quiet miracles that seek no
attention.
May you experience each day as a sacred gift woven around the
heart of wonder.

—John O'Donohue

February 2014

—·—— tender ——·—

As I sit writing, the world beyond my window is blanketed by snow. There is silence in the house, save for the hum of the refrigerator, the whisper of warm air rising from the grates in the floor. I've laid in groceries, mopped the salt and grit from the entryway, put some store-bought tulips in a vase on the table. The shoveling and snow-clearing can wait. There is no place to go, nothing I really need to do other than chop and roast some vegetables later for dinner. Time slows. Edges soften.

For a week I've been struggling with some old, familiar demons. The fear of not being enough. The need to protect my tenderest, most vulnerable feelings from the harsh light of day. Self-doubt. Regret for things said and unsaid in a relationship I cherish. The wish that I could feel less, hurt less, and slough off more. A piercing disappointment that try as I might to shape my life, there is and will always be so much that's beyond my control or understanding. The realization that I'm not quite as good at nonattachment as I like to think I am.

"The root of all suffering," the Buddhists say, "is the desire for things to be different than they are." I suffer.

But knowing why I suffer doesn't make the wanting and the wishing go away. And an intellectual understanding of melancholy does little to ease the sadness that is, I suspect, simply part of being alive, an essential ingredient of our muddling, hopeful humanness.

Yet, if growing older is teaching me anything—anything that makes me feel a bit more at home in my emotionally porous and decidedly solitary soul—it's that I can survive my own painful feelings. Instead of numbing them, I can allow them the full measure of their power, dark and humbling as that power sometimes is. Instead of turning and running in the direction of busyness or distraction, I can remind myself to be still, uncomfortable as stillness may be. Instead of masking my sadness and pretending I'm angry, I can let my tears fall and acknowledge that what I really am is hurt. Instead of pasting on a stiff upper lip and insisting that I'm fine, I can gather up my courage, invite a trusted friend into my murky corner, and concede that, for the moment anyway, I'm not fine at all.

And slowly, as always, the emotional weather changes. I finally know better than to think I can make myself stop feeling a certain way, any more than I can wish the snow to stop or the sun to shine. But eventually the sky does clear.

Every time. Sadness gives way to equanimity. Hopelessness is nudged aside by a moment of quiet, unexpected contentment. Gratitude turns grief a different color. Feelings go away because others come along to take their place. The trick, perhaps, is simply to keep the flow going. To watch and feel and wait and trust. To judge myself a little less harshly and to welcome all my feelings as reminders that I'm still learning—learning and fully engaged in the endlessly demanding but ultimately worthwhile task of being me. Which is to say: I'm doing the best I can. And I'm giving myself permission, again and again and again, to love and to receive love in return.

February 2014

—·—— a love story ——·—

My husband and I mark Valentine's Day as the anniversary of our falling in love nearly thirty years ago, over the course of a long-planned weekend alone at my parents' house on the coast of Maine. We'd been dating on and off for a couple of years by then, though not seriously or, on his part, exclusively.

I was living in New York City and he was in Cambridge, an office romance in that we both worked for the same company—but in different cities. Work threw us together often enough, and when it didn't we figured out ways to throw ourselves together. But as a couple, we weren't exactly achieving lift-off. He was nearly ten years older. We were opposites in every way (as he liked to remind me), and although I was crazy about him, our prospects for long-term togetherness seemed discouraging.

As we drove north from Logan Airport, Steve took his eyes from the road for a moment, glanced my way, handed me a small heart-shaped tin of six chocolates, and said, "I've been thinking about you this week. And I finally just said to myself, 'this girl is a peach.'"

It was the closest he'd come to acknowledging any serious feelings for me. Perhaps it was even a declaration of sorts from this guy who'd been insisting since we met that although he liked me well enough, I wasn't his type. I was a *peach?* It seemed to me a positive sign: don't give up all hope, but proceed with caution.

We arrived at my parents' vacation house after dark to discover that we'd been booby-trapped. My mom and her friend had spent the previous weekend at the house together. And they had amused themselves by "decorating" on our behalf.

There were hearts and flowers on every surface. Cupids taped to the windows. Candles strategically placed. Candy hearts tossed around with abandon. A book of love poetry open on the table, which was set for two with red cloth napkins and champagne glasses and a scattering of heart confetti. There were new (red!) sheets on the bed, heart balloons dangling from the light fixtures, Brie and champagne in the fridge.

I was mortified.

Having guarded my own smitten heart so carefully, lest it be broken by this man who seemed certain we weren't meant to last, I'd just had my cover totally blown—by my own mother. *Not* funny.

Steve laughed.

Shaking, heart pounding in my chest, I went through the house without even taking off my coat, gathering up all the offending knickknacks and brazen cupids, my face redder than any Valentine. By the time I got back to the kitchen, Steve had opened the champagne and lit the candles. I don't remember exactly what he said then, but the gist of it was: "Well, I guess we could fight this, or we could just give in."

Three months later, he asked me to marry him. I still have the little candy tin he gave me all those years ago. It's near the washing machine, full of his extra shirt buttons.

February 2014

——·—— otherwise ——·——

Long after most of my friends in their fifties had given up running, I continued. Not every day, and not very far, and not for very long. Better, I thought, to save my knees to run again another day than to push myself to go another mile or another twenty minutes. For the last few years, I've run less often in the hope of running longer. If I was careful, I figured, I would run right into my sixties.

Even so, there wasn't ever a morning that I laced up my sneakers and headed down the road with the wind in my hair, fresh air filling my lungs, and my beloved Gracie trotting at my heels, that a line by poet Jane Kenyon didn't cross my mind: "One day, I know, it will be otherwise."

"Otherwise" is Jane Kenyon's hymn of gratitude to her life just as it was on one blessed, ordinary day—gratitude that is burnished by her own profound awareness of life's fleetingness, of change, of mortality. The lines of this heartbreakingly prescient poem always give me pause. Jane Kenyon died of leukemia at forty-seven. Her "otherwise" came tragically soon, a stark reminder—as is every untimely death or freak accident or life-changing diagnosis—that our existence here is fragile, unpredictable, not to be taken for granted.

And yet, I suspect I'm not alone when I admit that most days it's a challenge to maintain such perspective. Perhaps it's human nature to weave ourselves a thin, protective mantle of denial about life's one and only absolute truth: nothing lasts.

Waking up in the morning, I set my sights on the beginnings of things, not the endings. I scan my to-do list, ponder the essay I want to write, wonder where I'll find the hour I need to exercise, think about the talk I'll give next week. The preciousness of life is rarely uppermost in my mind as I deal with what the day hands me. Too often, instead, I find myself succumbing to frustration at the way things are: not what I'd planned, not quite up to my expectations, not this, not that.

Fortunately, I know where to find a simple antidote to my own petty annoyances. No matter how out of sorts I am—with myself, with a family member, with the demands of a difficult day—I need only step outside to reconnect with my more mindful, expansive self. The clouds sailing overhead, a pair of cardinals taking turns at the feeder, a patch of damp earth newly revealed in a sunny corner by the front door, the slow erosion of last week's snow—noticing these things, I'm restored to my better self, refreshed by wonder. The world is at once sweet and harsh, living and dying, always in flux—and I'm just one small part of the infinitely complex, eternal flow.

Running in all kinds of weather, feeling that inimitable rush of endorphin-induced well-being, has long been my quickest, clearest path both to peace and into the present moment—a moment which, I remind myself with each step, is already in the process of turning into something else. How to respond, other than by giving thanks for my own healthy body, for my life as it is, for the simple fact that I'm *here,* heart pounding and two strong legs carrying me onward as the miles accumulate in my wake.

Over the last several months, I've had to confront the first chronic pain of my life. The initial problem, ironically, was the result not of running, but of too many hours spent sitting. It took me a year to write my book, and I spent a good part of that year sitting cross-legged with a lap desk for my computer balanced on my knees.

"A writing injury," I said at first, laughing it off, certain my pulled groin muscle was nothing a little time and a different position in the chair wouldn't fix. Unable to run, I settled for power walking instead. I grudgingly gave up jump-backs in yoga and then soon found I had to think carefully even before making a step forward. Some days,

I pushed through the discomfort to do exactly what I wanted to do, groin muscle be damned. Other days, the pain had its way with me, and I was forced to stillness.

But instead of healing, the injury deepened and, in a sort of domino effect, has led to yet more trouble. By January, I had to lift my left leg with both hands in order to get in and out of the car. Putting on my underpants required slow motion and deep breaths and even so resulted in sharp, shooting pains through my thigh. Stairs were agony. If I dropped something on the floor, I often left it there rather than endure the pain of bending over to pick it up. Yoga, always a joyful release and exploration, became just another challenge to get through, my attempts to modify poses finally resulting in more time spent sitting on my mat than doing asana practice. Lying in bed, with a pillow propping up my knee, my entire left hip and leg throbbed. There was no good position. There have been many nights with no sleep, either.

It's hard for me to admit what a struggle this has been. Being forced to give up the very activities I've long relied on for my peace of mind has been humbling, to say the least. An injured leg is hardly traumatic in the great scheme of things; I have friends and loved ones who are dealing with far more debilitating health issues. Yet as the weeks went by, the combination of discomfort and inactivity and sleeplessness brought me to my knees. Life felt constricted, narrowed down to a monochromatic prism of pain, frustration, exhaustion.

One day last month, after a long week of being cooped

up in the house and barely moving, my leg seemed just a bit better. I put on layers of warm clothes against the subfreezing temperatures, stepped outside, and eager to get some exercise at last, set off down the road at my usual clip—a fast, determined walk.

Two steps, four, six, *stop.* I hadn't even reached the mailbox before the spasms in my thigh had me gasping in pain. It was January and 12 degrees. Our beautiful dog had been gone two months, and I missed her desperately. My leg refused to do my bidding. Instead it pulsed back at me in furious protest. I turned toward the house in defeat, tears freezing on my cheeks.

And then I stopped again. I couldn't bear to give up and go back inside. But I couldn't take my walk, either. What to do? Slowly and with great care, I turned around once more. I took a long deep breath and one very, very small step. "Soften, soften, soften," I whispered to myself, to my heart, to the poor inflamed muscles in my hip and thigh. Instead of contracting the hurt place, I tried relaxing it completely. Instead of moving quickly, I barely moved at all. The pain eased a little, clearing space for another deep breath, another tiny step, a glimmer of understanding. Maybe, just maybe, I was ok right where I was. And maybe, if I released my white-knuckle grip on all I couldn't have and all I couldn't do, I could find a different way to move forward.

For weeks, I realized, I'd been angry. Perhaps moving forward really means moving beyond that impotent, helpless anger and surrendering instead to everything I can't fix or control. I've been annoyed at my body for letting me down. Why not be grateful to it for still holding me up? I've been disappointed by my failure to cope with grace and a stiff upper lip. Why not acknowledge that I've done the best I could? I've been secretly disgusted at my-self for not being invincible. Why not yield at last to my own fragile humanness?

I suspect now that the brief, halting, weepy walk I took on that bitter January day may have been my first step toward some kind of healing, spiritual if not physical. After months of ignoring and resisting the information my pain was offering me, I finally stood in the middle of the road, with no idea which way to turn next, and began to hear what my body had to say.

Letting go of my anger has meant letting go of the suffering I was bringing upon myself. There is nothing I can do about the pain in my leg, but I can do something about my attitude toward it. Perhaps what I most need to be cured of is not my sore muscle, but my swollen ego—the idea that I am unstoppable.

This does seem to be the central task of growing up and of growing old: learning to ride the waves of loss and sorrow as we come face to face with the truth of our own unimportance and our own impermanence. Life has offered me plenty of opportunities to practice of late. Suffice it to say, I don't have to look far to see things fall-ing apart. But as this winter is teaching me, to know loss in the mind isn't the same as learning it in the body or feeling it in the heart.

There is nothing quite like pain—be it physical or emotional—to shine a bright light on just how vulnerable we really are. We can put up a stoic front, or go down kicking and fighting. Or, if we're lucky, we may begin to glimpse some small measures of grace and meaning even in the midst of changes we couldn't have foreseen and circumstances we never would have chosen.

Over the last few weeks, I've been deeply moved by a friend's unwavering presence and empathy. I've been thankful for my husband's steady support and encouragement, for several sessions of bodywork that brought instant if temporary relief, for hot showers and Ibuprofen and for every hour of uninterrupted sleep. I've written more, read more, rested more. I've cried more. I've watched the snow fall day after day and left the shoveling to others. I've found a way to practice yoga that is slow and safe and therapeutic and, in my classes, a way to teach the poses that I can't do myself. I've stepped outside at dusk, buckled on my snowshoes, and taken a few brief, gentle expeditions through weightless powder into the silent woods. I've chosen gratitude as often as I could. I've taken time to appreciate each small, good thing.

And, a month later, I'm feeling a tiny bit better. Softness and acceptance creates a more fertile ground for healing than resentment and resistance. Instead of pushing myself each day, I'm finding that patience is its own kind of progress. I'm trying harder to listen to my body, rather than forcing it to listen to me. No longer adversaries, we're working together to find a new way forward—not running anymore, but still moving, albeit at a different pace.

Today, for the first time in a long time, I find that I can walk without severe pain. In Florida visiting my mom for the week, I feel liberated after these long, cold winter months spent mostly inside. It is tee-shirt weather here, and everything is green with life. I'm taking it slow, one step at a time, in no hurry to get anywhere. I'm thankful for the breeze on my cheek, the slow, measured rhythm of my steps on the pavement, the sweat needling my back, the ghost of a heart I discovered in the sidewalk. The hibiscus are in bloom. Palm fronds click in the breeze. A mockingbird delivers its exuberant medley as I pass beneath its perch. It is a joy just to be here, putting one foot carefully in front of the other.

One day, I know, it will be otherwise.

Otherwise
I got out of bed
on two strong legs.
It might have been
otherwise. I ate
cereal, sweet
milk, ripe, flawless
peach. It might
have been otherwise.
I took the dog uphill
to the birch wood.
All morning I did
the work I love.

At noon I lay down
with my mate. It might
have been otherwise.
We ate dinner together
at a table with silver
candlesticks. It might
have been otherwise.
I slept in a bed
in a room with paintings
on the walls, and
planned another day
just like this day.
But one day, I know,
it will be otherwise.
—Jane Kenyon
February 2014

——·—— remembering Laurie Colwin ——·——

I once bought a black-speckled canning pot, two boxes of Ball jars, and twelve pounds of dusky Italian plums in memory of an author I loved.

For years, I've suspected I was one of a few remaining Laurie Colwin fans, a smallish but loyal band of readers of a certain age and sensibility who still hold her close in our hearts, afford her books prime space on our shelves, and continue to make her signature dishes in our kitchens.

So it was wonderful, though a bit startling, to discover

in the pages of the *New York Times* recently that I'm not alone after all. That in fact, in the more than twenty years since her death, Laurie's following has only grown, attracting "a new, cultishly devoted generation of readers," many of whom are in their thirties or younger.

As it turns out, Laurie Colwin is more beloved than ever. Her books, never out of print, are selling briskly, although some of her most zealous disciples today were toddlers when she died in 1992. Somehow, just knowing about her expanding reader base gives me hope—not only for this new generation of secret romantics and home cooks, but also for the survival of such humble institutions as tea parties, picnics, and family dinners.

I knew Laurie only slightly. Back in the mid-eighties, she agreed to read in a short-story series a friend and I were producing, pairing well-known writers with our latest literary discoveries. We'd barely been introduced backstage when Laurie asked if I would retie her scarf, a slippery, oversized square of silk that proved impossible for either of us to get just right.

I was twenty-five, longing for love and domesticity, and she was, hands down, my favorite living writer. I often felt in those days as if I were meeting alternate versions of myself in Laurie Colwin's stories, which I read and reread as if they were medicinal. In a way, I guess they were. Newly separated from a miserable but well-intentioned first marriage, I was ashamed of the embarrassing mess I'd already made of my life. Laurie's characters—good, honorable souls all—often found themselves haplessly entangled as well. I found solace in their romantic missteps and hope in their ability to survive life's ambiguities. "Falling in love is not a mistake," insists a character in *The Lone Pilgrim*—curative words for my own bruised heart.

Backstage that night, my hands shook a bit as I fussed with the ends at her neck, trying to make them lie flat. I remember exactly what I was thinking: Life is full of astonishment—here I am standing in the wings of a New York theater, tying Laurie Colwin's scarf.

After that, a mutual publishing friend began inviting both of us to his dinner parties. For a time, our paths crossed. I was in awe of her wit and charm, and I think she, fourteen years older and almost preternaturally maternal, liked the idea of keeping a watchful eye on me.

Once, after I'd fallen in love with my future husband and left New York to marry him, Laurie and I met for lunch when I was back in the city. She loved a romantic story with a happy ending, and I was flattered that she wanted to hear every detail of mine. We sat outside at a deli around the corner from her Chelsea apartment. I know we shared an enormous corned-beef sandwich at her suggestion, because later I wrote it down. She asked me about children, and I told her, yes, I was trying—without success.

Laurie leaned across the table, intent, her face framed by a halo of untamable dark hair. What had I tried? What drugs had I taken? What was I doing and how often was I doing it? She was certain I needed to work less and eat more. Surely I needed more sleep, too. (She was right on all counts.) And I needed to see her doctor right away. She would make sure I got in. I was pushing thirty, she pointed out, and there was no time to waste.

It's funny, the details the mind files away. And for me this one remains indelible: an impassioned Laurie Colwin insisting I had no time to waste. She wrote her gynecologist's name on a white deli napkin and handed it to me. "Call him," she said. "The man can get a stone pregnant."

After lunch, we walked a few blocks to pick her daughter Rosa up at school and then back to their cozy, cluttered apartment. It seemed familiar, almost as if I'd been there before, though of course I hadn't; I'd just read enough of Laurie's descriptions of home to recognize hers: "small but crammed with artifacts: watercolors, family photographs, teapots, pitchers, and beautiful plates." We had tea in the kitchen as the late afternoon light streamed in. Less than six months later, I was pregnant. I never saw her again.

The news that Laurie had died, suddenly and in her sleep, of heart failure, on October 23, 1992, stunned everyone. Her death seemed unfathomable. She was only forty-eight. She had a young child, a husband. She was fully engaged in living and writing and volunteering at the soup kitchen near her home where she was on a first-name basis with all the regulars. And then she was gone.

I was eight months pregnant with my second son, standing in the sunshine on our back porch in the suburbs when the call came from a friend. Although Laurie and I weren't often in touch, I'd happened to talk with her just a few weeks earlier about being the guest editor the following year for

The Best American Short Stories. I promised her we'd have fun. She hadn't hesitated before saying yes. It took a few minutes before my tears began, as if my heart refused to admit the news.

Despite these brief but cherished memories, my real relationship with Laurie Colwin has always been that between a writer and a reader. As a twenty-three-year-old married too soon and to the wrong man, I took heart reading Laurie's short stories, encouraged by her conviction that there is a fine, flawed person at large in the world destined eventually to find his or her way to each of us. Love, she believed, was unpredictable, often painful, sometimes blind, always worth waiting for and worth fighting to keep. And, as her characters inevitably realize: even happiness takes work.

When I was home sick with a cold, or exhausted, or feeling sorry for myself, I'd often take to my bed with a box of tissues and my favorite novel of hers, *Happy All the Time.* I'd come across a description of a restorative cup of tea, or a perfect cheese omelet, or a full-bodied glass of wine—descriptions so seductive that I'd always be roused to get up and wander into the kitchen to fetch a little something for myself. It was simple: when I was faltering in my twenties—whether due to matters of the heart, the spirit, or the body—reading Laurie Colwin made me feel better.

Later, married and raising two children, I began to read Laurie's essays about food with the same kind of affinity I'd always felt for her fiction. She wrote about eating a tomato from the garden with as much rapture as another writer might bring to a love scene. She could make eggs sexy, cold coffee appealing, lentil soup sound festive, old British cookbooks compelling. She inspired me to throw more dinner parties, to make better sandwiches, to go in search of my first organic egg, and to exhaust my arm stirring my first pot of polenta. And she was the only writer on earth who could tempt me to cook a lima-bean casserole, simply by recounting the contentment her own had brought to the group of friends upon whom she bestowed it one wintry night.

For Laurie, it was all one in the same, romantic love blending seamlessly into culinary exuberance and from there into a generous passion for life itself. She was, like her heroine Polly in *The Lone Pilgrim,* a domestic sensualist, reveling in the enchantments of everyday existence. And although the essays that became *Home Cooking and More Home Cooking* were ostensibly about cooking and eating and feeding people, these two casually intimate volumes are in fact sublime celebrations of love and friendship and family—as much memoirs as cookbooks, the wealth of recipes not withstanding. To step into these pages was to find a friend not only to stand at my side in the kitchen but also to accompany me through the vagaries of my own newly domestic life as well.

Laurie's essays—in which she manages to be anecdotal, funny, affectionate, and informative all at once—shone a light on the path as I became a wife and a mother myself. Drawn into her confidence on the page, I felt as if I'd come to know at last this generous, quirky, brilliant woman who got dressed up every year for Halloween, ate stewed eggplant out of the saucepan, and baked gingerbread every week for her little girl.

"You do not have to be a housebound mother to make ginger-
bread. All you need is to put aside an hour or so to mix up the
batter and bake it, and then, provided you do not have a huge
mob waiting to devour the gingerbread immediately, it will pay
you back for a few days because it gets better as it ages."

Cooking, Laurie continually reminds us, needn't be
drudgery but rather an expression of affection and creativity.
And the dinner table isn't just a place to serve food, but also
the ideal setting to create and sustain traditions, to nurture
oneself and others, to weave the invisible mantle of memory
and intimacy and security that holds us gently in place in a
fast-moving world.

"It took me a long time to get over my fear of making jam. The
whole enterprise seemed terrifying. After all, entire factories were
devoted to its manufacture, so how was I, one small person in an
inadequate kitchen, supposed to compete?"

Reading about Laurie's "jam anxiety," I was surprised to
discover she'd been as leery of sterilizing jars as I was. She
was gone by the time I finally got around to trying jam
myself, but I liked to imagine that somehow, somewhere,
she was watching out for me still.

I bought the canner and my first load of ripe plums
because she convinced me I was up to the job. For many
years, making Laurie Colwin's plum jam each October
felt like a way of sustaining the ineffable thread that bound
us, a writer who left the world too soon and her grateful
reader, still here in it.

I suppose we all look for guides and mentors along the

way, people who suggest by example a way of being in their own skin that prompts us to take notice because it feels right to us, too—and worth emulating. Laurie Colwin was that kind of guide for me, simply by living her life so fully and writing about it so generously. I would seek her advice on roasting a chicken and what I received along with it, always, was a reminder to savor my hour in the kitchen and the precious people gathered at my table for the meal.

Throughout my years of editing and writing books and raising children to adulthood—as I brewed my morning cup of coffee, peeled carrots, baked bread with my little boys, put dinner after dinner on the table, listened to the rise and fall of deepening male voices and the clatter of silverware—I've thought of Laurie many times. The lessons she taught, both in her writing and by dying right in the middle of her living, have shaped me both as a person and as a writer. And certainly this is one: to fully embrace the delicious, irretrievable, ordinary moment that is now. *April 2014*

———·——— present moment ———·———

I'm still waiting for the last snow bank to melt outside the back door. My guess is it'll linger, grainy and gray, for another week or so. I suppose I could get out there today and attack winter's last frozen carapace with a shovel. If I were to break up that mound of snow and ice and spread it all out on the flattened, spongy lawn, it would disappear faster.

Instead, I look at winter's grimy remains and see an invitation to pay attention. The slowly dwindling snow bank reminds me once again: nothing lasts. Even the harsh, seemingly endless winter I've complained about and struggled against for months is finally on its way out, its last vestiges vanishing by the moment.

On this windy, chilly spring day, it's too early to do much of anything productive outside. And so, I walk around and survey the wreckage: the old front gate, broken off at the hinge, the fallen tree limbs, the cache of dead leaves in the window wells, the skeletal remains of the Christmas tree on the patio, the dead hydrangea blooms I never got around to pruning in the fall. I could easily get overwhelmed by the list forming in my head— so much work to be done.

Instead, I look around in wonder at the relentless, reassuring continuance of Nature. The year has its rhythms, its phases, as do I. There is a time to honor the winter of the soul, to turn inward and rest, gathering intention for the next season. And there's a time to gently clear space for what's greening inside, waiting its moment to emerge.

For today at least, we seem to be straddling two seasons here. I can step out my back door on the north side of the house, rest a bare palm on gritty snow that's been fallow since November's first storm, and recall the hard lessons of winter: accept the cauterizing cold, welcome the darkness, surrender your well-laid plans, let go into things as they are, practice patience, have faith.

Or, I can round the corner to the southern side of the

house and inhale the eager elation of spring. Out here where the sun shines for most of the day, an entire flock of robins have landed, as if to celebrate the thaw. They are busily extracting worms from the waterlogged grass. Meanwhile, over by the stone wall, a pair of yellow crocuses have asserted themselves where just yesterday there was nothing but bare ground. There are crimson peony shoots pushing forth just outside the kitchen door, too, as if they've been waiting impatiently to take their rightful place. It is mid-April, after all.

Standing out in my bare garden, face tipped up to the sun, I marvel at just how much life pulses in a single moment. It feels as if there's something stirring in me, too. Maybe it's an inner voice that's been quiet for a long while now, offering me permission to grow and stretch and break some new ground.

Present Moment
Don't get caught in the past,
because the past is gone.
Don't get upset about the future,
because the future is not yet here.
There is only one moment for you to be alive,
and that is the present moment.
Go back to the present moment
and live this moment deeply,
and you'll be free.
—Buddha
April 2014

—·— Mother's Day —·—

Every year, I tell my sons what I'd like for Mother's Day: a letter. Something, *anything,* on paper, that I can keep close at hand for a while, reread till I've memorized each line, and then tuck away in a drawer to save and read again. For me, words written from the heart are more precious than anything that could be bought from a store. I don't always get my wish, nor do I always take the time to write to my own mother. (It is so much easier to buy a card, choose some flowers, indulge in a nice dinner out.)

This year Jack is home for spring break and we'll spend the day together. With Steve and Henry both on a trip, Jack offered to join me in my annual spring "cleanse" and we've been partners all week in this challenging endeavor, juicing and eating raw fruits and veggies and practicing yoga. His presence, and his willingness to try what he calls "the mom lifestyle" for a week has been a gift in itself. (In a few minutes, we'll have our Mother's Day breakfast together: a green smoothie with kale and sunflower seeds. And then we'll head off to yoga class— my idea of a happy Mother's Day indeed.)

I used to mourn the end of my sons' childhoods, especially on Mother's Day, nostalgic for the years of breakfast in bed, Crayola cards, my sons' eager assistance as we planted the flowers my husband had helped them pick out at the nursery.But I think I've finally made peace with what is now long over. Last weekend we watched Henry's first class of high school jazz students perform at a May Day celebration. It was a full-circle moment. Nine years ago, he was the fourteen-year-old freshman trying out his jazz chops at the dessert cafe on May Day, and now he's returned to his old high school for a semester to teach jazz himself. My heart swelled, my eyes brimmed, just as they always did at every school event. "Now" may be the only time there is, but these days "now" comes with an even deeper appreciation for time passing, the moments layered with memories and associations and gratitude. As I grow older, "now" just becomes richer, deeper, and more precious.

Jack's life in Atlanta, far from us, suits him. He comes home these days as a young adult visiting, not as a child returning. And so, knowing our time together is brief, I sense a new willingness on both our parts to stretch toward one another, to find and inhabit the common ground, to accommodate each other's idiosyncrasies with affection. At twenty-one and twenty-four, my sons "get" me, and vice versa. And I think they know this, too—much as I will always love receiving a handwritten letter on Mother's Day, the best gift they can possibly give me is their own health and happiness, the very fact of their busy, full, well-lived lives.

I wonder if my own mother feels the same, having watched her two children grow up and marry, become parents and raise families themselves? I suspect so. What she wants at seventy-eight is not more "stuff." She's getting rid of things, not accumulating them. Nor does she have any desire to be the center of our lives. What she wants, surely what *every* mother wants, is more time to bear witness to her children's continuous unfolding, to share in the ups and downs of our everyday thises and thats.

I don't often pause to think about it, and yet my mom is the one person who has been right here, at my side and *on* my side, from the moment I drew my first breath. How to ever fully appreciate the woman whose presence and love and example have shaped me into the adult I am? How to capture even a small part of the sharing, sacrificing, and support she has given me over the years? Well, she'd probably appreciate a letter herself. And so.

Dear Mom,

I can't possibly do you justice in a letter or give voice to all the memories, but here are just a few that come to mind as I think back:

I remember the bracelet, dark red-and-blue shoe buttons strung on elastic, that I made for you in kindergarten when I was five, the first Mother's Day gift fashioned by my hand. I remember seeing it for years tucked in the corner of the jewelry box on your dresser where you kept it, loved and treasured if not worn.

I remember soft pajamas with feet and Sunday night suppers served on TV trays in the living room. Welsh rabbit on Saltines, milk in gray plastic mugs with brightly colored rims, *The Wonderful World of Disney,* and a bedtime that was the same every night. I remember lullabies and "Mairzie Doates" and "Tell Me Why the Stars Do Shine" and the comfort of knowing that I was good and well-loved and safe.

I remember the first deliberate lie I tried to get away with—"the cat did it"—and how you saw right through my five-year-old fabrication and gave me time to figure out for myself that the truth would be better.

I remember that I could not, would not, put my face underwater at the Air Force pool. I remember that you didn't make me do it. And I also remember two small Dutch dolls, a girl and a boy, with wooden shoes and painted faces. I remember your giving them to me on a hot summer day for no reason at all, except, perhaps, because that was the afternoon when I finally coaxed my terrified self all the way into that pool.

I remember peeking through the keyhole of your bedroom door late at night, hoping for a black-and-white glimpse of Danny Kaye on TV and hoping I wouldn't get in too much trouble if you found me crouching there. I remember you taking me by the hand and leading me back to bed and tucking me in with a kiss.

I remember the only good part about being sick: your hand on my forehead as I knelt in front of the toilet bowl, retching up dinner. The comfort of being held. A cool washcloth. Clean sheets, a night breeze through the window, peace.

I remember a bedroom done over just for me. A desk and chair of my own, a dressing table with a mirror, a record player, and your own beloved horse figurines handed down to me at just the right moment.

I remember a bright pink corduroy jumper that you sewed on the green Singer, and a shirt with daisies growing up the front, and playing dress up in your filmy blue nightgown and pearls, tottering down the driveway in your shoes, feeling like a princess in your grown-up things.

I remember Easter baskets and Easter dresses and your hand on my knee in church. Lighting the candles on the ting-a-ling on Christmas Eve, the tiny bronze angels pinging against the hot chimes as you read the story of Jesus's birth from the book of Matthew. I remember watching you stuff turkey after turkey after turkey, a lifetime's worth of turkeys roasted and holiday meals served and cleaned up after. I remember the kitchen table set with plates and silverware and folded napkins, every single night of our lives.

I remember finding your childhood books in a chest in Grammie Stanchfield's attic and studying your careful, girlish penmanship, absorbing the shock of your maiden name inscribed all those years ago on the faded inside cover of *Black Beauty.* I remember being stunned by the realization that you had once been a little girl yourself, and that you had had a whole, complete life before me.

I remember summer evenings, and you reading out loud as we sprawled on John's bed, scratching at mosquito bites and patches of poison ivy. *The Family Finds Out, The Borrowers, Misty of Chincoteague.* I remember wishing the books would never end, that you wouldn't turn out the light, that the day didn't have to be over so soon.

I remember that you always called your mother on the day of the first snowfall of winter. I remember the day you lost her. I remember thinking, when snow came the next year, that I should call you.

I remember when you allowed me to buy *Magical Mystery Tour* and bring my phonograph outside on the back deck and play the Beatles really loud. I remember being in the back seat of our red Plymouth Fury as you drove along, eyes on the road, and explained to me about sex. And I remember being disappointed that it sounded so weird and unfun. I remember the first bra you bought me and how embarrassed I was—by the color (red!), the name ("Little Me"), the prospect of wearing it, the very possibility of breasts.

I remember long walks in the woods and one picnic lunch on the stoop of an abandoned house, and an early-morning breakfast we carried up into the low, embracing branches of a special tree. I remember admitting to my best friend at school that you were my best friend.

I remember how good you looked on a horse. Back tall and straight, hands quiet, heels down. I remember how nervous you were about riding and that you did it anyway. I remember the day you flew a plane by yourself—and I remember thinking, "I will never do that."

I remember confiding in you ahead of time that I was going to sleep with my boyfriend and then realizing you might have preferred not to know. I remember wanting to tell you about it the next day and forcing myself, for your sake, to keep quiet.

I remember going out to lunch together the day before I left for college, at a long-gone place called the Avocado, and ordering a drink, and feeling sadness and excitement all mixed up together, already missing you on the one hand and, on the other, just itching to be gone.

I remember that you filled a house with hearts and flowers on Valentine's Day when you thought my lukewarm romance needed a little push, and that I was horrified and touched and then had to give you credit. (Would I be married today, if not for those ridiculous cupids and candy hearts?)

I remember the two of us eating lobster and drinking wine two nights before my wedding, and how much fun we had picking flowers and making bouquets for every guest room. I remember a moment just before the ceremony, when we stood in the bedroom in the house in Maine, and said something that felt like a good-bye and a hello at the same time. I remember your funny, relieved curtsy in the kitchen on the morning after, when every wedding task was done, and I was finally married to a good man, and you could relax at last.

I remember when Henry was born, how somehow— despite your dread of city driving, despite not having any idea where the hospital was in that pre-GPS era—you managed to get there anyway, to be at my side when I became a mother myself. I remember how glad I was to see you.

And I remember the night, three years later, when my water broke and I told you not to hurry, there was plenty of time. I remember that you ignored me and jumped in your car and came anyway—just in time for Steve to rush me to the hospital.

I remember all the ways you have loved and cared for my children these last twenty-four years, how gracefully and joyfully you became a grandmother. How much I've needed you to help me through the hard days of motherhood. And how, when there is something terrible or wonderful to report, you are always the first person I need to tell.

I remember—and I know this still—that you have always believed in me, even when I couldn't believe in myself. We have believed in each another, taken care of each other's hearts, and shared each other's joys and sorrows for more than half a century. On this Mother's Day, I rejoice in our good fortune and in our lives as mother and daughter.

Thank you, Mom.

Today, I wish for myself, for all mothers, for all who care for others, the simple gifts of love and gratitude. May we remember that in living our own lives well, we offer our loved ones the gift of good lives, too. Happy Mother's Day!
May 2014

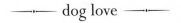

—·—— dog love ——·—

If we had power over the ends of the earth, it would not give us that fulfillment of existence which a quiet, devoted relationship to nearby life can give us.
—Martin Buber

Dear Tess,
So, okay, I was wrong.

Love at first sight is possible after all. I wonder, though, was it the same for you? Did you really know I was your person, and that we were your family, just as immediately as we knew you were our dog?

I can admit this now: I didn't actually believe I could give my heart away again—not so completely, not even to another black-and-white border collie with a paint-dipped tail and a coat of silken cowlicks.

Besides, I'd finally gotten sort of used to the pet-free life. Sleeping a little later. Saving money on dog food and vet bills. Skipping the morning walk, the poop patrols around the yard. Staying in out of the rain. No one's bladder to keep track of but my own. No dog hair on my black yoga pants, no stray bits of kibble crunching under foot, no new holes under the azalea or scratches in the pine floorboards. No one eating the appetizers off the coffee table or barking at the door to go in or out or staring at me with imploring eyes, telegraphing the unmistakable late-afternoon message: shut your laptop and put on your sneakers.

Sure, there was an emptiness around here, but I'd almost stopped noticing it. Just as the silence after Henry and Jack first left home, crushing at first, became part of the fabric of my days, my grief over the death of your predecessor had softened over the winter into, well, a new kind of normal. We humans can get used to anything.

And then May came. The last snow finally melted, revealing a backyard still scattered with faded tennis balls. The sun woke us up at six, then even earlier. Birds sang. The world beckoned. Our boys came home, both of them at once.

"You said spring," my dog-loving friend Debbie reminded me. "And it IS spring."

She gathered up all the old tennis balls and piled them in front of the garden Buddha, an offering of sorts. A nudge.

One night, Jack and I clicked on a link I'd bookmarked a while ago, back when Gracie was still with us—a border-collie rescue farm in upstate New York. And there they were: a hundred Gracie cousins all in need of homes, each one with a story to break your heart.

In truth, Tess, we skipped right over your photo that night, seduced by roly-poly puppies and cavorting adolescents.

I printed out the adoption application, only to be stopped in my tracks by its lengthy essay questions ("Describe a typical day in your dog's life. . .") and the many requirements. Would we be willing to install a hard fence? Would we promise to enroll with our puppy in obedience school? How many hours each day would our dog be alone? Would we use a crate? Would we take a dog with special emotional needs? With chronic health issues?

Finally, there was just a week left before the boys departed again. If we were going to welcome a new member to the family, it did seem as if the family should actually be here to say hello.

And so I returned to the website, scrolled down past the youngsters, and there you were, hiding in plain sight—a four-and-a-half-year-old orphan girl named Princess who'd seen way too much death and loss and change in your brief, chaotic life. Would you wait for us?

On a chilly Sunday, Henry, Debbie, and I made the five-hour drive to Morris, New York, knowing you might be gone by the time we got there. Another family was coming to meet you in the morning; they had first dibs.

Pulling up to the farm's gate after our long morning on the road, I offered up a little prayer to Gracie, who I knew must be watching these proceedings from somewhere. "This is in your hands, you know," I whispered. "Bring us the right dog."

Right at that moment, the cold rain that had been intermittent all morning stopped for good. The sun came out from behind the clouds. I told myself not to see this as a sign.

And then there you were. As soon as I knelt down, you put your soft cheek against mine. "Princess" became "Tess" in that instant—as if you'd whispered your new name in my ear. That pretty much sealed it. "She's the one," I must have said. Or something like that. Because it was obvious, we already belonged to you.

Nearly three weeks into our new life together, you have most of it figured out: chasing down tennis balls, barking at squirrels, come and sit and wait, leash walks and woods rambles.

You know the men who live in this house are different from the ones who hurt you in the past. You know early morning is the best time of day, that the dogs we meet on the road are friendly, that people who come to the door are welcome, that the bear who ambled into the yard at dusk the other night to raid the bird feeder was definitely not one of "us."

You know where to sleep and not to beg at the table and

to stay off the sofa. You know that pockets hold treats, that grass is for rolling in, that tennis balls are reliable, ever-ready companions and that brand new plush toys can be destroyed in less than ten minutes. You know that when I leave a room, I return. You know that car rides with your new family lead only to good places and that they will always end up right back where we started from: home.

You know the joys of rest and of play, and that here and now are the best places to be. Most important of all, you know how to ask for what you need the most. A paw placed on my knee means it's time for us to gaze deeply into each other's eyes, for one of our many long heart-to-heart chats. You squint up at me, nose lifted just so, to receive a kiss or to offer a delicate one of your own.

Tell me you love me, you insist. And I do.

June 2014

—·— bucket list —·—

On Tuesday afternoons this past year I've been a traveling yoga teacher, lugging a bag full of straps and foam blocks and lavender eye pillows to a small elementary school in a nearby town.

My students, a dedicated handful of regulars, are all in their sixties, including the school principal and her now-retired husband, who once taught English to my son Jack. We work gently together, accommodating a tricky hip (mine), chronic back pain, osteoporosis, balance issues, and the inevitable assortment of aches and injuries that are simply part of the territory now that we are no longer young.

Last fall, on the first afternoon I arrived at the school to teach, I was surprised by a few sudden tears the minute I walked through the front door. It hit me—suddenly, although certainly not for the first time—just how far down the road I've traveled from all that transpires each day in this tidy, welcoming brick building.

Everything I saw brought back a memory: the box of lost-and-found baseball caps and tangled sweatshirts, the collection of canned goods for the food pantry accumulating in the foyer, the children's bright artwork on the walls, the sight of a lone L. L. Bean backpack forgotten in a corner, the distinctive peanutty smell of kids and used books and half-eaten lunches.

The question rose up hot and fierce as a reprimand in my chest: *Have you loved your life enough?*

The honest answer? Probably not. Back when my own boys were small, what I now know to be evanescent felt as if it would go on forever. I made a hundred sandwiches, a thousand, with no end in sight. How many mornings did I urge my kids to hurry, warn them they'd be late for school, lose my patience as they whined or dawdled or resisted some obvious necessity—hair combing, boots on the right feet, raincoats?

Much as I tried to pay attention, tried to remind myself nothing lasts forever, and certainly not first grade or third or fifth or childhood itself, I couldn't possibly have anticipated the speed with which the years would fly by while I was mired in the details of doctors' appointments and homework assignments and T-ball practice.

Perhaps it is ever so. Perhaps it's only the lived experience of seasons passing that can teach us the truth of impermanence, as endings pile up willy-nilly. Perhaps it is only by enduring a progression of lasts that an ordinary *now* is transformed into an achingly precious present moment.

Perhaps it is only in pausing every now and then to gaze back at where we've been that we can face forward again with hearts full of gratitude for the ground beneath our feet.

With the school year over, my Tuesday afternoon classes have concluded as well. Over time, I did get more comfortable walking down the hall, nostalgia for the past giving way to a kind of cultivated ease in the present.

Still, I would always stop to look at the bulletin boards, to enjoy the children's artistic creations, to read their names, to remember just how it felt to visit my own sons' school all those years ago and see their latest efforts displayed in the hall.

As the last school day drew nigh, the children made summer "bucket lists," sharing their hopes and dreams for the months ahead. There were lots of pictures of sunscreen tacked to the board, along with aspirations for summer vacation: *play with my cousin, go to the beach, ride my bike, go camping.*

I thought about making a summer bucket list myself. What would be on it? Read a book a week. Meditate every morning. Take a walk every day. Be more disciplined about writing my blog posts. I got just about this far before I realized: my summer bucket list sounded suspiciously like a to-do list.

Last week, my husband, Steve, turned sixty-five. A big one any way you look at it. Medicare. Senior-citizen discounts. Fifteen years shy of eighty. Only thirty-five less than a hundred.

As it happened, I was away at a book festival on his actual birthday. We'd both been busy all week, running in opposite directions, no room on our calendars for a party or even a dinner out, both our sons away.

I wracked my brain for an appropriate gift and came up empty. There is nothing he needs. Nothing he really wants that he doesn't have already. Nothing except, of course, more *time*. The one gift money cannot buy. And then it dawned on me—time *was* a gift I could give. No receipt needed, no return possible.

Steve played hooky from work, and I planned a day for the two of us. "Trust me," I said.

We got up early, had breakfast with friends, then headed north to Vermont and our date with a rented double kayak. After a few hours of paddling down the Connecticut River and lunch at the Harpoon brewery, we made our way through an underground tunnel to enter an outdoor sculpture garden called, appropriately enough, The Path of Life.

Metaphors abounded—from the hemlock maze, signifying the adventures of childhood, all the way to the circle of dead oaks and charred carvings that evoke death, and finally the quiet grove of delicate white birches suggestive of rebirth and life's renewal.

It was a weekday afternoon, and we had all fourteen acres of this weirdly inspired, idiosyncratic garden to ourselves. It felt as if time had indeed slowed down a bit. There was space to talk, plenty of time to wander. "I still can't wrap my head around sixty-five," Steve said as we approached a towering jazz combo exuberantly constructed of old wood and metal scraps. "Sixty-five is old. But inside, I still feel the same. How can that be? I'm not even sure how I'm supposed to act at this age."

We looked up at the faded, venerable musicians playing their silent song for the ages, perfectly embodying the spirit of creativity. Maybe there is no *"supposed to,"* they seemed to say. Maybe the work of growing older is about finding your own song and singing it fearlessly, joyously; singing even when it seems no one is listening. And maybe aging doesn't have to be about submitting grudgingly to loss, but rather about accepting and choosing life as it is—and beating out a wild, heartfelt tune that acknowledges all of it, all the joys and pains and conflicts that are part of the human trip.

Knowing where our own journey would wind up, we took our time. Why rush down the path of life, when one can choose to sit for a while under the tree of knowledge, survey the view from the top of the hill of success, meditate with a full heart upon one's ancestors and absent loved ones from within the circle that represents family?

As the end approached, we moved even more slowly,

lingering, wanting to make it last, determined to drink fully of every experience along the way. (Another revelation: as it is in the garden, so it is in life.) We made an offering to the silent Buddha, walked the labyrinth, lay flat out on the grass and closed our eyes and each imagined our own final rest.

Back in the car at dusk, driving south toward a dinner of Thai food and listening to Willie Nelson sing "Just Breathe" on the mix tape I'd made him, we were both quiet. I found myself brushing back tears, as does seem to happen more and more often these days. But these tears weren't for the past, not at all. They were for the beauty of the moment, for our shared, richly layered present.

And it suddenly occurred to me that I do have a summer bucket list after all. It's not a to-do list. Nor does it include a fancy vacation or any grand ambitions or even the stack of books by the bed that I really do long to read.

What I want most this summer is to spend more time with the ones I love. To have more days just like this one. Enough presence of mind to pay attention. And enough presence of heart to make gratitude my song, acceptance my refrain.

Yes, I understand that every life must end, uh-huh
As we sit alone, I know someday we must go, uh-huh
Oh I'm a lucky man, to count on both hands the ones I love
Some folks just have one, yeah, others, they've got none.
Stay with me…
Let's just breathe…
June 2014

—·—— this life ——·—

We're all only fragile threads, but what a tapestry we make.
—Jerry Ellis

I didn't intend to go silent back in July.

And now all these weeks later, I'm not sure how to start again. Writing anything after a long time away from my desk is a bit like trying to reconnect with an old friend who hasn't been part of my every-days for a while. It doesn't just happen, it requires attention. *Intention.* But where to begin?

Perhaps just *here, now.* On this quiet Sunday afternoon the house is empty. The low, constant churr of crickets signals the change in season even as the nasturtiums sprawl exuberantly across the stone wall and the sunflowers stretch ever skyward. No blooms to speak of, but that's what I get for allowing the spilled seed from the bird feeder to go wild in my garden. It's September, yet the temperature hovers in the seventies. My bathing suit and towel are still in the backseat of the car. Driving past the pond earlier, I was tempted to swing in for a swim.

Instead, I came home, cleaned the kitchen, and carried my notebook and laptop out onto the porch. It's time to sit, to look out the window, to gather up at least a few thoughts and put them into some kind of order. The slant of the sun and the already-deepening shadows tell the story: summer has ended, as it always does, too soon.

Since the day—it feels like a lifetime ago—when I last

sat on this screened porch writing about a youthful trip to Paris and a review of a lovely new cookbook, life has unfurled in ways I couldn't have imagined.

What I remember about that sultry July afternoon was that I'd just finished writing when I took a break, picked up my phone, and saw the screen was full of missed texts and calls—several from my dear friend Lisa's husband and several more from my own. I called Steve back first, gazing out at the mountains, hands trembling a bit, already sensing something was wrong.

This is how life turns, right? You are chugging along, doing whatever it is you do, your mind full of plans and intentions—the work at hand, the grocery list, some petty annoyance, the eye you must keep on the clock, the dinner you have to make, the movie you want to see. And then news arrives that shatters one reality and, in an instant, constructs another.

The words "inoperable brain tumor" are life changers.

Your beloved, strong friend of twenty years, your sons' adored kindergarten teacher, your playmate and advisor and confidante, who was fine when you saw her for dinner just a couple of weeks ago, has been rushed to the hospital. And with that, everything that seemed important five minutes ago fades to insignificance. The world tilts, grows sharper and, for an eerie breathless second, silent. Your hands shake harder. For some reason, the words that come first to mind, right after "I can't believe this is happening," are the ones your father-in-law's best friend, gone now for over twenty years, used to keep above his desk, to remind him that life is short and precious and finite: "No one gets out of here alive."

It is just a little easier, I realize, to write about this by slipping into the third person, as if I'm telling a story rather than struggling to articulate feelings that are painful and raw and complicated. But perhaps I don't even need to say much more. We've all received some version of that phone call. We've all planned for one future and suddenly found ourselves confronted with another. And isn't sadness a theme in every life that achieves some span of time? Growing older means losing things we care about and people we love. And yet even so, we wish for our loved ones to be healthy and happy, safe and at ease and long-lived. Of course, to think about that yearning for even five minutes is to realize we wish such well-being not only for our nearest and dearest, but for everyone, everywhere, always. How could we not?

Meanwhile, what life hands us, catching us off guard every time, is not the simple ease we ask for but something different: challenge, grief, pain. What choice do we have but to figure out how to accept it, all of it—the carefree afternoons; the charmed moments; the ordinary days; and, too, the unexpected blows that bring us to our knees, the news that makes us want to curl into a ball on the floor and weep. Maybe growing old—or, rather, growing *up*—means realizing that there will always be charmed moments, even in the bleakest of times, if we're attuned to notice them, and that there is no such thing as a charmed life. Not for me, or for you, or for anyone.

So it is that I've spent most of this lovely, mild, gone-too-soon summer finding my way in territory that is at once brand new and profoundly familiar. I know from past experience that grief and grace are two sides of the same coin. That healing is always possible even when a cure is not, and that it happens in the most unexpected ways. That laughter and tears can share the same moment, the same breath. That there is light even in the darkest night. That faith and mystery are inextricably intertwined, bound by wonder. And I know that showing up and quietly doing whatever most needs to be done in the moment is a more helpful response than unsolicited advice, dramatic gestures, or worry.

For me, perhaps the greatest surprise of the last couple of months has been discovering how much gratitude and sadness it's possible for one heart to hold at once.

My friend Lisa is much loved and day by day the circle of support around her grows. Volunteers sign up to cook, and meals appear each night in the cooler by the front door. Family and friends share driving duties in the daily round-trips to radiation. Notes and prayers and flowers and good wishes pour in from far and wide. Nothing is easy, nothing is as it was before, and yet she is wholly, unmistakably herself—engaged, curious, calm, and kind. By her own quiet example she inspires the rest of us to live in the moment, to be with her right here, rather than dreading the unknowable future.

She is more than halfway through her treatment, feeling better for now, taking it one day at a time, choosing gratitude for what is good rather than despairing about what can't be changed. And because I'm lucky enough to live eight minutes away, and because I'm not bound by a regular schedule or by the demands of a "real" job, we are having lots of sweet, precious time together—good visits and long talks and outdoor lunches and movies that make us laugh.

Even our rides to radiation are times to cherish, and every short walk in the driveway or candlelit dinner on the porch with our husbands is a special pleasure. This is what I do now—work of my own choosing that never, ever feels like work. It is really nothing more than friendship. To be a part of this network of love and concern is to embrace the true privilege of being human, each of us doing our best to be present, both for Lisa and for each other, gently offering comfort and connection where we can.

Even so, finding meaning in a situation that seems utterly meaningless, random, and unfair is difficult. The "new normal" keeps changing. It's only human to want answers and plans and promises. And instead we have questions and chemo and fragile bits of hope. Slowly, bit by bit, the incomprehensible becomes more manageable.

Surrendering to things as they are, we find a new way forward. Despair softens into acceptance. Fear of what might be in the future gives way to a desire to ease the path for today. Meaning goes hand-in-hand with connection. And the one thing I know for sure is that I become my best, most compassionate, most resilient self by stepping outside myself. By just showing up.

I suspect we all do better when our hearts are fully engaged. And really, as we grow older and as things we love are taken away one after another, what choice do we have but to learn to give even more? To love even more? To bring more and more peace and more and more kindness into the world?

As Buddhist teacher Sylvia Boorstein writes in *Happiness Is an Inside Job,* the small, wise, deeply consoling book that has lived in my purse and that has nourished my soul all summer: "Perhaps [this is] the clue about the happiness inherent in caring connections. The frightened 'I' who struggles is replaced by the 'we' who do this difficult life together, looking after one another. Holding hands." Yes. Oh, yes.

So, I return to a simple theme, one that many of the writers I most love devote themselves to as well: to live fully is to allow ourselves to be broken open time after time, even as we grow in awareness and appreciation of all the ways we are held and mended and supported by one another. This is life as it really is. So much goodness and beauty, so much unwarranted suffering, so many fragile hearts beating as one.

This morning I woke up early, while it was still dark, and lay in bed for a long while, listening as the birds began their song, one solo voice at first and then, within moments, a full-scale dawn chorus. Just after sunrise, Steve and I headed out for a walk with Tess, pausing to marvel at the layers of mist draped over the mountains; at the clear, golden light above; and at the sun breaking through clouds. Later, drinking coffee on the porch and reading the Sunday *New York Times,* I came across some lines excerpted from a letter by Steven Sottloff, the second American journalist slain by ISIS.

Reading these words, words written in captivity and smuggled out by a former cell mate of Sottloff's, I also grieve for this innocent man, for his family, for the needless suffering that yielded such urgent wisdom. And now, sharing them here, weaving this small connection between you and me and a young man whose life was violently taken, my soul heals just a little bit, too. We each awaken by degrees, our bruised hearts softening and growing more supple as we learn just how much is at stake, how much we need each other, how much we have to offer, what a beautiful tapestry we make.

"Live your life to the fullest and fight to be happy," Steven urged his family before he died. And then, this quote from Confucius:"Each of us has two lives.The second one begins when you realize you have only one."

September 2014

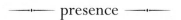 presence

Last week I drove through lashing winds and wild rains to a small town in Connecticut, to give a talk to a group of library friends. Afterward, a woman from the audience approached me as I stepped between the podium and the book table. It was clear she had a question, one she preferred not to share with the whole crowd.

We chatted for just a few minutes, barely long enough for her to articulate her thoughts about being lost on the path of midlife and for me to respond with a few words that might be helpful. It was a conversation that really called for a walk, a cup of tea, time—not the rushed reassurance I tried to offer while people were lining up to buy books.

But I've been thinking about her over the last few days, as I've done the mundane tasks of keeping my own life on track: watering the houseplants, vacuuming, walking the dog, paying bills and answering mail, raking leaves, planning dinner and shopping for groceries. Nothing exciting or important, just the ordinary work of being me.

The woman's children are grown and she's recently retired from a full-time career that satisfied her for years. She's neither young nor old; her health is good—her *life* is good. Her days, she told me, are busy still, taken up with family, volunteer work, seeing friends, and caring for others. She is making a difference in her world, grateful her new freedom means she's able to be there for those who need her.

And yet, she said, there's something missing. She's not quite certain that what she's doing is "enough." There's a nagging guilt, a sense of inadequacy, a suspicion that she's not being productive enough or successful enough or impressive enough.

"I know that feeling," I said to her. "I have it, too."

Looking back over the last few months, I have little to show for my time. I've barely written a blog post, let alone an essay someone might actually be willing to pay for. I keep moving the words "book proposal" to the next page of my calendar, without ever actually getting started. Apart from teaching one weekly yoga class, I'm essentially unemployed.

I've let the garden go this fall. There are no chrysanthe-mums in pots on our doorstep, no cornstalks propped at the threshold. I've not done a very good job of staying in touch with my friends, or made it to my book group, or truth be told, even found time to read the book. My summer clothes are still in the closet, augmented by the few sweaters and pairs of jeans that live there year round. I haven't thrown a dinner party or taken my mom out to lunch. I haven't upgraded the operating system on my computer, or cleaned the pantry, or sorted through the old magazines piled up on the coffee table. I not only forgot a good friend's birthday, but when I finally did call her, I had a momentary brain warp and had her age wrong by three years.

In addition, my sense of myself as a strong, sturdy, physical person has come up against a new reality. Months of shifting but chronic pain have led me down one road after another, in search of an "answer." I've spent a lot of money at the chiropractor's, trying to keep my spine in alignment and my hips open and my legs moving, and lots more money at the office of the nurse practitioner who's treating me for Lyme disease. The kitchen countertop is littered with homeopathic remedies and supplements, my closet floor is a jumble of shoe boxes. (I'm still trying to decide which pair of new orthotic shoes will give me the best hope of walking this winter without limping, and which ones should go back to Zappos.) And I'm typing these words while perched upon my new Tush-Cush Orthopedic Seat Cushion, which is supposed to prevent me from further compressing my vertebrae.

Not exactly a picture of a high-achiever. As I confessed to my husband the other night, I sometimes worry I've become more of a liability in our household than a contributor. I'm definitely writing more checks than I'm depositing at the bank. (Thank goodness for royalty payments of any size.)

When I look around at what my friends are doing—settling a ten-million-dollar lawsuit in a client's favor, creating an early-childhood program in South Africa, counseling families, writing books, hosting tours of their gardens, creating prize-winning websites—I'm proud of them and their accomplishments. At the same time, I have to admit to feeling considerably "less than."

And yet from a distance, to the woman in the audience, I appeared to be someone who had it together and was doing a lot. "You've published these books," she said, "and you also teach, you do Reiki, you have a website, you stood up here today and gave a talk." And then, in the next breath, "And I'm not doing anything. At least, not anything that really matters."

Ah, and there it was again, this age-old, heartbreakingly cruel thing we women do to ourselves. We compare ourselves to someone else and come up wanting. We look at what someone else is doing and feel our own contributions mean less, are worth less, amount to less. We assume other women must have things all figured out, and that we must be the only ones stumbling along in the dark, unsure of our choices, managing invisible aches and pains, uncertain of our purpose, hesitating to take the next step.

"No, no," I rushed to assure her. "I haven't actually written anything for weeks. I only teach a little. I mostly practice Reiki on myself these days." It seemed important for me to let her know, in the two minutes we had together, that we were in the same boat.

But thinking about that brief conversation over the last few days, I realize we both had shortchanged ourselves. The woman who berated herself for not doing anything that "matters" had just told me about her family, her friends, and her volunteer work in her town. She offers her best self in places where she's needed and she gives her time as a gift from the heart. Tell me that doesn't matter.

And, although it's true I've been quiet lately, writing less and doing less out in the world, I also know deep down that what I have been doing is no less meaningful for being invisible.

Not having a 9-to-5 job, or even the regular editing work I did for years, means it's been possible for me to be there for my friend who is sick. "Can you believe we're doing this?" Lisa said the other day as I pushed her wheelchair through the hospital halls, on our way to her weekly blood test. I had just been thinking of the afternoon runs we used to take, the mountain we used to climb, the last hike we made on snowshoes. She's right—no one could have foreseen this latest installment in our twenty-year friendship. But at least we both chose in that moment to laugh, glad—as always—to be together and making the best of things as they are. And it didn't escape me that my own presence on this journey is a privilege. I can be at my friend's side—driving her to appointments, dropping in midday with some lunch, cooking something healthy for dinner—because I'm not needed more someplace else.

I've been steadily available, too, for a friend in crisis, just as I know she would be for me if the tables were turned. One step at a time, she's negotiating the end of an old life and navigating the scary, unknown territory of a new one—the kind of venture no one should have to undertake without a companionable fellow traveler with whom to share the inevitable twists and turns of the road. Being present here means talking things over, going to court, reading the small print, hashing out a plan. I travel this rocky terrain with my friend because I can. Again, a privilege.

In both of these situations, I'm reminded every day that being present for someone else isn't about swooping in to rescue them, solving their problems, or even helping them manage the day's challenges. Sometimes being present is simply about, well, presence. We live in a busy world, surrounded by people bent on getting things done. Our culture is fueled by our notions of doing—more, faster, better. But action isn't always the answer. And a lot of what I'm doing these days involves a willingness to shift gears, to move gracefully and gratefully into a state of *not* doing. Sometimes, the best I have to offer is a willingness to listen, and to simply *be*—with whatever the moment brings.

And so, I join my sick friend as we float along in the slow current of her "new normal." We take a little walk and stop to watch the leaves fall as she catches her breath.

Or we sit on the grass and pick shriveled beans off the vine. Or we lie on our backs on an unseasonably warm October afternoon, gazing up at the sky, our thoughts drifting with the clouds. Back at home, brimming with emotion, I find myself drawn to solitude and silence, needing this time to feel my own sadness at her prognosis and to reconnect with my own quiet center.

Sitting down to dinner at the end of the day with my husband and our grown son, both home from work and with news to share, I look across the table and am overcome, as always, by the simple truth of life's abundance, intertwined as always now with a sharper sense of loss.

I may or may not get the book proposal written. I definitely need some new shoes. I'll take my cat's claw and my magnesium and my various other pills and potions and do my daily stretches and hope for the best. I'll fill the birdfeeder and make another meal and answer another letter from a reader. I'll drive my friend to the doctor and make beautiful salads for her lunch and cradle her head in my hands when she's in pain.

Meanwhile, to my own chiding inner critic and to the woman at lunch last week, I want to say this: it's never *what* we do that matters, but rather, how we do it. The secret ingredient isn't ambition but love. We make a gift of our lives, of ourselves, in simple ways—by being kind, by being compassionate, by paying attention, by being useful in whatever way we can, wherever we happen to be, in whatever time we have.

October 2014

—·—— finding goodness ——·—

When I was child, my dad's dental office was attached to our house. On one side of the door was our private, domestic world: home. Pass through the back room with its overflowing bookcases full of dental textbooks and journals, maneuver around the desk piled high with bills and paperwork, step through the small brown door by the laundry room, and you were in the reception area of my parents' busy practice. Many afternoons I'd forgo the TV reruns my brother was watching in our den and slip into my dad's quiet waiting room to read magazines. I loved the jokes in the *Reader's Digest,* the photographs in *Life,* the lavish meals in *Gourmet,* and most of all, the hidden pictures in *Highlights.*

There was a trick to solving those optical-illusion puzzles with their lists of random objects hiding in plain sight. At first glance, all you'd see was the scene itself, a dense drawing of animals in the jungle, perhaps, or a crowded playground scene. But squint your eyes just enough to change focus, and you could begin to discern the outlines of those other things: a slice of bread, a pencil, a teacup, a button.

The only way to find the button amid the tangle of palm fronds and swinging monkeys was to blot out everything else. You had to narrow your gaze and go in search of that one thing you most wanted to see.

My life lately has felt as complex as those multilayered drawings of my childhood. On the surface, things appear orderly enough. But what I've experienced internally is a series of invisible, painful losses—each a challenge to my equanimity, to my sense of the universe as a fair and benign place. Feeling fragile and overwhelmed, I've been experimenting with an emotional version of that old eye-squinting thing. I keep thinking I'll suffer less if I can just look more deeply into the picture. Somewhere, I know, goodness is hiding in plain sight. My task is simply to find it.

And so I repeat these words to myself like a mantra: "Look for the good." And then I narrow my focus until I begin to see what I'm hunting for: the delicate outline of a blessing, some well-camouflaged scrap of goodness amid the sadness, some small, random thing to be grateful for.

"Look for the good," was also the intention I carried with me to Georgia last week, as I flew south to see my son Jack for the first time in six months. Six months! It's still almost inconceivable to me that I could go so long without seeing one of my children. Since he left New Hampshire in May to change schools and begin working toward a degree in sound engineering in Atlanta, Jack hasn't slept under this roof for one night. We stay in touch by phone and text, but I'd never seen where he lives or met his roommates or ridden in his car. He was about to turn twenty-two. It was time to go.

Jack invited me to stay at his place, on the futon in their spare upstairs room. Although I had a plan B—the serene guest suite of a young friend of ours who happens to live a mile away—I really did want to be with Jack, to see his life up close. And I was grateful that these three guys (and one nearly live-in girlfriend) were willing to welcome me into their midst for four days.

"I'd love it," I said. "All I ask is a clean set of sheets and that you wipe down the toilet seat for me."

I got a quick glimpse of the picture on my first night. Jack seemed too thin to me. I wasn't crazy about the beard, dark and straggly. Although he'd washed some sheets, they hadn't actually made it onto the bed. The spare room, my room, was a jumble of cast-off furniture, various cords and cables no one needed, a lamp that didn't work. The toilet seat had definitely not been wiped. A cockroach skittered across the kitchen counter. There was clutter. A massage table but no sofa. Random piles of clothes in the living room. Dirty spoons and empty glasses.

The fact is, twenty-two-year-old guys don't set up housekeeping the way fifty-plus-year-old women do. There are different standards for just about everything, but especially for how often a male face needs shaving, or a floor needs washing, or a toilet needs scrubbing.

But I wasn't there to approve Jack's facial hair or to pass judgment on his home or to grade the tidying skills of its occupants. I was there to spend time with my son and get to know his friends. My only agenda for the visit: enjoy Jack's company for four days and depart with a sense of what his life is like. I narrowed my focus. "Look for the good."

Jack and I made up my bed. We sat in the kitchen with his roommates and drank hibiscus tea. I saw how they were with each other: kind and easy and attentive. There was lots of laughter. It was obvious that Jack was happy and comfortable, that these kids don't just live together, they care about each other.

I'd worried four days might seem too long for a mother to hang around, but it didn't turn out that way. The time flew by. We shopped for groceries and cleaning supplies. (I was so happy to buy cleaning supplies!) Jack made me eggs and veggies for breakfast. The two of us hiked up Kennesaw Mountain with their new foster dog, Clyde, a sweet ten-month-old Lab–pit-bull mix waiting for a permanent home, and we talked and talked.

On Friday, two days in, I swept the floor, donned a pair of rubber gloves, and scrubbed the bathroom. That night Jack and I made a huge pot of spicy lentil soup and a salad with oranges, grapefruits, avocados, and pomegranate. A couple of his friends came over, and we had a dinner party. That's when I "got" the décor. With the exception of Jack now, all these young people are chiropractic students. They don't sit around after dinner. They work on each other's bodies and adjust each other's necks and spines and occiputs. The living room, with its massage table and bongo drums and resistance bands and keyboard, works for them—a place to lift weights, exercise, stretch, make music, play with the puppy, and practice the art and craft of healing themselves and each other. The conversation was lively. And after the dishes were done, I got my cervical spine adjusted.

By then it was apparent to me: things aren't perfect or even perfectly figured out, yet an aspiration to live healthfully is what binds this small household together. There isn't a bag of Doritos or a soda in sight. But there are two refrigerators, and they are full of kale, carrots, apples, broccoli, and almond milk. There are good knives, good cutting boards, good pans. Two blenders. A compost bin. Purified water on tap. A sign on the wall that says, "NO ICE CREAM." Jars of coconut oil and bags of raw almonds. Kombucha mushrooms growing on the counter, wrapped in dish towels.

By Saturday morning, as we all piled into two cars to go to the farmers' market, I was feeling like part of the household. Later, as we unpacked our bags, I asked Jack about the cockroaches.

"Yeah, we have a few," he said. "We ignore them till they get big, then we do catch and release, and put them outside. They're just trying to survive, like the rest of us."

On the last night, Jack's birthday, I offered to take everyone out to dinner. Jack shaved off his beard. They chose a funky raw/vegan restaurant in midtown Atlanta, their favorite "special occasion" place. There were four of us, me and Jack, his roommate Jules, and Jules's girlfriend, who had led us in a "high-intensity" interval workout in the park that afternoon. We passed on the "shots" (coconut water), and ordered a raw platter to share, quinoa bowls, salad. The food was fabulous. When the bill came, Jules reached for it.

"Actually, we decided we want to take *you* out to dinner," he said. "To thank you for cleaning our bathroom. It feels so nice to walk in there now, I don't really know why we never did it before. I even took a bath this afternoon, and it was so relaxing."

I told them what a great time I'd had, how grateful I was to them for making me feel welcome. "You guys have created a really wonderful home together," I said. They agreed.

"Yeah," Jules said. "It's even better when there's a mom around." Goodness in plain sight.

November 2014

———·— spark joy ———·—

When our sons were young, there was no holding off Christmas. Henry, born December 18, absorbed holiday melodies in the womb, from "Jingle Bells" to *The Messiah*. His in-utero nickname was Bing, for Crosby, which morphed into Der Bingle after a visiting friend introduced us to the German diminutive. (Of course, we had no way of knowing then that music would turn out to be his "language" of choice, but now, looking back, it seems almost preordained; he arrived in a season of shimmer and twinkle, surrounded by love and borne into our arms on a wave of joyful noise.)

That year, in the final weeks of my first pregnancy and with a December due date looming, my husband and I were organized in a way we've never been before or since: all our gifts bought and wrapped and shipped weeks in advance. A tree up and decorated the day after Thanksgiving. Holiday cards mailed December first, and a newly painted yellow room awaiting its tiny occupant. All was in readiness, every diaper and onesie neatly folded and stacked, every holiday ornament shining in its place.

Four days before Christmas we brought our newborn home from the hospital, dressed him up in the miniature velveteen Santa suit my brother had given him, and snapped our first family photo in front of the tree. And so it was that the holiday and Henry were linked for life. At three, he donned his own Santa hat and sat at the dinner table on Christmas eve singing "The Twelve Days of Christmas" by heart, while his newborn brother, Jack, dozed in my lap, just over a month old but already a bit too big to be squeezed into that tiny hand-me-down Santa suit.

The traditions accumulated with the years: driving through nearby towns on a wintry evening to view Christmas lights in all the different neighborhoods with Bing Crosby and Leon Redbone providing a familiar soundtrack in the warm, dark car and the kids singing along from the backseat. Unpacking the boxes full of miniature fir trees I've collected over the years and creating small forests of them on the mantel and shelves. Placing the slender metal angel silhouette on the top of the tree. Taking turns opening the tiny, crooked doors of the Advent calendar. Baking cookies and cranberry bread and spiced nuts. Attending the Christmas Revels in Cambridge with our dear friends and former next-door neighbors. Reading Truman Capote's *A Christmas Memory* and *Harvey Slumfenburger's Christmas Present* out loud in front of the fire.

Always, Henry has been the instigator of Christmas in our household, and the rest of us are content to let him take the lead. It was Henry who made sure the box of

Christmas books was carried up the basement stairs and unpacked the day after Thanksgiving. And it's Henry who insists our Christmas morning breakfast include both oatmeal scones *and* Jimmy Dean sausage balls, which he willingly makes and freezes a few days early, knowing that if I had my druthers we would quietly eliminate Jimmy D. from the menu.

It was Henry who, at age six, organized the first of many annual Christmas shows, with all the kids in the neighborhood singing carols under his direction and, in later years, performing on their various musical instruments. And this year it was Henry, now teaching for a semester at his old high school, who guided the students through the choral arrangements for the annual Nativity pageant—yet another tradition embraced and passed on.

But this year, as Thanksgiving came and went, I found myself resisting Christmas even as those around me were eager to embrace it. The very thought of hauling the decorations out made me feel irritable and tired and overwhelmed. It seemed as if there was already too much—too much to think about, too much to do, too much stuff in every nook and cranny of the house.

Maybe everyone has their moment: the sudden realization that you simply can't move forward without first turning around and digging into what's been piling up around you. I do wish my own flash of motivation had come a few months ago, when things were just a little less hectic, but we can't control these things. I hit my breaking point the day Steve and Henry arrived home with a Christmas tree tied to the top of the car.

"I just don't think I can start Christmas yet," I admitted to them. "Please, give me a couple of days."

And then I picked up a small book that's been sitting by my bed for a while now, *The Life-Changing Magic of Tidying Up*. According to author Marie Kondo, there is magic in order, happiness in tidying, transformation just waiting to happen as soon as we start taking out the trash. A few weeks earlier I'd read the first few pages and immediately decided I probably could part with the years' worth of old *New Yorker* magazines I'd piled into the bookshelves in our bedroom.

That first, heady purge led to several bags of books pulled off the shelves and donated to the local library. The newly emptied spaces in our bedroom seemed to glow in the sunlight, and the newfound sense of spaciousness inspired me to vacuum under the bed and clean my bathroom drawers. Pretty soon, though, I got busy again, and the cleaning came to a halt. But I didn't forget the sense of relief I'd felt at finally tackling just a few of my cluttered spaces.

The *New York Times* has called Marie Kondo a kind of "zen nanny," and so she is, at once likable and firm. She's a little woo-woo, too. Socks have souls? Sweaters prefer to be neatly folded? Our personal possessions have lives of their own and brighten under our care? And she's nothing if not down-to-earth: "Effective tidying involves only two essential actions: discarding and deciding where to store things. Of the two, discarding must come first."

I was in.

Marie has one rule of thumb, and it makes me laugh.

"The best way to choose what to keep and what to throw away," she suggests, "is to take each item in one's hand and ask: 'Does this spark joy?' If it does, keep it. If not, throw it out."

And so I spent the first few days of December in search of some joy of my own—not stringing lights or shopping for gifts or baking cookies, but cleaning out the basement and holding one random item after another in my hands.

I applied the "joy test" to old clothes, to winter hats and gloves, to boxes of my own unsold books, including multiple copies of foreign editions. What to do with ten copies of *Mitten Strings for God* in German? (Toss.) I applied it to the kids' school papers, tablecloths and dishes from a suburban life that ended a decade ago, lamps without shades—still perfectly good but hardly harbingers of happiness. I texted photos to Jack in Atlanta: a moldy basketball, a box of Magic cards, an old guitar amp, a tangle of cables, and a box of unidentifiable electronics. By the time I got down to vacuuming mouse poop and swabbing grimy hidden corners and sweeping spiderwebs away, I didn't even mind doing the dirty work.

The basement led, a day later, to the cellar storage freezer where I discovered, among other hoary artifacts, rock-solid remnants of the 2010 Christmas ham, carefully wrapped and labeled. The bags of blueberries we picked last summer? Yes, there is joy in every one; we will be eating blueberries on our morning oatmeal all winter long. Those petrified loaves of bread covered with freezer frost? Not so much. Another trash bag, filled and carried out the door.

On a roll, I headed up the stairs to the pantry. There, I was met with half-gone boxes of pasta, a small shop's worth of expired spices, old cans of things and old things in cans. There is no joy in an unlabeled bag of unidentifiable grain, nor in a bottle of cloudy vinegar, nor in that dusty box of farro purchased for some summer salad that never got made. But it was, indeed, a joy to take every single thing off the shelves, wash every surface, and carefully choose what went back. It was a joy to send a box of still-good things to the local food bank. And how happy I was to find the blackberry jam I bought at the farm stand last July and then forgot all about.

By day three of my cleaning extravaganza, I felt as if I'd set down a heavy burden I hadn't even been aware of carrying. I kept slipping into the pantry, just to have a look and smile. My step was lighter, my holiday spirit finally starting to simmer.

"You know, Mom," Henry pointed out, "if you don't stop cleaning and start decorating, Christmas will come and go, and the tree will still be in the corner in the garage."

He was right. The office, the linen closet, and the laundry room would have to wait. We've spent the last few days readying the house for Christmas, in no hurry at all, playing our favorite Christmas music and carefully choosing what goes up and what gets put into a box to take to the swap table at the recycling center so that someone else can find a treasure and bring joy home.

It feels as if getting rid of some things that no longer serve us well, that no longer make us happy, that no one in our family really needs or wants has opened up some emotional space as well as physical space. Confronting my own possessions has made me less inclined to shop and more inclined to offer Christmas gifts of time, of food made with love, of experiences that can be shared. As Marie says, "We need to show consideration for others by helping them avoid the burden of owning more than they need or can enjoy." Exactly so.

I could have spent Tuesday at the mall, but instead I spent it in the kitchen, making granola for everyone on our list. Thursday, it was spiced nuts: the perfect stocking stuffer or holiday hostess gift. Saturday morning, as sun poured into the kitchen, I made a double batch of cranberry orange bread from the recipe my mom always used and then went out for a walk while the loaves baked. When I got back to the house and opened the door, the sights and smells of Christmas at home did indeed lifted my heart: baking bread in the oven, holiday greens in pitchers, cherished decorations carefully arranged.

As my mom begins to pack up a lifetime's worth of things from her home, some of her favorite decorations have made their way to me this week, and now the Santa who once graced her mantel has found a new home on ours.

In a few days, Henry will turn twenty-five and, as always, Christmas and his birthday will be all wrapped up together. Jack will fly home, and our family will be under one roof at last. As always, we will gather with our friends this weekend for the Christmas Revels and for chili and cornbread around their table afterward. Our grown children will make the same jokes they always make about the sword dancers' dwindling numbers and the shuffling guys holding up reindeer antlers in the second act.

Some night next week, we'll sit in our living room and I'll read Truman Capote aloud till the last page, when I'll pass the book over to someone else to finish so I don't have to read through my silly, predictable tears. On Christmas Eve, Henry will play the service in the church where he served as musical director when he was just out of college. Our friends Lisa and Kerby will come for dinner, and we will not speak of inoperable cancers or of what the year to come may bring. And the next day our house will be full with family and friends and dogs and all the stuff of Christmas.

There will be joy. There already is. Joy slipped in quietly and took up residence in the space I cleared for it.

December 2014

The little things? The little moments? They aren't little.
— *Jon Kabat-Zinn*

—·—— emptiness ——·—

I awake this morning to a leaden, pre-storm sky, not yet light, the room silent but for my sleeping husband's quiet breathing. The holiday season over, the work of this new year not yet begun, I gaze out the window near our bed, studying the dark shadows of the mountains beyond and searching for the right word to put to my feelings.

Melancholic. Yes, a little.

We said good-bye to Jack yesterday, knowing it will be early June before he's home again. The departure of a grown child always brings with it a quick, sharp pang of parting. And although it's only January 3 by the calendar, I'm more aware of endings at this moment than new be-ginnings. The year ahead will hold unexpected blessings, certainly, but there will undoubtedly be heartbreak, too. The poignancy of more comings and goings, changes and transformations, as well as more permanent losses. And my soul, anticipating, has already shouldered some of that grief.

Tired. That, too.

It's been a tough few weeks. First there was the bustle and preparation of Christmas, the shopping and cooking and cleaning, the care taken to uphold traditions, to create a special season, a good day, a whole series of delectable meals. There was an unspoken yet ever-present awareness of "lasts" as I spent time with my friend Lisa. And then, no sooner was the holiday ushered out and the house set to rights than we found ourselves entertaining an uninvited guest. Jack and I, and our neighbor Debbie, were all knocked flat within the same hour by a violent intestinal bug. Instead of the movies and dinners, winter hikes, and family activities I'd envisioned for the wide-open days after Christmas, we shared a catalog of unspeakable symptoms, trips to the ER, twin IVs, slow recoveries. *Tired* is an understatement.

Gratitude. Of course, always.

In the midst of our sickness, Steve and Henry leapt to the rescue, cleaning bathrooms and running loads of wash, making countless trips up and down the stairs with buckets and rags, glasses of Pedialyte, cups of tea, stacks of Saltines. My friend Maude brought ginger ale and home-made turkey soup and healing potions. We were well nursed, and yesterday, finally, six days into the ordeal, our bellies rumbled once again with hunger. (I was so sure I'd feed Jack up while he was home and send him back to school carrying a few more pounds on his tall, lean frame; instead, I'm pretty sure he's had to tighten his belt another notch.)

And so, perhaps it's fitting that the word I finally land on to describe my inner state is this one: *empty*. It's not just that my innards have been thoroughly scoured this week, although I'm definitely feeling emptied in a physical way. But my spirit feels as if it's been poured out, too. I am in need of sustenance of every kind—soul food and real food, replenishment both spiritual and literal.

Later, after the breakfast dishes are done and Steve and Henry have left for the day, I pull my worn, well-read copy of *Gift from the Sea* from the bedroom shelf. I'm not even surprised when the book falls open to the very passage I've come in search of: "Traditionally we are taught, and instinctively we long, to give where it is needed—and immediately. Eternally, woman spills herself away in driblets to the thirsty, seldom being allowed the time, the quiet, the peace, to let the pitcher fill up to the brim."

Yes. How satisfying it is to see another's need and to meet it, quietly, without a fuss. How swift I am to find my own purpose in easing the way for someone else. And the more uncertain I'm feeling about myself, the more insistently I ask, "How can I be useful here?" Usually, I find that just answering the question reveals a path forward.

But as we all know, it's easier to give to others than to ourselves. Easier to spill our energies than to replenish them. Easier to quench another's thirst than to acknowledge our own.

Today is a day to fill my own pitcher. I turn up the heat, start the dishwasher, and sit down in the kitchen, a stack of books and notes at my side. I read a few more pages of Anne Morrow Lindbergh, grateful as always for this uncanny sense of kinship that transcends time and space, amazed that a woman writing before I was born remains so vibrantly alive in my imagination, as if she is herself a trusted friend, nearby, ready at any moment to whisper straight into the ear of my heart.

"I do not believe that suffering teaches," Anne insists. "If suffering alone taught, all the world would be wise, since everyone suffers. To suffering must be added mourning, understanding, patience, love, openness, and the willingness to remain vulnerable." Yes, again.

Her words remind me: there is no escape from the reality of things falling apart. "Everyone suffers." The choice I have, the only choice really, is to plumb the possibilities for growth and healing even in the midst of pain. And growth can't happen in the dark. Growth requires sunlight, water, care, and space. Healing doesn't occur in a vacuum. Healing goes hand-in-hand with allowing, accepting, softening.

Filling the pitcher means taking time—time to reflect, to rest, to read poetry, to look at beautiful art, to get lost in a novel, to walk through the woods at dusk, to sift through thoughts and feelings and to make room for all of them. Grief and joy, fear and courage, despair and hope.

After a while, I close the book, turn off my laptop, and set all of my things aside. It is indeed both wisdom and solace I'm thirsty for; these are the qualities with which I long to fill my pitcher. But perhaps on a cold, sere January morning, "empty" is not a bad place to be.

Emptiness is also readiness. Emptiness is potential. Emptiness is a space swept bare. Emptiness is a willingness to sit here quietly, for as long as it takes, allowing things to be just as they are.

January 2015

————— in awe of the subtle —————

I am perched on a stool in my friend's kitchen, looking out at the same mountains I see from my own kitchen on the other side of town. A reverse view. On the sill above the sink, a row of single paperwhites rising out of cobalt blue jars. Beyond the tiny star blossoms, on the other side of the window, a few flakes of snow dancing through the air. And then, in the time it takes me to type a sentence and look up again, the storm quickens, and the solid, slumbering mountains disappear behind a swirling veil of white.

My friend sleeps in the bedroom down the hall. When she wakes up, I'll be here. We'll have a late breakfast together, drink tea, listen to the wild wind, and watch the snow fall. I suspect there will be comfort for both of us in that.

A sentence sent by another friend over the weekend about sums it up: "Sitting silently beside a friend who is hurting may be the best gift we have to give." Sitting silently is something I'm always happy to do. The gift, needless to say, goes both ways. We are all hungry for silence. To dive down, to find the beauty in a moment's passing, to inhabit time with a breath, to be fully present to another's beating heart is both an act of perception and imagination. I love that even a time of stillness can be shared through the gift of presence. There is no need to chatter or to fill the space between us with words. For me there's a comfort in knowing that silence, too, speaks a language of caring and connection.

At my own house, we've put the holiday decorations away and stripped the rooms down to a bare winter austerity that pleases me. I relish this gradual return to a simpler existence. I find beauty in the empty surfaces, relief in the absence of stuff, a serenity and quiet order that meets my January soul where it is.

Over these last few days, I've allowed myself space to linger, to look, to savor. What better time than the frozen month of January to ponder the quiet miracles of everyday life? What better moment than this to remind ourselves that the potential for healing is always at hand, and that we begin to access it as soon as we say yes to whatever is true in this moment. Whether we like it or not, whether it's what we expected or not, we can still say yes. And suddenly, with that small gesture of acceptance, we discover not only that life is manageable after all, but that our own spirits are more resilient, more compassionate, more capable of gratitude and joy than we imagined.

As yoga teacher Rodney Yee has said, "Train yourself to live in awe of the subtle, and you will live in a world of beauty and ease." That, it seems to me, is a practice worth pursuing. And to guide the way, could there be any better words than these, a blessing for the senses from John O'Donohue:

May your inner eye see through the surfaces
And glean the real presence
Of everything that meets you.
May your soul beautify the desire of your eyes
That you might glimpse
The infinity that hides
In the simple sights
That seem worn to your usual eyes.
January 2015

——·—— to love like a grandmother ——·——

Break a vase, and the love that reassembles the fragments is stronger than that love which took its symmetry for granted when it was whole.
—Derek Wolcott

I was not the best little girl. Shy, bookish, solitary, dreamy, not athletic, a bit chubby, I was certainly no troublemaker. At school, a year younger than most of my classmates, clueless about fashion, part of no clique and always two steps behind on the latest trend, I kept my head down and my mouth shut, hoping not to be noticed. At home, where repercussions for misbehavior were swift, I did as I was told and tried to stay out of the way. I read a lot. I wrote. I colored, painstakingly, in a beloved, finely drawn coloring book with my colored pencils. I sat contentedly on the floor of my bedroom, making tiny dolls from wooden clothespins and sewing clothes for them.

But the truth is, at my grandmother's house, where love was unconditional, I pushed the limits. When my brother and I were little, we spent many weekends with our grandparents, who were happy to give my young, overworked parents a break. My grandmother, who at the age I'm remembering her, was just a few years older than I am now, seemed to me at once frail, elderly, and immortal. She was tiny, less than a hundred pounds, with feet the size of a small child's. Asthma sometimes forced her to lie down on the couch in the middle of the day, wheezing with each breath. Her heart was weak. She was in and out of the hospital, for gallstones and kidney stones and I don't know what else. And yet, because I'd never known anyone to die, it never occurred to me that someday she would. I couldn't imagine her other than as she was, up in the morning before anyone else, her breath rattling a bit in her chest, frying eggs at the stove, tending to her home, to my grandfather, to us pesky children with our endless questions and demands.

My grandmother—Wilda was her name—was a housedress-and-apron kind of grandmother. There were always cookies in the jar, a dried-up Lipton tea bag by the sink waiting to be used a second time, a half stick of butter softening in a dish by the stove. She kept her collection of china teacups on proud display in the dining room, a stack of magazines—the *Ladies Home Journal, Family Circle,* and *McCall's*—by her chair, recipes copied by hand into a falling-apart notebook, antimacassars tacked into place along the back of the sofa, hard butterscotch candies in a covered glass dish, Laurence Welk on the TV, witch hazel and a big blue jar of Vicks and a flesh-colored bottle of calamine lotion in the bathroom cabinet, lace-trimmed hankies in the top right dresser drawer, a pack of Wrigley's spearmint gum down at the bottom of her black handbag, amid the lipstick-stained tissues. (Gum that she would generously dispense, though always by the half piece, to make it last longer.)

I see her now in my mind's eye, this small, kind, busy woman, pushing her huge brown Hoover vacuum across the flowered carpet, it's bright headlight illuminating the path ahead. There was always a seriousness to her work, care taken but no fuss made, simply another dinner to be prepared, more dishes to wash, a shopping list to be written out on the back of an envelope.

I remember standing by her side in the huge old Baptist church she and my grandfather attended, smelling her powdery smell, listening to her sing the hymns in a high, thin, warbly voice, feeling at once terribly bored and completely safe. I remember five-minute trips in her boat-sized white Oldsmobile—she could barely see over the wheel, despite the extra height afforded by a square pillow she sat upon to drive—to the little store down the road. There, my brother and I would pester her for treats—something we never would have dared with our parents—and she would always give in, extracting quarters from her change purse to pay for our orange popsicles and Pixy Stix and cheap plastic toys.

I loved her. And yet.

When I came across this beautiful line by Derek Wolcott yesterday, the first thought that came into my head was a memory of the evening I broke my grandmother's antique, hand-painted kerosene globe lamp that had once belonged to *her* mother. The lamp, one of the only things that had accompanied my grandmother throughout her modest life, from her childhood in a small town in the Maine woods to the tidy ranch house where she would end her days, had been wired with electricity for the twentieth century. It was delicate and beautiful, her most precious possession.

My brother and I had had our after-dinner baths. We were probably still dripping, damp skin sticking to our pajamas, revved up and acting silly because, at our grandparents' house, no one cared if we made noise or danced like wild little savages in the living room. He was three, a toddler imitating his big sister. I was six, old enough to know better than to swing a big wet towel around over my head like a lasso. My grandmother asked us, kindly I'm sure, to stop. We pretended not to hear. She asked again, firmly this time, warning, "Something is going to get broken."

Something did. I whipped my towel around with a mighty flourish, one last time. It caught the lamp and sent it flying. The glass shattered, scattering everywhere. My grandmother burst into tears.

I remember little else about that night, except that there were no raised voices or spankings as there would have been at home. I was not shouted at or punished, though I fled down the hall to my bed, in tears myself. There was no hope of reassembling the fragments. From behind the closed door, I could hear my grandmother weeping, the tinkle of glass being swept into the dustpan, the roar of the Hoover getting up the last bits.

As I write this story now, my heart still hurts to recall it. The lesson, too, is fresh and raw; in fact, I am learning it anew these days. And it has nothing to do with obeying my elders or refraining from roughhousing in the living room.

My grandmother's beautiful heirloom was shattered, but her love for me was intact, not even chipped or cracked. In the morning, there was no mention of the lamp I had broken. Instead my grandmother took me into her arms and reassembled the fragments of *me,* gluing my broken, heartsick, remorseful self back together.

I did not know, at six, whether I was a good person or not.

I was very much afraid that I might not be very good after all, that I wasn't worthy of love—or even of the Pixy Stix and gingersnaps and half sticks of gum my grandmother gave me. I did not know that good people say and do stupid, reckless stuff, which does not make them bad, only foolish. I did not know that a broken *thing* doesn't matter nearly as much as a broken heart, or a broken word, or a broken trust. I did not know that the glue that mends a broken relationship is forgiveness. Or that in choosing to forgive someone who has wronged or hurt us, we do indeed reassemble a shattered love into a stronger whole.

I did not know when I was six that, fifty years later, with my grandmother long gone from this earth, I would sit in my kitchen on a snowy winter day thinking about her, yearning for the kind of openhearted pardon she offered me so long ago. For, although I do now believe in my own essential goodness, I can still, unwittingly, break things that are precious. I can be wrong and graceless and dumb. Recently, I wrote and sent a letter I should have kept to myself, the emotional equivalent of swinging a towel in the living room. I caused a friend to suffer.

Whether this particular vase can be reassembled by love I don't know. I can only do my best to gather up the broken pieces, to make amends, to wait patiently and see. But in the meantime, I want to do a better job of loving like my grandmother, quietly and wholeheartedly— without feeling so compelled to have my say or my way, without expectation or attachment.

To love like a grandmother means to offer pardon without need of an apology. It means to apologize without asking for or expecting absolution. It means to love with no strings attached or conditions to be met. To love like a grandmother is to know: we all make mistakes and we all need to be hugged and held and forgiven the errors of our clumsy ways. To love like a grandmother is to remember that no one gets out of bed in the morning with the intention of sending a lamp flying through the air or doing harm to someone we love, and yet our lives and our needs inevitably bump up painfully against the lives and needs of others. A wrong word, a rash action, a hurtful gesture, or a simple lapse of attention—we are all guilty. To love like a grandmother means to tenderly forgive these human errors in others, in ourselves. It is to see the beauty and the value in the vase that's been broken and painstakingly, imperfectly repaired.

January 2015

———·——— the shape of a year ———·———

It's snowing again, for the third time in a week. In New England, and certainly here in our part of New Hampshire, it's a season of enforced respite from the comings and goings of our everyday lives. We can fight the weather (not much of a contest there), or we can rise to the challenge of an un-compromising northern winter, layering on fleeces and wool socks, planning ahead, slowing down. I choose to acquiesce to this season of storms, keeping more food in the refrig-erator, making pots of soup that last for days, shopping less, driving less, snowshoeing more, writing more, reading more, gazing out the window more.

This morning, it's pretty wild outside—a bitter, relentless wind drives swirling curtains of powder across the field and sends silent clumps of snow crashing from tree limbs. With the temperature dropping steadily and the snow already thigh deep, it would be easy to view yet another four or six or sixteen inches as an annoying inconvenience. But I'm seeing this latest storm as a muffled blessing, an invitation to stay put today—no place to go and nothing to do, at least not until the roads are cleared.

Looking up from my stool in the kitchen, I spot the empty bird feeder swinging in the wind and a sturdy cardinal, all puffed up and hunkered down in a nearby snowdrift, bright as a jewel against the blanket of white, patiently waiting for his breakfast. We all need to eat.

I slip on Steve's tall black boots to trudge out and fill the bird feeder, scattering some extra nibbles along the top of the snow-covered stone wall—a sunflower-seed buffet for the squirrels and the jays. A pair of chickadees arrives before I'm even back to the door, the two of them too hungry to be shy. I stand there quietly for a moment, close as I dare, to watch them take turns plucking seeds from between the wires. But my fingers are already numb with cold. I'll skip even the short walk today.

Back inside my cozy kitchen, second cup of coffee in hand, I pick up my book. More and more these days, I want to close my computer, silence my phone, and steep in the silence. And yet, being quiet in both body and soul can be its own kind of challenge—especially given the countless distractions, obligations, needs, and desires that tug at the coat sleeves of my attention each day.

And so, I've been giving myself this small gift of time,

a few minutes of uninterrupted reading before the work of the day begins. I have a stack of new books waiting on the bedside table. But in the silent expansiveness of these winter mornings, as I set a tone for my day, I'm drawn not to the latest literary releases on my shelf or to the novel half read on my iPad, but to a modest, gently worn, long-out-of-print memoir called *The Shape of a Year*, by Jean Hersey.

I have a special place my heart for such chronicles of daily life as it was once lived by women who have long since left this earth. (May Sarton's *Plant Dreaming Deep* is probably my favorite, but there are others, too, memoirs by Louise Dickinson Rich, Elizabeth Coatsworth, Florida Scott-Maxwell, Gladys Taber, and Madeleine L'Engle.) These graceful, unaffected writers feel like soul friends to me, kindred spirits who are still alive on the page, their own ordinary days eternally vivid and fresh simply because they took the time to notice, to watch, to reflect, and to write things down.

In a world that's constantly urging me—all of us—on to the next new thing, these quiet, bygone voices are rarely heard now. Yet there's a certain pleasure to be found in turning back instead of pressing forward, and in discovering the worth and beauty in a book that's old, unknown, unsung, unavailable on any bookseller's front table. (Maybe I also like the idea of some yet-to-be-born woman sitting at her kitchen table on a winter's morning fifty years from now, reading a timeworn copy of *The Gift of an Ordinary Day* and feeling a stirring of kinship with its long-gone author.)

And so it is that this is humble lineage feels precious to

me, a reminder that throughout the ages we humans, and perhaps women especially, have expressed our love for the world by noticing it. No matter what century or country we inhabit, we learn, each of us in our own way and our own time, to nourish our souls by paying attention.

It's true that our mortal lives are fleeting. We don't last, but the words we commit to the page do. Ten years ago, when my husband and I bought the old summer cottage that became our first home in New Hampshire, *The Shape of a Year* was one of many forgotten volumes left behind in the bookshelves here. Although the cottage itself eventually had to come down, I couldn't part with all those dear, dusty, old books—relics of other lives, other summers, other readers who must have whiled away August afternoons on the screened porch that would soon vanish, to exist in memory only. I packed the books away before the wreckers came.

Much later, when our new house was finally built on the site of the old, I put a few of them back on my shelves, honoring the past by inviting these abandoned volumes to reside with us in the present. Recently, while searching for some other memoir, I found myself pausing with Jean Hersey's book open in my hands. It was a January afternoon in the year 2015. And, too, it was January 1967. Another time, another woman, another life.

Quiet and smooth, fresh and untouched, the new snow lies across our meadow. Its pristine surface catches the sunlight, and tree shadows stretch like great blue pencils over the unbroken white. The snow folds gently over rocks and hummocks half concealing, half revealing a variety of different shapes.

So lies our year ahead, its basic ingredients sun and shadow and suggested shapes of things to come. I wonder what we will do with this year, what it will do with us, and what together we and life will create during the twelve months ahead.

The words captured my attention, as if I were being summoned to stop what I was doing and to allow time to fold in upon itself. And what I discovered, reading on, was something entrancing and lasting between the faded covers: an intimate record of one quiet life well-lived. A deep awareness of what matters and of what endures—the pulse of nature, our human yearning for connection, the turning of the seasons, the patterns beneath the surface of daily life, the unadorned beauty of simple prose.

On this blustery February morning, with our own birds well supplied with seed, I accompany my new friend into her long-ago February observations. These winter mornings, she writes, "are like opals, soft, milky white and pink around the edges." Yes. I know those colors, too. Across the span of years, a hand extends for mine. I take it, and read on:

It's a joy to feed the birds during the winter. In a blizzard we are literally a lifeline to these lovely creatures. You get to know the different kinds and sometimes certain birds themselves. One particular chickadee is my friend. Each day I'm especially pleased when he comes for his sunflower seed. He perches near me while I scatter food.

And with that, our bond today is secured—she's watching her birds as I look out for mine. Not much happens in *The Shape of a Year,* beyond one woman's close observations of the world as she finds it. The world I live in today is much changed from Jean Hersey's world of 1967, but the things that matter remain the same: compassion, love, nature's eternal rhythms, shared laughter, a sense of wonder. My new friend writes about the very things I notice.

The scent of February:

February air has a flavor all its own. It is not only crisp and cold and tingles in your nose when you go walking, but something more. We hear a lot about spring air, summer air, and that of autumn. But do pause briefly and appreciate the air that nature sends us in midwinter.

A full moon on snow:

It was beautiful outside. Shadows cast by moonlight weave their own magic spell. Moonlight was streaming over the garden where seeds will sprout and grow, where vegetables will nourish and fragrant flowers bloom. It seemed to me as I stood looking out that many of the things we get all stirred up about have less value in the overall pattern than the sight of a full moon shining down on a sleeping garden, or tangled up in the bare branches of a maple tree along a stone wall.

The awkwardness of change:

A restlessness in our bones responds to the wild restless winds of the month. The wind in January awakens a kind of strength. February storms rouse our spirits and hearten our defenses. But a tearing March wind howls through us exposing lonely and unfamiliar areas. We are not at home with the strange impulses and wild, undisciplined thoughts that go blowing through our minds and emotions. Some days, confidence shrinks to the size of a pea, the backbone feels like a feather. We want to be somewhere else, and don't know where; we want to be someone else and don't know who.

Time marches on, and the details and demands of our daily lives evolve. The laptop I'm typing on bears little resemblance to the typewriter I imagine must have sat upon Jean Hersey's desk. And yet, the inner life, the quiet work of seeing deeply into the nature of things, the familiar duties that accompany each hour of a writer's day and each change of season—these things are a constant thread, connecting us. We water plants, mix pancake batter for breakfast, wrestle with a paragraph till the words are just right to the ear, relish an evening spent alone reading in bed. If we lived next door to each other, we would be friends. Instead, for a few minutes each morning, we share a silent conversation, a kinship that transcends time and space.

And it occurs to me that what draws me to this thoughtful, introspective woman, and to her unassuming record of a long-ago year, is something as simple and as challenging as this: a mutual if unspoken yearning to heed Mary Oliver's instructions for living a life: "Pay attention, be astonished, tell about it."

February 2015

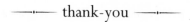 thank-you

If the only prayer you ever say in your entire life is thank you, it will be enough.
—Meister Eckhart

If you had visited my friend Lisa last week, the first thing you would have seen upon entering her living room is a large bright mobile hanging near the window—a thousand and one paper cranes strung on thread and suspended from a curved branch.

The cranes were created over the last couple of months by visitors to the Hilltop Café, a small coffeehouse at the farm up the road from the Pine Hill School, where Lisa has been a beloved kindergarten teacher for many years. Anyone who came into the cafe this winter to eat or grab a coffee to go was invited to pause for a few moments to craft an origami crane and send healing thoughts Lisa's way. The result: the beautiful wall hanging in her living room. Love made visible.

The phrase "it takes a village" comes to my mind many times a day lately, for that's what we have here, a village of caring friends and thoughtful strangers who show up in all sorts of ways and who do what they do in a spirit of love. There have been months of beautiful dinners, massages, flowers, stories written and pictures painted and cards sent. There have been donations large and small from across the land, photos and memories shared, housecleaning, rides given, family and friends arriving to brighten the days. An abundance of much-needed, much-appreciated assistance, care, and concern.

No one can change Lisa's diagnosis. And there's no denying the challenges she faces each day: pills to take and transfusions to endure and a new port to contend with. There are side effects to every medication. There is the unknowable yet all too predictable future. There is no cure. But there is always healing, and healing is what she's choosing to focus on. There is also the beauty of the present moment. I think of it as a bubble of grace, this sacred territory in which goodness and gratitude coexist with illness.

Some day, I know I'll look back on these winter days and the hours I'm privileged to spend with my dear friend. And the prayer I'll say then is the same one I'm saying now: "Thank-you." I'll remember the record-breaking snows of 2015, the frigid cold, the racing start I need in order to get my car up the steep, icy hill to her house, and also the warmth that envelops me as soon as I walk through the door. I'll remember the hours we've spent on the couch, talking about everything. I'll remember fires in the fireplace and wedding plans (her son will be married next week, and Lisa will be there, having the first dance with her boy). I'll remember reading Anne Lamott out loud to her and how we both got laughing so hard tears came to our eyes. I'll remember the two of us doing her PT exercises together side-by-side on her bed. I'll remember afternoon meds and Reiki and cups of turmeric-ginger tea. I'll remember a flock of handmade paper cranes taking flight.

After a rough holiday season, Lisa's medical team decided to try a new medication to reduce swelling from the tumor in her brain. She is one of the lucky ones. The drug is often ineffective, but for the moment it's working for her. It's given her a window of feeling better—*much* better. It's allowed her to take a short walk in the snow, to go downtown for lunch, to do some of the things that nausea and seizures and collapsing legs and headaches have kept her from enjoying for months.

"I don't know where my will has gone," Lisa said many times throughout the fall, as the hours ticked by and she found herself too weak and too weary get up off the couch. Now, she wants to make up for lost time. And what is she doing with this unexpected gift of energy? Writing thank-you notes. Given a day, a moment, an opportunity to ask, "What now?" my friend is choosing to affirm the abundance in her life. She is choosing to say "thank-you."

And then, as more and more snow piled up outside last week, and as the temperatures hovered around zero, Lisa asked her husband to carry all their boxes of photos up from the basement. Homebound but grateful to be up and about at last, she embarked on an ambitious journey through the past.

When I arrived last Monday, every surface in the dining room was covered with pictures; there were more boxes on the floor, a new photo collage artfully arranged on the refrigerator door, an arrangement taking shape on the table of pictures to be hung on the wall going down the hallway.

So many memories! And such a reminder that life is long, full of twists and turns, love and loss, laughter and forgetting. Here was her husband, Kerby, today a distinguished, white-haired, eighth-grade teacher; once, long ago, a seven-year-old boy in shorts and tap shoes, ready to twirl his somewhat heftier partner. Here, Lisa, a fresh-faced young mom with her three tow-headed little boys on a summer afternoon.

Here, her son Morgan in his senior year of college, just off the lacrosse field, grinning, his arm around his beautiful girlfriend—a photo so full of life and energy that, thirteen years later, it's still hard to fathom that this was to be his last day. Or that after saying good-bye to his family that night, he would lose his life while trying to help a young team-mate who was being beaten up on a street near the Bates campus. For many years, these photos were just too hard to revisit. Now, Lisa is wading in with courage, drawing both the beauty and the tragedy of the past right into the present.

Here, Lisa and her beloved horse, Bentley, gone himself just three months ago, but a soul gift in that time of great sorrow, around whom Lisa began to construct another life, one that included a new home for her and Kerby, where she could ride and create her remarkable summer camps for children. Out of that deepest grief: more love.

Together, we began sorting the stray photos into envelopes: good times, boyhood, early days, cherished animal friends, married life, family. . . . We studied a photo of her on a long-ago beach, tanned and stunning in her bathing suit, legs long and lean, hair wind-whipped. Gorgeous. "Look at this," she said, a note of wistfulness in her voice. "There's no going back there," I said. "Not for any of us." And we agreed: it's ok. No one gets to go back. But we all have a choice about how we inhabit our *now*.

At one point Lisa looked up, turning to gaze out the window where the afternoon sun was turning the distant snow-covered mountains shades of rose and violet. "Even if I knew this was to be my last week," she said, "I don't think I'd want to be doing anything else."

And in that moment, I looked at my friend with something that approached awe. She could have been regretting every single loss in her life, of which there have been many. Instead, she was choosing gratitude for all the good, for all the abundance, for all the love. What better way to pass a winter afternoon?

In the kitchen, there were enticing smells—dinner coming together. Risë, the nurse who's been living at our house in exchange for helping to care for Lisa, was making pasta sauce.

Over the last month, Risë, who arrived in our midst as a stranger, has become both dear friend and an essential member of the team. She knows her stuff, she keeps us laughing, and she does whatever needs to be done—organizing Lisa' medications, driving her to doctor appointments, making sure there's something good to eat on the table on the nights friends don't deliver meals to the door. (And, on the days when we've all been completely snowed in, Risë has organized the linen closets at *my* house; she's made sourdough bread, folded laundry, chopped vegetables with me for soup.) Sometimes, I pause and wonder: how did we get so lucky? I find myself praying all the time these days. "Thank-you."

"Gratitude," writes Melody Beattie, "turns what we have into enough, and more. It turns denial into acceptance, chaos into order, confusion into clarity. . . . It makes sense of our past, brings peace for today, and creates a vision for tomorrow."

Lisa and I are both journal keepers. Lately we've been talking about putting all our diaries and random writings together and burning them, something we've both thought about for years but haven't quite been able to do. And yet, the words written in our ratty old notebooks were never meant for others' eyes. They were outpourings and rants, inner struggles brought to the page for resolution, private conversations with our most pathetic, angry, confused, uncertain selves. Sending them up in flames, we suspect, will be a kind of spiritual cleansing. She's pretty much ready to go for it, and I'm pretty much ready to join her.

So, we've been envisioning a little ceremony—a few kind words of remembrance and a good strong fire. Lisa's already started going through her writings. The other day, she told me there was one journal she'd found and decided to keep: the gratitude journal I'd encouraged her to start during a particularly dark time many years ago.

"I found an entry in there about making Morgan dinner," she said, "and how happy it made him. Reading that, I wasn't sad. It made me happy to remember it."

And with that discovery, Lisa was inspired to begin another project: writing a new gratitude journal. She found a simple, red, blank book and gave that one to Risë, suggesting she might wish to begin a gratitude journal of her own. (Later that night, I asked Risë if she's ever had a cancer patient encourage her to keep a journal of each day's blessings. She has not.) I've got a new notebook, too. In it, I'm already praying. "Thank-you."

February 2015

—·—— spring thaw ——·—

I step out of the shower and stand dripping with my towel wrapped around me, looking out the bathroom window. The new day seems luminous, worth pausing for and gazing into even as my toes curl on the freezing tile floor.

The fields below the house are still covered with snow although the tops of the stone walls are finally visible. The sky seems a bit less austere, the sun more committed to its silent shining. It really doesn't look like spring out there yet, with everything still bare and frozen, but something seems to have yielded. Something ineffable has changed. It's as if the air itself is richer.

Something subtle has changed inside me, too. Everything external appears the same: upper-arm skin a bit saggy, belly soft, hair thinning and in need of a cut, the face in the mirror looking less and less like the younger person I still feel myself inside to be and more like my Grammie Stanchfield every day. (Those puckery little vertical lines above my upper lip! Where did *they* come from? Her.)

And yet, my heart is lighter.

A few weeks ago, I sat on the couch in my kitchen, brushing away tears, wondering how to respond to the most recent words of someone who has hurt me deeply. I thought I would write her a letter and instead what came out onto the page was a prayer. Not the words I needed to say to someone else, but the words I most needed to hear myself.

When the going gets tough may I have faith that things are unfolding as they are meant to.

It helps me to remember that there's a bigger picture, a story being written that's larger than the one I can see in front of my nose. And try as I might to avoid heartache, life will continue to have its way with me. To be human is to hurt, to worry, to wonder, to suffer, to stare at the ceiling at three am.

And yet, if there's one more thing I know for sure, it's this: whatever is happening in this moment is already in the process of turning into something else. Change is continual, and for that I can be either fearful or grateful. Today, I choose grateful.

Recently my friend Amy posted a quote I love on her beautiful blog *My Path with Stars Bestrewn:* "No winter lasts forever; no spring skips its turn."

Another good, necessary reminder. For as it is in nature, so it is in life. For every dark night of the soul there is a sunrise, a brightening of the inner landscape. Smiles always follow tears. Joy will find a way, if I let it, to push up and out, through the rich, dark loam of heartache. And I am here on this earth to feel everything, to experience every-thing—the ups and the downs, the dark and the light, the freeze and the thaw, the drama and the denouement, the whole human catastrophe.

I can hunch my shoulders and duck my head and resist what is. (And oh, I've been so tempted this winter to resist, to hunch, to hide.) Or, with quiet curiosity, I can simply allow the fragile pages of my days to turn. *What now? What next?*

Still naked at my spot at the window, I watch a sleek,

copper-colored fox trot delicately across the crusty snow and hop up onto a rock, surveying her domain. Against the blanket of white, her tail flicks like a flame. I'm delighted to see her. I know this animal. To discover her here this morning is a lovely validation of life and the cyclical nature of things. For the last two springs, we have watched this beautiful wild girl as she raised her litters in in our field.

Each year as the trees bud and the matted winter grasses give way to new growth, the cubs emerge from their den beneath the rock pile, ready to meet the world.

From our own home on the hill we humans spend hours observing the goings-on at the neighbors' place. The wonder of new life never ceases to amaze. We hand the binoculars back and forth, entranced by the hunting expeditions of this watchful, dedicated mother and delighted by the cavorting pups, so hesitant at first to leave the security of their broad, flat, rock roof, but soon enough venturing farther afield, bent on exploration.

And, always, there is drama. Five babies become four become three. Coyotes, we suspect. The first year, the family moved from one hole in the ground to another, leaving a single kit with a broken leg behind. All through one freezing night, we fretted about the tiny fox cub, wondering if the mother would return to fetch it. In the morning, my neighbor Debbie and I intervened: we scooped up the abandoned baby and took it to a wildlife rehab center, hoping for the best. It died a few hours later. Life and death inexorably intertwined. The fragile pages turn.

Maybe this year, I think, the fox family will do better. But the mother entertains no such hope or expectation. For her, the only moment is right here, right now. The days are lengthening, warming; it's time to prepare a den, to hunt, to assess the landscape, to get ready to begin again.

I pull on the same clothes I wore yesterday, come down to the kitchen, start coffee. And I assess my own landscape. It occurs to me that for the first time in months my heart feels unburdened, as if a stone has fallen off it and rolled quietly away.

It's taken time, many sleepless nights, both patience *and* prayer, but I think I finally understand how I must make my peace with the person who has hurt me. I'm ready to accept an apology that's not been offered, that probably never will be. I choose to forgive her anyway, wholeheartedly, as much for my sake as for hers.

If I can make room in my own heart for what she's said and done, then I can also move toward healing—here, now, without needing to understand her motives, without needing to be right, without needing to explain my version, without, in fact, needing anything at all—other than my own willingness to let go and move on.

"The only path to forgiveness," suggests writer Kent Nerburn, "is learning to see the world through different eyes. The world will not change; we must change. We must find a way to replace yearning for what life has withheld with gratitude for what we have been given."

At last, this long hard winter is coming to an end. Soon, there will be yellow nubs on the forsythia, the first bright crocus pushing up through warming soil, robins arriving to build nests in the lilacs, a new family born in a snug hole in the field, hungry coyotes on the prowl. Endings, beginnings, life having its way—fierce and beautiful and fleeting.

Always, there is loss entangled with growth. Always, there is mystery beyond human understanding. Always, we are challenged to see the world through different eyes, to surrender, to accept, to let go, to change.

The world beckons. Silently, somewhere deep within me, an invisible page turns. Forgiveness, it seems, goes hand-in-hand with faith, with humility. It is the soul work of a winter-weary heart in spring: thawing, softening, opening to the light, to whatever is meant to be.

March 2015

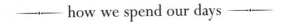 how we spend our days ——

How we spend our days is, of course, how we spend our lives.
—Annie Dillard

It begins just before first light, like a wave breaking gently at the shore, the slow rising of consciousness. A fragment of self, swimming up toward the surface of being, dispelling the textures of dreams. Awakening. The day arrives in shadow and sparse birdsong, the music of bare, wind-rustled branches running with sap. With it, a sense of possibility. Who knows what will happen next? Annie Dillard's words "How we spend our days" nibble at the ragged edges of my first thoughts, inviting attention. *Intention.* Or maybe it's just pressure I feel: *Make it good. Make it count.*

Today, there's no place I need to be. Clear space beckons, a parade of solitary hours: a writing day. Already I am itching for it here among the warm, tossed bedclothes. I crave the empty moment—the place where stillness meets silence, time unhinges from itself, and words begin to stir.

A red sliver of sun inscribes itself across the ridge of mountains, the familiar backdrop to our days here. The bedroom lightens. My husband rolls over, still half asleep, and lays a hand on my hip, the one that needs replacing, that always hurts, that his touch seems almost magically to ease. It is in these small ways that we care for each other. There's a part of me that wants to jump up now, spin the shower knob to hot, get on with things—breakfast, coffee, a kiss at the door, good-bye, good-bye, exhale, and breathe it in: the hushed tranquility of an empty house.

But first, this.

A large part of my writing practice these days seems to be about letting go of the idea that if I'm *not* writing, I'm not being productive. I have to keep reminding myself: meaning isn't found in accomplishment; one thing isn't better or worse, or more or less, than another thing. The page awaits. But life is full. And I'm trying day by day to trust that if I'm fully present then I *am* where I'm meant to be, whether it's at my laptop composing sentences or in the laundry room folding towels or turning to meet my husband's sleepy embrace. *How we spend our days. . .*

The sun inches higher, proclaiming the dawn in a seamless

sky. The dog dances her impatient little dance by the bed, barks once, twice, louder, demanding: attention must be paid.

On the bedside table, my phone buzzes. It is not yet seven. A text from a friend: "She died." This death is not unexpected but is shattering nonetheless. The world has lost a person. Hearts are breaking.

Buddhist teacher Jack Kornfield writes about the possibility of creating, within ourselves, our own monastery. As we work to quiet the inner chatter, letting go of our notions about the way things *should* be, we create a compassionate space that allows for all things as they arise—sorrow, grief, shame, regret, frustration, joy. Already, the orderly, productive morning I've envisioned has shape-shifted.

"This too, ah, this too," are the simple words Kornfield uses to remind the heart to soften. And so it is that I repeat them now, alongside Annie Dillard's potent phrase. I need both. For the truth is, my days rarely unfold as I expect them to. But I can choose, again and again, to stay open to whatever the moment brings.

I prop myself up on the pillows, reach for the covers, my eyeglasses, and search my brain for words to peck onto the screen, a few sentences to convey all that can't possibly be said. "I'm so sorry. I'm here. So sad. Talk later. Love you."

In the kitchen I heat water, slice bananas, shake vitamins into my palm, stare out the window at the sky. I think about my friend, suffering the loss of *her* friend. Soon, before I get down to writing, I will call her. I think about beginnings and first sentences and plans for the day, and how they so often get abducted by one thing or another.

My husband props up his iPad at the breakfast table, eats his oatmeal, and reads the *Times* online. Yesterday morning, I did the same—a mistake. The front-page story was about a young black vet in Atlanta suffering from PTSD who was running naked through his apartment complex. It was perfectly clear to anyone with eyes that he was unarmed. A cop shot him anyway. Twice through the chest. Once my tears began, they wouldn't stop. I spent the day in aimless mourning, grieving for all that is wrong—with me, with us, with our country, our world. I took a long walk and made soup and talked with both my sons and didn't write a word.

Today I sit down with my bowl of fruit and the book that arrived in the mail yesterday, Abigail Thomas's new memoir about aging and writing, illness and grief and friendship. The title is perfect for those of us who've rounded that corner into the homestretch of middle-age, who struggle daily to make our own peace with life as it is: *What Comes Next and How to Like It*. We are all hoping to learn the secret.

"I wasn't writing all the time," this marvelous writer admits on page nineteen. "Days, sometimes weeks would go by without my doing anything at all. I began to feel like something left too long in the vegetable drawer. Then I had the bright idea of starting a weekly writing work-shop. There would be a point to me!"

No wonder I love her. And oh, the joy of beginning the day with good sentences—priming the pump rather than bleeding the heart. One thing I'm still learning as a writer is that I do have to protect myself, to be careful about what I allow *in,* if I'm to have any hope at all of bringing my own words forth. There's a time to read the morning news, but not when my own intention is to write.

My husband fills a Tupperware container with the remains of last night's dinner, brushes his teeth, claps a baseball cap on his head, and makes his exit. I'm grateful for his good cheer, his work, his steadiness. It's not lost on me these days that while I'm between books, he's earning the salary that allows my life to be what it is: a luxury of time. For the next nine hours, the house is mine.

Resisting Abby's good company (this is hard, but it's a *writing* day), I close my book and survey the scene.

Once, a student in my own weekly writing class told us that she writes every day, all the time—in doctors' waiting rooms, at stoplights, while on hold on the telephone, in the middle of the night. She flipped open a well-used notebook full of her dense scribbles—snippets of essays and scenes and dialogue and prose poems awaiting her finishing touch. I was in awe of her output. It occurred to me that, really, *I* should be taking a writing class from her.

Were it not for the words I somehow *have* managed to write, and all the hours I've spent sitting in my kitchen and staring out the window in order to produce them, I could not call myself a writer. I do not write at stoplights or in the middle of the night or while on hold. Not ever. I write in hard-won secret pockets of time, in solitude. I sit still as a hunter perched in a blind in the forest, breathing quietly, waiting for words to come into view.

This morning, before I reach for my laptop, I need to get a few things done. I water the houseplants, fill the bird feeder, start a load of laundry, and vacuum the dog hair off the floor. Scrub the stubborn remnants from last night's roasting pan, carry the recycling out to the bin, straighten the magazines on the coffee table, scribble a grocery list for later.

Setting the house to rights is unavoidably, irrevocably, part of my process. It's not always easy to know where to draw the line. The other day my friend Maezen, author of three fine books and an archive of brilliant articles, and a Buddhist priest who knows a thing or two about discipline, posted this on Facebook: "I've washed every shower curtain in the house. I think this means it is time to write again."

My first thought: "No, no, there must be grout to clean yet." My house is never tidier than when I'm preparing to head off into the silent woods of myself. Before I can slip away, I must always rinse out the sink, fold the dish towel.

Now, these duties done, I stand once again at the kitchen counter, gaze out to the mountains, and call my friend. I listen to a heart-rending account of last days and final hours, family members arriving, memories spilling forth. My task in this moment is simply to be here, phone at my ear, holding space for her tears. It occurs to me that *"how we spend our days"* goes hand-in-hand with "*this too, and this too."* Perhaps they are two sides of the same coin, reminding us simply to embrace all the truths of our lives with wise and tender hearts.

Already the sun has climbed to the top of the pine trees. Slender icicles release a steady stream of drips from the roof. The snow is receding at long last but not soon enough for me. A ravenous hairy woodpecker has made its way through half of the sunflower seed I just put out.

The fox trots by. (I think of her as my totem, this bold, graceful animal, for rarely does a day pass lately that I don't catch sight of her going about her own business in the world on the other side of the windowpane.) She glances briefly up at me and continues on her way, alongside the stone wall, down the driveway, across the road. She knows what she's about, is as much a tenant of this patch of earth as I am. I watch a squirrel poised on the lip of the birdbath, sipping at a bit of ice melt there. Everywhere, life is resuming, poised to be quickened by warmth and thaw and rain.

Across town, my friend Maude is presiding over the daily births of spring lambs. My laptop pings with the arrival of her photos, newborns so impossibly delicate and adorable they defy description or belief. She sends videos capturing first steps, hops, tiny bleats. And then, inevitably, e-mails entitled "sad news." Each lamb lost is another small heartbreak; she feels every death deeply. The mothers cry piteously for their babies, and Maude weeps with them and then reports the toll. I write her back, a sympathy note for every lamb she cannot save. *"This too, ah, this too"*: the only solace I can offer.

All days are numbered, and the world shall keep turning with and without us, life and death inextricably linked. We hurt and find a way to bear the sorrow, for it is surely our awareness of life's brevity that allows us to fully grasp its beauty.

My writing day is already half over. "I haven't yet begun," I think anxiously. "It's slipping away." In fact, I haven't missed it. I will never separate my writing from my living or my living from the work of tending whatever is in front of me in the moment—the bread crumbs on the counter, a friend in need, the pink geranium's falling petals, the words that arrive so slowly on the page. It is all one, as continuous as the sky.

And perhaps I *have* begun, almost without knowing it. Perhaps I began hours ago, in the diffused light of sunrise, listening to a husband's quiet breathing, to mourning doves and wind murmur. We live surrounded by story. To write is simply to pay attention, to allow the day its ebb and flow, to summon up its riches and find some way to give them form. I sit down, curl my toes around the rung of the kitchen stool and begin to type.

"It begins just before first light, like a wave breaking gently at the shore, the slow rising of consciousness…"
March 2015

———•——— mother, daughter ———•———

My mom and I just spent ten days together at my parents' house in Florida. We didn't go anyplace and we didn't do much. What I most loved about our time was that it was so quiet, so spacious, and so much our own. Introverts by nature, my mother and I have this in common—we are connoisseurs of companionable silence. We like to relax into our own rhythms, side-by-side but with plenty of breathing room between us.

She brought me coffee in the mornings. I made us healthy salads for dinner, except for the night we ordered a pizza to share in bed while watching TV. Most afternoons she took a nap and I swam naked in the pool. We read a lot. And in the evenings we got into our pajamas before the sun went down and then stayed up till after midnight, catching up on the last three seasons of *Mad Men*.

I didn't blow-dry my hair or put on lipstick for a week. There is something to be said for letting things slide. It wasn't at all exciting but it was what we each needed—time to hang out, time to read and write and think and be. There was no one to cook for or take care of, no one to worry about or sleep with. A perfect mother-daughter vacation.

At seventy-eight, my mom is moving more slowly, more cautiously than she used to. She's not a great fan of the cane she needs for walking distances but it's better than the alternative, better than risking a fall. She has dizzy spells and she can't always trust her balance. She tires more easily. So, she paces herself. And when we run out of avocados or half and half, she lets me drive to the grocery store rather than insisting on going herself.

I'm moving more slowly these days, too. It's been nearly six months since my orthopedist pointed to a narrow, shadowy place on the x-ray of my hip and showed me why it hurts so much to walk up the stairs: bone on bone. I guess I've just needed this time to get used to the idea of a surgeon replacing my own worn-out hip joint with some new parts. It wasn't so long ago that I was out running. Just last spring, I still thought I'd simply pulled a groin muscle and would be back to doing pigeon pose any day now.

In September I walked twenty-six miles in one day without much pain and believed I was finally "over it." But really, all I'd done was take enough ibuprofen to quiet the inflammation for a few hours.

By now, I've grown accustomed to taking smaller steps, to the popping sound when I shift in my chair, to the nagging ache as I lie in bed at night. But I can't say I'm used to it. This is not the "me" I believe myself to be—and so I keep being surprised to find myself hurting, hesitating to bend over to pick my socks up off the floor, easing myself into the driver's seat of the car in slow motion.

"I never thought I'd feel this way at fifty-six!" I said to my mom, a bit of petulance creeping into my voice.

"Well I never thought I'd feel this way ever," she replied, without the slightest trace of self-pity. "But I can't complain. Life is still so good. The only thing I can't get used to is the idea that there's not going to be much more of it. I can hardly believe Dad and I are reaching the end. I hate to think of all I'm going to miss when I'm gone."

I know exactly what she means.

My writing's been interrupted this morning by phone calls from both my sons. Jack sent me his résumé to proofread. He's got projects to finish as the school year winds down, internships to apply for, a job he's hoping to have a crack at. Henry checked in on his lunch break, calling from Louisville en route to Ohio. He's got three more weeks on tour, and playing in a different city every night is still a thrill for him.

Nothing makes me happier than hearing from my children.

As Barbara Kingsolver writes, "Kids don't stay with you if you do it right. It's the one job where, the better you are, the more surely you won't be needed in the long run." True enough. But every text lifts my heart a little and a phone call just to say hi is even better. I love knowing simply from the tone of a voice that, for today anyway, all is well. And I can't imagine missing any of it, either. I can't wait to see where my sons' careers will take them, who they'll meet and fall in love with, where they'll finally land, whether they, too, will become parents. Someday, I want to hold a grandchild in my arms. And it goes without saying: I'll want to be around to see that child grow up.

My own parents recently sold the home where my brother and I were raised; a year or so from now the small retirement cottage they're building near a pond just a couple of miles from our house will be ready. They will spend the next chapter living close by, so close I can go back and forth between our two houses as many times a day as I wish. Or, as many times a day as I need to. No one's really talking about it, but we all know things are changing. The family plotline is bound to become more complicated. Does anyone survive their eighties without some kind of surprise or setback?

In the meantime, I feel blessed to have my parents nearby. For the truth is, time is having its way with all of us. As my sons make their way into adult lives, I have no choice but to confront the evidence of my own encroaching old age. Bodies break down and hair turns gray and minds aren't quite as sharp as they were. My husband, Steve, nine years older than I am, endures a creaky knee without complaint. He buys a senior ticket at the movie theater and then adjusts his hearing aids to be in synch with the sound system. (At least, since he got them, our dinner-table conversation has grown softer, easier, more intimate.) I dab concealer under my eyes and try to ignore the wrinkles deepening at the corners of my mouth. My mom laughs when I confess how much I spend on a jar of face cream. She knows there's no stopping the vicissitudes of time.

For now, though, minor aches and pains aside, we are all fine. And this mere fact of life itself, of human resilience and fortitude, really is gratifying enough. We have each other. We take care of each other. We show up for each other. The days are good, and the loving and the caring flow both ways.

And here's the best thing: I'm a mother, yes, but that's only half of it. When I need to, I can still just be a daughter, too. There is nothing lovelier or more precious to me right now than this. I am allowed, for a while longer, to inhabit both of these roles at once. And not a day goes by that I'm not grateful.

April 2015

—·—— a deep form of love ——·—

A midsummer Monday morning. After a weekend away, I've just spent a couple of hours setting the house back to rights. Emptying jars and vases of their dead flowers, vacuuming up the scattered petals, watering plants and deadheading lilies, gathering laundry into a hamper and getting the first load going in the basement.

The kitchen is peaceful. Beyond the windows, which are all cranked open to their fullest on this steamy day, cardinals and blue jays vie for turns at the feeder— unaware, for the moment anyway, of the blueberries ripening on bushes just a few feet away. As always, it's a race between me and the birds to see who will get there first to harvest the small crop. (Usually, I lose. A watchful catbird is already hopping along the top of the chaise lounge in the yard, taking stock of the bounty.)

I'm feeling a bit unsure about what to write this morning after a few months of not writing at all. No excuses for that really, other than that I've been busy elsewhere. Yet, sitting quietly on my kitchen stool, I discover there are a few thoughts that have been waiting their moment to emerge after all. I can't find words for everything that's on my mind, but I can say this: I feel softened by the season, slowed down in my thinking but perhaps a bit more raw and open in my emotions. Life this summer has been tender and bittersweet, suffused with beauty, laughter, and tears.

There have been no big revelations, but rather countless variations on this one small truth: joy and sadness are not opposites. In fact, they coexist, all tangled up together in the same day, the same moment, the same unguarded heart. Knowing this, it's become a little easier for me to trust that where I am is where I'm meant to be: open to what life hands me, feeling my feelings (even the painful ones), sensing what needs to be done in any given moment, doing it, and moving on.

The view that greets my eyes when I look up from my writing—a panorama of delicate, blue-tinged clouds and hazy, shadowed mountains—is silent but insistent, drawing my attention away from the screen in front of me to the pulsing, irresistible world of living, breathing things.

So it has been for months now. Given a choice between my computer keyboard and the weedy, burgeoning garden; between making a good meal for hungry loved ones or holing up alone with my thoughts; between taking a long walk with a friend or sitting at my desk crafting sentences, I'm pulled inexorably these days toward love and life and shared moments.

The world beckons in all its intoxicating beauty. And I'm reminded with every passing shower, with every unfurling and fading daylily or blooming nasturtium, with every candle lit and extinguished, with every summer dinner prepared and eaten on the porch, with every golden sunset and every soundless moonrise, to be even more deeply present.

My friend Lisa, diagnosed just over a year ago with an inoperable brain tumor, has been having a good summer. After months of worsening symptoms last fall, she responded remarkably well over the winter to a drug that works for only a few. Her tumor stopped growing. There were no side effects. Many of her symptoms disappeared. It seemed miraculous: she danced at her son's wedding, visited her mom in Florida, planted flowers in the spring, went to the beach with her husband, reorganized the guest room, and created a photo collage in the hallway at her house. Week by week, she actually began to feel like herself again. Like herself, but different, for living with a terminal diagnosis changes everything.

Illness demands a subtle but profound shift of attention. No longer physically able to race from one thing to the next, we have little choice but to slow down. Relieved of the constant pressure to produce and perfect and display our achievements, we are free to tune in to a different frequency. Knowing time is short, we begin to take heed, to appreciate the little things, which become ever more precious—a hug, sunshine after rain, a cup of good coffee, a poem read aloud, a hand to hold. We have a clearer sense of what really matters and a powerful yearning to more fully inhabit the moments we do have left. Instead of taking life for granted, we're suddenly stunned by the simple, inexhaustible miracle of being alive. The great, gorgeous dance is ongoing. And yet now we know this one thing for sure: we ourselves are here but briefly.

"I'm never bored," Lisa has said more than once from her spot on the living room couch. "I could look out this window and watch the sky forever." I think I understand what she means. Paying attention leads to wonder. And wonder gives birth to reverence. When life itself hangs in the balance, even the familiar becomes dear, imbued with meaning and beauty.

Over the course of this last year, I've had the incredibly moving, humbling honor of being at my friend's side through good days and many hard ones. And so I've also been privileged to observe this deep, essential transformation as she adjusted to living *in* the present rather than *for* an imagined, unlikely future. Bearing witness to her soul growth, seeing her gradually let go of resistance and open to a quiet acceptance of things as they are, I've sensed a kind of subtle, internal shift in myself as well. Thinking about mortality, confronting the truth of it, inspires here-and-now living. Why waste any more time and energy holding grudges, regretting past mistakes, or fearing what's around the corner? In this, as in so many things these days, Lisa is my guide. When she feels well, she works a bit in her garden. When she doesn't, she finds solace in the beauty of a single flower. "I've become very good friends with this petunia," she said one afternoon, turning a quiet day into an opportunity to pay attention.

And so, taking my cue from her, I choose to let a lot of inconsequential stuff go. Things that once annoyed me are surprisingly easy to ignore. There are more important things to think about. Worries that used to keep me awake at night no longer do. I feel less need to control, a bit more willingness to trust that my own life, too, is unfolding according to a pattern that's perfect—but that is also beyond my understanding or design. As my yoga teacher–friend

Pam used to say at the beginning of class, "Things have already worked out." They have. They do. They will.

A while back, Lisa asked her doctor about the possibility of returning to work this fall. Gently, he reminded her that the drug that's been working so well can offer her only temporary respite. It is a treatment, not a cure. "I think you should use this time," he suggested, "to go home and do the things that make you happy."

What an assignment.

I suspect I'm not the only one who would struggle with that. Don't most of us spend too much time trying to figure out what we *should* be doing and how we *should* be feeling, rather than listening to and trusting our own inner compass? We live in a culture fueled by the notion that happiness is "out there" somewhere—something we need to earn or acquire rather than quietly cultivate from within. Happiness, we're led to assume, depends on our owning certain things, living in a particular place, advancing in a chosen career, landing in the right relationship, being recognized for our achievements and good deeds, piling up some savings, having a clean bill of health, and going somewhere nice for vacation.

Just keep reaching for it, the advertisements and billboards and song lyrics insist, *and someday, just maybe, if you work hard enough and play your cards right, happiness will be yours.*

Lisa's task these days is a bit different. There is nothing for her to buy and nowhere she wants to go. There's no job advancement or fancy vacation in the offing. There's no magic pill that will make her brain tumor go away, either. Yet I think it's fair to say she has accepted the challenge the universe has sent her. Each day, she wakes up with a quiet determination to find joy in living.

Everyone who loves her wishes our friend's prognosis could be otherwise. She is held in the hearts and in the daily prayers of many, and there is no denying the sadness and pain of this journey.

But pain can also be an invitation to be present. And joy, as poet David Whyte suggests, is not only a "deep form of love," it is also "the raw engagement with the passing seasonality of existence." In allowing herself to laugh, to love, and to be joyful—here, now, and in spite of everything— Lisa is giving all of us a tremendously powerful lesson in how to find meaning and purpose in *today*. What matters, she reminds us by her own gentle example, isn't what happens, but how we respond. We can let today unfold. We can feel today's feelings, solve today's problems, enjoy today's gifts. We can laugh and dispel darkness. We can smile and make someone else's day better. We can choose happiness over despair, joy in the moment over fear of the future, faith in what is rather than fantasy about what might have been. To live this way isn't just courageous, it is profoundly creative and extraordinarily generous.

The sun is high in the sky. It's hot outside. And suddenly my cell phone is ringing. "Hey, we're going swimming at the pond," Lisa says. "Do you want to meet us over there?"

"I do," I say. "I'm on my way."

July 2015

—·— solitude —·—

Solitude is the soul's holiday, an opportunity to stop doing for others and to surprise and delight ourselves instead. —KK

There comes a moment.

You love your life and the dear people in it. And yet, suddenly the very intimacy you cherish feels like a burden you can no longer carry. You want to see yourself as a person who is competent and sturdy and kind. And yet, today you are able to be none of these things.

You can't plan one more meal or push the cart through the frigid produce aisles one more time or carry one more bag of groceries in from the car. You can't cook another balanced dinner or sit at the table and have one more meaningful conversation. You can't anticipate or meet one more need or set one more thing to rights.

You want to sleep alone in a narrow, clean bed and wake up in silence and let things go their own way. You want to take a vacation from worrying and fretting and fixing. You want to have breakfast at ten and skip lunch and eat salad from the serving bowl for dinner—with your book propped in front of you.

You want to take a walk at your own pace, slowly. You long for a conversation in which the only one you have to listen to is the small quiet voice inside, the voice that speaks without words.

You imagine what a relief it would be to spend a whole day without talking. Without cleaning or washing or weeding or folding anything. Without makeup, without good cheer, without a to-do list, without getting in the car, without reaching for your wallet or your phone or the dog leash or the sponge.

You wonder if anyone else hits this wall. The wall of too much. The hard unforgiving place of feeling crowded and tired and overwhelmed. Of knowing you simply cannot accomplish all that needs to be done. Or make good on all the promises you've made to others. Or live up to the expectations you've set for yourself.

You find yourself imagining solitude, craving it. The dark quiet cave of aloneness beckons.

And you think about where you might go, just for a little while, to privately fall apart and put yourself back together again, without causing anyone you love too much fuss or inconvenience.

You e-mail a friend who has a cabin on a country road, the place you went once before to grieve the loss of a friend and to write the first, halting chapter of a book you weren't sure you'd be able to finish. *Yes,* she responds moments later. *Yes. Go.*

You tell your husband, who knows better than anyone how frayed and fragile you are. Who worried when you burst into tears after breakfast for no reason, but whose hugs and rational words of advice just made you cry harder. *Go,* he says. *I hope it's what you need.*

You undo some plans, cancel this and that, make a pot of soup to leave behind, water the houseplants, throw some things in a bag and drive. At the market you've never been to before, the items in your green plastic basket tell the story: cherries, an avocado, yogurt, kale, raspberries and blueberries, and M&Ms. The food choices of a person who is not intending to feed anyone else.

You arrive at dusk in a downpour and lug your things up the twisty path. The cabin door is sticky but unlocked, like a magic place in a fairy tale. Everything you brought with you is soaked but it doesn't matter. The rain has washed away some outer layer you were ready to shed anyway. Arriving drenched, with your hair plastered to your head and your feet squishing in your sandals, feels like a beginning. Already you are inhabiting your body in a different way, curious and raw. Defenseless. Hopeful.

Inside, the damp, musky scent of old wood, old seasons, summers past, gives rise to sharp childhood memories: a cabin rented long ago, the familiar textures of leisurely afternoons spent reading and dozing under old quilts while waves lapped a nearby shore. Solitude has always been your home territory. A daddy longlegs skitters across the floor. The rain pounds the roof. You open windows, put clothes on a shelf, line your wet shoes up. As darkness falls you feel lighter. Peaceful. Better.

In the morning, without any sort of plan, you walk up the road, going nowhere. *Focus on today,* you remind your-self. *All is well,* you say, to no one. And it is. With every step you are clearing a space, coming closer to a self you almost forgot you knew. The good news is, that self hasn't abandoned you. She has been here all along, waiting patiently for you to turn away from all your busy comings and goings, to recognize her, greet her, and welcome her home.

The sun is shining and you are sweating and your legs are moving. You listen to the sounds of a summer day. Kids playing soccer at the boys' camp on the lake. The encouraging shouts of counselors and the wild ruckus of competition. Further on, from a shed in a field: the sounds of an orchestra tuning up for rehearsal. A solo flute traveling up and down the scales. The breeze rustling leaves in the dense canopy of maples overhead. A lawn mower churning back and forth across a expanse of green. The drone of bees in a jumbled roadside garden, colorful as a piñata. Everything has its marvels. You are here to pay attention.

Alone, your life begins to feel like a choice again. You find yourself drawn into harmony with the sweet, easy flow of the day, unfolding according to its own rhythm. Slowly, something that was stuck deep inside begins to move. You ride the gentle currents of sadness, regret, joy, longing, acceptance. Surprised by tears, you lift your face to the sky and allow the sun to dry them.

There is the necessary, satisfying work of serving others in all the places where you are loved and needed. But there is also this: the soul's work, which you ignore at your peril.

And so, for today anyway, you commit yourself to it fully: The journey inward to find your own truth. The stillness of your mind behind the noise of your doing. The willingness to see the beauty inside yourself, and to honor that. You are a little rusty and awkward in your quest. The privilege of solitude is also a skill that requires practice.

At the far end of a field, a granite bench awaits under the shade of a tree. The words "Sit a while" are engraved across the top. You do. And you take in the view, the gentle, slumbering hills, the drifting clouds. This, too, is a kind of compassion—resting, listening, waiting in the silence of your heart to feel the next step. There is a new energy moving in you. A reverence. You can do this. You can dive down, naked, into the sacred quiet. You can learn to be at ease here. To be grateful for these hidden treasures. In this secret, spacious place you remember something beyond the moment, a strength on which to build.

In a little while you will walk the long road back. You will return home tomorrow the same but different, still holding the hand of your wilder self, having touched for just a moment your own infinity.

The grace of God means something like:
Here is your life.
You might never have been, but you are,
because the party wouldn't have been complete without you.
Here is the world.
Beautiful and terrible things will happen.
Don't be afraid.
I am with you.
—Frederick Buechner
August 2015

———·——— beautiful things ———·———

This quiet morning. My friend asleep in her bed, snuggled deep in a nest of pillows, her faithful terrier molded to the curve of her back. The gentle rise and fall of the covers, her breath coming slow and steady when I peek in to check on her.

It is 6 am. My shift. The house is still but for the steady tick of the kitchen clock, empty but for the two of us. What turns of fate have brought us to this moment? One woman engaged in the deep inner work of letting go of life. And the other, me, still here, striving to see this world as perfect, to love it as it is.

I pour coffee, slice a peach, and carry my breakfast to the back deck where the two of us have spent so many companionable hours over the last year. The dark trees are still silhouetted against the sky. Clouds at the horizon melt to shades of rose. The sky lightens. In the new light, dragonflies stitch invisible seams through the morning. A blue heron wings by, heading from one secret pond to another.

My notebook is open before me, the empty white page. I tip my full heart over and pour myself out. A list takes shape: all the hard, sad things. It doesn't take long to write them down. Just putting words to these feelings brings a swift, unexpected relief, like setting down a bag full of rocks. Tears come. This, too, is a relief.

And then, as I read through my list, one thing becomes suddenly clear. Most of the things on it are out of my control:

my friend's progressive, inevitable decline; the behavior of others; the chronic pain in both my hips and lower back; the plight of Syrian refugees; the end of summer; a loved one's harsh words; a lie I've been told and asked to believe; deepening wrinkles and upcoming hip surgeries and canceled plans.

For a while now I've been stuck in this place—waiting, fragile, hurting. Feeling as if my life is on hold until I'm no longer needed here as a caregiver, or until I can walk and bend over without pain, or until a difficult relationship is resolved.

I'm wrong, of course. I'm not waiting. I'm living.

And this moment is neither "good" nor "bad." It's life as it is—complex and messy, painful and beautiful. There is the immense mystery of a loved one's slow dying and the gossamer thread from which life hangs. The tenderness she inspires in those at her side and our profound awareness of the transience of all things. My own body growing older, the first leaves changing color, a criticism that stings, someone else's kind words, a ripe peach for breakfast, a blue heron in flight, a September day dawning.

On the wooden table where I sit, there is a tiny pile of stones. I pick them up and spread them out before me, each a rough yet recognizable shape. Hearts.

And with that, I begin another list. Beautiful things. I need only look up to see them.

And I need only awaken to the varied territory of my life in this moment to feel awe at all I have, awe for all that is. I easily fill a page and then another. Soon my heart feels full once again, but in a different way now. No longer heavy, but spacious. Buoyant, even.

Perhaps this is the invisible gift offered to one who is blessed to accompany a loved one through the final days of his or her journey: an invitation to open, to go deep and to feel everything, to be less afraid. For surely we can trust that life will continue to offer us great joy and great sorrow, and that we are here to know both intimately, even as we grow ever more attuned to the small, daily, simple things like breathing and walking and whispering and hugging.

Paying attention changes everything. Gratitude multiplies and transforms a day, a life, the world. Choosing to see beauty creates more beauty. Nothing is on hold. Nothing lasts. Nothing is wasted. And so, this really is it: the mystery, the miracle, the pain, the joy, the tears, the laughter, the love, all of it. And we get to be here. Now.

That, surely, is a beautiful thing.

And so, in the presence of both grace and grief, I find myself drawn to the idea of seeing beauty as my daily practice, a slight variation on the gratitude journal I've kept over these last few months. What would happen if I chose to begin every day by noticing and writing down a short list of beautiful things? The world wouldn't change, but I would.

All that matters is what you love
and what you love is who you are
and who you are is where you are

and where you are is where you will be
when death takes you across the river.
You can't avoid the journey but
you can wake up… now
and see where you've been
and where you are going.
—John Squadra, from "Circle of the One" in *This Ecstasy*
September 2015

---·— oasis —·---

The surgeon was running a little late. I was right on time. I'd also followed every pre-op instruction to the letter: donated a unit of my own blood to receive back during surgery, had an MRI and new x-rays taken, swallowed my liquid iron and B vitamins and blood thinner and Celebrex, met with an anesthesiologist, a physical therapist, a pharmacist. I'd given up coffee and my evening glass of wine days ago, had my teeth cleaned (from now on, that will involve a precautionary dose of antibiotics), tidied up the house and paid the bills, and scrubbed my right hip twice a day for three days with Hibiclense. I even got my hair cut.

Through it all, I worried and wondered. Was I doing the right thing? Would I be better off to accept my lot, grit my teeth, and carry on with my own two painfully arthritic hips? Was I trying too hard to hold on to youth? Was I being greedy to want to hike or do triangle pose or ride a bike again? Or would I look back, as a few hip-replacement veterans predicted, and wonder why I waited so long to get new parts?

By the time I climbed into my assigned bed in a small pre-op cubicle at New England Baptist Hospital last Friday, there was nothing more for me to do. And there was certainly no point to any more mental dithering and debating. A curious, unexpected calm descended.

I was warm and comfortable. Whatever happened next was out of my hands. I'd expected to find myself at this juncture feeling terrified, with clammy palms and a heart pounding with anxiety—my typical response to stress. Instead I was peaceful. It occurred to me that this is what faith feels like—the quiet, still, rather unfamiliar place Khalil Gibran calls "an oasis in the heart which will never be reached by the caravan of thinking."

Somehow, moments away from the first major surgery of my life, I had found my way to that oasis. An accidental destination, deep and mysterious and welcome.

"We'll give you something to make you relax before we take you in to the operating room," a nurse promised as she deftly slipped an IV needle into a vein in my wrist. As it turned out, there wasn't time to administer the drug meant to soothe my nerves. When the doctor was finally ready, he wanted me delivered to his table, pronto. It didn't matter. Some invisible current had already begun to flow. And I had given myself over to it.

As I sit on the screened porch at my parents' house six days later, typing these words, there are many small details of the last month that come bubbling up. Two weeks before my surgery, my beloved friend Lisa died after a long journey with brain cancer. The intensity of her final weeks and the intimacy, wonder, and grace of the three-day vigil friends and loved ones created in her home after her passing—sitting with her body, reading and singing and praying and speaking to accompany her soul as it departed—every bit of this is all still vivid in my mind.

The grief I feel is fresh still, but not raw. There is a quiet oasis in my heart for this sadness, too. This has been a long road and the destination was never in question. Those of us who loved this special woman have been grieving since the day she was diagnosed eighteen months ago. And yet, I keep thinking of the dream I had in the recovery room on Friday, exactly two weeks after Lisa's death. While swimming my way back to consciousness after surgery, I experienced something that was perhaps more illumination, or visitation, than dream: Lisa and I sitting together having a picnic by a lake, a shared sense that all was well, that there was nothing very unusual here, just our simple joy in seeing each other.

Moments later—or maybe an hour later? who knows?—I woke up from that shimmering picnic, surrounded by nurses speaking my name. It felt as if I were returning from a distant place and, at the same time, as if I'd just blinked my eyes shut for a second—the strange effect of drugs and loss and wishful thinking. And maybe it doesn't matter; dream sightings and anesthesia experiences aren't to be analyzed but appreciated.

The first days with my new hip were more than I'd bargained for: the pain; the nausea; the foggy brain; the plugged-up digestive system; the pulley hanging over the bed for slowly moving my leg; the first hesitant steps on crutches; the mushy, marshy nowhere land between sleep and wakefulness, neither of which was fully achievable.

And yet. Somewhat to my surprise, I was still in the oasis, still at peace, still surrounded by kindness and love. Held afloat by the good wishes and prayers of a whole circle of dear friends, I had only one task: to relax into that love and allow it to bear me forward.

On Sunday afternoon, my husband drove us from the hospital to my parents' house, the finest rehab facility anyone could wish for. My mother ceded to us their king-sized bed and bathroom on the first floor and greeted me with turkey soup, tulips, and the ice pack of my dreams. And so, just months before my parents leave this dear old family homestead forever and move into the new small cottage they're building closer to us, I find myself back in the rooms of my childhood for one last time.

The autumn leaves drift down, a golden dance of deliverance. In the backyard, the apple tree—so much broader now than when we two first met nearly forty-five years ago—has released her generous crop of golden apples, spread around her like a skirt. As I make my way slowly around the backyard on my crutches, I must be mindful of fallen acorns thick underfoot, the oak trees' abundant yield. Everywhere I look, it seems, something is letting go.

Even as my parents await their moving day, the new owners of this land have begun to realize their own vision for it, carving out roads and house lots and felling trees.

Each day, we listen as the forest my brother and I wandered as children disappears. Early this morning the huge machine was right at the edge of the yard. For my mother, who has spent most of her adult life in silent conversation with these trees, it was wrenching to see them shudder and fall, one after another, each loss forever changing the landscape of this place we all still think of as home. Little wonder that we found ourselves in tears.

"You knew this was going to happen," my dad reminded her. And of course we did. Still, for a few moments there, as I stood on my crutches and my mother leaned on her cane in the unseasonably mild sunshine and the trees crashed down one by one, the symbolism was almost too much to bear.

But in a little while the workers moved on, out of sight. The felled trees were silent, the view out past the field so much bigger than before.

My parents spent many years creating a home here, but they leave it behind knowing the time has come to let go. In one sense, the letting go happened already, as they chose a new place to live, sold this one, began cleaning out sheds and cellars and drawers. For them, too, the debating and deliberating is over, but there's no denying how hard the final good-bye will be. There is nothing for them to do but have faith in their own next steps.

A few days before my surgery, I admitted to my husband that I want a break from lessons in letting go. The last year has been hard and sad, marked by one loss after another. And the two hip replacements, though my own choice and surgeries from which I expect to fully recover—well, they represent a kind of loss as well.

It's been a long time since I went up the stairs without grimacing or walked without pain. The two-year-long medical journey that led me to this decision has been humbling in every way. And, too, there's a vulnerability after surgery that's altogether new to me, as challenging in its own way as any of the physical trauma. Like most of us, I much prefer the role of capable caregiver to that of needy patient. But here I am. My husband spots me as I step gingerly into the shower. My mom wrestles my tight support stockings up over my calves. My friends are offering meals. A nurse comes every couple of days to check my INR levels. I look at the pharmacy's worth of medications and vitamins on the counter and can hardly believe they belong to me, the girl who hardly ever takes even Tylenol.

And so, moment by moment and day by day, even as I heal and graduate to one crutch and learn to use the four-foot-long shoehorn to get my sneakers onto my feet, I also have to surrender over and over again to this new vulnerability. I must make some sort of enduring peace with the loss of my young, fit, able body that served me so well for so many years with all its own parts intact.

Right now, my newly operated-on right leg is nearly a whole inch longer than the left. The next surgery, no longer optional, will even me out. Or so I hope. Till then, I'll wear different kinds of shoes on each foot – a flat sneaker on the right, a thick-soled clog left. No matter. I've had to let go of my fashion aspirations, too.

But just now, as I have the time and space at last to sit quietly and begin to reflect on all that's happened this autumn, I'm beginning to see things a little differently. Perhaps the hard lessons I've been learning haven't been so much about letting *go* as they have been about letting *be*. "Letting go" suggests a need to actively do something: let go of hurt, let go of fear, let go of what's over, let go of expectations of what will be next.

What if there is a path to the oasis in the heart after all? And what if that path opens at our feet when we stop trying so hard to decipher the roadmap through life and allow ourselves instead to simply be more at ease with what is?

Everything comes and goes: the green of springtime and the fleeting gold of fall, the apple blossoms of May and the ripe fruits of October, the tiny acorn and the mighty oak, the seasons of the heart and the seasons of the fields. Not to mention youth and age, homes and bodies, hopes and dreams, life and death. We want so much to hold on to what we love, and then when the time comes to say good-bye, we work just as hard at letting go. But perhaps there is another way. Neither holding on tight nor letting go. Instead, just letting be.

"People who have faith in life are like swimmers who entrust themselves to a rushing river," says the wise Benedictine monk David Stendhal-Rast. "They neither abandon themselves to its current nor try to resist it. Rather they adjust their every movement to the watercourse, use it with purpose and skill, and try to enjoy the adventure."

Enjoy the adventure. I love this idea just as much as I love the image of an oasis in my heart. And it seems that "letting it be" is both a profound affirmation of faith and an opening to possibility. I am savoring this quiet, healing time in my old family home more than I ever would have expected. After many, many months of doing, *being* is a welcome relief. After all that worrying and second-guessing, it is lovely to allow my own caravan of thinking to come to a halt for a while. After a long chapter of caregiving, offered with all my love, I'm grateful to those who are showing up now to care for me. I do my new hip exercises. I read and take naps. Slow walks up and down the driveway. Some chair yoga. The oasis in my heart is green and quiet, its waters undisturbed. The days fly by.

November 2015

Joy is the happiness that doesn't depend on what happens.
— *David Steindl-Rast*

——·—— lessons ——·——

It's been two and a half weeks since my second hip replacement, a bit more than two months since the first. And I'm finally approaching the moment when I can look back at all this and say, "It was worth it." As of a few days ago, I'm getting around the house on one crutch, which leaves a hand free for pouring tea or emptying the dishwasher. I can pull on my own compression socks and cut my toenails and drive downtown. Best of all, I can press up slowly and carefully from all fours into a downward-facing dog.

What I didn't expect yesterday, as I spread my palms wide on my yoga mat and lifted my tailbone to the sky, were the tears. Moving from crutches into my first post-op yoga pose was a bit like coming home after a long trek through another land. Things are the same, but different.

After twenty years of yoga practice, I arrive on my mat a beginner again, feeling my way forward tenderly. These two prosthetic hips? They are my new teachers. And I am an uncertain, humbled student.

There have been so many times over the last two years when I found myself thinking, "I want my old life back." This morning, sitting once again at my writing spot in the kitchen, healing and breathing, I find myself writing different words: "This *is* my life." And every moment? Another opportunity to practice. Here, four lessons I've learned so far.

Some day your body will surprise you.

No matter what you see on the x-ray, no matter what the lab results show, no matter what the doctor has just diagnosed, no matter what operation you've just found out is in your future, one thing is for certain: the disturbing thing going on deep inside your body wasn't part of your plan. Perhaps we all presume, in our secret hearts, invincibility. I certainly did. But my body has begun to teach me that there's no special protection from pain, from aging, from death.

The moment my orthopedist flipped the switch on the light box and brought up the ghostly x-ray images of my two arthritic hips was the first time it really hit me: I'm not indestructible after all. In fact, I'm not even in charge here. I'd done everything "right"—exercised regularly, eaten well, practiced yoga for years, bought well-cushioned new sneakers every spring. I was pretty sure all that good living was buying me both time and health.

And yet, the pain I'd believed for months to be a groin

pull was suddenly revealed to be something else entirely. And with that my illusions were shattered.

"Looks like you'll be needing a couple of hip replacements," the doctor said, pointing first to the bone spur that was not a groin pull at all. It looked like a shark's tooth, sharp and vicious; no wonder I was gasping every time I moved my leg to either side. And then, "Bone on bone here," he went on, tracing the fuzzy line at the head of my left femur. "And clearly degenerating over here as well," he said, pointing to the other hip.

And so, standing there staring at the first of what would be many x-rays, I got a little wiser. I learned what advanced osteoarthritis looks like. And I realized I'm not in control of the way my body is succumbing to the realities of wear and tear, age, and mortality.

How you respond to that surprise is up to you.

You probably already knew this would be the second lesson. It took me a while to learn it, though. Looking back, I now see I went through something akin to the stages of grief as I absorbed the news that at age fifty-seven—still youthful in my mind—I already needed replacement parts.

There was *denial*. Surely, if I juiced every morning and cut out sugar entirely and chewed turmeric and sipped ginger tea and took glucosamine and saw a chiropractor and tried acupuncture and stretched a few times a day, I could avoid surgery. I did all those things. There were good days and bad days—that's the way it is with arthritis—but the pain got worse.

There was *anger.* No, I didn't have an incurable disease or even a frightening diagnosis. Even so, I indulged in my share of "why me?" moments. I watched a stream of college students running along the river in Cambridge one spring day, annoyed that they all clearly took their strong, straight legs and well-lubricated hip joints for granted. I waved to my adorable eighty-year-old neighbor as she slowly jogged past my house, and silently cursed my own bad genes and bad luck. She was loping along, smiling, her white hair blowing in the breeze, and I was hobbling out to the mailbox. Yeah, I was pissed. (And perhaps this goes without saying—I was scared, too.)

Bargaining was irresistible. Ok, I would give up running for good, and tennis, too, if only I could hike. And then, fine, I could even let the hiking go, as long as I could manage a nice long walk. Or, even a short walk. I would modify my yoga practice, become more yin than yang, sit on two blocks, no on a *chair,* and I'd promise never, ever to even try to cross my legs again. Eventually, just walking up the stairs was hard. I gave up everything in the bargain, except the pain. (And although we don't often admit this, pain is scary.)

I'm not the sort of person to sink into depression. But eventually *depression* and physical pain become inextricably intertwined. I think of all the days my husband and I would get up early for our morning walk, as we have always done, and how, after just a few minutes I'd have to turn back, admitting that the idea of a walk had become way more appealing than the actual experience.

One by one, I lost all the physical outlets that have always relieved my stress and kept me strong and made me happy. Just getting in and out of the car became a project. Increasingly sedentary I also became, almost imperceptibly, sad. "I feel as if I'm watching you get old before my eyes," Steve said, more than once. That made me sad, too. (And it also made me scared—would I ever feel like *me* again?)

Acceptance, when it finally came, was a relief. A few days after the diagnosis, when I made an appointment with a surgeon in Boston, I was pretty sure I'd end up canceling it. Certainly in the eight long months between that initial phone call and his first available consultation, I'd cure myself! (See *"denial."*) By the time I finally made my way to the surgeon's office, all I wanted was two dates, one for the right hip and one for the left.

I had to wait five more months for the first surgery, and during that time my self-pity slowly gave way to gratitude that I had good options. I couldn't control everything, but I could control some things. And my own attitude was at the top of that list. Soon, soon, I kept telling myself, I would shift gears at last, from coping to healing. I would begin the new year with two new hips. I hadn't failed myself, I was taking care of myself. I was on a new path, toward renewed health and strength and mobility. I had family and friends ready and willing to support me. I could begin to make plans for the future. There was so much to be thankful for. It took a while, but I got there. (And perhaps this goes without saying—I was still really scared.)

Ask for help. Then accept it.

This seems obvious. And yet as an able-bodied, nurturing, middle-aged mom I've been so much more comfortable being a caretaker than receiving care myself. I suspect I'm not alone in this. But people *do* want to help, and it's our job to let them know how.

A year or so ago, on the evening before going into the hospital to have a kidney removed, a friend of mine sent out a group e-mail, asking each recipient to pause the next day and send her healing vibes at the hour of her surgery. I felt so privileged to be on that list, glad both to be reminded of my friend's surgery and honored that she wanted me to be part of her circle of support. Later, she said she *felt* all the love coming her way, that she rode that wave right into the operating room.

And so, the night before my first surgery, I followed her example. From Maine to Hawaii, good wishes poured into my e-mail box. The next day, lying on the gurney in the pre-op room, watching the old-fashioned clock on the wall tick toward the appointed hour, I grew strangely, unexpectedly calm, even before the sedatives began to drip into the vein in my arm. The fear that had dogged me for weeks leading up to this moment melted away, replaced by something I can name only as peace. Was I held in an invisible web of care? Maybe so. Seven weeks later, the same thing happened again. Silent, stealthy, sacred: this is soul territory, the mysterious awakening of the energies of love.

Coming home from the hospital on Christmas eve, with little choice but to accept helplessness, I watched from my chair as a meal came together in the kitchen, one son making soup, the other assembling a salad with a friend, Steve pouring champagne and fixing my plate. Christmas cookies arrived at the door.

Saying yes to help was new to me. Allowing my husband to help me into my underpants was new to me. Having my mom accompany me to the bathroom was new to me. Asking a friend to vacuum my kitchen floor was new to me. Accepting every offer of assistance that came my way was new to me. And yet, what lovely gifts these weeks have brought: delicious dinners, bags of groceries, fresh juice and homemade biscotti, a clean garage, rides to appointments, flowers and cards and books to read, an exercise bike for home, a hospital bed for daytime naps.

Saying yes to help is a way of saying yes to things as they are. Saying yes to help is about softening around the edges and loosening the boundaries. It's about accepting that life is not to be controlled but surrendered to. And in that surrender, something new and beautiful begins to grow: the kind of openness and intimacy that deepens and fortifies a friendship, that burnishes a marriage, that acknowledges how very much we need each other.

Someday your body will surprise you again.

It happened sometime around 3 am, two nights ago. I was awake, content to be snug in my own bed, listening to the rise and fall of my husband's breath. It was as cold as it's been all winter, the sky crystalline, the bright crescent moon climbing higher, until it slipped into a dark tangle of branches in the maple tree outside the bedroom window.

Stretching one leg out long and then the other, flexing my feet, I realized that for the first time in recent memory I felt no pain: no pain from arthritis, no pain from an incision, no pain from a new prosthesis, no pain from traumatized muscles. Nothing hurt.

Lying there in bed, at peace, relaxed and comfortable, I was acutely aware that something had shifted, deep beneath my awareness, from struggling to healing. *This is me,* I thought. *Not perfect or intact, but not broken, either.* It felt like a miracle.

While I have been diligently doing my exercises and taking my vitamins, drinking water and eating green veggies, resting and celebrating each small step of progress, my body has been doing its own invisible work. Day by day, I'm getting better. And for me that's been the other big surprise: it turns out that even my wrinkled, saggy, puckery fifty-seven-year-old body is possessed of extraordinary regenerative powers.

And so, this paradox. So much of growing older is about learning to surrender, relaxing our attachment to what was and trusting that where we are is where we're meant to be. At the same time, for as long as we're alive, our minds dance in partnership with these mortal, resilient, remarkable, vulnerable bodies. And being a good partner means treating these bodies with loving care and respect. It means listening carefully to what they are telling us, and creating a calm, nurturing environment in which self-repair can continue to happen. We are all aging *and* healing at the same time. Growing a little every day and dying a little, too. This, it seems to me, is the holy wonder of the human journey, its beauty and its frailty. As Rilke writes, "Life always says Yes and No simultaneously."

"I feel lucky," I said to my mom this morning. "I have all this time now that's just for me." It's true. Although I knew I'd spend the month of January recovering from surgery, I didn't ever expect these post-op weeks to feel like either a vacation or a gift. It turns out they are both.

I'm grateful for each quiet, solitary, elongated day. For expanses of time to nap and read and stretch and be. For nourishing food provided by dear friends, for texts that ping on my phone to say "I'm thinking of you." I'm grateful for good books and dark chocolate and fresh coffee. Grateful to have no place to go and nothing much to do. (Except for PT appointments, my calendar is strangely, beautifully empty.) I'm grateful for a fire to sit beside and for my husband's evening foot rubs and for early bedtimes. For starry night skies and crystalline winter sunrises, for the cardinal at the bird feeder and for the pure rose light at dusk. I'm grateful for every step I take without pain. And I'm gratefully still learning all these lessons, it seems. Yes, always learning to be fully present.

We look with uncertainty
We look with uncertainty
beyond the old choices for
clear-cut answers
to a softer, more permeable aliveness
which is every moment

at the brink of death;
for something new is being born in us
if we but let it.
We stand at a new doorway,
awaiting that which comes…
daring to be human creatures,
vulnerable to the beauty of existence.
—Anne Hillman
January 2016

———— first steps ————

I just got off the phone with my son Jack. He touched in as he often does these days after school, to say hi, to tell me about the few questions he missed on a test, to let me know he's going to AA tonight, where he'll receive a thirty-day sobriety chip.

It's been a month since Jack had a beer or used any other substance, eighty days since he last smoked pot, his drug of choice.

At twenty-three, he is meeting his own sober adult self for the first time. In a way, so am I. These have not been ordinary days. But in all my years as his mother, I have never been so proud.

A month ago, on his fiftieth consecutive day of not getting high, Jack told me he was going to write a status update on Facebook to share what he'd been going through. My first response was concern for him, for his privacy and for the fragility of his still-new sobriety.

"Think carefully before you do that," I said. He already had. He'd led a double life for years, he explained. And he didn't want to do it anymore. So he was choosing to put it out there for all to see:

"These last couple months some things have happened for me that really forced me to step back and look at myself objectively. After countless past attempts and failures I have finally committed to confronting my deep-seated patterns of addiction. After today I will have successfully stayed sober for a full 50 days. This is the longest time for me since I began smoking weed when I was 15 years old. I am writing this status because the reason I fell into this pattern was because I neglected to be open and honest with people about how I was suffering, and instead opted to portray myself as someone who had all their shit together and was always happy and enthusiastic. The truth is I was so ashamed and guilty about how I could not control myself, that it was too frightening to let people see what was really going on. I can't think of a better way to facilitate a change than by being honest right here on FB for everyone I know to see. So there it is. Thank you to every one of my friends who are supporting me through this drastic life change."

I'm not yet well versed in the twelve steps of recovery. But my sense is that these early days are a particularly vulnerable time—a kind of tender, bare-naked limbo between the old, ingrained ways of numbing and escaping and the delicate beginnings of new coping skills and healthy habits.

For Jack, a huge part of this process has been about stripping away the layers he's hidden behind for years. Smart, funny, creative, athletic, passionate, my son has always been a natural leader and a loyal friend. He has prevailed, almost effortlessly, in many areas of his life—on the pitching mound as a kid, on the tennis court in high school, in challenging AP classes, in the sound-engineering program he's now completing in Atlanta, and most recently in a physically and emotionally demanding job that requires deep commitment on his part.

At the same time, he's lived another life, one he's put enormous energy into keeping hidden from many who know and love him. There was the charismatic, easygoing, self-confident guy who could inspire a team to victory, improvise a guitar riff, or step out on a stage and juggle five balls without breaking a sweat. There was the non-chalant student who could always pull out a decent grade at the last minute. There was the defiant, impulsive teenager who acted first and regretted later. There was the young man living on his own, going to school and going to work, and assuring his parents that he was "fine."

And there was someone else, too: a boy who found his own chaotic emotions too uncomfortable to bear, a teenager who numbed his feelings of inadequacy with hits of pot, a young adult who lied to cover up his feelings of weakness, who found himself increasingly powerless to live the life he dreamed of, and who felt like more of a fraud and a failure with each passing year.

In recent weeks, Jack and his dad and I have been engaged in a painstaking process of getting to the truth of things. A necessary reckoning, a first tentative step toward healing.

Hard as it was to look back on some of the darker moments of these last few years, we each wrote letters—raw, no-holds-barred letters—that gave full voice to our memories, our worries, our fears. We let our true selves be seen, in all our sadness.

For his part, Jack gave us a full accounting. Coming clean was a step in his recovery; absorbing all he had to tell us was part of ours. None of it has been easy.

But I can say this: each of us told the truth. Each of us listened. Each of us was heard. And dismantling the old walls, on both sides, was a relief. There was nothing more to separate us. And so we could reach right back out and touch each other again, for real—with love, with forgiveness, and with a commitment to move forward from here. Together.

Truth, as Jack is discovering, is a powerful antidote to shame. It takes such courage to step out of hiding and be seen as we really are: imperfect, striving, hopeful, scared. And now he is widening the circle. With each new day of sobriety, with each twelve-step meeting he attends, with each conversation in which he shares his struggle, his network of support grows larger. Bit by bit, the loneliness and isolation that have been his secret prison are transformed—into both accountability and connection. But as my son reminds me every time we speak, it's a slow, at times excruciatingly painful process.

The other day, I suggested that hard as this is, he has much to be grateful for. "The thing I'm most grateful for," he said, "is that I don't hate myself anymore."

Hearing the son I love so much speak those words nearly broke my heart. But it also made me think about the profound value of standing tall in all our vulnerability, allowing our deeply flawed, most authentic selves to be fully seen.

I can't help but wonder how many other teenagers and young adults are living lives that look good on the outside, while suffering on the inside. I know there are many who can ride life's ups and downs with ease, who can enjoy alcohol and marijuana without ill effects, who experiment with drugs without becoming dependent or addicted. But I also believe the fear of being not enough, of being unlovable, of being inadequate runs deep through our culture. And no, a loving home and caring attentive parents are no guarantee against either inner suffering or self-harm. We are all wired for struggle, and some of us are wired for addiction. That is a battle no one can fight alone.

Jack has a long road ahead. Recovery, as we know already, isn't a destination but a lifelong journey. But he's put his feet down on the path. He's walking it. I can't clear away the obstacles in front of him or take on the work that's his alone to do. I can be here, though, listening each day, sharing both his struggles and his victories. I can resist the impulse to offer unsolicited advice. I can let him know how proud I am of his progress and of his courage. And, with Jack's permission, I can follow his example by telling the truth, entrusting each of you reading this with the first chapter of his new story.

Courage is a heart word. The root of the word courage is cor—the Latin word for heart. In one of its earliest forms, the word cour-

age meant "To speak one's mind by telling all one's heart." Over time, this definition has changed, and today, we typically associate courage with heroic and brave deeds. But in my opinion, this definition fails to recognize the inner strength and level of commitment required for us to actually speak honestly and openly about who we are and about our experiences—good and bad. Speaking from our hearts is what I think of as ordinary courage.
—Brene Brown
February 2016

——·—— the family we choose ——·——

An invisible red thread connects those who are destined to meet, regardless of time, place, or circumstance. The thread may stretch or tangle, but it will never break.
—Chinese proverb

I always wanted a daughter. Last year, I finally got one.

She arrived not as a newborn into my arms, but into my heart instead, and fully grown. And yet the mysterious, compelling process of attachment has changed us both. Perhaps that's because as long as we're fully engaged in forging deeper relationships with others, we're also continuously being formed ourselves, sculpted and honed by the invisible hand of love.

The first e-mail from my daughter-to-be came a couple of years ago, through my website:

Hello. Today I watched your Ordinary Day video on YouTube

and found myself crying in my cube at work. I am not a mother (yet). I am a Connecticut native who became a transplant in Atlanta—working and dating with no long-lasting luck.

Your video moved me because even though I am 32 years old, I have always longed for my parents, or perhaps more so my Mom, to share with me her feelings like you did. . . . Funny enough, I am much like you: Nostalgic, and with a plethora of stories of the five kids I grew up babysitting, and I long for those "ordinary days" even for myself!

Lauren wanted to order a book for herself and one to give to her cousin for Mother's Day. And, Lauren being Lauren, she wanted to make her gift special by having me inscribe it.

That was the beginning—an innocuous exchange similar to hundreds of others I've had over the years. But, Lauren being Lauren, she followed up her request for books with a thank-you note after she received them. What's more, she told me she'd now read *The Gift of an Ordinary Day* herself and sensed in me a kindred spirit, the kind of mother she herself aspired to be one day.

Fast forward a few months, to early autumn 2013. My son Jack was moving to Atlanta to begin school in October, and I was flying down with him, to rent a car and help him set up housekeeping in a new apartment. Lauren, now a regular reader of my blog, sent an e-mail.

The gist: I live about ten minutes from where Jack will be. I'm sure you'll be busy, but if you have time for a cup of coffee, I'd love to dash over to the campus and meet you two. And then, if Jack ever needs a ride to the airport,

or tickets to a Hawks game, or a friend in Smyrna, he'll
have someone to call.

The three of us had that cup of coffee. We hit it off. We
both had the same sunglasses on. Conversation flowed
easily. In fact, it seemed like the most natural thing in
the world to part on that bright October morning with
hugs and promises to stay in touch. And we did. Jack and
Lauren met for breakfast a few times, and he took her up
on her offer to drive him to the airport. He played his
music for her and invited her to parties at his house. We
exchanged more letters. When Jack lost his wallet, it was
Lauren I called to take him some cash. When she came
home to Connecticut for Christmas, I invited her to New
Hampshire for a visit.

"Boundaries," my friend the therapist cautioned when
I told him. "I know," I said. And then I wrote to her:
"Come!"

This is so *not* the usual me. Introverted by nature, protective of my space, I don't enter into new relationships
lightly or often. But from the beginning there was something different here—what Lauren called "a wink"—as if
some larger forces were at work.

And so it was that within minutes of arriving at our
house for the first time, Lauren was up to her elbows in
dough, making sausage balls with Henry for Christmas
breakfast. When I flew to Georgia to visit Jack last February,
she invited me to stay in her guest room. And once again,
the universe winked: what was meant to be a quick three-
night stay turned into a whole week, as one snowstorm

after another, all up and down the East Coast, resulted in a series of canceled flights.

Lauren loaned me a cozy bathrobe and a winter hat, brought me coffee in bed each morning and, on long walks through her neighborhood, shared with me the story of her life, from her parents' divorce when she was eleven through the ups and downs of her online dating career. I taught her how to make my salad dressing, introduced her to the short stories of Laurie Colwin, and to the grace our family says when we're all gathered at the table. We took Jack out for dinner one night and on another invited him over for a candlelit meal at *her* table.

We spent our time just the way I'd have spent a lovely, uneventful week with my own flesh-and-blood daughter, if I had one. And moment by moment, as we walked and talked and listened, we got to know each other better. Stirring soup and making banana bread, watching *Downton Abbey,* browsing the neighborhood shops, reading side-by-side in silence or working quietly on our laptops, our easy, companionable togetherness slowly, imperceptibly turned into something more, something I can describe only as kinship.

By the time I finally did get on a northbound plane, Lauren and I were a done deal: bound for life. And when I landed in New Hampshire, there was an e-mail waiting for me: "I'm completely charmed by your nurturing presence and big heart. I also think you would have been an ideal mother to a daughter, so I'll gladly and graciously be your girl, if you'll have me!"

These days, I often refer—only half jokingly—to "my three kids." In fact, those three young adults have grown close, forging their own sibling relationships with each other, just as Lauren and Steve have created an affectionate father-daughter bond. Without any urging from me, our family simply got bigger. And better.

What I've learned over the last year, as these unexpected, tender relationships have deepened, is that motherhood isn't just a matter of biology and blood. To mother another human being is to love that person wholeheartedly, both for who they are and also for who they could yet be. It's a willingness to be present, to bear witness to another's journey. It's an act of recognition.

Here's what I think: Just as in the exhilarating moments after birth, when two souls meet, so too can a mother and her spiritual child find each other at any time when hearts are open, and at any twist or turn in the path. And when it happens, there's a flash of affinity, a kind of deep acknowledgment, a sense of ancient, inexplicable knowing.

I can't say whether it was grace or God or serendipity that offered me and a sensitive young woman from Atlanta the opportunity to forge a connection that satisfies a longing in us both, but ours is surely a sacred alliance. To me, being a mom these days—whether to my own two sons or to my cherished surrogate daughter—is about seeing and nurturing the essential beauty in each of these young people, believing in their growth, inspiring them to realize their deepest potential even as they inspire me, in return, to realize mine.

"I think I willed you to me," Lauren wrote me the other day, in a letter that prompted me to ponder our special bond—and to write these reflections down. She continued:

I don't know any other way to express this thought other than to say my soul had been searching for you. . . . Perhaps the biggest misconception is that we assume that you can only mother little kids, and that adults don't need to be mothered. But look at us—I'm 35 and you're 57. There's no right or wrong time to connect, or to mother someone you didn't bring into the world. Your kids grew up and flew the nest, and doesn't that just mean they need you now in a different way?

And now you've got me, too, updating you on potential matches, sharing books, advice, love, stories. I think about how I met you after years of working on some really difficult things, and while I don't view myself as a wounded bird, there is a part of me that you saved. This entire last year would have been a completely different experience for me if you weren't in my life. I believe that deeply. And no one would have been able to predict this connection on that morning you first treated me to coffee at Life University.

I'm glad the love flows in both directions, and I'm glad I have you as a mother in my life. I may no longer be held safely within the village of my youth, but I'm pretty sure your presence in my village today is just as special and important, simply because I choose you every day.

It's often said we can choose our friends but not our families. Not so. I've chosen a daughter, and she's chosen me. There are years we missed (no adolescent angst to recall, no funny anecdotes from childhood to laugh about), but no matter. Being a mother is only partly about giving birth to people and almost entirely about our willingness to love them.

At this point, I can't imagine a life without my young adult daughter in it. Ours is a potent alchemy, one in which we are both being asked to stretch, to trust, to reveal our own vulnerabilities and shadows and yet to remain in sight, present for one another through life's sweet joys and its inevitable sorrows. An invisible thread has connected us and the blessing flows both ways.

February 2016

———•——— expectations ———•———

Before we can change anything in our life, we have to recognize that this is the way it is meant to be right now. For me, acceptance has become what I call the long sigh of the soul. It's the closed eyes in prayer, perhaps even the quiet tears. It's "all right," as in "All right, You lead, I'll follow." And it's "all right" as in "Everything is going to turn out all right." This is simply part of the journey.
—Sarah Ban Breathnach

I was pretty confident I would be a kind of poster child for hip-replacement recovery. I'm relatively young, not overweight, in decent shape for someone who's been slowed down by advancing osteoarthritis for two years. In all that time, despite encroaching pain, I did my best to keep exercising. I continued my daily yoga practice, albeit a modified practice using blocks and a chair and bolsters. I waited a full year to see a highly recommended surgeon at one of the country's best orthopedic hospitals. I scheduled my surgeries for six weeks apart at the end of 2015, so I could begin the new year with two new hips.

And I figured that if I followed every instruction to the letter, did my physical therapy religiously, and didn't push too far or too fast, I'd soon resume my old, normal life. Some people had warned, "This is major surgery." But others said, "It's no big deal." Those were the ones I chose to believe. I was nervous, of course. But this had already been a long road. And within a few days of my second surgery, I had myself convinced I would negotiate this little patch of rough ground easily and soon be back on course with my life.

Yes, that's called an "expectation." And you'd think I'd know by now that getting attached to an expectation is a good recipe for disappointment.

About six weeks ago, I had to ask well-intentioned friends to stop sending me YouTube videos meant to lift my spirits and urge me on. There are plenty of inspiring hip-replacement stories out there. I've watched the sixty-year-old woman doing yoga three weeks after her hip replacement. And the forty-eight-year-old former gymnast as she kicked her legs up around her shoulders without missing a beat.

I marveled at the guy who threw his crutches away three days after surgery and was doing martial arts and kickboxing a few months later. I visited the website for post-op runners and read their stories of training for and completing marathons with bionic hips. The fifty-five-year-old Alvin Ailey dancer is gorgeous and amazing. As is the tap dancer. Yep, tap dancing, three weeks after surgery.

So impressive, every one of them. And so not my story.

Which is to say, I will not be joining the HipRunners club or sharing my recovery on dancerhips.com.

A few weeks after my second hip replacement, on the left side, I began to notice increasing pain and weakness in my left leg. Having already relegated my crutches to the basement, I hobbled down the stairs and retrieved them. The pain got worse. And then it became excruciating. X-rays showed there was nothing wrong with the new hardware, and blood work confirmed there was no infection. And with that, my highly respected surgeon pretty much lost interest. "Take it easy," he said.

The day after that appointment, I flew to Florida, fighting back tears with every step and dependent on the kindness of strangers to help me board the plane. My parents met me at the other end, surprised to see how much ground I'd lost. I'd planned this trip to their house here months ago, with the thought (the *expectation*) that by the time I arrived, I'd be almost back to "normal." I pictured myself outside walking every day, adding miles, getting back to full speed.

Instead, for the first couple of weeks here, my mom took care of me. I spent hours those first days online, until I was finally able to diagnose myself: ischial bursitis. This debilitating inflammation can be caused by a discrepancy in leg length (check), extended periods of sitting (check), trauma to the region (check). There is no cure but rest and time, pain management, and then, eventually, gentle exercises to begin to strengthen the traumatized, atrophied muscles.

I'm better now. Most of the pain is finally gone, but some simple movements are beyond me. It's been almost three months since my last surgery, and I'm a long way from taking a normal walk or going upstairs without support, let alone kicking up my heels. I still have weakness in my groin area. I have a limp. My left leg is shorter than my right, and that is something I'm going to have to live with. None of this is what I expected.

And so I've done a lot of thinking over these last weeks about expectations. I can certainly relate to *Calvin and Hobbes* creator Bill Watterson's line, "I find my life is a lot easier the lower I keep my expectations."

Because, really, so much of the disappointment we experience in life has to do with the gap between the way we think something ought to be and the reality of what actually pans out. In retrospect, I wish I hadn't watched all those videos of the hip-replacement superstars. I might have had an easier time, psychologically anyway, if I'd set out down this path with a bit less ego and expectation, and with more humility and curiosity instead. Bodies are unpredictable, after all, and surgery is an art not a science. There are no guarantees.

I come to the end of this long-awaited time in Florida with new perspective on the process of healing. The physical setback of bursitis meant I had no choice but to go into one-day-at a-time mode. And having to readjust all my expectations brought me to a place I didn't expect to be: starting over again at square one. Instead of sailing through these surgeries and the aftermath with flying colors, I sat on the edge of the bed here at my parents' house six weeks ago and wondered how I was going to lift my foot high enough to get my underpants on.

"In the beginner's mind there are many possibilities," observes Zen master Shunryu Suzuki, "but in the expert's there are few."

Pain makes you a beginner. Moment by moment, day by day, you learn what your body will tolerate. You figure out what helps and which movements to avoid at all costs. And suddenly, with pain as your teacher, you are really, really awake and really, really paying attention. Simple tasks that you once did mindlessly—carrying the teakettle to the stove, shifting in bed, standing up from the toilet—demand the kind of awareness and integrity you used to bring to an advanced yoga pose you were trying for the first time.

I've had nearly two months in this lovely house with a pool and a hot tub overlooking a canal. I've had time with my mom, time with Henry, and now, before Steve joins me for a short vacation, I have two utterly quiet weeks all alone. I've had hours each day to stretch, to do exercises in the water, and to experiment on my yoga mat, slowly, painstakingly rebuilding some strength and flexibility. What I've accomplished wouldn't make for much of a video, but it feels like progress to me. Both of my legs are getting stronger. And I've also learned a few hard lessons about releasing expectations.

When it comes to my body now, I have to accept that there's much I can't control. What I can do instead is attend to it. The difference is major. Attending means listening, observing, accepting. It means working with what is rather than grasping for something out of reach. The path to wellness turns out to be more mysterious and unpredictable than I ever knew, which makes it scarier and more confusing. But it also makes it beautiful. Because as pain slowly eases its grip, what comes seeping into that tender place is gratitude.

Yesterday, I took my first real walk outside without using hiking poles for support. It felt like liberation—and like cause for celebration. I walked slowly, thinking about every step, carefully placing heels and toes, focusing on creating a smooth gait. And what I thought about wasn't that I'm not running or dancing or executing pigeon poses on my yoga mat. I thought about how fabulous it felt to take a walk.

I watched the sky change colors and the clouds turn golden as the sun sank away. I listened to the mourning doves calling back and forth from their perches on the utility wires above my head. I felt the breeze on my skin and the long muscles in my inner thighs that still need strengthening and the awkwardness of having legs that don't quite match up. But I also felt like myself. Not the old self, who used to run through these neighborhoods, pounding the pavement and dripping sweat, but me, nonetheless: present, in my body, in the world, and still moving. Oh, and grateful.

March 2016

——·—— happy reports ——·——

The other morning, I snapped the leash onto Tess's collar and headed out for a walk. We followed our old route, down the hill from our house, onto the bike path toward town, and home again. Nothing too ambitious, yet this was the first time in two years I've taken this particular four-mile walk without feeling pain. It was also the first time since having both of my hips replaced last winter that I felt confident enough in my new hardware, and in my healing, to risk having Tess lunge unexpectedly or pull me off balance. I'm strong enough now to hold onto her, strong enough to hike back up the hill without pausing to catch my breath, strong enough to do the whole loop in under an hour. And so it is that a daily ritual I once took for granted has been transformed into an experience that feels special, one I'm grateful for.

So much of what I've struggled with, and written about, over the last couple of years has had to do with loss and grief, what Jack Kornfield so evocatively calls "the storm clouds of the heart." Sitting alone in a quiet room, finding words that both pay homage to the richness of human experience while also acknowledging how vulnerable I often feel in the face of that experience, has given me a way to come to terms with some of the inevitable challenges of growing older—the illnesses and deaths of dear friends, concern for the struggles of a young adult son, life chapters ending, intimate relationships transforming, elderly parents facing their mortality, a body that's showing the wear and tear of nearly six decades of hard use.

I've sometimes wondered whether "ordinary days" would ever return. Or if in fact the best days were behind me now and my own "ordinary" would forever more be tinged with sadness, a kind of constant, chronic, low-grade grief, like the slight limp I'm learning to live with as result of having one leg that ended up being an eighth of an inch longer than the other.

The answer, it turns out, is no. The hitch in my gait is ever present. But sadness, most definitely, is not. The slow, demanding work of mourning what's over gives way, in time, to the quiet peace of accepting what is. And just as the sky clears after a heavy rain, the storm clouds of the heart disperse. The sun shines again. It's shining now.

A couple of weeks ago our family pulled off the rare accomplishment of gathering in the same town at the same time. Jack, who finished school in April, moved to Asheville, North Carolina, in May and resumed his job working in a wilderness therapy program for troubled adolescents. His schedule is such that he's on duty out in the woods for a week and then off for a week. Fortuitously, one of Jack's off-shifts coincided with a week-long break from touring for Henry, who flew in to Asheville to meet us. We rented a cabin and a car. Our surrogate daughter, Lauren, drove up from Atlanta to join us. And suddenly there we were—along with Jack's new dog, Carol—walking along a trail through the botanical gardens on a beautiful spring morning.

Time was (not so very long ago) when an outing with the kids was utterly routine. As the mother of two boys I was always in search of some simple diversion to fill the day. But boys grow up. Life separates parents from their adult children. Jobs and friends and distant places take priority and even brief moments of togetherness can be nearly impossible to achieve. So this leisurely family walk felt somewhat miraculous—worthy of gratitude if not outright celebration.

And lately, gratitude, especially for the little things, has been my daily theme. Our family has always made a dinnertime practice when we're together of going around the table and sharing something we feel grateful for. As we recently discovered, Lauren and her roommate Lindsay do the same thing at their house, but they have a special name for it, a hold-over from Lindsay's childhood: Happy Reports.

I love this practice and I particularly love the way these two young women share the news of their day and the doings of their lives by choosing to focus, first and foremost, on what's good. The words, "I am happy to report" can't help but bring a smile to a listener's face.

We all did Happy Reports in Asheville and found that our evening meals began on just the right note of intimacy and gratitude as a result.

Steve and I carried Happy Reports home with us and are doing them still – a powerful antidote to a day's petty grievances or the grim realities of the evening news. Happy reports are a reminder that even the most challenging day contains its moment of grace, if we are willing to seek it out. Happy reports are a way of affirming that we can choose our own responses to the roadblocks fate places in our way. Best of all, happy reports have a way of generating, well, more happiness.

And so, to that end:

I'm happy to report it's June and once again the days are long and warm and generous. In our yard the lupines, iris, and foxgloves are in full, harmonious bloom. The lilacs were more lush and fragrant this year than they've ever been and the peonies are awaiting their moment to take center stage.

I'm happy to report that I can work all day in the garden, come in tired and dirty at dusk, and not even think of reaching for the bottle of ibuprofen. (This feels like a gift.)

I'm happy to report that I've cleaned the screened porch and we've already had four dinners and one birthday party out there, listening to the birds sing their evening songs as the sun slips behind the mountains.

I'm happy to report that our son Jack continues to walk his path of sobriety with a commitment and humility that makes me proud to be his mom. I'm happy to report that we talk on the phone just about every day. I'm happy to report that he's happy.

I'm happy to report that Steve and I will spend this Sunday night in Providence to catch a matinee of *Bullets Over Broadway* and a glimpse of Henry in the orchestra pit. After the show, he'll have a week off before heading to Texas for the last leg of this long national tour. I'm happy to report he'll be home in his old bedroom for the next seven days.

I'm happy to report that our expanded family means there's more love to go around. Having Lauren join us in Asheville simply made it better—more conversation, more laughter, more fun, more precious memories stored up. And we are all nuts about Carol, a sweet little pup who appeared on Jack's doorstep a few months ago in need of a home. Perhaps there was a bit of divine intervention there, for Carol came to Jack just as Jack found his way to the twelve steps. He was immediately smitten with her, adopted her, began to train her, and got her certified so she can accompany him to work in the woods. They are a good team both on the job and at home, and Carol is proving to have a knack for the therapeutic intervention: kisses, sock stealing, and tail chasing are all effective tension diffusers. (And although I don't expect to be a grandmother any time soon, I'm happy to report that Carol seemed to awaken some of my dormant maternal hormones the moment I met her.)

I'm happy to report that my parents have completed the herculean task of emptying out the family homestead of forty-five years and letting go of an enormous mountain of possessions—with grace and good humor and remarkable energy. I'm happy to report that, after living with us for three weeks, they are finally at home in their new, light-filled cottage and we are now almost-neighbors. I'm happy to report that I can go have lunch with my mom any day—and the drive from my door to hers takes exactly eight minutes.

Although there's no turning away from the truth of loss or suffering, I'm happy to report that at this particular moment no one in our immediate family is sick or struggling or in crisis. I'm happy to report that I'm old enough to know that such a brief, blessed reprieve is all any of us can ever hope for. The clear skies won't (*can't*) last. And when the storm clouds roll back in and the emotional weather of my own life once again takes a dark turn, I also know I'll somehow manage to gather my courage, reach for a friend's hand, brave the elements, and carry on.

I'm happy to report that with each passing year, the ordinary feels more extraordinary, simple kindnesses matter more, time with family and cherished loved ones becomes increasingly precious, and life's small enrichments bring greater contentment to my heart than any material riches ever could.

Done! And now, my friends, it's your turn. What is *your* happy report today?

June 2016

—·— when the going gets tough —·—

When the going gets tough may I resist my first impulse to wade in, fix, explain, resolve, and restore. May I sit down instead.

When the going gets tough may I be quiet. May I steep for a while in stillness.

When the going gets tough may I have faith that things are unfolding as they are meant to. May I remember that my life is what it is, not what I ask for. May I find the strength to bear it, the grace to accept it, the faith to embrace it.

When the going gets tough may I practice with what I'm given, rather than wish for something else. When the going gets tough may I assume nothing. May I not take it personally. May I opt for trust over doubt, compassion over suspicion, vulnerability over vengeance.

When the going gets tough may I open my heart before I open my mouth.

When the going gets tough may I be the first to apologize. May I leave it at that. May I bend with all my being toward forgiveness.

When the going gets tough may I look for a door to step through rather than a wall to hide behind.

When the going gets tough may I turn my gaze up to the sky above my head, rather than down to the mess at my feet. May I count my blessings.

When the going gets tough may I pause, reach out a hand, and make the way easier for someone else. When the going gets tough may I remember that I'm not alone. May I be kind.

When the going gets tough may I choose love over fear. Every time.

———•———

Cooking is at once child's play and adult joy.
And cooking done with care is an act of love.
— *Craig Claiborne*

———•——— recipes ———•———

I've had enough readers write me saying they've made my lemon cake, or asking me to point them to the lentil soup recipe I once shared, that I decided to include this appendix of all the recipes I've put on my site over these last years. Dates are with each recipe, so if you're inclined to find them online or to read the accompanying essays, you can do so. But for ease here, recipes only. Bon appetit!

spicy chai (also known as yogi yea)

I learned how to make this delicious tea from my Kundalini yoga teacher, who prepares it according to Yogi Bhajan's instructions. Here is the original recipe. I brew mine strong and let it steep for a long time for maximum intensity, then strain it into jars to store in the fridge. I heat up just one cup at a time, adding *almond milk and raw honey to each individual cup as I go. It's also delicious iced. And you can use any milk you prefer.*

ingredients

  1 gallon water
30 cloves
30 whole green cardamom pods
30 whole black peppercorns
  1 large finger of fresh ginger, thinly sliced
  5 sticks cinnamon
  2 tea bags, pure black tea
milk and honey to taste (optional)

steps

Bring water to boil.

Add all spices *except* black tea bags. Simmer on low heat for 30 to 45 minutes. Longer is stronger.

Finally, add tea bags and simmer another 5 minutes.

The black tea is added last because it amalgamates the spices and sort of seals them. Also, the tannins help assimilate the spices into the body. If caffeine is an issue, you can choose decaf tea.

If adding milk and honey, do so after adding the tea and letting it steep—or, better, add milk and honey to each individual cup or to a small batch. That way you can store the leftover tea in the fridge and prepare with milk and honey as you go.

Milk helps to ease the spiciness on the stomach and intestines, so do be sure to drink with milk if you're sensitive. For a stronger tea you can let the spices sit and sink to the bottom. If the tea gets really strong, you can cut it with more milk or reconstitute with a little water.

It is said that yogi tea purifies the blood, lungs, and circulatory system and has many more unseen benefits. I do know that it lifts the spirits. For a premade blend, the best I've found comes from a small Vermont company called Chai-Walla. You can order online at www.chai-wallah.com. Just add water, milk, and sweetener.

November 6, 2009

Heidi Swanson's ginger cookies

"Let the beauty we love be what we do," Rumi reminds us. "There are hundreds of ways to kneel and kiss the ground." Loving this life, cherishing these perfectly ordinary, radiantly beautiful summer days, I do aspire to be attentive, to be thankful for all that is. Sometimes I kneel and kiss the ground by sitting at my desk, fingers hovering over this keyboard. Sometimes, I just bake cookies.

If you were plunked down in my kitchen right now, I'd turn the oven on, start scooping bits of fragrant dough onto the pan, and ask you to tell me the news of your day. Instead, I'll do the next best thing—share Heidi Swanson's lovely recipe.

ingredients
½ cup large-grain raw or turbinado sugar
6 ounces bittersweet 70% cacao dark chocolate

  2 cups whole wheat pastry flour
  1 teaspoon baking soda
1½ tablespoons ground ginger
  ½ teaspoon fine grain sea salt
  ½ cup unsalted butter cut into small cubes
  ¼ cup unsulphured blackstrap molasses
  ⅔ cup fine grain natural cane sugar
  2 tablespoons peeled and grated fresh ginger
  1 large egg, well beaten
  1 cup plump dried apricots, finely chopped

steps

Preheat the oven to 350 degrees and place the racks in the top and bottom third of the oven. Line two baking sheets with unbleached parchment paper or a Silpat mat and place the large-grain sugar in a small bowl. Set aside. Finely chop the chocolate bar into ⅛-inch pieces, more like shavings really.

In a large bowl, whisk together the flour, baking soda, ground ginger, and salt.

Heat the butter in a saucepan until it is just barely melted. Remove from heat and stir in the molasses, sugar, and fresh ginger. The mixture should be warm, but not hot, at this point; if it is hot to the touch, let it cool a bit.

Whisk in the egg.

Now pour this over the flour mixture, add apricots, and stir until just combined. Fold in the chocolate.

Chill for 30 minutes, long enough for the dough to firm up a bit.

I like these cookies tiny, barely bite-sized, so I scoop out the dough in exact, level tablespoons. I then tear those pieces of dough in two before rolling each ½ tablespoon of dough into a ball shape. From there, grab a small handful of the big sugar you set aside earlier and roll each ball between your palms to heavily coat the outside of each dough ball. Place dough a few inches apart on prepared baking sheets. Bake for 7 to 10 minutes or until the cookies puff up, darken a bit, and get quite fragrant. (In my oven, 8 minutes is just perfect.)

Makes roughly 4 dozen cookies
Prep time: 30 minutes; cook time: 10 minutes
June 9, 2011

lentil soup

When my friend and writing colleague Margaret Roach and I were preparing to go out on book tour together, we spent a weekend honing our show before taking it on the road. I took a pot of this unusual lentil soup to her house, and we've both been making it ever since.

ingredients
- 2   tablespoons olive oil
- 1   red onion, chopped finely, or one large shallot chopped
- 1   leek, white part only, chopped finely

2 celery stalks, diced finely
4 cloves of garlic, chopped
4 twigs of thyme, chopped finely
½ teaspoon saffron
1 teaspoon cumin
1 teaspoon turmeric
3 branches of parsley or cilantro, plus more to garnish
sea salt and pepper
large can of diced tomatoes with their juice
2 tablespoons tomato paste
2 cups dry French green lentils
2 carrots, peeled and sliced
2 cups peeled and diced butternut squash
4 cups water
2 cups white wine (or vegetable broth)
2 bay leaves

steps

In large pot, heat oil, add thyme, cumin, turmeric, garlic, saffron, shallot, leek, and celery; cook, stirring, about 5 minutes, till veggies are softening.

Add tomatoes and tomato paste; cook 1 minute.

Add lentils, carrots, and squash; cook 1 to 2 minutes.

Add water, wine, bay leaves, and cilantro; season with salt and pepper. Cover and simmer till lentils are tender, about 25 minutes.

To serve: ladle soup into deep bowls, top with a poached egg (totally optional, but delicious), a heaping tablespoon of crème fraiche (sour cream or yogurt can substitute), chopped cilantro or parsley leaves, and a dash of paprika.

(Recipe liberally adapted from *La Tartine Gourmande: Recipes for an Inspired Life,* by Beatrice Peltre.)

December 7, 2012

my go-to glazed lemon cake

I long ago lost count of how many times I've made this lemon cake. The recipe, clipped from the Boston Globe *in the pre-Internet age, is pasted with rubber cement into a notebook of recipes I began keeping the year before I got married in 1987. The pages are all loose now, held together with a rubber band. But I know exactly where the yellowed, glaze-spattered cake recipe is, should I ever need a quick refresher. In fact, I don't really refer to the recipe anymore. I know it by heart. Simple. Dense. Lemony. Sturdy. Good.*

ingredients
2 sticks unsalted butter, room temperature

2 cups sugar (I use half a cup less)

3 eggs slightly beaten

3 cups flour

½ teaspoon baking soda

½ teaspoon salt

1 cup buttermilk

2 heaping teaspoons grated lemon rind

3 tablespoons fresh-squeezed lemon juice

glaze

2 cups confectioners sugar
3 tablespoons butter
3 tablespoons grated lemon rind
¼ cup fresh lemon juice

steps

Preheat the oven to 325 degrees. Grease a 10-inch tube pan, line the bottom with a piece of waxed paper cut to fit exactly, grease the paper, and then lightly flour the pan. Set aside.

In the bowl of an electric mixer, cream the butter and sugar until light and fluffy.

Add eggs 1 tablespoonful at a time, beating well after each addition.

Sift together the flour, baking soda, and salt, and add to dry ingredients with mixer on its lowest speed, alternating with the buttermilk and beginning and ending with the flour.

Beat in lemon rind and juice.

Pour the batter into the pan and bake on the middle rack of oven for 65 minutes, until the cake begins to pull away from sides of pan. Cool for 10 minutes, then remove from pan and glaze (optional) while still warm.

For the glaze: In a mixer, cream together 2 cups confectioners sugar and 3 tablespoons butter. Add 3 heaping tablespoons grated lemon rind and ¼ cup fresh lemon juice.

April 29, 2013

applesauce

I think of this simple recipe as "time in a bottle." To me it is the essence of fall.

ingredients
6 to 8 pounds of organic apples
juice of half a lemon
3-inch-wide strips of lemon peel
3   cinnamon sticks
3   whole star anise
dollop of raw honey (to taste; I use about 3 tablespoons)
¼   cup water
raspberries (optional)

steps
Cut apples into quarters. Add the rest of the ingredients and place everything in a large, heavy pot over low heat. Stir occasionally, for about 15 minutes, till apples are completely soft and sauce is thick.

Taste for sweetness. The lemon and sweetness should achieve a nice balance, enhancing the apple flavor.

You can eat as is, run through a food mill, or whiz in a blender. If I have frozen raspberries on hand, I will add a generous handful for the last minutes of cooking—a beautiful rose hue results. Applesauce will keep in the freezer for a year.
September 20, 2013

a glorious granola recipe (with plenty to give away)

My grandmother Kenison crocheted afghans and made the world's best donuts, two skills I still wish I'd learned from her before it was too late.

She was also the first person I ever knew who made her own granola, back in the days when "health food" was considered a fad, "organic" might as well have been a foreign word, and the cereal boxes in our kitchen cupboard at home ran from Raisin Bran to Cap'n Crunch.

At least, on a visit years ago when I was newly married, I did have the foresight to write down Grammie's recipe. My granola isn't exactly like my grandmother's. I've taken some license with her original recipe over the years. It's fun to play with new combinations of ingredients, and it never turns out quite the same twice anyway. (She liked carob powder in hers; lately, I've been experimenting with cardamom in mine.)

The one thing I always do, though, is make a lot. And it's always delicious. I think of my grandmother every time I start gathering the ingredients, and I feel happier creating something simple from scratch than clicking a "buy now" button on my computer or wandering through stores looking for the "perfect" gift.

ingredients
1   14-ounce jar of organic coconut oil
4   tablespooons unsalted butter (more butter = more
    clumps; feel free to increase or decrease here)
2   tablespoons dark brown sugar
1   cup dark maple syrup

1   tablespoon vanilla extract
1   tablespoon good-quality cinnamon
8 to 10 cups old-fashioned rolled oats
4 to 6 cups raw, unsalted seeds and nuts (I generally
       use a combination of sliced almonds, sunflower
       seeds, walnuts, and pumpkin seeds, but sometimes I
       add in cashews, pistachios, and/or pecans)
1 to 2 cups raw sesame seeds
       sea salt or Maldon salt flakes, to taste
4   cups mixed, chopped dried fruit in any combination
       you like (sour cherries, cranberries, apricots, raisins,
       golden raisins, dates, plums, blueberries)
1   cup of organic unsweetened coconut flakes (optional)
½   cup finely chopped crystalized ginger (optional)
2   teaspoons cardamom (optional)

steps
Heat the oven to 325 degrees.

In a saucepan over medium-low heat, heat the coconut oil, brown sugar, maple syrup, and butter until oil and butter are melted, stirring occasionally. Remove from the heat and stir in a generous pinch of salt, the vanilla extract, cinnamon, and cardamom if using.

Place the rolled oats and the mixed nuts in a large mixing bowl and pour the oil/syrup mixture over. Stir with a spatula to coat the oats and nuts evenly. Divide the mixture among three jelly-roll pans. (Make thin, even layers; you should have enough left in the bowl for at least three more pans after the first batches are done. If you like, line the pans with parchment—sometimes I do, but not always.) Taste for balance of flavors.

Bake until golden brown, about 30 minutes, rotating the sheets and stirring every 10 minutes.

While still warm, stir in the dried fruit and ginger and sprinkle with more salt flakes to taste. Cool completely before covering. The mixture will keep in a tightly covered container at room temperature for at least a week. Store the rest in your freezer in zip-lock bags or pack into jars to share.
December 13, 2013

a few tips
• Feel free to play around with this basic recipe. As long as you don't oversweeten or overcook, you can't go wrong. Taste your way along.

• You can use more butter for a toastier, richer flavor and more clumps. Or just use coconut oil for vegan granola. Olive oil is good, too, for a richer, more complex taste. Any neutral oil will do. Try fruit puree (apple is good) in place of the oil for a lighter, crunchier result. Cut back on the syrup or leave out the brown sugar if you prefer your granola less sweet.

• Be liberal with the Maldon salt flakes and taste to get desired result. What sets my granola apart is the perfect, subtle balance between slightly sweet and slightly salty.

• Try different combinations of spices, sweeteners, nuts, and fruits. (Choose organic ingredients whenever possible.)

• I like these: apricot/cardamom/crystalized ginger; grated orange zest (mix in with the oats and bake)/cranberry/maple; lavender buds/lemon zest (again, bake in with oat mixture)/honey.

• Other things you can add, or not: carob powder, flax seeds, hemp seeds, dried mulberries, goji berries. The recipe above is gluten free; you can add wheat germ if gluten free isn't a requirement for you.

• Don't overcook but make sure granola is evenly browned throughout; stir every 10 minutes. Never bake the fruits; always mix them in to your still-warm granola.

• Cool completely before covering, stirring occasionally.

• Consider the recipe above a work in progress and allow it to evolve as you go. This recipe will make plenty of granola to divide up into generous gift portions, with some left for you.

• For a lovely presentation, pack your granola into classic Weck tulip jars, available online at weckjars.com.

heart cookies for Valentine's Day

When my sons were young, we always made Valentines. It was a joy for me to join my boys at our old Formica table in the playroom and, for a few February afternoons each year, devote ourselves to frilly matters of the heart. I still have our old box of Valentine paraphernalia in the basement, though it's been many years since the three of us made cards together, and the glue sticks have no doubt turned rock hard. I considered the box briefly the other day: should I carry it all upstairs? Sit down by myself and cut up a few red doilies for old times' sake? No, I realized; that would just feel weird.

Instead, I satisfied my hands-on urge by making some grown-up Valentines for the people I carry closest to my heart. Baking these cookies turned out to be as pleasurably messy as the arts-and-crafts productions of old—and even more gratifying: the results were edible.

So, a new tradition is born, I think, thanks to two recipes that are most definitely keepers.

dark chocolate espresso hearts

ingredients
  2 sticks (1 cup) butter, softened
1½ cups sugar
  2 eggs
  3 teaspoons vanilla extract
  4 teaspoons instant espresso powder
 ⅔ cup unsweetened cocoa powder
  3 cups flour
 ½ teaspoon salt
 ½ teaspoon baking powder

steps

Preheat the oven to 350 degrees.

Cream together butter and sugar in a large mixing bowl.

Mix in eggs and then cocoa.

Place vanilla and espresso powder together in a small cup until coffee dissolves. Add this mixture to the batter and mix until completely incorporated.

Gradually add dry ingredients and mix until smooth (use clean hands at the end, to knead into a soft ball of dough). Wrap in plastic and chill for at least 1 hour.

Allow cookie dough to soften a little at room temperature and then roll out the dough on a floured counter.

Cut into hearts and place on a parchment-lined baking sheet.

Bake for 8 to 11 minutes until the edges are firm. Gently slide parchment paper off of cookie sheet and onto a flat surface. Cool completely before removing cookies from paper. You can serve the hearts plain, or with a little cocoa powder sprinkled on top, or you can ice them. I embellished mine with a glaze made of 1 cup of confectioners sugar, 2 teaspoons milk, 2 teaspoons strong cold coffee, mixed well. Scoop the icing into a plastic bag, snip a corner, and decorate cooled cookies as desired.

Makes 36 medium-size cookies

(Recipe adapted from *Easybaked.com*)

chocolate-dipped espresso hearts

ingredients

  8 ounces cold unsalted butter, cut into small pieces

  ½ cup granulated sugar

  ½ teaspoon salt

2¼ cups flour (measure carefully or weigh to get exactly 10 ounces of flour)

  3 tablespoons finely ground espresso coffee beans

steps

Preheat the oven to 300 degrees.

Combine butter, sugar, and salt in bowl of electric mixer. Mix on low speed until butter is combined with sugar but not completely smooth (1 to 2 minutes).

Add the flour and ground espresso and mix on low till dough comes together, about 3 minutes. Warning: this is a crumbly, dry dough. You will have to gather it into a ball in your hands, and press it together.

On a lightly floured surface, roll dough to ¼ inch thickness. Cut hearts as close together as possible, arrange cookies on two parchment-lined baking sheets, and refrigerate for 20 minutes.

Bake cookies until golden on the bottom and edges and pale to golden on top—in my oven, this took about 40 minutes.

For glaze: Melt 3 ounces of dark bittersweet chocolate with 1 teaspoon shortening in a small bowl over boiling water, stirring—don't let it get hot. Set a sheet of parchment paper on your work surface. Dip the edge of each cooled cookie in warm chocolate and cool on parchment till chocolate is set, about 2 hours.

(Recipe adapted from *FineCooking.com*)

February 14, 2014

Buvette's asparagus Milanese

I don't get to New York often, but if I did, Buvette would be my go-to spot for a morning coffee or an unhurried dinner with friends. So, it's probably not surprising that Buvette *has also turned out to be the cookbook I find myself pulling off the shelf most all summer. I made Jody Adams's Asparagus Milanese about once a week during the season.*

(This recipe serves two, but it is easily doubled.)

ingredients
Coarse salt
Small handful of asparagus, tough ends removed
2   tablespoons unsalted butter
2   good-quality large eggs
Freshly ground black pepper
Finely grated Parmesan cheese

steps
Bring a small pot of water to boil, season with salt, add the asparagus, and cook until just tender, about 2 minutes.

Drain immediately and transfer to paper towels and let dry for a minute or so.

Heat the butter in a skillet over medium heat. Add the asparagus to the butter, with the spears together in the center of the pan.

Crack the eggs directly into the pan at the edges of the asparagus, sprinkle with a bit of salt, cover, and cook until the whites are just set, about 2 minutes.

Sprinkle with a generous dusting of Parmesan cheese and a few healthy grinds of black pepper. (I like a bit of chopped parsley, too.)

July 15, 2014

my mom's cranberry orange bread

This recipe will make two loaves; I often double the recipe, working in two separate bowls, so I can slip four loaves into the oven at once instead of two. I've also cut back on the sugar and upped the spices from her original.

ingredients
    2 cups whole wheat flour
    2 cups white flour
    1 tablespoon baking powder
    1 teaspoon salt
    1 teaspoon cinnamon
    ½ teaspoon nutmeg

1 teaspoon ground cloves
1 cup brown sugar
½ cup white sugar
½ cup unsalted butter
1 heaping tablespoon grated orange rind
2 eggs
1½ cup fresh orange juice
2 cups fresh cranberries
1 cup chopped walnuts
1 cup raisins

steps

Preheat the oven to 350 degrees.

Combine dry ingredients. Cut in butter.

Combine orange juice, eggs, orange rind. Add to flour mixture and mix until just wet.

Fold in cranberries, nuts, and raisins.

Pour into 2 greased and floured loaf pans. Bake 55 to 60 minutes. Cool on wire rack after removing from pan.

December 16, 2014

the only apple cake recipe you'll ever need

I found this cake on the wonderful (and highly addictive) Food52 site and have tweaked it a bit over the course of many bakings.

¾ cup chopped dates

½ to ½ cup apple brandy (actually any brandy will do)

2 cups unbleached, all purpose flour

1½ cups sugar (I use half white and half brown sugar)

2 teaspoons baking soda

1 teaspoons ground cinnamon

1 teaspoon ground nutmeg

1 teaspoon cardamom

¾ teaspoon salt

4 cups slightly tart apples: peeled, cored and roughly chopped

1 cup roughly chopped walnuts or pecans

½ cup melted sweet butter

2 eggs, lightly beaten

confectioners sugar for sprinkling on top

steps

About one hour before starting to bake, place the dates in a small bowl and cover with the brandy. Stir from time to time and if they get too dry, just add more brandy.

Preheat the oven to 325 degrees. Using butter, grease a baking pan that is approximately 13 x 9 x 2 inches.

Into a large bowl, sift together flour, sugar, baking soda, cinnamon, cardamom, nutmeg, and salt.

Add the chopped apples, dates, nuts, melted butter, and the eggs. This will be a very heavy, thick batter but don't worry—just be sure to mix it well.

Spread in the prepared pan, place on a rack in center of the oven. and bake for 1 hour. Test with a skewer—if it comes out still a bit gooey, bake for another 5 to 10 minutes. You'll know when it's done. It will be a nice dark tan color and will spring back to a light touch. Remove from oven and let cool a bit.

This is delicious hot, warm, or cold and for breakfast, lunch, or dinner. It's as good served with a slice of sharp cheddar as it is with a scoop of vanilla ice cream. It's a rough looking cake; if you want to dress it up for guests, sprinkle each serving with a dusting of confectioners sugar.

November 22, 2015

—— acknowledgments ——

My greatest debt is to the many readers who have accompanied me on this journey—reading faithfully, leaving comments on my website, writing personal letters, sharing stories, and offering me the gift of your companionship as we travel this road through life. These pieces exist in book form not only for you but *because* of you. I am deeply grateful.

Moments of Seeing is the result of a team effort. I couldn't have brought this collection into being without the help and support of the talented, generous people who offered their time and skill to make it happen.

Heartfelt appreciation to Rickie Harvey for copyediting my daunting manuscript with such sensitivity, smarts, and care, and for then for jumping in at the eleventh hour to cast a keen eye over the final pages. (Little did we know, when we first met in a Boston birthing class twenty-seven years ago, that life would lead us to the same New Hampshire town and, at long last, to a chance to work together.)

Thank you to Ellen Klempner-Béguin, for cheerleading me on through two hip replacements, for becoming my friend in the process, and for then agreeing to design my book. I'm doubly grateful, both for this new friendship and for a beautiful, readable design. It has been a pleasure, and you made it so.

When I first saw Sue Callihan's lovely still-life hanging on a gallery wall, I knew: if I were ever to collect these essays into a book, her painting would be my first choice for a cover. I'm grateful to this extraordinary New Hampshire artist, neighbor, and friend for so exquisitely evoking the beauty of ordinary life. Thank you, Sue, for allowing your work to grace mine.

A humble bow to Scott Allen for being such a patient, good-natured webmaster, for solving all my tech problems as they arise, and for bringing your vast WordPress knowledge to my online home.

Mike Ribaudo at Kase Printing reminded me how beautiful a physical book can be. The Kase team's dedication to quality and attention to detail is an inspiration. Thank you for letting me keep it local.

Special thanks to my husband, Steven Lewers, for being my partner in life, but also for assuming the role of my most devoted and forgiving reader. Thanks, too, for first having the idea of collecting these essays between two covers, for offering to be my publisher, and then for so willingly undertaking all the forethought and footwork this project has entailed, from start to finish. You have greatly expanded upon the job description of "husband."

I'm grateful to everyone at Earth Sky + Water for stretching their boundaries to include the publication of my book.

Of course, were it not for the tolerance and trust of my family and friends, I couldn't write as I do of our lives together and the experiences we share. My gratitude to each of you knows no bounds, but, in addition to Steve, special love and thanks are due to my parents, John and Marilyn Kenison; to my sons, Henry and Jack; to my surrogate daughter, Lauren Seabourne; and to my friend, neighbor, and tireless caretaker of dogs and plants, Debbie Day. Margaret Roach, I can't quite imagine how I managed before you became my writing pal, colleague, and sounding board for all things written and lived. Maude Odgers, your steady presence, unconditional and true, is one of the great blessings in my life. Big thanks to each of you. Together, we keep all the balls in the air.